An Introduction to Political Philosophy

Now revised and updated and containing several entirely new chapters, this book provides a comprehensive introduction to political philosophy. It discusses historical and contemporary figures and covers a vast range of topics and debates, including immigration, war, national and global economics, the ethical and political implications of climate change, and the persistence of racial oppression and injustice. It also presents accessible, nontechnical discussions of perfectionism, utilitarianism, theories of the social contract, and the Marxian tradition of social criticism. Real-life examples introduce students to ways of using philosophical reflection and debates, and open up new perspectives on politics and political issues. Throughout, this book challenges readers to think critically about political arguments and institutions that they might otherwise take for granted. It will be a vital and provocative resource for any student of philosophy or political science.

COLIN BIRD is Associate Professor of Politics at the University of Virginia. He is the author of *The Myth of Liberal Individualism* (Cambridge, 1999), and his work has also appeared in numerous major academic journals including *Ethics*, *Philosophy and Public Affairs*, the *American Political Science Review*, *Political Theory*, *Polity*, and the *European Journal of Philosophy*.

An Introduction to Political Philosophy

Second Edition

COLIN BIRD

University of Virginia

CAMBRIDGE
UNIVERSITY PRESS

CAMBRIDGE
UNIVERSITY PRESS

University Printing House, Cambridge CB2 8BS, United Kingdom

One Liberty Plaza, 20th Floor, New York, NY 10006, USA

477 Williamstown Road, Port Melbourne, VIC 3207, Australia

314–321, 3rd Floor, Plot 3, Splendor Forum, Jasola District Centre,
New Delhi – 110025, India

79 Anson Road, #06-04/06, Singapore 079906

Cambridge University Press is part of the University of Cambridge.

It furthers the University's mission by disseminating knowledge in the pursuit of
education, learning, and research at the highest international levels of excellence.

www.cambridge.org
Information on this title: www.cambridge.org/9781108423434
DOI: 10.1017/9781108526067

First published 2006
Second edition 2019
Reprinted 2019

Printed in the United Kingdom by TJ International Ltd. Padstow, Cornwall

A catalogue record for this publication is available from the British Library.

Library of Congress Cataloging-in-Publication Data
Names: Bird, Colin, author.
Title: An introduction to political philosophy / Colin Bird.
Description: Second edition. | Cambridge; New York, NY: Cambridge
University Press, [2019] | Includes bibliographical references and index.
Identifiers: LCCN 2018048988 | ISBN 9781108423434 (hardback) |
ISBN 9781108437554 (pbk.)
Subjects: LCSH: Political science – Philosophy.
Classification: LCC JA71.B528 2019 | DDC 320.01–dc23
LC record available at https://lccn.loc.gov/2018048988

ISBN 978-1-108-42343-4 Hardback
ISBN 978-1-108-43755-4 Paperback

Contents

Preface to the Second Edition

This book has two aims: first, to stimulate critical reflection on political institutions and practices, and on the various arguments that might be offered for and against them; and second, to give readers an appreciation of the most provocative historical and contemporary contributions to political philosophy. The book could be used as a free-standing text in an introductory course, or in conjunction with assigned readings from some of the major texts discussed (Plato, Hobbes, Rawls, and others). Although I have aimed for wide coverage, the immense scope of the field necessitates some selection, and this book does not pretend to be comprehensive or exhaustive.

The topics addressed in this second edition differ from those included in the first. The extensive discussions of the problem of political obligation and of the value of toleration that formed Chapters 7 and 11 of the original edition have made way for new chapters covering territorial rights and immigration (Chapter 9), the political implications of climate change (Chapter 10), and the utility of so-called "ideal theory" as an approach to "non-ideal" problems, especially those posed by the ongoing struggle against racism and racial injustice (Chapter 15). I have introduced these topics because they are of increasing relevance both in public discussion and within academic political philosophy.

Although they cover much the same ground as their counterparts in the old edition, the remaining chapters have also been revised, in some cases extensively. Chapter 1 now includes a discussion of the recently influential "realist" turn in political philosophy, aspects of which are taken up in the largely new Chapter 14. Chapter 2 introduces the idea of a "common good" in a new way. Chapters 3 and 4 offer a much more detailed account of classical utilitarianism and its problems, both in order to remedy some aspects of the earlier discussion with which I became dissatisfied and to take account of important new work by de Lazari-Radek and Singer on Sidgwick. The argument of Chapter 7, which considers and rejects arguments for the unregulated free market as an agent of economic justice, has been recast and, I hope, clarified. A key distinction between blame-responsibility and remedy-responsibility, which was implicit in the earlier discussion of free-market justice, and plays a role in other chapters, is now flagged more directly. Chapter 12, on freedom, has been restructured and now includes a discussion of sweatshops as a test case.

As with the first edition, I have not attempted to provide extensive or comprehensive references to the large and growing academic literatures on these topics. Such websites as the "Stanford Encyclopedia of Philosophy" give students today unprecedentedly easy access to bibliographic databases on any number of topics. These online resources effectively supplant the textbook as a source of bibliographic information and, because they are regularly updated as new literature emerges, they perform that function rather more effectively than a book published at a particular moment ever could. Accordingly, I have written the book, not to reproduce academic resources already available online, but to orient readers to the central philosophical problems raised by various political questions, hopefully in a fresh, efficient, and provocative way. It will have succeeded if it provides them with reliable, and critically aware, frameworks to guide them as they venture into the dauntingly vast academic literatures on these subjects, and as they reflect for themselves on the adequacy of the political practices and structures that surround them.

For related reasons, I have tried as far as possible to steer clear of excessive technical jargon, and of those contemporary debates that seem to me to have become boringly scholastic (e.g. "equality of resources" vs. "equality of welfare"; "individualism" vs. "communitarianism," and so on). Although I have not avoided *all* references to schools of thought, I have also deliberately chosen not to organize the book around ideological worldviews like "liberalism," "libertarianism," "socialism," "feminism," or "conservatism." The most interesting arguments too often flow between these various positions. Moreover, I have found that emphasizing them encourages the false view that these ideological fixtures are natural kinds when in fact they reflect highly parochial political divisions. Focusing on them also implies that political philosophers are servants of ideologies, helping to make them more plausible, systematic, and rhetorically effective. We should discourage this perception. Political philosophers need not be loyal to particular ideological positions or movements and define their activities in these terms. Of course, there are many who today write in this vein – a liberal theory of this, a feminist theory of that, a libertarian defense of such and so – but I think this is clearly the *wrong* way to make philosophy politically relevant. I hope this book helps readers to see a better way.

I am grateful to Hilary Gaskin at Cambridge University Press for encouraging me to update the book, and for her guidance in thinking about how best to revise it. In the closing stages of the writing, I taxed both her and Sophie Taylor's generosity and patience, and I greatly appreciate their accommodation and assistance. Bob Amdur, Ross Mittiga, and Harrison Frye provided me with invaluable advice on the chapters on climate change and freedom, for which I am very grateful.

Finally, special thanks go to my wife, Adrienne, and my three children, Nicholas, Teddy, and Tatiana, for their support, affection, and forbearance. I dedicate this book, like its predecessor, to them.

Introduction

Like the weather, politics presents two starkly contrasting faces. Often, it comes in the form of calm and seemingly cloudless routine, stability, predictability, and consensus. When we survey the political landscape, for example, we find widespread acquiescence in particular modes of political organization and acceptance of the values generally thought to underlie them; entrenched rules and principles widely affirmed within particular communities as a legitimate basis on which to criticize the conduct of their members; the regular circulation of bureaucratic forms and instructions, passports issued and honored, wills written and upheld, contracts enforced, wrongdoers peacefully brought to justice in accordance with accepted procedures.

As often, however, politics brings conflict, struggle, disruption, coercion, brutality, uncertainty, disorder, violence, destruction, fear, subversion, and menace: one thinks of bombing raids, pogroms, terrorist attacks, genocides and "collateral damage"; of coups, revolutions, sweeping legislative change, invasions, electoral reversals, forced evacuations, conscription, hijackings, martial law, and the imposition of violent legal sanctions and penalties; of divided loyalties, naked ambition, sharp moral and religious disagreements, international realignments, and ethnic hatreds; and of intrusive surveillance, invasions of privacy, confiscations of property, arrest, interrogation, and torture.

Some might say that these two faces of politics represent the Jekyll and Hyde of political life. Just as we distinguish between good and bad weather, so we might straightforwardly identify *bad* politics with instability, subversion, and the disconcerting threat of violence and *good* politics with stability, order, and routine.

But a moment's reflection reveals that this Jekyll-and-Hyde theory of politics is far too simple. When we imagine the menacing hum of bomber formations approaching from the far horizon, our first instinct may indeed be to identify with the potential victims, quietly going about their business without realizing that their homes and communities are in grave danger. But while the raid may be terrible for them, in at least some cases we might reluctantly conclude that it could be justified for the greater good. Rather few, if any, significant political achievements have been entirely bloodless, and it is not obvious that we should never be prepared to use violence for the sake of legitimate political ends. Today, the nuclear bombings of Hiroshima and Nagasaki that ended the Second World War, or even the "conventional" bombings of Tokyo, Dresden, and Hamburg, are no longer widely defended. But almost no one says we should not have done *anything* about the Nazis, and there are still many who defend the policy of nuclear deterrence as it was practiced during the Cold War, despite the obvious fact that it involved threatening literally *millions* of innocent civilians with incineration. Even if we doubt that these very drastic forms of violence can be justified under any circumstances, we might still concede that the more familiar forms of coercion and violence involved in the regular operation of criminal punishment can be more readily defended.

Furthermore, the mere fact that certain patterns of political cooperation are stable, enduring, and routine does not mean that they are therefore desirable or legitimate. Slavery has very often been a routine and widely accepted practice; so have (and are) child labor, the subordination of women, religious intolerance, and racial and ethnic discrimination. On reflection, then, we will often agree that some of these practices, even when hallowed by tradition, deserve to be swept aside in the name of freedom, equality, justice, and other important social ideals.

So political disruption and subversion, even when violent, may sometimes be good, and acquiescence in stable political routines may often be very bad. If there is a distinction between good and bad politics, then, it is not just the same as the difference between order and disorder, or between stability and instability. But when is politics good and when is it bad? Which forms of political action might be justifiable under what circumstances? When ought we to regard the stability of certain public institutions as a good thing and when ought they to be resisted or destabilized? And destabilized by what means and in favor of ... what?

The Quest for Justification

Humans are not, as Aristotle noted, political animals in the way that ants and bees are, simply programmed by natural instinct to organize themselves in certain iterating structures like nests and hives.[1] Rather, our political communities and institutional practices take many incompatible forms, and people have differed sharply on their relative merits. For example, almost everybody now claims to be for democracy. But until the last couple of centuries "democracy" was more often a term of abuse, rather like the word "fascist" is today. (And we tend to forget, of course, that not *all* fascists were the power-crazed crackpots we find in old war movies – at least some of them were serious, well-intentioned intellectuals who quite sincerely hoped to improve the world.) More generally, there have been theocracies, aristocracies, oligarchies, monarchies, and each has had its defenders and detractors. The variability of human political forms and our judgments about them is one of the most striking facts about us. It means that we cannot avoid thinking of our political practices as alterable, and even (if only in retrospect) as possible objects of choice. We can always ask: why should we continue to organize ourselves *this* way when we could have done it *that* way instead?

To ask such questions is to demand a justification for the current way of organizing things. That demand seems misplaced when behavior is determined by instinct or reflex. Swarming bees and herds of terrified wildebeest fleeing a predator do not have doubts about or demand justifications for what they are doing. Humans have instincts and reflexes, too, and doubtless much of our political activity is habitual and unreflective. But we strongly resist the idea that our political practices are wholly mindless. "Well, I just *do*" may be a perfectly reasonable reply to the question: "Why do you like strawberry ice-cream?" But "We just *do*" does not seem a satisfactory answer to such questions as: why do we enslave people? Why do we allow enormous disparities of wealth between citizens of the prosperous Western nations and the poor around the world? Why are we sometimes prepared to sacrifice innocent life in war? Such questions demand well-reasoned answers. If we are not convinced by any of the proposed justifications, we may conclude that the relevant practices should be

---

[1] Aristotle 1981, p. 60.

changed or eliminated. This assumes that, at some level, our political arrangements are subject to rational criticism and choice. This assumption lies behind the effort to distinguish political practices and forms of political action that can be justified and those that cannot. That effort, more than anything else, defines the general project of political philosophy.

Ideas and Concepts in Political Life

Aristotle put his finger on another, closely related, reason why our political interaction is not like that of bees, ants, and herds of wildebeest. Wildebeest do not talk and they do not use concepts. They do not recognize "*authority*," they have no notion of what it is to be "*represented*" by other wildebeest, and they do not fuss about "*wildebeest rights*." Nor do they urge allegiance or resistance to various practices within their herds for the sake of "*freedom and equality*," or on the grounds that they are "*required*" as a matter of "*justice*," that they possess or lack "*legitimacy*," that they are part of or inimical to the "*common good*," and so forth. However, such concepts seem central to human politics and to our efforts to justify our political arrangements to each other.

Broadly, these concepts are of two kinds. Some of them, like the concepts of "justice" or "the common good," refer to certain ethical *ideals* routinely cited in justifications for (or objections to) political practices and actions. Thus we are often urged to reject slavery as unjust, to embrace democracy for the sake of equality and justice, or to topple dictatorships abroad in the name of freedom. Other concepts, such as those of "authority," "representation," "rights," "property," "coercion," or "sovereignty" pick out aspects of political practice that themselves stand in need of justification.

Obviously, concepts of the first sort are most directly relevant to the search for justification in politics. We mainly want to know what justice requires, what a truly free society would look like, what is ruled out as subversive of the "common good," and so on. And clearly this requires that we reflect on exactly what appeals to "justice" or the "common good" involve, how such concepts have the capacity to justify anything (if indeed they do), how we certify *what* they justify and so forth.

But concepts of the second kind raise philosophical questions as well. If we are asking (say) whether political authority can be justified, and if so when, we had better be clear on what exactly political authority *is*. Are we? Do we immediately understand, for example, how authority differs from power (does it?), or what exactly it means to say that a judge, rather than my next-door neighbor, has authority over me? Is political authority similar to, or different from, the kind of authority that expert archeologists claim? Facing these questions often leaves us unexpectedly puzzled about things we at first thought we understood. When we ask them, we are not necessarily directly seeking a justification for a mode of political organization. But in order to understand *what* they are trying to justify, political philosophers must address these questions as well.

"Theory and Practice"

We have seen how, in the course of investigating the possible justifications that might be offered for different modes of political organization, we are led to reflect on the nature of political concepts like justice, freedom, authority, the state, and so forth. But some become quickly impatient with the resulting focus on concepts and ideas, and complain that it makes political philosophy an unduly "theoretical" as opposed to "practical" endeavor. Such critics charge that political philosophy is an academic diversion from active political engagement, from going out and "making a difference." Instead of wasting our time with philosophy, we should go out and join the Labour Party, become a Young Republican, or sign up for the Peace Corps.

Plainly, doing philosophy is not exactly like working for Oxfam, running the country, or implementing public policy. Still, this does not make it helpful to understand the relation between political philosophy and political activity in terms of a broad opposition between "theory" and "practice." Presumably those who want to "make a difference" by becoming politically active do not want to make *just any* sort of difference. They want to make *the right sort of difference.* The Nazi Party made a big difference, but we would not have much patience for someone who said: "Who cares about justice, equality, and all that? That's merely theory. Practice is what matters. So I'm off to do my bit for the Third Reich – at least *that* way I'll make a difference."

In other words, we need to think intelligently about *where* to try to make a difference, about *which* political causes merit investments of our time and energy. This obviously requires some reflection on the proper goals and aims of political activity. Mostly, when people are asked why they become politically involved, they will cite beliefs about justice, the common good, freedom, oppression, and equality, among others. As we have seen, these beliefs, and the question of their soundness, form a major part of the subject matter of political philosophy. But rarely can we separate these beliefs about the goals of political action from our actions themselves; usually the two are seamlessly connected. For example, there is not some bit of my voting in an election that is "pure activity," neatly separable from my beliefs about why a particular candidate deserves my support, or about why I should bother to vote in the first place. My vote and these beliefs about it are of a piece.

This has an important consequence. If the beliefs on which we act in politics do not make sense, our actions may not make sense either. In principle, then, philosophical reflection on these beliefs has the power to expose certain of our political activities as confused, to make it clear that we ought to behave otherwise than we do. Neat and tidy distinctions between "theory" and "practice" obscure this point. The important contrast is not between some pure realm of moral ideals ("theory") and a disconnected world of political action ("practice"). Rather, it is between political activity informed by relatively sophisticated and defensible beliefs about its goals and political activity guided by beliefs that are indefensible, confused, or simply stupid.

This is not just a point for those who consciously decide to become politically active in various ways. To adapt a famous remark of Leon Trotsky's: "You may not be interested in politics, but politics is interested in you." The point here is that, independently of our decisions to become politically active, we nonetheless find ourselves dragooned into concerted political action in a variety of other ways. This is why so much of our political involvement is expressed in the passive voice. In politics, we are constantly being expected, required, ordered, authorized (etc.) to ..., being manipulated, coerced, recruited, bullied, conscripted (etc.) into ..., and being organized, regulated, controlled (etc.) so that ... Very little of this is in any sense voluntary; much of it goes on without our even noticing, like sales taxes.

Consider, for example, our relationship to the modern state. This immensely powerful and ubiquitous political agency makes significant claims on us. In order to reproduce itself, to promote its goals, to perform its functions, to fight its wars, citizens are recruited, usually involuntarily, into organized action. In this sense, the state makes us all politically active despite ourselves – it transforms us into the agents of *its* projects. Most go along with this out of habit and socialization, encouraged from an early age to believe (perhaps) that the state promotes justice and our common good, that we have some sort of obligation to comply with it, that it represents us and our interests, that it is an agent of our collective self-government, and so forth. These familiar beliefs and habits of thought purport to justify the state and the forms of collective action over which it presides. But as before, when political philosophers ask whether those beliefs make sense, they are also asking whether these forms of collective action and organization themselves make sense. Insofar as these practices and beliefs partly constitute the terms on which we understand and conduct our own lives, the question of whether they make sense is hardly a purely abstract or "theoretical" one.

The Plan of the Book

This book is divided into three parts. Part I (Chapters 1–6) raises the general question of how philosophers can gain appropriate critical distance on public affairs. Chapter 1 explains why the effort to achieve such critical perspective has proven notoriously problematic, and elaborates some of the philosophical challenges it faces. The next three chapters discuss and evaluate one family of attempts to meet those challenges, organized around a framing ideal of the "common good." Chapter 2 introduces the general idea of a "common good" in politics before setting out some challenging features of Plato's perfectionist approach to it. Chapters 3 and 4 cover the contrasting account of the "common good" developed by classical utilitarianism. The following pair of chapters discuss the tradition of social-contract theory, which differs from the common-good approach in that it organizes political criticism, not around a conception of well-being, but rather around notions of willing agreement. In Chapter 5, I discuss the classical theory of the social contract as developed in the seventeenth century by Hobbes and Locke, and explain why it fell into disfavor in the eighteenth century. Chapter 6 describes and evaluates John Rawls's attempt (in the late twentieth century) to revive social-contract theory for contemporary use.

Part II (Chapters 7–13) moves away from these more general issues of philosophical approach to address more overtly political questions. It deals directly with several largely independent, free-standing political topics: economic inequality and distributive justice (Chapters 7–8); territorial rights and immigration (Chapter 9); climate change and environmental justice (Chapter 10); war and international conflict (Chapter 11); political freedom (Chapter 12); and democracy (Chapter 13).

Part III (Chapters 14–15) returns to some of the more general questions left over from Part I and reconsiders them in the light of the intervening discussion. Chapter 14 asks how philosophical arguments might inform political practice, and engages extensively with Marx's views on this topic. Although it dissents from some Marxian claims, it cautiously endorses others. The final chapter addresses a major contemporary debate over the value of "ideal theory" as it was influentially conceived by Rawls, which has recently been called into question by several critics. Though influenced by Marx, these critics have often been more interested in the plight of marginalized identity groups (especially groups defined by race, gender, and sexual orientation) than he was. Chapter 15 accordingly sets this general debate about "ideal theory" in the context of racial exclusion.

The three parts of the book are loosely cumulative. Part III presupposes acquaintance with the material in the first two parts. However, Part II is largely written as a free-standing discussion, as are each of its constituent chapters. Readers should therefore be able to dip into them without having read any of the earlier chapters, and in any order they like.

Part I

Politics and Critical Morality

1   Forms of Political Criticism

Mary Midgely once suggested that philosophy is like plumbing: nobody notices it until something goes wrong.[1] Whatever might be said about other areas of philosophical inquiry, Midgely's thought provides a helpful point of entry into reflection about the scope and purposes of political philosophy, and about the challenges it faces in accomplishing its critical aims. This opening chapter explores some of these general issues.

Exposing the Pipes

We noted in the Introduction that, although often sustained by habit and unreflective conformity, political practices are not wholly mindless. They are rather underpinned by at least tacit understandings of why they matter, of their purposes and value, and of our reasons for maintaining them. We rarely think very deeply, or even at all, before complying with legal requirements to pay our taxes, to have our car inspected annually, or to stop at a red light, but if someone asks us why we bother to do these things, we are not left speechless. To the contrary, various reasons for doing so will come readily to mind: considerations of fairness, safety, reciprocity, etc. Similarly, citizens of Western liberal democracies frequently take for granted their rights to vote, to speak and associate freely, and to engage in their preferred forms of religious worship. But again, they will not greet someone who argues that they should be stripped of these rights with shrugs of indifference. More likely, they will unleash a tirade about the importance of such rights for justice, equality, personal liberty, or the realization of democratic ideals.

[1] Midgley 1992.

Much of the time, these underlying assumptions about the value and purpose of political practices and institutions remain largely in the background, like a well-functioning plumbing system. Under the pressure of social conflicts and historical circumstance, however, such background beliefs and commitments sometimes burst out into the open, forcing agents to reconsider assumptions that have hitherto gone unquestioned. Do the material benefits of economic integration warrant the surrender of national sovereignty required by membership in the European Union? Does the commitment to protect the liberty of all citizens require or forbid public welfare provision? When states refuse to admit immigrants do they violate a human right to free movement or exercise a rightful power to exclude people from their territory? Once made explicit, however, and especially where agents have strong vested interests in alternative answers, such questions become insistent, stimulating enduring disagreements and in some cases violent struggle.

Defusing and Mobilizing Arguments

Political disagreements of this kind are typically provoked, and sustained, by a perception on the part of at least some that *all is not well*, that *something is not right here*, much as one might become concerned about low water pressure in the shower. Such concern focuses agents' attention in something like the way in which recurring pain or discomfort leads them to fear that they are seriously ill and to seek medical advice. Hopefully, a doctor will be able to reassure them that their pain is asymptomatic and that nothing is seriously wrong. In that case, she will *defuse* their concerns; although this will not necessarily remove the pain, it should change the patient's attitude to it, eliminating further anxiety about its significance. Alternatively, medical investigation may reveal that their pain is indeed caused by an underlying illness requiring treatment. In that case, the doctor's findings are *mobilizing*; they argue for more or less urgent action aiming to cure or remit the relevant disease.

When a parallel unease that something seems to be seriously wrong arises in politics, both types of response – defusing and mobilizing – are in principle available. That is, one possible outcome of further inquiry is the conclusion that the political grievances motivating it are not, after all, a real reason for concern. As in the medical case, this need not remove the feeling of unease; but it may change our attitude to it, reassuring us that we should classify it with the unavoidable frustrations of human existence, not as a serious flaw calling for urgent remedial action.

The wide economic inequalities characteristically induced by capitalist economic systems are today often defended in these defusing terms. I have in mind the proponent of capitalism who denies neither that such inequalities exist, nor that those who are relatively poor suffer quite genuine hardship and disadvantage, but who goes on to claim that the challenges they face are within acceptable limits given the impossibility of eliminating all suffering from human life. Arguments along these lines do not pretend to make the challenges faced by the poor any less severe, but rather aim to change everyone's attitude to them. They purport to show that they are not instances of rank injustice or oppression calling for redress, but endemic, albeit sad, features of human life with which we must learn to live. Once defused and put in their proper perspective, exponents of this sort of argument claim, concerns about inequality need no longer distract us from appreciating the prodigious wealth-creating capacities of a free-market economy, which (they think) constitute a powerful reason to make peace with a capitalist order.

Compare this defusing argument in defense of capitalism with those arguments that led the right to vote to be extended to women in modern times. By the late nineteenth century, as ideals of democracy gained widespread traction in the West, the conflict between basic democratic aspirations and the exclusion of women from the franchise became painfully apparent. If the point of democratic institutions is to make rulers accountable to the ruled, why should responsibility for calling governments to account fall solely on men? If the virtue of democratic representation is to communicate information about the interests and preferences of *all* those affected by political decisions, why deny it to half the adult population? If, as a matter of justice, the rights of democratic citizenship should be granted to people on an impartial basis, without regard to irrelevant differences between them (like height or eye color), why should they be conditioned on gender or sex? Defusing answers to these questions are very hard to find, and as people gradually realized this, they increasingly concluded that denying women the vote was indefensible, a glaring flaw in any purportedly democratic society. This realization was *mobilizing*: many found themselves unable to reconcile themselves to the *status quo*, given their commitments to justice and democratic inclusion. This provoked a sustained, and ultimately successful, campaign to secure women the vote.

Subjective and Objective

What I am calling defusing and mobilizing arguments in politics, then, aim to affirm or change their addressees' attitudes toward political practices. The relevant attitudes are ones of appraisal, consisting, at the broadest level, in forms of approval or disapproval. Such arguments purport, at least implicitly, to answer the question "Should we approve or disapprove of these political institutions and practices?"

Political philosophy, as conceived in this book, is largely the attempt to critically assess, in a more systematic way than is normally possible in the pressured circumstances of actual politics, arguments of these kinds. Since those arguments themselves claim to pass judgment on political institutions and practices, efforts to analyze them philosophically should automatically carry critical implications for the practices under scrutiny. The hope is that introducing greater philosophical clarity and discernment into such arguments can bring into focus our deepest reasons to approve or criticize modes of social and political organization that we tend to take for granted.

So understood, the political philosopher aims to *inform* us of our reasons to judge aspects of coordinated political life favorably or unfavorably. This informative aim can be compared to that of the scientist, who similarly aims to inform us of reasons to endorse or reject alternative theories about the nature of matter, space and time, chemical properties, or speciation in the animal world. Both forms of investigation succeed in being informative to the extent that they move us beyond obvious, trivial platitudes, to more interesting, surprising conclusions that we would otherwise lack reasons to believe. You will not win the Nobel prize for pointing out that objects on Earth are subject to some force of gravity that impels them toward the ground; establish that gravity is actually equivalent to acceleration,[2] and is therefore as much a temporal as a spatial phenomenon, and you are in with a shout.

---

[2] Einstein 2012.

Similarly, it is uninteresting to claim that we have reasons to deplore forced labor, torture, and the deliberate infliction of agony for personal amusement, to resent injustice, to abhor political corruption, to protest against arbitrary discrimination, to find mass genocide tragic, or to have contempt for serial rapists. Although disputing such claims is pointless, they provide no new information about which social and political practices we have reason to approve or disapprove. We already know, or at least have no reason to deny, that states ought to criminalize rape, refrain from genocide, suppress injustice, discrimination, or political corruption, and prevent suffering when it can. A political argument can be genuinely informative only if it justifies more controversial judgments, for example: that private property produces oppression, not freedom; that redistributive taxation is as bad as forced labor; or that the authority claimed by the state is illegitimate and that citizens lack general reasons to obey the law.

At this point, however, the enterprise of political philosophy faces a commonly expressed challenge, one that, although confused, commands a high level of credibility in contemporary culture. Since this challenge, if it goes through, threatens to undermine that enterprise at the outset, we need to assess it now, for otherwise the rest of this book is in vain. The challenge draws attention to an apparent, though as we shall see spurious, difference between science and political philosophy. It goes like this: science is concerned with "objectively" verifiable *facts*; but the arguments addressed by political philosophers purport, not to establish facts, but rather *value judgments*. To use the now standard academic lingo, science is "positive," aiming at the empirical interpretation of the facts, while political philosophy is "normative," advancing evaluative claims. Clearly, both defusing and mobilizing arguments in politics are in this sense normative: they appeal to such values as justice, equality, democratic ideals, reciprocity, well-being, and so forth. They claim to inform us, in other words, not about what is the case, but about what ought to be the case, and about whether social and political practices are acceptable by the lights of relevant standards. The problem is that many believe that claims about something's value, be it a political arrangement or anything (a work of art, a personal experience, a commodity), cannot be validated because they are essentially "subjective" rather than "objective."

The model of "objectivity" to which this distinction appeals is usually provided by modern empirical science. The thought here is that scientific inquiry involves the impartial investigation of hard, verifiable, "objective" facts. Our value judgments, however, are not objectively verifiable facts, or so goes the challenge. Rather, they reflect nonrational preferences and emotional reactions. Like our taste for different flavors of ice-cream, they vary from person to person, and are tainted by personal interests and biases. Unlike the question of whether the earth is flat or revolves around the sun, these claims cannot be "objectively" or impartially tested. Some see great value in political arrangements that promote equality; others those that prioritize freedom; still others decry "freedom and equality" as bourgeois illusions; and even when parties agree that justice is vitally important, they interpret its requirements in radically divergent ways. These differences of outlook, on this line of thinking, are in principle nonrational: they are determined, not by an impartial consideration of the facts, but rather by the varying psychological propensities of the speaker.

This line threatens the enterprise of political philosophy. If judgments approving or disapproving of various political practices are in this way "subjective," how can we assess them from a rational or impartial point of view? Many allege that this is impossible. According to them, claims about the value of different political arrangements lie beyond rational assessment. If they are right, the idea that political philosophy can be genuinely informative is confused. They might allow that reading the works of political philosophers, past and present, can inform us about the personal values of the writer. They might also concede that we can learn something from political philosophers about which forms of rhetoric and propaganda are in fact effective in persuading people to support various political causes. However, they regard the idea that one can rationally adjudicate between political value judgments, establishing that some are more plausible than others, as an illusion.

This sort of skepticism is ubiquitous nowadays. It is therefore particularly important to expose its inadequacy.

Defusing Skepticism, Mobilizing Criticism

A first point is that the distinction between "objective" and "subjective" is far less clear than many suppose. Below are a few of the various different meanings that hide behind it:

Subjective	Objective
might mean …	
Difficult to prove	Easy to prove
Biased	Unbiased
About values	About facts
Matters of opinion	Matters of fact
Matters of the "heart"	Matters of the "mind"
Untestable	Testable
Doubtful	Certain
Normative	Positive
Sentimental	Dispassionate
Nonrational	Rational
Expressive	Informative
Unreflective	Reflective
Controversial	Uncontroversial
Prescriptive	Descriptive
Preferences	Judgments
Partial	Impartial
Emotional	Reasoned
Unscientific	Scientific
Moral	Nonmoral
Personal	Impersonal
Neither true nor false	True or false
Discretionary	Mandatory

The important point about this list, which could be extended, is that there are clear differences between these various distinctions. Crucially, moreover, it is not obvious that they match up with each other: not all of the items in each column necessarily go together. But the opposition of subjective and objective indiscriminately blends all this into a single omnibus distinction. This is imprecise, because we have no reason to assume that everything on the left is incompatible with everything on the right.

For example, couldn't some normative claims be testable judgments rather than unverifiable preferences ("on balance, the industrial revolution did more harm than good" [think of climate change])? Aren't some moral claims relatively uncontroversial (killing innocents for no reason is wrong)?

Is it not possible that some value judgments could be impartial rather than partial (convicting someone of a crime based on the evidence rather than personal animus)? Couldn't some be based on reasons rather than emotions (don't you have a reason not to discriminate against a job applicant even if you find their sexual or religious preferences disgusting?)? When the awarding of a penalty is at the referee's discretion, does it follow that the referee can never be mistaken in calling a foul? I am not saying that these possibilities are easy to explain or completely unproblematic. The point, rather, is that the objective/subjective distinction simply discounts these possibilities at the outset, more or less by definition. This prejudges the very questions at issue.

A second problem with this appeal to the "subjectivity" of value judgment is that it implausibly insinuates that judgments about "matters of fact" are systematically easier to validate than claims about what we have reason to value. Sometimes, of course, they may be. Compared to the question of (say) whether justice requires or prohibits affirmative action, it certainly seems easier to determine (say) whether the cat really is on the mat. But this is just one example. In other cases, the comparison seems to go the other way.

Consider, for example, starvation, disease, depression, rejection, exclusion, loss, fear, ignorance, delusion, war, violence, insecurity, rape, humiliation, and pain. Is it complicated or difficult to validate the claim that these are evils that anyone has reasons to avoid? Do we even need to validate it? Consider falling in love, encountering great beauty, laughing so hard that tears come to your eyes, bringing some important and difficult project to completion, experiencing intensely pleasurable sensations, enjoying the trust of a loyal friend, successfully raising healthy children, and achieving knowledge or understanding. Should we hesitate before granting that these things (among others) usually enhance our lives?

Now compare these normative claims with the answers one might offer to the following "factual" questions: what caused the French Revolution? Did the universe begin with a "Big Bang"? How does the human brain process visual images? Why did the dinosaurs go extinct? How can physical matter be conscious? Why is it dark at night when so many stars far more powerful than our sun are still shining?[3] Answers to these "factual" questions look as if they will be much harder to validate than claims about the value of such basic goods as friendship, pleasure, or beauty. It is not as

---

[3] This is, of course, the famous "Olbers' Paradox." See Harrison 1989.

if historians and scientists are in complete agreement about the causes of the French Revolution, about the status of "string theory," about the nature of consciousness, or about how to interpret the peculiar implications of quantum mechanics. Does this mean that science is "subjective"?

A third point follows on from this. That science and political philosophy have different subject matters and ask different types of questions need not entail that they are fundamentally different in kind. To the contrary, a more basic logic of rational argumentation underlies both, and once we grasp this, naïve oppositions between "objectivity" and "subjectivity" collapse. Even within the empirical sciences (broadly understood), very different questions are asked. Consider: "Is this reactor design safe?" "Is someone with high blood pressure ill?" "Are photons waves or particles?" "(Why) is the universe expanding?" "What causes economic inflation?" "Are the French, American, and Russian revolutions tokens of the same type?" Each of these questions could be rephrased so that it is prefixed with such formulae as: "Do we have reason to think …?"; "What justifies the view that …"; or "What reasons do we have for believing that …?" Despite their different subject matter, then, inquiry in all of these areas is a search for *reasons* warranting particular conclusions, supporting certain judgments, or undermining common assumptions about the topic under scrutiny. We uncover such reasons, in all these areas, by advancing and assessing arguments purporting to offer better, more perceptive, answers to our questions.

To present an argument is simply to put an interlocutor through an experience intended to reveal their reasons to accept or reject some claim. Some arguments, like those used in geometry and logic, are proofs: given certain starting assumptions, a proof demonstrates how certain conclusions are irresistible. Many arguments, however, and most of those in political philosophy, are not proofs in this strict sense: they purport merely to give grounds for finding a conclusion more or less plausible, or so implausible compared to the alternatives that we can safely discard it as wrong. Such informal arguments rarely approximate logical proofs, but they can still be compelling in many cases. There is no obvious reason to deny that this could also be true of arguments advanced for or against political judgments, even controversial ones.

One might point out here that the scientific method remains distinctive in that it relies on empirical experimentation in a way that philosophical arguments about politics cannot. Although it is true that political philosophers can rarely establish their conclusions by doing experiments, we should be careful not to infer too much from this observation. Data and empirical evidence turned up in experiments cannot ground scientific conclusions unaided. The scientist must also offer a compelling interpretation of her results, explain why her experiment is apt, and why it, rather than some experiment with an alternative design, supplies us with relevant information about the hypotheses under consideration. These further explanations are needed, in part, to certify the presumption that the scientist is motivated by a good-faith search for the truth, rather than massaging the evidence for the purposes of persuasion and self-advancement. The requisite arguments are neither matters of strict proof nor unadorned lists of raw data. To the contrary, classic scientific experiments (like the Michelson–Morley experiment, which undermined the once prevalent theory that light moves through a physical medium called the "luminiferous aether") and empirical research projects (like Darwin's famous voyage on the *Beagle*) were important not simply because they churned out data. They were path-breaking, rather, because their findings had a scientific *significance* in relation to accepted views. Data alone cannot explain that significance. It can be appreciated only through informal, non-empirical arguments that tell us why the data are newsworthy, how they require accepted assumptions to be revised or dropped.

Notice that argumentation along these informal lines, even in the realm of science, already has normative content because it presupposes certain value judgments: to say that an assertion (scientific or otherwise) is reasonable is to *commend* it. An unreasonable assumption is a *bad* assumption; a warranted claim is *worthy* to be believed; one who refuses to accept a conclusion overwhelmingly supported by reasoned argument is open to criticism as a *fool.* This point undermines the idea that the subject matter of political philosophy is in principle beyond the reach of rational assessment just because it involves normative claims. Once one appreciates that all reasoned argumentation, whether scientific, empirical, or otherwise, presupposes the validity of some normative standards, one can no longer cordon skepticism about the reasonableness of value judgments within any particular domain of inquiry. This suggests that either *both* science and political philosophy are governed by reasoned judgment or *neither* is.

Recall the arguments that helped bring about the enfranchisement of women in the West. Under the influence of these mobilizing arguments, people acquired a conviction that women's exclusion from the right to vote was unjust, and/or incompatible with democratic ideals. Clearly, this conviction is evaluative – it condemns a certain practice as unjust or undemocratic. But it is not for that reason "subjective" in a sense that helpfully contrasts with the "objectivity" of scientific judgment. For one thing, it is nothing like a brute psychological preference for e.g. chocolate ice-cream, which it would anyway be eccentric to describe as a *conviction* about what kinds of ice-cream are worth eating.

More importantly, like conclusions warranted by scientific experimentation, we can identify several very plausible grounds for enfranchising women, and quite easily expose the most familiar arguments against doing so as implausible. For example, we have no reason to accept the claim, which has historically been advanced in this context, that when compared to men, women as a group lack the intelligence or judgment needed to participate effectively in political deliberation. (At the very least, such a claim grossly exaggerates male intelligence.) And, insofar as justice requires that we not discriminate against people on the basis of entirely arbitrary considerations (skin color, religious belief, sexual orientation, eye color, etc.), we have good reasons to regard the exclusion of women from the vote as unjust. Moreover, restricting voting rights to men conflicts with the assumption, basic to the very idea of democracy, that all adults affected by public decisions should have a say in calling governments to account. Given the combined force of these considerations, the case for enfranchising women seems unassailable, at least given a commitment to justice and democracy. Viewed from this angle, denying that women should enjoy the right to vote seems just as unreasonable as rejecting Darwinian natural selection or insisting, against massive evidence to the contrary, that God created the world in six days.

To be sure, the fact that the reasons for enfranchising women overwhelm those against it hardly guarantees that die-hard chauvinists will actually give up their opinion that women have no place in the polling station. But their imperviousness is beside the point. Despite the devastating objections advanced by Darwinian biology, many also stubbornly refuse to abandon the theory that animal speciation must have been effected by an "intelligent designer." But the bare fact of their resistance hardly refutes Darwin; it merely reminds us that irrationality is quite common. Whether a reasoned argument is plausible depends not on whether people are in fact convinced by it, but rather on whether they ought to be. The empirical prevalence or obstinacy of particular beliefs is one thing, their defensibility quite another.

This reinforces both of the main claims that I have advanced here against flabby contrasts between the "objective" and the "subjective": first, that standards of rational judgment across the range of human inquiry do not differ in any fundamental way; and second, that because they are indeed *standards*, they are already normative. Whether we are investigating the causes of war, the nature of light, or the justice of social practices, we are inquiring into what we have *good* reason to believe, and presuming that rationally justified, as opposed to irrational or unwarranted, conclusions are worth wanting.

We have seen, then, that conventional dogmas about "objective" facts and "subjective" value judgments are too confused to daunt inquiry in political philosophy. One might well ask, however, why they nonetheless persist and command cultural credibility despite their manifest shortcomings.

One explanation, which I will not pursue, but is well worth thinking about, turns on the possibility that these dogmas endure because it serves the interests of dominant institutions and power structures that they do so. This possibility is a live one because the view that political judgments are hopelessly "subjective" has a defusing, rather than mobilizing, effect on complaints and grievances directed against the existing order. Insofar as criticisms of regnant institutions and practices are presumed to be merely "subjective" opinions beyond rational assessment, their claim to our attention diminishes. They will not be received as rational arguments carrying general probative force, giving anyone reasons to disapprove of the practices in question. They will rather seem merely to exemplify the critic's personal dissatisfaction and frustration, special pleading on behalf of some narrow, partisan, constituency, or the sort of grumbling that can never be eliminated from organized human life. Once defused in this fashion, the critic's complaints assume the guise of background noise with which we must learn to live, not a mobilizing reason to think that anything is seriously amiss. Since this line of thinking may predispose us against recognizing in such grievances any reasons to suspect that something is fundamentally wrong, the allegation that it tends to protect the existing state of affairs from critical scrutiny is therefore quite plausible.

In reply, one might point out that the dogma of "subjectivism" will have the same defusing effect on judgments purporting to *defend* the existing order; they, too, will appear as merely "subjective" expressions of approval, presumably reflecting speakers' personal interests in maintaining it. However, precisely because it *is* the *status quo*, this may not matter very much. By hypothesis, it already enjoys dominion over the men and women whose allegiance is in question; the critic, by contrast, is usually a voice crying in the wilderness, occupying a position of comparative social weakness. This makes it safe for the existing regime to simply concede that apologists and critics are on an equal footing, both equally entitled to their "subjective" opinions. As Marx pointed out "between equal rights, force decides."[4] If it helps the "powers that be" win by default, then, the dogma of "subjectivism" may be among their most important allies.

Pacifica and Atlantis

Another, simpler and less sinister, reason why that dogma persists is that many confuse it with a more plausible set of doubts about the enterprise of political philosophy. This more sophisticated form of skepticism stems, not from hazy distinctions between "objectivity" and "subjectivity," but rather from an appreciation of the depth and extent of *reasonable disagreement* in politics.

I suggested earlier that, like scientific research, political philosophy aims to *inform* its addressees by justifying nontrivial conclusions. To make good on this informative ambition, arguments must somehow narrow the range of reasonable disagreement about the topic under consideration. They must, in other words, uncover reasons that promote judgments previously in dispute into ones that can no longer be reasonably denied. To illustrate, before Copernicus and Galileo, agents could reasonably disagree over whether the Earth orbits the Sun or vice versa: the available evidence permitted either interpretation. Their more precise measures of the Sun's true trajectory would ultimately render geocentric views untenable and put heliocentrism beyond reasonable dispute. They advanced cosmology by informing us that, far from being the center of anything, the Earth is actually part of a *solar* system.

One might doubt, however, whether philosophical arguments about the justifiability of alternative *political* arrangements can be genuinely

---

[4] Marx 1992, p. 344.

informative in the same way. Can we reasonably expect such arguments to significantly narrow the range of reasonable disagreement about how societies should be politically organized? One reason for pessimism is that political arguments, whether defusing or mobilizing, characteristically invoke evaluative assumptions and concepts that themselves proliferate, rather than reduce, reasonable disagreements. Ideals like justice, fairness, equality, the "free society," or the "common good," for example, often figure prominently in arguments for or against political arrangements and actions. But these concepts are controversial and notoriously difficult to pin down. Different people and political cultures interpret them in radically conflicting ways.

To highlight the character of such disagreements, consider two fictional countries, Atlantis and Pacifica, whose public life revolves around two very different conceptions of justice. Atlantis is a democratic regime and its political culture dedicates itself to an egalitarian ideal of justice. All Atlantans are assumed to be independent, free beings, each with an equal right, founded upon justice, to be respected as such by their fellows and the social institutions that regulate their common life. On this basis, freedom of speech and religion are upheld, and the Atlantan state represents itself as a wholly secular institution, entirely independent of any church or devotional creed. A commitment to these norms is woven into the day-to-day practices of Atlantan public life – judges, citizens, and public officials accept the Atlantan political system because they believe that it accords, broadly, with the egalitarian conception of justice they endorse. Atlantis has a market economy and although holdings of income and wealth are highly unequal, broadly speaking both rich and poor accept the prevailing economic distribution as just. Basic political entitlements, such as the right to vote or run for office, are, however, not conditioned on economic wealth.

In nearby Pacifica, however, things are very different. Pacifica is an oligarchical regime, whose political culture and entrenched social practices revolve around a quite opposed, and strongly inegalitarian, understanding of justice. Pacifica is a caste hierarchy whose members enjoy different social entitlements and privileges: some are born into aristocratic status, others attain it through economic success or by becoming government officials; others belong to a middle class of gentleman professionals, who enjoy some, though restricted, rights of political participation; the rest are peasants or manual laborers who are barred from positions of public responsibility. Although Pacifica has abolished slavery, most of the peasants and laborers come from previously enslaved families, and are tainted by a resulting social stigma. Women are excluded from positions of public responsibility and status and are expected to remain at home raising children and running households; a widely accepted norm of modesty forbids them from wearing clothes that expose too much of their skin. The Pacifican constitution explicitly endorses a particular religious doctrine, practiced by a majority, but also conscientiously rejected by many others. It does not guarantee freedom of worship outside the mainstream religious tradition. Religious and political speech is subject to government censorship. Although a market economy exists in Pacifica, it is highly regulated, with the ownership and operation of industrial and other enterprises largely in the hands of oligarchs drawn from the aristocratic castes. The dominant religious beliefs also restrict economic activity in certain ways: prostitution and the sale of pornographic materials are forbidden as sinful; the right to accumulate wealth is conditioned by a religious expectation of liberality, requiring support for the poor. Let us suppose that these practices are stable and that they are widely accepted as just by members of Pacifican society. Even those who are disadvantaged by them – women and religious dissenters, for example – largely acquiesce in them, socialized to accept that it is not their place to question their subordinate status.

Although Pacifican and Atlantan ideals of justice are so different as to be mutually incompatible, they nonetheless play similar roles in the two societies. Each is the object of a local, although somewhat open-ended, consensus about the basic expectations of justice. That is, although they commit Pacificans and Atlantans to definite visions of a good society, these frameworks are not so fixed as to preclude any further discussion about how they should be interpreted and applied in specific cases. For example, the Atlantan commitment to freedom of worship presupposes some general assumptions about what counts as a genuine religion, and in borderline cases Atlantans may disagree over which devotional practices should be protected by it. The Atlantan ideal of "equal respect for all" is also open-ended with respect to the public provision of welfare; some Atlantans may think that that ideal requires such provision, others that it forbids it. Similar internal disagreements are possible in Pacifica: Pacificans may not be of one mind over exactly what forms of female dress are "immodest";

and they may disagree over the terms on which individuals might earn or lose aristocratic status.

Notice again that the language of "subjectivity" fails to capture the character of these disagreements. Those debating these issues within each society are surely doing more than simply expressing unreasoned preferences, like likes and dislikes for ice-cream flavors. The parties will offer each other reasoned arguments for interpreting Pacifican and Atlantan ideals of justice in different ways. And it is at least possible that some of them will have the better of the argument. This was true, as noted earlier, of those who, in our own societies, appealed to a broadly Atlantan understanding of justice and democracy to mount a virtually unassailable case for women's suffrage.

However, such arguments were compelling precisely because they addressed people who already take that democratic vision of justice for granted. They will not impress Pacificans, whose discourse about justice proceeds from a radically opposed starting point. Even one who concedes that an Atlantan conception of justice entails women's suffrage might still ask why we should accept that conception in the first place. After all, the Pacificans seem to manage perfectly well without it, and clearly their understanding of justice will not support extending political rights to women.

Putting these internal debates in Atlantis and Pacifica side by side thus exposes a deeper form of disagreement about justice. In thinking of their societies as just, Pacificans and Atlantans both appeal to the same concept. At a sufficiently general level they might agree on certain elements of that concept: that it involves notions of fairness, of giving people their due, applying the rules impartially, and so forth. But the way in which these two societies interpret this basic concept results in radically opposed *conceptions* of justice. From a conventional Atlantan point of view, societies count as just rather than unjust to the extent that they approximate some principle of basic equality; but from a Pacifican perspective societies count as just insofar as they perpetuate and respond to various sorts of inequality. These views exclude each other. But it is also difficult to see how we might resolve the disagreement between them. For here there seems to be no consensus in place, no obvious fund of shared assumptions to which Pacificans or Atlantans might appeal to try to vindicate their underlying views about justice against each other.

Those impressed by these seemingly intractable disagreements often regard them as illustrating a more general phenomenon: that normative ideals like justice exemplify what W. B. Gallie called "essentially contested concepts." According to Gallie, "when we examine the different uses of these [concepts] and the characteristic arguments in which they figure we soon see that there is no one clearly definable general use of any of them which can be set up as the correct or standard use." As a result, we can expect "endless disputes" about the proper uses and implications of these concepts.[5] And what goes for justice, we may fear, also goes for other "essentially contestable" concepts that figure prominently in political argument: "the common good," "equality," "democracy," and so on. How can we demonstrate that some of these rival interpretations are superior to the others? Beyond informing us about *how* people reasonably disagree over the meaning of justice, can political philosophers supply nontrivial information about whose interpretations are more and less plausible?

Positive and Critical Morality

These questions pose a deeper challenge for political philosophy than the dogma of "subjectivism" rejected earlier. The sort of radical disagreement over justice and other political ideals just introduced is disturbing precisely because those party to them seem to be disagreeing *about* something, and to care about being in the right. If they were merely emoting or voicing simple appetites and aversions, why would they waste their time trying to convince others that they should share the same inclinations? One can hardly *argue* someone out of a food allergy. But defusing and mobilizing arguments circulating in political discourse presuppose that political judgment is not like this: people bother to advance them because they believe they offer genuine reasons to judge political practices favorably or unfavorably. Yet, even though they are more than just expressions of "subjective" opinion, if these arguments turn on "essentially contested" concepts, their capacity to significantly narrow the range of reasonable disagreement in politics still seems doubtful.

One might try to downplay this challenge. Perhaps political philosophers should accept the inherent locality and cultural relativity of the standards

---

[5] Gallie 1956, pp. 168–9.

implicit in political criticism and work exclusively within particular traditions, not worrying too much about the interface between different political cultures like those of Pacifica and Atlantis. This line is implicitly taken by an influential strand in contemporary political philosophy that takes for granted a "liberal" or "liberal democratic" political culture dominant today in the West and seeks to determine what its leading precepts imply about a range of specific issues (free speech, democratic representation, minority rights, welfare provision, punishment, etc.).[6] In effect, these political philosophers are like Atlantans who suggest that the criticism of Atlantan institutions can best proceed within terms that Atlantans already accept. After all, we can hardly expect political arguments to gain much traction with Atlantans if they rest on assumptions that they in fact do not or cannot accept. More generally, as long as Pacifica and Atlantis keep out of each other's way, why should these radical disagreements bother citizens of either society? Why not simply encourage Atlantans to get on with organizing their civic life in their own way and Pacificans to do the same? Why not just say, "diff'rent strokes for diff'rent folks"?

But this effort to sidestep the issue proves ultimately unsatisfying. As a practical matter, we cannot usually assume, as our stylized example has done to this point, that deep disagreements of this kind coincide neatly with the boundaries of different communities. The more standard case is one in which – to adapt the example – citizens with Pacifican and Atlantan understandings of justice must live side by side within a common civic order. In such circumstances we do not really have the luxury of saying: "Let the Pacificans and Atlantans amongst us go their separate ways." Unless Pacificans and Atlantans secede from each other, then their civic association will be marked by a troubling, and potentially destabilizing, dissensus about its orienting values. Under these conditions, it will surely be difficult for Pacificans and Atlantans (and, for that matter, Mediterraneans, Caspians, etc.) to ignore their profound differences over the fundamental requirements of justice.

This points to a deeper philosophical reason why we cannot simply sidestep deep disagreements between rival conceptions of justice, and why it is complacent to simply relativize the remit of political philosophy to locally entrenched traditions like "liberalism." To appreciate it, consider

[6] Johnston 1996; Tomasi 2012; see also Walzer 1993, 1994.

an important distinction drawn by the twentieth-century legal philosopher H. L. A. Hart between "positive" and "critical" morality.[7]

As Hart defined it, "critical morality" refers to the perspective one adopts when one steps back from existing practices and institutions in order to assess their adequacy, rationality, or overall value. To do this, the critical moralist canvasses "universally applicable" or "rationally acceptable" principles for "the evaluation or criticism of social institutions generally." She thus postulates, and tries to specify, "the legitimacy of a standpoint which permits criticism of the institutions of any society, in the light of general principles and knowledge of the facts."[8]

In contrast, "positive" morality refers to any set of norms (they might be legal, ethical, cultural, religious, professional, political, sporting, to do with manners or courtesy, etc.) that are *in fact* internalized and accepted among agents participating in activities, associations, or organizations. For example, the norm that one remove one's hat when entering a church, the rule that in the UK one drives on the left, the prohibition on handling the ball in soccer, or the expectation that married persons should not commit adultery, are all aspects of various positive moralities. Some of these expectations, like rules of the road, have the force of law; others, like the rules of a game, are similarly formalized but not strictly legal matters; still others are enforced informally, by shaming, ostracizing, or openly reviling violators (as in the Me Too movement).

Unlike the principles applied in "critical morality," the norms constituting "positive moralities" in Hart's sense need not be rational, ethically defensible, or in any way good. Criminal organizations like the Mafia, for example, sometimes operate according to a code of honor requiring the immediate assassination of traitors. That code remains a positive morality despite its brutality. Innocuous traditions, like the expectation that one ruin a perfectly good Christmas lunch by serving disgusting plum pudding for dessert, is a positive moral norm even though nauseating (to some of us). Often, we can know what positive moral norms require even though we ourselves disapprove of them. For example, a staunch opponent of monarchy may think that the customs to be observed at a royal wedding are utterly ridiculous, but still recognize when to curtsy and correctly identify

[7] Hart 1963.
[8] Hart 1963, pp. 19–21.

breaches of protocol. Something becomes a "positive morality," then, not in virtue of its justifiability, mode of enforcement or value. What matters, rather, is that the relevant norms are, as a matter of social fact, observed and generally recognized as valid within some community.

Can we understand the Atlantan and Pacifican conceptions of justice simply as positive moralities in this sense? Certainly, as I have depicted them, they partly function as such, for, as a matter of social fact, Pacificans and Atlantans will routinely make judgments about proper and improper conduct by appealing to those conceptions. In this sense, each conception of justice is implicated in an entrenched social practice of *recognition* or *accreditation*. That is, they make available to members of both societies certain criteria to determine whether actual procedures, practices, and conduct in their societies *count* as just or unjust.

Yet, this cannot be the whole story, because the concept of justice also brings with it an element of *valuation*. Justice purports to be a *value-conferring* property: just societies are *good* societies and worthy of our allegiance for that reason. So, in judging social arrangements to be just, we are not merely applying a bloodless checklist of conventionally accepted criteria. We are also appraising them as *superior* to those that are unjust or less just – and not merely along any old dimension, either. Unlike trivial expectations like the rules of the card game patience, or some stupid tradition that we could easily abandon, the requirements of justice purport to be of enormous importance in public life. To contend, then, that Atlantan institutions are just is to say more than that they satisfy some set of positive moral standards. It is also to assert that we have a strong reason to value the Atlantan regime *because* it satisfies those standards.

This value-conferring feature seems to be a fixed point in our ordinary understandings. It would be strange to say that there could be an essentially just society that is in no important respect better than an unjust one. "Hooray, we just punished an innocent man!" "Damn the courts for seeing that justice is done!" seem incoherent statements. We normally assume that just societies are in some absolutely vital sense superior to unjust ones. We are likely to believe this even when the adjective "just" is applied to things we otherwise regard as bad. We may think, for example, that war is always regrettable, but would nonetheless accept that a *just* war is in some important respect better, or at any rate less bad, than an unjust one.

So Pacificans and Atlantans do not merely differ over matters of accreditation, i.e. over how they apply locally accepted criteria to recognize justice and injustice. In applying those criteria, they implicitly assert that we ought to value certain ways of doing things rather than others, and that we have overriding reasons to approve of certain institutions and not others.

This evaluative dimension takes us beyond mere positive morality and into Hart's domain of critical moral reflection. And when viewed from this angle, Pacifica and Atlantis are not merely doing different things, but asserting mutually exclusive ideals. Yet we cannot easily sweep the conflict between these ideals under the rug with trite slogans about "diff'rent strokes for diff'rent folks." The reason for this is straightforward: presumably the same value cannot make contradictory demands. To be sure, something can be good in one respect and bad in another. But it is hard to understand how it can be both good and bad *in the same respect.*

That is why it makes no sense to say that it can be just *both* to subordinate women *and* uphold gender equality. As long as justice is some sort of value, it has to be one or the other. White supremacist practices cannot be simultaneously just and unjust, even though they have sometimes been conventionally regarded as essential to the justice and health of the social order and sometimes repudiated in other political cultures as outrageous injustices. If democratic societies are better than dictatorships because the former are more just, it cannot be the case that dictatorships are more just than democracies. And so on.

These points are obvious. But that they entail disturbing conclusions is not always clearly appreciated. If we grant that concepts like justice are "essentially contested" then we may have to admit that we cannot significantly reduce reasonable disagreement about what they imply. This is an unsatisfying result. It makes our earlier canvassed proposal that political philosophers should decline to look beyond the positive moralities and political cultures regnant in their own societies hard to live with. Operating exclusively *within* some locally accepted, but contested, understanding of justice like that of Atlantis, Pacifica, or the tradition of modern "liberalism," leaves some nagging questions. No doubt we learn something by figuring out how we should think about justice *if* we are committed to "liberalism." But if we are being asked to conform our whole lives to its requirements, and sometimes to sacrifice our own interests to them, do we not also need to know why *it* can legitimately claim our allegiance?

Critical Morality as Introspective

So, to make good on their ambition to inform agents about how they ought to evaluate institutions, practices, and policies, political philosophers cannot be content to operate merely within the accepted conventions of particular societies (whether their own or others). They must somehow get beyond the local positive moralities that sustain historically entrenched social practices and judge them from the more encompassing, independent standpoint of critical morality. But how can they attain the requisite critical distance? Why, and on what basis, can we trust philosophical arguments to reliably inform us about the value of different political arrangements from a suitably detached perspective? What are the principles that apply in critical moral reflection? This issue has haunted Western political philosophy from its beginnings in antiquity.

Traditionally, it has been approached by trying to distinguish between (on the one hand) a set of universal, common standards that all rational agents would, on due reflection, affirm, and (on the other) the various psychological dispositions, cultural biases, and narrowly personal concerns that dominate the particular perspectives from which they lead their lives. The task of the critical moralist, in this picture, is to deploy philosophical argument in a way that allows agents to abstract from their particular interests, proclivities, and cultural orientations and to converge on a common rational standpoint from which they can assess their form of life on something like an impartial basis. This approach hopes that agents occupying a wide variety of personal perspectives can be led, through a process of philosophically guided introspection, to transcend their many differences and agree on a set of criteria whose critical authority and import *anyone* should recognize.

The next five chapters consider two families of historically influential theories that develop this basic line, one committed to the idea of a "common good" (Chapters 2–4), and the other proposing the idea of a "social contract" (Chapters 5–6). Despite the many differences between and within these two paradigms, their exponents all try to reach a critical understanding of the goals of political association by inviting agents to rationally introspect on their interests, circumstances, and commitments.

For example, Thomas Hobbes and John Locke, the two most important theorists of the classical "social contract," ask each of us to reflect, from within our own points of view, on what we most fundamentally care about.

When we do this, Hobbes and Locke maintain, we discover that, starting from any idiosyncratic perspective agents in fact occupy, the rational interest in personal security and survival emerges as prior to all others.

In emphasizing the importance of self-preservation, Hobbes and Locke were building on a long-standing theory which they themselves accepted and that goes back to Roman antiquity.[9] That theory postulates the exist-ence of a so-called "natural law," comprising a set of universal ethical precepts ("do not kill innocents," "do not lie," "do not steal," "show impar-tiality," etc.) standing behind, and conditioning the legitimacy of, systems of "positive law" and other conventionally accepted ethical expectations. According to this theory, the natural law affords an authoritative and uni-versal standard by which "critical moral" reflection can proceed. When a positive law (or accepted moral norm) conflicts with the natural law (e.g. "ugly babies are to be strangled at birth"), it ceases to be a valid law.[10]

The natural lawyers equated the "natural law" with "right reason," and so they claimed that to determine its content and authority, rational agents need only look within themselves. As St. Paul put it, in a formula still cited by the Church today, all rational creatures already have the "requirements of the law ... written on their hearts." If we sometimes fail to recognize or act on these requirements, it is on this view because the internal voice of reason is easily drowned out by the din of externally oriented appetites, emotions, personal ambitions, cultural biases, and partiality to self. To dis-cover it, we must silence the call of our idiosyncratic personal interests and let our common reason speak from within.

Hobbes and Locke argued that when we introspect in this way, we find that the most fundamental precept of the natural law is the rational imperative of self-preservation and survival. They contended that this is the one, uncontentious, rational principle that *anyone* introspecting on their deepest personal concerns must acknowledge as the foundation for all reasoning about politics and practical action. In Chapters 5 and 6, we will explore how this idea led Hobbes and Locke, and some more recent fig-ures, to develop the modern theory of the social contract (which eventually came to float free of their concern with self-preservation).

---

[9] Cicero 2009.

[10] Hence the natural lawyers' famous slogan "lex iniusta non est lex" – an unjust law is not law.

Another, much older, variant of this introspective approach forms the topic of the next three chapters. It first appears in a clear and sophisticated form in Plato's *Republic*,[11] which, despite its antiquity, has had an enormous and continuing impact on Western political thought down to the present. Plato's argument hinges on a point noted earlier: virtues like justice purport to enhance the societies or individuals that display or (as Plato put it) "possess" them. A just action is *better* than an unjust one; the presence of injustice reflects *badly* on those responsible; and to say of an institution that it guarantees justice is to praise it as *good*.

If justice is value-conferring in this way, it seems to follow that no fully adequate conception of justice could actually make those who accept and comply with it worse off. Plato inferred that no social order that harms its own members can be truly just. He accordingly invited readers to abstract from their conventional beliefs about justice, to introspect on their deepest rational interests and to consider how different conceptions of justice, if followed and internalized by themselves and others, would secure or undermine those interests. In pursuing this line of argument, Plato helped to launch the idea that a society is only truly just when its political arrangements work impartially to the advantage of all. As Plato himself put it, his project in the *Republic* was to "determine which whole way of life would make living most worthwhile for each of us."[12] Plato's attempt to answer this question in the *Republic* became the prototype for a whole tradition of inquiry into the proper requirements of a "common good," because it led him to investigate how differently configured conventions and institutions might successfully or unsuccessfully coordinate social interaction so that it genuinely secures mutual advantage. Theories of the "common good" raise many questions: how do we determine whether someone's life is enhanced in the relevant sense? Compared to what? How do we ensure that everyone's interests are taken impartially into consideration? What is the relevant standard of impartiality? The history of inquiry into the nature of the common good is the story of various efforts to confront and answer these questions. The next three chapters survey and assess some of the most provocative efforts to tackle them.

[11] Plato 1992.
[12] Plato 1992, p. 21.

Critical Morality as Historical

Before considering theories of the common good, however, I close this chapter by describing an alternative approach to critical moral reflection that dissents from the traditional approaches just described, and especially their reliance on introspection as a propitious vehicle for political criticism. For reasons that shortly emerge, I will refer to it as a *historical* approach. This "historical" alternative will, where relevant, make occasional appearances throughout the book, and receives more extensive attention in Chapter 14. This different approach is of much more recent provenance, with few clear precursors before the mid eighteenth century. Its founding text is Rousseau's *Discourse on the Origin of Inequality* (1755),[13] but it matured only with Marx in the nineteenth century,[14] and the various intellectual movements he helped inspire.

Since they form a very diverse group of thinkers,[15] generalizing about those committed to this historical alternative is a little dangerous, but it seems safe to attribute to them a basic organizing intuition. Although they fully endorse the general goal of considering conventional morality and political practice from an independent standpoint, these critics have followed Marx in rejecting as naïve the assumption that mere introspection can afford the needed critical perspective. Marx's objection runs essentially as follows: to make any sense, that assumption requires that agents can clearly distinguish, within their own introspection, between two types of concerns:

(1) those that matter to them only because of features peculiar to their socialization, historical context, personal experience, and contingent characteristics;

and

(2) those that matter to them because all rational agents *as such* universally endorse them, regardless of any historically, psychologically, or culturally specific circumstances in which they find themselves.

---

[13] Rousseau 1992.
[14] Marx and Engels 1978, pp. 146–202.
[15] Foucault 1984; Geuss 1981, 2005; Held 1980; Horkheimer 1982.

Marx, however, denied that any such clear distinction is available because he doubted that "introspection" ever operates in isolation from the particular cultural, psychological, and historical influences determining agents' consciousness quite generally. He held, to the contrary, that agents can introspect at all only because and to the extent that they have absorbed vocabularies, concepts, categories, and beliefs that give them both means and objects of philosophical reflection. But these vocabularies and concepts are not, Marx insisted, independent of history, culture, and psychology, but are themselves entirely conditioned by such particularities. For that reason, they are also highly varied.

To illustrate, contrast medieval Christians with those (like us) for whom the structures of commercial capitalism are so pervasive as to be axiomatic. When they introspect, these differently primed agents will bring to bear quite divergent repertoires of concepts shaped by their own upbringings and social experiences. The medieval Christian's introspection will be populated by such categories as "sin," "redemption," "resurrection," "sacrament," "the Trinity," etc. Those socialized into modern commercial societies will absorb a distinct, sometimes opposed, set of concepts, and these will shape how they introspect on their own social circumstances. These newer concepts permit, for example, various reinterpretations of the categories central in medieval theism: "sinners" can be recast as "consumers"; churches compared with "firms," "corporations," or "businesses"; the wafers and wine administered in the Eucharist assimilated to "commodities"; the sin of "usury" redefined as rational "investment"; and marriage regarded less as a "sacrament" than a "contract," etc. This suggests that introspection is no less partial and historically conditioned than the various positive moralities and social practices we are trying to critically evaluate.

Marx concluded that the traditional effort to gain critical perspective on social practices and positive morality by addressing arguments to agents' introspection is fundamentally confused. Rather than opening a genuinely critical angle on current practice, philosophically guided introspection can at best repackage in a generalized, abstract form aspects of the very forms of life we are seeking to critically assess. Since, on this view, introspective plausibility is itself a culturally and historically relative variable, it will remain entrapped within what Marx called the "illusion[s] of the epoch." Marx used the term "ideology" to denote all beliefs that appear introspectively credible to agents in the light of their particular historical experience and situation.

This technical Marxian notion of "ideology" departs from the usual meaning of that term today. We typically use the word "ideology" to refer to rival political positions like "socialism," "liberalism," "conservatism," "eco-feminism," etc. Such partisan allegiances may be related to "ideology" in Marx's sense, but they do not define it. For Marx, *any* merely intro-spective conception of one's interests and circumstances (whether or not it corresponds to a recognized political stance or movement) will exemplify "ideology," since he denied that bare introspection can escape assumptions and prejudices given by the introspecter's cultural and historical context.

Why, for example, does the idea that agents have "natural rights" to private property seem so plausible to many in our society? Is it because the concept of a natural property right commends itself to the introspection of any rational agent independently of their socialization into a historically particular form of life? If so, one would need to explain why such a concept seems to have occurred to virtually no one before the mid seventeenth century, and has only recently acquired any currency at all. According to Marx, in the face of this inconvenient fact, the more plausible hypothesis is that the concept of a "natural property right" is simply an ideological (in his sense) generalization of the routines of capitalist market exchange, which (not coincidentally?) became increasingly dominant after the seven-teenth century. Its credibility to agents today on this view reflects the dom-inance of a historically contingent ideology, not a universal truth of reason revealed through impartial introspection.

If introspective reflection is in this way always a child of its time and cul-ture, what alternative is available for those seeking to introduce critical dis-tance on their ways of life? Those who have followed Marx's lead have not all been of one mind in their answers to this question, but most, including Marx himself, have stressed the importance of historical awareness. They argue that, by understanding how one's form of life evolved from earlier, quite contrasting, historical formations, one can appreciate their particular characteristics and structure with fresh eyes. One comes to realize that assumptions that appear to the contemporary mind self-evident, natural, and beyond criticism would not have been obvious to (and indeed were often explicitly rejected by) agents in earlier times. At the very least, such historical awareness will tend to loosen the grip of prevailing orthodoxies, attuning agents to the possibility that their most basic assumptions about their place in the world are not set in stone, but are open to revision.

For example, the discovery that specific beliefs about the nature and social position of women, or about the basis of property rights, have been historically very fluid, and have gained traction at particular times for complex social and political reasons, should automatically lead agents to reflect critically on how and why *they* have acquired the particular beliefs about men and women or about the importance of private property toward which they in fact incline. Through such historical perspective, women may find that their self-conception need not be captive to entrenched assumptions about traditional gender roles; or agents may reconsider whether, as they may unreflectively assume, private property must be a sacrosanct "natural right." By pursuing a historically minded approach, then, critical moralists hope to enlighten agents about the real character of their political situation.

They can do so, moreover, without postulating that abstract philosophical introspection on one's interests as a rational agent gives access to some universal, impartial standpoint from which institutions and practices can be authoritatively judged. To be sure, critical reflection of this historical kind may have the *effect* of altering agents' introspective self-awareness. Unlike more traditional approaches, however, it does not claim to achieve such transformations in self-understanding *through* introspection conducted in abstraction from historical particulars. To the contrary, it aims to do so, rather, by careful historical investigation into the external social and political forces that condition agents' own consciousness of their actual political circumstances. In this sense, it tries to get people out of their own heads, by getting them to contemplate the reality of their external political predicament.

For this reason, contemporary exponents of this broadly Marxian approach often cast themselves as political "realists."[16] They do not use this label because they are anti-utopians or inherently opposed to the pursuit of ideals in politics. They do so, rather, because they believe that the only way to achieve an informative critical perspective in political philosophy is to investigate, in an honest, unsentimental, and empirically rigorous way, the real historical forces that at once shape agents' actual political situation while perhaps disguising its real character.

---

[16] Geuss 2008; Williams 2005.

We might put their point in the terms with which this chapter began. If we want to understand how the plumbing actually works, where it is malfunctioning, and what we might do about it, introspecting on whatever beliefs we may have acquired about maintaining water pressure, likely causes of leaks, and so on can only get us so far. If we want to appreciate what is really going on, and what might be wrong with our form of life, in the final analysis we have to punch through the walls to expose the pipes.

2   The Common Good

The last chapter concluded by noting Marx's reasons for doubting that, simply by engaging in philosophical introspection, agents can escape the conventional "positive" practices into which they are socialized (in different places and historical epochs) and assess them from an independent, critically informative perspective. His challenge to that aspiration is powerful, but before endorsing it, we need to at least consider the most promising versions of the more traditional approaches to critical moral reflection he rejected. As I mentioned in Chapter 1, one of these approaches is centered on the postulation of a *common good*. This chapter presents a very old, but still influential, version of the common-good approach, first pioneered in antiquity by Plato and his pupil Aristotle. The next considers a more recent effort to update this approach for use under modern conditions – that of classical utilitarianism. Chapter 4 then considers some criticisms of these various construals of the common good.

The Idea of a "Common Good"

In the seventeenth century, Louis XIV of France is reputed to have declared "l'état, c'est moi" (I am the state). The story is probably apocryphal, but in any case most instinctively resist the suggestion implicit in Louis's boast: that political associations, or other corporate forms like universities, clubs, or firms, are appropriately ruled by any particular person, as if their resources, inhabitants, or territory are exclusively at the disposal of a specific individual just as means for promoting his or her ends. Against that view, Aristotle insisted that the state is not simply the plaything of the ruler, slavishly subordinate to his or her personal whims. Rather, political rule is exercised appropriately on behalf, not of any particular individual, but of the community as a whole. It is rather, as the later tradition would put it, a *res publica* (a "public thing") – the locus of a self-conscious "we" with a good of its own. This Aristotelian idea implies that properly *political* association is oriented toward securing those interests that can be attributed to this corporate "we." Those interests form a "common good" in that they are not simply those of any particular individual or group within the state, but constitute the good of the community itself.

But how is this public "we," with capacities and interests of its own, constituted and identified? In the case of private individuals, we can rely on the natural fact of biological integrity to help identify the locus, jurisdiction, and remit of the relevant agents. Each natural person is born with a body over which they enjoy some mental control, equipped with various inherent assets and resources, and granted a finite (and roughly predictable) life expectancy during which "I," "you," "he," or "she" pursue their particular interests as best we or they can.

In one way, political agency is analogous: just as "you" and "I" are like personal pilots wielding power in own interest, in politics "We, the people" act together in our collective interest, aiming to secure our "common good." Clearly, however, biology is of no help in identifying the "we" whose interests form such a common good. "Belgium" is a social and historical construct, not a token of a biological type. States have, moreover, no definite life expectancy ordained by nature: they often outlive individuals by centuries, and whereas the resurrection of natural persons like Lazarus and Jesus is miraculous, we find nothing magical in Poland's reconstitution in 1918 after a century of nonexistence following its dismemberment at the end of the eighteenth century.

How, then, can we account for, and detect, the presence of a public "we" that intercedes, in an institutionalized form, between the affairs of private individuals for the sake of their "common good"? Surveying and assessing all of the possible answers to this question would require a comprehensive history of Western political thought. Fortunately, we do not have to rummage through this attic now. We need note only that the notion of a "positive morality" elaborated earlier is likely an important part of any plausible answer. The reason for this is that, in order for a set of norms and expectations to constitute *any* sort of positive morality, it cannot be the case that agents who recognize their validity do so *simply* because of pressure exerted on them by any identifiable private individual, any particular "I."[1] They must instead view those norms as providing a kind of *impersonal* guidance, in that their authority does not depend on the power of any specific individual or group to compel compliance.

To be sure, many sets of positive norms include rules that permit certain designated agents (officials, judges, police officers) to use power to force agents to comply. But when this is so, it is not that the validity of the rules reflects the *de facto* power of the relevant officials, but rather that those officials' *de jure* warrant to exercise such power depends on a prior and independent recognition of rules authorizing them to do so under specified circumstances. So the operation of a positive morality cannot be fully analyzed as bilateral exercises of power by specific persons over others. Once one sees this, one can begin to think of it as the locus of a kind of "we," formed around a common recognition of certain norms as valid. This provides a vital clue to demystifying the philosophical idea of a common good.

To develop this crucial but subtle point, consider how the rules of certain games empower particular officials (e.g. referees) to interpret and apply certain rules. When (say) a soccer player is sent off, their acknowledgement of the referee's authority to call a foul and order them to the dressing room is not simply a function of the power of the referee to enforce his decision. After all, the referee might in fact lose control of the situation and the game descend into chaos as open fighting breaks out among the players. But this would not show that the referee lacked the right to send the player off, merely that the players have chosen to ignore rules that they, and the spectators, independently recognize as essential to the orderly playing of the game.

Insofar as the rules are independently recognized in this way, they form a common point of reference by which a relevant community – in this case the community of soccer players and aficionados – can deliberate coherently about (e.g.) whether the referee was right to call a penalty on some occasion, whether certain teams are playing well or badly, whether certain rules (like the notorious "offside" rule in soccer) should be modified or relaxed, or "what a bloody disgrace" it was that the players chose to

---

[1] The classic statement of this point was provided by H. L. A. Hart in his critique of the "command theory of law" defended by the utilitarian thinker John Austin (Austin 1995; Hart 1994).

riot rather than respect the referee's decision. In engaging in such discussion, soccer players and fans effectively affirm a common responsibility to ensure that the game is properly played and continues to flourish. What makes this possible is their shared understanding of the rules and traditions of the game, and especially their recognition that these expectations are valid, not because anyone is bullying people into accepting them, but because members of the soccer community accept them and know that other members do so as well. In this sense, the game is a common good for them.

Why Politics Excludes Slavery

The same idea lies behind Aristotle's insistence, noted already, that relationships of absolute subordination, such as that of slavery, cannot be genuinely political or civic ones. In the master–slave relation, one party (the slave) is simply a "tool" for promoting the master's ends and needs. For Aristotle, however, such unilateral domination precludes any authentically *civic* or *political* bond. For civic relations presuppose at least minimal forms of mutual parity and partnership among those involved. The parties to political association must at least acknowledge each other as independent sources of potentially conflicting claims and needs that must be somehow reconciled on a reasonable and reciprocal basis. The unilateral domination of masters over slaves destroys any such parity; there is here only one real agent – the master – and only his interests count. The slave is simply added to the list of powers available to the master to meet his needs, like a jet plane acquired by a wealthy individual. The slave's powers are to the master as the thrust of a jet is to its new owner. In no sense does the engine *willingly* participate in propulsion, but as and when the pilot in the cockpit chooses to open the throttle.[2]

So, for Aristotle, authentically civic or political association begins when citizens pool their powers and resources and cooperate in assuming responsibility for each other's independent needs and interests on reasonable terms. It ends either in the absolute subordination typified by slavery,

---

[2] Aristotle's recognition of this conceptual point about slavery makes his own endorsement of "natural slavery" all the more horrifying. See Aristotle 1981, 1254b16–21.

or when the various groups constituting a society become so alienated and factionalized that they cease to function as an integrated "we," and instead fall into open conflict to be resolved, not through communal deliberation about how to move forward together, but by the outcomes of blind (and perhaps violent) contests for power.

From this Aristotelian point of view, then, the absorption of various expectations of justice into a society's positive morality is both symptom and agent of the archetypically *civic* effort to cooperate in assuming proper responsibility for the flourishing of a shared community and its common assets. On this model, the norms and expectations around which public life revolves are not unilateral commands imposed by others bent only on securing their own narrow interests. Rather, like the rules of a game, they are *ours*, demands we make of ourselves as we play. They frame a common form of life, based on the assumption, always open to challenge, that the demands members place on each other are reasonable. In reflecting together on the value and purpose of these rules, and on how they might reasonably be configured or modified, citizens deliberate about their common good.

The Common Good in Politics

The game analogy usefully illustrates the general *idea* of the common good, but mobilizing that idea in the context of politics faces two immediate complications. One is that if we are not interested in chess or soccer, no one is going to force us to play. Political association, however, is virtually inescapable, and so submission to the positive norms regulating public life is typically compulsory in a way that following the rules of a game is not.

The other is by now familiar: although we possess certain concepts – like justice – that purport to describe desiderata that *any* good polity must satisfy, different countries and political cultures have notoriously disagreed on what exactly justice requires. The project of realizing political justice therefore appears to be far more open-ended than the rules of any particular game. If we radically alter its rules, chess would cease to *be* chess. But Pacifica and Atlantis both purport to be doing the *same* thing – pursuing justice as a common good – despite the radically different content of their respective conceptions of justice. As we have seen, it is difficult to believe that they can both be correct in their surmise that the particular vision of justice they aim to secure is really to the credit, rather than to the detriment, of their respective forms of life.

Plato was among the first to realize, however, that the challenge of determining whether, and in what sense, justice enhances societies might open up the critical perspective that political philosophers need to step back from the prejudices of regnant positive moralities. That is why his most powerful and influential work in political philosophy, the *Republic*, is framed around the effort to show that "justice benefits its possessor." His gambit is this: if, as that phrase indicates, justice is a value-conferring property, we may be able to invalidate or vindicate the credentials of alternative conceptions of justice by asking whether they make life better for those whose common life is structured by them.

Plato's question, then, is this: what is some realized positive morality of justice really worth to those who internalize its precepts and act accordingly (who, in Plato's language, "possess it")? That question immediately opens up others. In what sense is life made "better" under some scheme of rules than under others? Better how, and for whom? These questions are not easy to answer, but Plato was surely right to suspect that their answers promise to shed fruitful light on the real value of different ways of organizing society. The reason for this can be appreciated by invoking an analogy with medicine that Plato himself emphasized.

Anyone following a medically prescribed regimen will (i) internalize certain rules (take these pills twice a day, no coffee after 4pm, boil the entrails of a sacrificed animal and inhale the fumes for breakfast, etc.) and (ii) follow these rules because they believe that doing so is good for them. Like internalized conceptions of justice, all medical regimens *purport* to be good, in that they are supposed to advance the health of the patient. But it is one thing for someone to follow such a regimen in the belief that it is doing them good, and another for that belief to be sound. Some regimens may be effective, some less so, and others may be positively harmful. Insofar as we can establish that some are actually toxic, we can falsify their medical credentials and expose patients' beliefs about their value as confused. Plato proposed that we assess possible or actual positive moralities of justice in an exactly analogous way, by demanding that they prove their implicit claim to be enhancing the lives of those who follow them. To meet that demand, such positive moralities must at a minimum show that, unlike quack medical therapies that actually poison those who undergo them, they do not harm those who internalize their expectations. Positive moralities that fail that test form, not a genuine common good, but a common *bad*.

Clearly, just as medical judgment presupposes some implicit understanding of physical health, pursuing this line of inquiry requires a working account of human well-being to determine the beneficial and harmful effects of organizing common life around alternative positive moralities of justice. To introduce Plato's efforts in that direction, and to highlight their critical potential, I first consider, in schematic form, the positive morality of political justice regnant in liberal democratic societies like ours. For among the most challenging implications of Plato's argument is that the liberal democratic understandings of justice must be fundamentally defective. It suggests that far from serving as the framework for a common good encompassing everyone's well-being, it inevitably harms some of those living under it. If Plato is right about this, some of our deeply held convictions about the value of liberal democratic institutions are confused: what we take to be common goods are actually common bads, like quack medical treatments that hurt, rather than help, their patients. As we shall see, his challenge remains powerful even today.

Public and Private

In the following extract, the poet W. H. Auden gives us a rough but beautiful summary of the "positive morality" around which today's liberal democratic societies revolve:

> There are two atlases: the one
> The public space where acts are done,
> In theory common to us all,
> Where we are needed and feel small,
> The *agora* of work and news
> Where each one has the right to choose
> His trade, his corner and his way,
> And can, again, in theory, say
> For whose protection he will pay,
> And loyalty is help we give
> The place where we prefer to live;
> The other is the inner space

Of private ownership, the place
That each of us is forced to own,
Like his own life from which it's grown,
The landscape of his will and need
Where he is sovereign indeed,
The state created by his acts
Where he patrols the forest tracts
Planted in childhood, farms the belt
Of doings memorized and felt,
And even if he find it hell
May neither leave it nor rebel.
Two worlds describing their rewards,
That one in tangents, this in chords;
Each lives in one, all in the other,
Here all are kings, there each a brother.

W. H. Auden, from *New Year Letter* (January 1, 1940)[3]

Implicit in Auden's poem is a certain vision of justice, centered on a distinction between a public and a private realm. As his geometrical metaphor nicely suggests, this broadly liberal democratic conception of justice asserts the importance of maintaining the integrity of a sphere of private, individual, discretion, a zone within which (as it were) "Captain 'I'" and "Captain 'You'" enjoy a kind of sovereignty. Justice is on this view fundamentally a matter of policing the "tangents" at which our separately led lives might collide. It is a purely external virtue, organizing the relations between persons, but as far as possible refusing to dictate the internal structure of individuals' own lives, the shadowy "chords" by which each of us chooses to order our inward lives. This private, "inner space" is to be protected from outside interference so that each of us enjoys maximum discretion to develop it as we will. My life thus becomes my responsibility and your life yours, such that *my* life is none of *your* business and vice versa. It would, on this view, be fundamentally unjust for others to meddle in our rights to "pursue our own good in our own way."

Since it captures core features of the positive morality entrenched in liberal democratic political culture, Auden's "two atlas" image does not merely offer a poetic redescription of an abstract philosophical ideal. It

---

[3] Auden 1991, pp. 225–6.

also represents a vision of justice that concretely orders our own public life. As we internalize that vision through education and socialization, we liberal democratic citizens learn to recognize just and unjust conduct in its light, to resent behavior or criticize policies inconsistent with it, to advocate actions and institutions that support or are required by it, and to reconcile our own aspirations with its demands.

That is why, in our societies, accusations that a fellow citizen has (say) stolen your property, or violated your rights to practice your preferred religion, do not usually precipitate any debate about whether theft or intolerance are indeed unjust and invite punishment. The accused will not gain much sympathy by asking "What's so bad about theft/persecution?" Such a line is as futile as responding to a soccer referee who has just awarded a penalty with "Who says handling the ball is a foul?" To be sure, other lines of defense enjoy more social credibility. The accused might, for example, deny that they were really the culprits and demand that proof be publicly given. Or, they might claim that in this case they should not be held fully responsible for their actions (perhaps they acted under duress, under the influence of some powerful drug, or met some legal standard of "insanity" such that they were "out of their minds" at the time). Perhaps they can argue that for some other special reason their conduct should not count as theft or wrongful persecution, and convince a judge or jury to let them off.

Clearly, however, none of these lines of self-defense questions the underlying injustice of theft or religious intolerance. To the contrary, they reinforce the conventional liberal democratic account of when one agent's interference with another constitutes unjust meddling (e.g. theft/intolerance) and when it involves a permissible or required form of intervention in others' lives (e.g. punishing thieves/persecutors). In taking the trouble to advance extenuating or exculpating considerations, they implicitly acknowledge the legitimacy of punishment when those considerations do not apply. They therefore presuppose that coercively imposed penalties (e.g. imprisonment, fines, community service) may legitimately disrupt agents' private atlas when necessary to maintain a general pattern of just mutual forbearance (the role characteristically assigned in liberal democratic societies to the public authorities and the police).

Those who defend themselves in these ways also implicitly assert the right to do so and indeed in our societies expect the state to provide them with public resources (law courts, forms of legal representation) to exercise that right. Although their provision will normally require some interference with private individuals – for presumably we must tax people to pay for these legal services – we take them to be justified as an incident of the same "two atlas" conception of justice Auden describes. For, clearly, punishing innocents is one way in which some agents (public officials, police officers, prison guards, etc.) can illegitimately interfere in the private lives of others. To guard against this danger, we need some mechanism for protecting innocent individuals wrongly accused of injustice toward others. That is how the "rule of law" is usually understood in liberal democratic societies.

All of this is likely to strike liberal democratic citizens as an entirely legitimate, and indeed valuable, way of thinking about the common good. Plato's argument in the *Republic*, however, suggests otherwise.

Down with Liberal Democracy

To appreciate his worry, we should first notice an important point of agreement between Plato and proponents of the liberal democratic "two atlas" model. Like the liberal democrat, Plato accepts that the normal function of ideals of justice is to determine the bounds of proper and improper interference between different agencies – in the liberal democratic model, for example, between the jurisdiction of public institutions and private individuals and organizations. In this sense, his basic concept of justice is entirely familiar to us – he assumes that justice is fundamentally an organizational virtue, presupposing a plurality of people, offices, agencies whose functions, responsibilities, competences, and activities need to be harmonized and reconciled according to some set of agreed principles. The need for coordination arises simply because these agencies, and the responsibilities we allot to them, potentially conflict, and may get in each other's way. For a society to run smoothly, then, its members must agree on a set of rules stipulating when it is appropriate and inappropriate for different people and offices to fulfill certain defined responsibilities. They must, in other words, accept, internalize, and follow a public positive morality.

Plato's most original and challenging insight in the *Republic* is his realization that this circumstance carries two important implications: first, that such a positive morality, and the scheme of coordination it protects, depends for its entrenchment and stable reproduction on the cultivation of various attitudes and beliefs within the general population; and second, that cultivating these attitudes and beliefs inevitably places psychological demands on members of society who are called upon to sustain the relevant coordinating practices. They have to become particular kinds of people, motivated in certain ways and not others, repressing drives and urges that might disrupt conventional routines and expectations, while emphasizing others and developing associated dispositions, attitudes, skills, and traits of character. When concretely realized in settled positive moralities, then, alternative organizing principles of social justice will tax human psychology in different ways. For example, the distinctive social and political routines of Pacifica and Atlantis will correspond to particular patterns of psychological organization within individual Pacificans and Atlantans.

Crucially, however, these psychological states may or may not enhance individuals' well-being. So, one way to evaluate different schemes of positive morality is to ask how far their psychological preconditions make people better or worse off. That is why Plato says at one point early in the *Republic* that his concern is with justice and injustice as "an inherent condition in the *psyche*." A positive morality that causes the agents who sustain it to become psychologically ill-adjusted, and therefore unhappy, cannot really be worth affirming. However, Plato's argument implies that when we apply this test to liberal democratic conceptions of justice, we will find that they fail.

Auden's poem hints at Plato's basic worry. Under the "two atlas" model, each of us is "forced to own" an "inner space of private ownership," one that we cannot escape even if we "find it hell." In putting it this way, Auden tacitly acknowledges that individuals might willingly conform to liberal democratic principles regulating their outward relations (e.g. "respect the rights of others," "tolerate religious difference," etc.) yet still suffer great distress in their inward lives. Even those who are never (or very rarely) the victims of theft, assault, persecution, or violence at the hands of others may still be insistently plagued by self-doubt, a deep sense of personal frustration or failure, mental conflict, stress, and anxiety. As Auden's judicious metaphors nicely emphasize, such private, introspective distress takes on a peculiar "hellish" intensity because, and to the extent that, it is seen as self-inflicted. Yet in a "two atlas" world, in which each person is the planter and farmer of the "forest tracts" constituting their inner lives, such unease is virtually guaranteed to appear self-inflicted.

Ideally, we would wish to be able to "patrol" these internal plantations with something like the pride an accomplished gardener can take from ambling through a beautiful, thriving, well-designed garden that she has created. All too often, however, as we reflect on our own lives from within, we instead find ourselves picking our way painfully through an overwhelming, overgrown thicket of weeds, nettles, and thorns that we have allowed to run wild. If, as Voltaire, one of the great prophets of modern liberal democracy, said, "Il faut cultiver notre jardin" (each of us must tend to our own garden),[4] then we only have ourselves to blame if our horticultural efforts fail. Yet such a realization is bound to be intensely distressing.

The major Platonic worry about the positive morality of liberal democratic justice is that, in "forcing" individuals to "own" responsibility for their own well-being in this way, it is inevitably complicit in unnecessary and acute suffering of that kind.

Plato's claim need not be that *everyone* will be unhappy under liberal democratic rules. Some may be up to the responsibility those rules thrust upon them and flourish in spite of them. Plato could also accept that, *if* human beings were quite naturally adept at recognizing what is good for them, making wise choices for themselves, and exercising the judgment, moderation, and self-control needed to secure their best interests, the "two atlas" approach would make sense. However, Plato thought that this was a very big "if." Indeed, he saw no reason to assume that, left to themselves, agents will automatically develop the personalities, strength of will, and capacities of discernment needed to identify their real interests and pursue them successfully. These character traits do not just develop by themselves, like biologically programmed growth patterns. They are complex social and psychological achievements. Without the right kind of guidance, education, habituation, and exemplars to emulate, the necessary skills and traits will atrophy, or develop only partially. When this happens, agents will tend to make poor choices; and, as their mistakes compound, their lives may become unfulfilled and profoundly unhappy.

Today, we often use the language of "depression" to capture the kind of suffering that Plato was particularly worried about. A standard symptom

---

[4] Voltaire 2005.

of major depression is profound and insistent self-accusation: depressed people often spend inordinate energy dwelling on their failures, errors of judgment, and shortcomings. It would be very convenient if we could always put this down to delusion and exaggeration, and certainly these tendencies are often implicated in depressive behavior. Unfortunately, however, things are more complicated.

For the problem is not only that, because of artificially low self-esteem, depressives fail to see how wonderful they really are. To the contrary, the deeper problem is that they are all too aware of dark truths about themselves. More often than not, people become depressed because they quite correctly perceive their own failures and inadequacies. They see their indolence, selfishness, cruelty, weakness, lack of self-control, cowardice, fickleness, mendacity, mediocrity, humiliations and so forth with some clarity, and can accurately catalogue incidents in their lives that evince them. These life events are the characteristic focus of depressive rumination.

If this characterization of depression is correct, then the best way to prevent agents from suffering it is to create conditions under which they can affirm themselves and their lives as success stories. To carry conviction, however, such affirmation must correspond to the truth about their lives. A mere illusion of self-esteem in the face of actual failure is not enough. People must actually *live well* and *know* that this is so. This requires a social condition that can give them that assurance. Yet this is exactly what Plato's argument claims the "two atlas" model denies us.

Some Replies

For us denizens of liberal democracy, surrounded on all sides by people whose lives are unsatisfying to them, who are addicted to substances they wish they could give up, whose relationships fail, who find themselves unemployed and unwanted, working at tedious and soul-destroying jobs, disillusioned by the idiots who run their countries, this argument is disturbing. In the next chapter, we will consider J. S. Mill's utilitarian reasons for reaching a more optimistic conclusion about liberal democratic forms of life. But we should note that the Platonic worry is not easy to dismiss.

One might respond by suggesting that Plato is confused about the kind of value that justice is. A just society is one in which agents fulfill certain duties simply for their own sake, and without regard, not only to their own interests, but also to interests more generally. As one contemporary political philosopher writes: "The idea that considerations of advantage are distinct from those of morality, and that it might be rational to allow the latter to override the former, seems to be at the core of our intuitions about morality."[5] This position is often associated with the great Prussian philosopher Immanuel Kant. He argued that it is a mistake to confuse "moral" values like justice and the duties and obligations they impose with prudential calculations or considerations of rational advantage. On his view, the defining feature of the rules of justice and morality is that they require me to fulfill my duties and obligations *on principle*, regardless of the ways in which I, or others, might benefit. But if this Kantian view is on target, Plato's project seems confused at the outset.

Yet the Kantian assumption that moral evaluation and considerations of advantage must be entirely distinct is in some ways even more puzzling than Plato's suggested alternative. If complying with justice and other moral requirements does literally *nothing* to promote anyone's interests, or actually works against them, it surely becomes significantly harder to explain why we have reasons to value doing so nonetheless. What is the value of a social order whose rules are followed punctiliously but whose members all suffer misery, self-doubt, stress, anxiety, depression, and a sense of worthlessness? Decoupled from claims about their tendency to advance one's interests, justifications that appeal to the free-standing value of conformity of the rules for its own sake seem question-begging: what kind of value is this? The appeal of Plato's strategy is that it can answer that question: it connects the value of justice with outcomes that should uncontroversially command our rational approval – the realization of interests, happiness, and well-being.

One might be tempted here to excavate a notion we tried to bury in the last chapter by retorting that the question of what would make each of us happy is a purely "subjective" one. It is therefore presumptuous for Plato to suppose that he or anyone else could know what would make others happy. Insofar as this sort of objection has any real meaning, it alleges that there is no authoritative standpoint outside each individual's own perspective from which we can evaluate judgments about their own good. There is

---

[5] Beitz 1999, p. 16.

only *my* good understood from *my* perspective, *your* good understood from *your* perspective, *his* good understood from *his* perspective, and so on.

Yet this view is very implausible, and may seem attractive to us only because we have been socialized to accept the "two atlas" model, in which each of us is left to determine how to live by our own lights. People plainly do make sometimes catastrophic mistakes about their own interests, and observers are often rightly confident in their judgment that this is the case. Indeed it often seems painfully true that outsiders are *more* aware of our own mistakes than we are. We can all think of examples of people who continually "mess up" by pursuing relationships with the wrong people, indulging foolish desires and temptations, lapsing into wasteful and unhealthy addictions, nursing inappropriate ambitions, sabotaging important long-term goals for the sake of trivial short-term gains, and so forth. And, as we know from our own political culture, democratic citizens do not deny that they often make mistakes of this kind. Faced with criticism or advice from others, for example, they often say, in a defiant tone: "Well, you may be right that *X* is a mistake, but it is a free country, and I have a right to make my own mistakes: *mind your own business!*" Or, invoking Frank Sinatra: "Even if I am making a mistake, at least I will be able to say that *I did it my way.*" These claims concede that people sometimes make mistakes about their own interests and that others can know that this is the case. The liberal democratic view is that it would nonetheless be unjust to interfere in individuals' personal affairs to stop them from making them.

One of the enduring merits of Plato's argument in the *Republic* is that it draws our attention to the puzzling quality of such familiar claims, and hence the stability of the "two atlas" model presented by Auden. What sort of interest do we have in a system of rights that exposes us to an undue risk of a failed life? To ask this question is to return to the challenge of showing how justice "benefits its possessor." Plato's objection to liberal democratic conceptions of justice is that they cannot meet this challenge and therefore cannot be adequate interpretations of the concept of justice. To "possess" liberal democratic justice, in the Platonic sense, is to be socialized into the belief that each of us is a self-sufficient individual with our own idiosyncratic goals and interests, and to be disposed to respect others' "Sinatra-rights" – their rights to live their lives *their way*. But if Plato is right, one can possess justice in this sense and lead a miserable, damaged, self-defeated life. In that case, what good is democratic justice to me? If I have wrecked my life, what consolation is it to know that I did it "my way"?

Moreover, as we noted earlier, it is precisely our conviction that they reflect "our way" that can make our private hells so hellish. That conviction implicates us in our own failures; they reflect on us, revealing who we really are. Consider depression again. Is the bare knowledge of inadequacy sufficient to trigger a depressive response? Not really. The distinctive pain of depression arises when consciousness of personal vice, irresponsibility, and failure is combined with the assumption that the relevant shortcomings can be no one's responsibility but one's own. They cease to be merely evidence *of* failings, but a reason to denounce ourselves *as* failures. That is why depressed people often speak of being unable to live with themselves, and waste energy "beating themselves up," as we put it today. It is also why the underlying psychological attitudes are so dangerous, sometimes leading to suicide or to something worse: for some may try to relieve the bitterness of personal failure by indulging the fantasy that others are to blame for their humiliation and must be punished. In their eyes, shooting up a school, blowing up a government building, raping women, driving trucks through crowds of protesters, joining a hate group, organizing a pogrom, and so on can represent the recovery of self-respect. In a less dramatic form, the petty vengefulness, manipulativeness, arrogance, narcissism, cruelty, and self-righteousness of ordinary private life, much of which is rooted in a desire to deflect personal insecurity and self-doubt, illustrate the same phenomenon.

So it is important to notice that Plato's critique is concerned not only with immiserating effects of certain forms of life *on* those who internalize their positive moral requirements. It is also that the resulting psychological maladjustment will characteristically produce other harmful effects on others, poisoning social life and triggering further unhealthy forms of internalization. As Jonathan Lear has argued, Plato's theory asks us to face up to the complex cycles of internalization and externalization that underlie organized forms of human life.[6] The political theory of the *Republic* remains important because this is its central insight: what is ultimately at stake in the claim that we are responsible for our own common good is the healthy or unhealthy functioning of this cyclical interaction

[6] Lear 1992.

between the social and the psychological. For Plato, these cycles constitute a *single* public atlas. If so, to think that there are two atlases – the private, inner standpoints from which we each captain our lives, and the public, external one, in which independent rules regulate self-enclosed, atomized, private lives – is to fail to comprehend the common good.

Perfectionism

I close this chapter by outlining the model of critical moral reflection that is implicit in Plato's critique. For this purpose, we can ignore the fine details of Plato's (various, highly speculative, and often quite crazy) counterproposals for an ideally structured society likely to fully realize the common good. Only the *general* features of Plato's approach are relevant here, the main lines by which he thinks we can theorize the common good for the purposes of critical reflection on politics.

First, his approach is *perfectionist.* It is built around a depiction of a perfectly rational agent directed intelligently and effectively toward the fulfillment of her deepest interests, making the best of her life. These interests define a set of rational ends. Plato grouped these rational ends under three categories:

(1) interests in satisfying certain physical needs, for food, drink, sex, the removal of discomfort and pain;
(2) interests in our character, efforts and activities being appreciated by those around us, i.e., interests in friendship, love, recognition, honor, and respect;
(3) interests in achieving knowledge and understanding, and especially in a justified consciousness of our lives as success stories.

Plato's perfectionism asserts that to flourish as a human being requires that you be properly oriented toward those ends and as far as possible realize them.

Second, agents attain such "proper orientation" through *practical reasoning*, that is, by rationally deliberating about how to act, about what they should try to achieve and avoid, and judge whether something deserves their approval or disapproval. Practical rationality in this sense is concerned with identifying *reasons* to (dis)value things, act for their sake, protect or destroy them, and to pursue worthwhile goals while ignoring or discouraging worthless ones. It contrasts with (what Aristotle would call) *the-oretical* reasoning, which is the kind of rationality implicated in describing the world, and especially in scientific and empirical research. Here, agents deliberate not about the worthy and unworthy objects of choice, action, and organized social practices, but rather about which beliefs, propositions, empirical hypotheses, or descriptions of objects or events they should accept. When you ask me "Did the train leave on time?" and I say "Yes, I checked my watch when we left," I give you a reason to *believe* that you have missed it. This is a theoretical reason in Aristotle's sense. If I say "The train will leave any minute" and I know you intend to catch it, I point out a valid (practical) reason for you to take action – you should hurry up.

Third, since our rational ends are several and potentially conflicting, practical judgment is often a matter of figuring out how to balance, coordinate, and prioritize them in particular contexts. Our mutual sexual attraction gives us a reason to make love (it will satisfy a rational desire for pleasure and joy) but if I am married to someone else and you are my parliamentary secretary, concern for my political reputation and my sense of pride in not betraying people I love supply overriding reasons to refrain.

Fourth, and this is the lesson of the Platonic critique of liberal dem-ocracy, whether agents succeed in displaying practical rationality in this sense, correctly judging the relative importance and priority of these com-peting reasons, depends on whether their society educates and socializes them propitiously, emphasizing the practical skills, aptitudes, emotional dispositions, character traits, and rational discernment they will need to orient themselves toward, properly balance, and realize their rational ends. This is itself a matter of coordinating the various different and poten-tially conflicting capacities scattered across the human population so that they are mobilized toward the achievement of its constituents' flourishing. Crucially, *some* coordination of capabilities and ends is unavoidable under any organized scheme of human association. So for Plato the choice is not between a condition in which agents live without such coordinating social practices and those in which they do. It is between associations that do it badly and do it well.

So construed, critical morality is not like computer programming, in which there is a fixed hardware that we can, by loading different software, make perform an open-ended set of possible functions (browsing the Web, composing documents, simulating flight, helping us meditate, analyzing data sets, etc.). Rather, critical moral reflection is an activity that arises among members of a social system that is self-programming in that it adopts, follows, various alterable positive moral conventions (e.g. different conceptions of justice) to organize its common life. This modifiable code of positive morality mediates between, on the one hand, the needs and rational ends of the individuals making up the system and, on the other, the various powers and capacities scattered across the population that are available to meet those needs and goals. The challenge for the critical moralist is to specify how this self-programming should best coordinate these various capacities and needs. Insofar as a society programs itself around a propitious positive morality (conceptions of justice, etc.), it configures itself so as to secure its common good and promote the well-being of its members. Conversely, if it adopts and follows a defective set of positive moral conventions, a society will fail to secure the common good, to the detriment of its members' well-being.

Plato and Aristotle developed this project against the backdrop of a very particular model of political community – the classical Greek city-state. These were largely self-sufficient, culturally homogenous political communities whose territory comprised the immediate environs of individual cities, such as Athens, Sparta, Miletus, Corinth, and Argos. By modern standards, these city-states were extremely small. The payroll of some multinational corporations today significantly exceeds the total population of Athens in the time of Plato and Aristotle. Because their speculations about how to realize the common good tend to presuppose this now extinct political form, many modern critics have charged that this Platonic and Aristotelian project, inspiring as it is, is of historical interest only. They argue that the research program they initiated has been rendered irrelevant by the subsequent development of political organization on an incomparably larger scale. The size, cultural diversity, and complexity of modern nation-states make it implausible to suppose that their citizens could ever share in the sort of rich common good Plato and Aristotle hoped to promote by political means.

But the common-good approach did not simply die out with the Greek city-states. One of the most influential paradigms in recent political philosophy – utilitarianism – can be thought of as an attempt to revive that research program and to adapt it to the transformed conditions of modern political life.

3   Classical Utilitarianism

Utilitarianism as a philosophical movement got underway toward the end of the eighteenth century in Europe and really took off in England in the nineteenth. Its pioneers were Helvetius, David Hume, William Paley, John Austin, James and John Stuart Mill and, of course, Jeremy Bentham.[1] Later utilitarians include Henry Sidgwick, G. E. Moore, R. M. Hare, and Peter Singer.[2] For reasons considered below, utilitarian approaches to political philosophy find themselves today very firmly on the defensive. Yet utilitarianism remains influential in both popular and academic discourse. When politicians and commentators complain that the benefits of certain public policies are outweighed by their costs, they are arguing in utilitarian terms, whether or not they realize it. Utilitarianism, albeit in an attenuated form, is also fundamental to modern economic theory and, as a result, has exerted a continuous influence on the human sciences down to the present.

These later adaptations of utilitarianism in academic economics and social science are, however, of limited interest to political philosophers. It is the *classical* version of utilitarianism, as represented especially in the writings of Bentham and (John Stuart) Mill, that remains most relevant and provocative in the context of political philosophy. Yet, as we shall see, our perception of classical utilitarianism has been clouded by naïve stereotypes and preconceptions which can easily lead one to underestimate its challenging reworking of the common-good tradition.

---

[1] Bentham 1996, 1988; Troyer 2003.
[2] Hare 1981; Sidgwick 1981; Singer 2011.

The Utility Principle

At the most general level, utilitarianism holds that rational evaluations of human activities and practices should be guided ultimately by the answer to a single question: do they increase or depress the overall welfare of all sentient beings? This welfarist focus brings with it an inherently consequentialist orientation, such that the value of actions, institutions, schemes of "positive morality," and so on is to be judged solely by considering their consequences for the welfare of those they will likely affect. However, utilitarianism is a distinctive form of consequentialism in that most versions add a *maximizing* expectation: it is not enough, on standard utilitarian views, to aim for merely *adequate* consequences. Its most basic first principle – "the utility principle" – is more demanding: it asserts that actions and social practices are good insofar as they promote the best possible outcome. As Bentham famously put it, his "fundamental axiom" is that "it is the greatest happiness of the greatest number" that ultimately "measure[s] … right and wrong."[3]

Although it is important to underline the consequentialist character of utilitarian judgment, it is equally important not to make too much of it. Many intuitively think that certain actions – killing or torturing innocents, cheating when one can get away with it, etc. – are intrinsically wrong, bad, or unjust even if they produce a better outcome overall. A stock caricature of – and objection to – utilitarianism is that it cannot make any sense of this intuition. If, in some instance, torturing innocents is necessary to maximize overall welfare, it would seem that the utilitarian must say, contrary to common sense, that such acts of cruelty can actually be right or morally good. We will consider more sophisticated versions of this worry later, but as it stands the objection moves too quickly. Classical utilitarians need not be, and historically have not been, committed to dismissing intuitions about the intrinsically ethical or unethical character of certain forms of conduct so lightly.

To see why, note that while (in utilitarian parlance) X has "utility" insofar as it tends to promote overall welfare, and "disutility" insofar as it tends to increase overall suffering, classical utilitarianism is entirely open-ended as to what kind of thing "X" might be. The stock caricature

[3] Bentham 1996, p. 393.

assumes that, for a utilitarian, X always or normally refers to some specific action contemplated under particular circumstances, such as the decision to torture a suspected terrorist to foil an imminent plot. Now, Bentham and Mill certainly did not *exclude* such one-off decisions from the set of all Xs that in principle invite utilitarian evaluation. However, they did not take such cases to be representative, common, or even particularly important, members of that set.

Here, one should keep in mind that the classical utilitarians thought of themselves primarily as social critics and political reformers, concerned with the evaluation of large-scale social practices, not with highly localized, often unique, micro-contexts of choice that specific private agents or public officials might confront day to day. Accordingly, they assumed that utilitarian judgment is most urgently invited by those Xs that form entrenched, iterating, macrostructural features of the social and political landscape – for example, basic institutions such as the law, the family, the education system, the state, the customs and conventions constituting prevailing "positive moralities," and the most prominent psychological dispositions developed and emphasized in a society's culture and modes of socialization. These features, after all, are among the most consequential aspects of human life, shaping its contours in particularly profound and far-reaching ways, and so according priority to their assessment is an entirely natural focus for utilitarians to adopt.

These considerations force a reconsideration of the original charge that utilitarianism cannot acknowledge certain actions to be intrinsically wrong apart from their consequences. For among the most important Xs calling for utilitarian assessment are settled moral beliefs, entrenched schemes of positive morality, and various supporting psychological attitudes, such as dispositions to strongly resent or abhor certain forms of conduct (betrayal, cruelty, wanton killing of innocents, etc.). Is there anything more to our common-sense intuition that certain actions are intrinsically unethical or inherently noble apart from their consequences than our *de facto* socialization into ethical attitudes and positive moral beliefs of these kinds? If not, classical utilitarians need not discount such intuitions as irrational or worthless. It is precisely this complex ensemble of positive moral expectations in place in particular societies, along with the ingrained psychological attitudes standing behind them, that they wish to submit to utilitarian assessment. If we can show that such ensembles, or large parts of them, are actually necessary to maximizing overall welfare, they might well survive utilitarian scrutiny.

Indeed, on reflection, one might ask what real value such an ensemble could possibly have, why it is worth anyone's allegiance, if not because aggregate welfare would be threatened by its absence. Wouldn't overall happiness be greatly diminished if agents were able to lie, cheat, steal, murder, and maim each other with complete impunity and if we didn't inculcate in the general population powerful psychological aversions to these actions? When we condemn societies whose positive moralities permit slavery, indulge racism, subordinate women, and repress human sexuality, isn't our most basic reason that these practices cause an enormous amount of unnecessary misery and suffering? If our answer to these questions is "yes," we are on the way to endorsing a classical utilitarian position.

Indirect Utilitarianism

The textbook image of the classical utilitarians as peddling a definitive algorithm whereby agents can decide, in any given situation, on the most ethical or moral course of action in the circumstances is thus a naïve stereotype. That image depicts Bentham and Mill as "direct utilitarians" who urged agents to apply the "utility principle" systematically to their own choices as far as they can. Yet this characterization cannot be reconciled with what Bentham and Mill actually wrote. For the most part their texts adopt a wholly realistic account of ordinary human behavior, seeing it as motivated largely by a familiar combination of self-interest, emotional drives, habits, rule-following, and unreflective obedience to conventional expectations. They never suggest that agents can reasonably be expected to spend their lives minutely calculating the utilitarian consequences of their daily and hourly choices.

Moreover, whatever Bentham and Mill themselves intended, such a suggestion is in any case an implausible one for a utilitarian to make. Attending in detail to the overall consequences of one's actions is a tedious and unpleasant activity, about as enjoyable as filling out a tax return; asking agents to engage in constant actuarial estimation is thus a recipe for misery and frustration. For a utilitarian, these costs in terms of human welfare would be worth incurring only if outweighed by greater benefits resulting from agents' efforts to conduct themselves in an optimizing way. But surely this is unlikely to be the case.

Agents are, after all, highly fallible. Their utility calculations will often be tainted by error or personal bias. And their judgments will only be as good as their predictions about how others will act and how events will pan out. Since their access to reliable information and capacity to make such predictions are surely sharply limited, a "direct utilitarian" strategy is almost certainly self-defeating. So if everyone is left to apply the utility principle themselves, actions will likely be poorly coordinated, depressing rather than promoting overall utility. Agents will do better if they are guided by various rules, expectations, institutions, and motives likely to coordinate their activities in ways that limit unnecessary suffering.[4] The most plausible versions of utilitarianism are therefore ones in which the utility principle plays a largely indirect role in guiding human action, applied mainly in high-altitude critical reflection about the overall value of the routines by which ordered social life proceeds.

Bentham and Mill were fairly clearly "indirect utilitarians" of this kind. They took for granted that most day-to-day conduct is, and will remain, determined by habitual obedience to legal and moral rules, local calculations of self-interest, affects and emotional commitments, and the acceptance of various ideals of virtue and probity. The question for them was whether these immediate determinants of human conduct and interaction are, in the circumstances, configured in ways likely to promote or diminish overall happiness. If they cause significant unnecessary suffering, the utilitarian will call for their elimination. If, to the contrary, they play an essential role in reducing such suffering and securing overall welfare, utilitarians will want to retain and reinforce them.

To illustrate, consider traditional taboos against and legal prohibitions on homosexual activity. These have been stable and entrenched features of positive morality in many societies for a very long time. Bentham and the classical utilitarians, however, thought that these norms, although conventionally understood to be good and morally vital, were in fact pernicious, repressing harmless yet deeply felt impulses for no obvious social benefit. From a utilitarian standpoint, then, the astonishingly rapid transformation in social attitudes to homosexuality in the West over the past

---

[4] See Mill on "secondary principles." Troyer 2003, p. 113.

few generations, going from outright criminalization to the full legal recognition of same-sex marriages, represents a long overdue advance, liberating agents to explore their sexuality without stigma or the pain of self-accusation. Bentham and Mill would also have welcomed the recent relaxation of repressive attitudes toward sex more generally (although it has doubtless brought its own problems).[5]

Worth emphasizing in this context is Bentham's and Mill's attitude to the moral psychology of shame and guilt, as it highlights the logic of utilitarian evaluation in a particularly clear way. On the classical utilitarian view, shame and guilt are presumptively bad because they involve *painful* feelings. It is no fun to be "wracked" with guilt or feel ashamed of oneself; indeed, a standard symptom of clinical depression (which surely excludes well-being or happiness on any account) is a highly exaggerated and utterly debilitating sense of guilt and worthlessness. The fact that such feelings are painful, however, does not mean that classical utilitarians must call for the complete elimination of the unpleasant pricks and pangs of conscience. It rather means that, on a utilitarian account, it is *worth* cultivating these unpleasant dispositions only if doing so averts even greater suffering and/or promotes a net increase in well-being. The feelings of shame and personal guilt that, in the past, attended (e.g.) masturbation, lust, sex before or outside marriage, homosexual or bisexual desires, and so forth likely fail this test. It is at least unclear that these feelings accomplish anything other than clouding innocent pleasures with unnecessary pain. If so, they have net disutility, tending always to reduce overall welfare.

Sometimes, however, cultivating shame, guilt, and certain social stigmas may pass the utilitarian test. For example, guilt and shame about (e.g.) bigotry, chauvinism, racism, propensities toward sexual violence and abuse, cruelty, deceit, envy, arrogance, aggressiveness, etc. likely have considerable utility. When unpleasant feelings of guilt or shame (and also exposure to painful social disapproval or ostracism) become psychologically associated with these dispositions, they may discourage agents from nursing and acting upon them, sparing others their typically far more painful consequences (exclusion, discrimination, misogyny, betrayal, assault, etc.). In these cases, cultivating innocent, shameless, immoralism seems guaranteed to depress overall utility. Insofar as this is the case, the

---

[5] Bentham 2014.

pain involved in guilt and shame can be justified by the greater welfare resulting from their inhibitory effects.

Bentham and Mill applied essentially the same analysis to the criminal law: like the pain of guilt, the unpleasant effects of legal punishment create a utilitarian presumption against imposing it. That presumption can be overcome, in their view, only insofar as punishing criminals averts even greater harms by deterring crimes, or by producing other beneficial consequences that together outweigh the costs incurred by those punished (and those who care about them). Insofar as this condition is not met, the classical utilitarian will see no strong case for legal punishment, and regard any further calls to impose it (perhaps in the name of "just deserts") as an irrational and often vindictive effort to inflict pointless suffering. This condition is likely to be violated, as Bentham for example explicitly acknowledged, when we punish what are today called "victimless crimes" (e.g. consensual use and sale of recreational drugs).[6] It again bears emphasizing that, in entertaining the idea that the threat of legal punishment is sometimes needed to deter agents from objectionable action they would otherwise be motivated to perform, Bentham and Mill clearly presumed that most ordinary conduct is prompted by self-interest and narrow personal motives (hatred, anger, love, loyalty, etc.), not by direct efforts to conform to the principle of utility.

Expanding the Circle

Bentham and Mill, then, were not utilitarian moralists advocating the utility principle as an ethical imperative to be followed by all morally upright individuals in their daily lives. They were, rather, progressive *critics* of positive moralities, legal systems, and institutional practices, canvassing the utility principle as the ultimate foundation for intelligent deliberation about social reform. Once we appreciate this, the clear affinity between their approach and that of Plato and Aristotle becomes apparent. As with the Greek perfectionists, the classical utilitarian position is centered on a conception of welfare that it is rational to promote. That conception of welfare functions, in all these theories, not as an immediate "criterion of moral right and wrong" from which one can directly read off a table of duties,

---

[6] Troyer 2003, pp. 26–8.

but rather as the rational keystone of critical morality (as introduced in Chapter 1).

Like the perfectionism of the ancient Greeks, the resulting model of critical morality is potentially revisionary, demanding that existing institutions, and the various positive moral conventions, ideals of virtue, and psychological dispositions that support them, prove their worth before the tribunal of human well-being. We noted in the last chapter how Plato's perfectionism casts critical doubt on the credentials of liberal democratic understandings of justice. And we have just seen, in our discussion of sexual mores, how utilitarian social criticism can be a similarly powerful solvent of traditional dogmas and taboos.

Despite these formal affinities, classical utilitarianism departs from the Platonist and Aristotelian approach in two fundamental and connected respects. First, unlike the utilitarian one, the implicit account of the common good mobilized in the thought of the Greek perfectionists is a highly localized one. Plato and Aristotle presumed that politically relevant common goods are realizable only in the context of relatively small communities like the city-states of the ancient Mediterranean world. They had no clear notion that much larger political units – like empires or modern nation-states – might be analyzed as having a common good of their own. It is true that later Hellenistic thought began, quite soon after Plato and Aristotle, to embrace a more universalist, cosmopolitan conception in which humanity *as such* shares in a kind of global common good. This move was encouraged by the expansion of the Roman Empire, which brought a multiplicity of local jurisdictions under common legal control. The development of natural law theory, mentioned briefly in Chapter 1, and which drew on the Roman *jus gentium* (the "law of peoples"), promoted this broader view of the common good as embracing the interests of all rational beings. But the tenor of classical Greek perfectionism militated strongly against any such cosmopolitan extension.

To be sure, Plato and Aristotle presumably thought that the general conditions under which a public "common good" can be felicitously pursued are the same for any social group seeking to establish a successful political community somewhere on the planet. To that extent, their political theories make universalist claims. However, they presumed that among the most important of these putatively universal truths is that a genuine common good can exist only in communities small enough to allow citizens to be acquainted directly with the specific needs and circumstances of their fellows. Critical reflection on how such a community can best assume responsibility for its common good remains, for them, bounded by a concern for the fate and flourishing of a relatively small circle of compatriots. In their view, without the intense and well-informed mutual concern that small-scale community permits, intelligent deliberation about shared political goals is difficult, if not impossible.

The classical utilitarian conception of critical morality, in contrast, denies that responsibility for the common good is inherently localized in this way. Against that claim, utilitarians insist that no such parochial or particular affiliations may confine the scope of critical moral reflection, because they hold that rational criticism can carry philosophical authority only if it takes the interests of *all* affected parties into consideration.

This is a radical move; it widens the circle of critical moral concern beyond that envisaged by even the most cosmopolitan of natural law theorists. Since the latter identified the "natural law" with "right reason," they accordingly presumed that critical moral reflection should address itself primarily to the interests of rational beings. But Bentham drew the circle of critical moral concern still more expansively when he asked what qualifies something for inclusion within it:

> Is it the faculty of reason, or perhaps, the faculty for discourse? ... [T]he question is not, Can they reason? nor, Can they talk? but, Can they suffer?[7]
>
> Why should the law refuse its protection to any sensitive being? ... The time will come when humanity will extend its mantle over everything which breathes.[8]

So, for Bentham and the subsequent utilitarian tradition, what ultimately matters in critical moral reflection is *sentience.* The welfare of nonrational animals, at least those capable of experiencing pain, must be taken into consideration as well. This explains why utilitarian thinkers have been among the most powerful advocates for animal welfare in the modern world. For them, the common good in principle encompasses not only the

---

[7] Bentham 1996, p. 283n.
[8] Bentham 1838–43, p. 562.

claims of human beings, but also all the sentient animals with whom we share the planet.[9]

Perfectionism and Hedonism

This brings us to the second major point of divergence between classical utilitarianism and its ancient Greek precursors. Although both approaches are organized around a conception of well-being, or happiness, that it is rational to promote, their respective conceptions of human welfare are quite different. The term that Plato and Aristotle used for well-being was the Greek word "eudaimonia." This is standardly translated into English as "happiness." But as many have pointed out, this translation is not ideal. The English word "happiness" tends to connote certain experiential or emotional states, but Plato and Aristotle had something different in mind. For them, *eudaimonia* consists in the realization of rational interests, projects, and desires. While they acknowledged that experiencing enjoyment (and being free of suffering) is among our rational interests, they refused to treat it as a basic, all-encompassing, rational end subsuming all others. They rather recognized a plurality of independent rational aims – for example, being loved and respected, encountering and appreciating beauty, fully realizing one's talents, or achieving knowledge and understanding – that cannot be analyzed merely as species of a more general, master, interest in certain pleasurable or painless forms of experience. So, the sort of human "fulfillment" (a better translation of *eudaimonia*) that Plato and Aristotle equated with well-being is not reducible simply to the quality or duration of the experiential states that succeed each other in the life of a sentient being. From their perfectionist standpoint, happiness does not consist fundamentally in mental states and forms of experience.

If this perfectionist conception of well-being seems odd, consider how variable and ambivalent the day-to-day experiences occasioned by such worthwhile projects as raising a family, becoming an Olympic athlete, or developing a musical talent are. Yes, there may be moments of joy and

---

[9] Singer 2009. If the idea of sharing a civic common good with animals seems far-fetched, see Donaldson and Kymlicka 2013, although Kymlicka and Donaldson are not utilitarians.

pleasure along the way, yet more often than not doing these things well also entails stress, hardship, graft, and self-denial. Moreover, thanks to good and bad luck or their contrasting personalities, people often experience these same pursuits very differently. Those who love being around children will find parenthood much more enjoyable than those for whom a screaming baby means an instant migraine. Competing in an Olympic event will tend to feel different to the extent that one is under immense pressure to win gold for one's country. Writing great music will feel like a terrible struggle if, like Beethoven, one is stricken with deafness. Some great artists or novelists produce masterpieces effortlessly; others are tortured geniuses, realizing their talents at enormous psychic cost.

Perfectionists conclude from all of this that quality of experience cannot yield a stable standard of well-being and instead invest in *success* as the appropriate criterion. From this point of view, the question of whether, and to what extent, agents prosper should be decided by determining: (a) whether their lives are oriented toward the pursuit of projects and aims that it is rational for them to pursue; and (b) how far they actually realize them. A person is happy (fulfilled), in this sense, to the extent that their efforts to advance independently worthy ends meet with success. Accordingly, perfectionist critical morality postulates that certain rational ends are valuable for their own sake, identifies well-being with the fulfillment of those ends, and then goes on to judge the merits and demerits of different social and political practices by investigating whether they help or hinder agents in achieving well-being so understood.

Like perfectionists, utilitarians accept that there can be rational ends worth pursuing for their own sake. However, where perfectionists usually acknowledge a plurality of such ends, classical utilitarianism insists that our reasons to value actions, practices, and institutions all ultimately reduce to a *single* rational end: increasing overall welfare as much as possible. In this sense, the utilitarian understands practical rationality in a monistic, rather than pluralistic, way. It follows that, from a utilitarian point of view, the value of everything other than welfare must be in some sense instrumental. Or, to put it differently, nothing can have any utilitarian value except as a means toward producing more of the only thing that utilitarians take to be worth having for its own sake: welfare.

Further, unlike the perfectionist view just described, classical utilitarianism *does* understand that rational end in terms of qualities of sentient experience. For they hold that the only things worth obtaining (or avoiding) for their own sake are the hedonic states of pleasure (and pain). All rational action, in other words, must ultimately aim to secure pleasure – what Henry Sidgwick, the most systematic of the classical utilitarians, described more precisely as "desirable consciousness."[10]

Rational Ends and Rational Constraints

Stated most abstractly, then, the utilitarian view is that the rationality of practical judgments (whether they be conscious decisions to act, evaluations of actions or practices, justifications of public policy, or merely implicit in unreflective, emotional, or habitual responses to events) depends ultimately on whether they are successfully oriented toward the intrinsically valuable end of "desirable consciousness."

Here it is important to avoid two confusions. Notice first that the claim here is *not* that we should be rational because, and insofar as, being so will have beneficial consequences. Rather it is that practical rationality itself presupposes, and is constituted by, the aim of promoting pleasure or "desirable consciousness." That aim determines *what is* rational and irrational on a utilitarian view, not *whether* we should act or judge rationally. Consider an ascetic who deliberately spurns pleasures, or a misanthrope who strongly approves of some social practice precisely because it produces massive unnecessary suffering. Utilitarians regard such stances as patently irrational. They condemn them as such, however, not because they think that the presence of people with ascetic or misanthropic attitudes must have really bad consequences (though it may). The problem is simply that the utilitarian's concept of practical rationality unconditionally precludes anyone's ever having a genuine reason to adopt such attitudes. Doing so would contradict the axiom that rational agents must aim at, or approve of, anything that promotes "desirable consciousness." For utilitarians, the irrationality involved is analogous to that displayed by a mathematician who, misled by a logical fallacy, wrongly believes that he has proved a theorem.

Second, this hedonist conception of practical reasoning and the utility principle itself, though closely related, are distinct components of the

---

[10] Sidgwick 1981, pp. 395–7.

utilitarian scheme. To see this, consider again the case of asceticism. Although utilitarians believe asceticism is irrational, their objection to it does not (or anyway need not) turn on the utility principle. That principle, remember, directs us to evaluate actions, practices, positive moralities, psychological dispositions, etc. according as they promote *aggregate* welfare. However, to appreciate what is irrational about asceticism, on the utilitarian view, we need only consider its consequences for the ascetic himself. Insofar as an ascetic's decision to (say) engage in private self-flagellation rather than succumb to the temptation to eat a chocolate bar affects no one but himself, "aggregate" welfare is not in point. In this instance, the ultimate object of utilitarian practical reasoning materializes only in the form of his own welfare. Yet the ascetic's self-flagellation remains irrational from a utilitarian standpoint because he is forgoing an opportunity to advance the intrinsically valuable end of "desirable consciousness" (the pleasure of eating chocolate) in his own case and, worse, choosing the (presumably) highly undesirable consciousness induced by flogging himself.

The utility principle only kicks in when we are assessing things likely to affect the welfare of many in ways that we can realistically estimate. It mostly applies, then, in the context of critical moral reflection, where we are considering the rationality of retaining, modifying, or eliminating large-scale social practices. Once we make this jump to the perspective of critical morality, however, we face a new question: how are we to weigh the "desirable consciousness" of affected parties against each other for the purposes of aggregating welfare overall?

The standard utilitarian answer to this question appeals to an ideal of impartiality: the welfare of each affected party should be given equal weight in our estimates of overall utility. Although the utilitarians rarely defend this principle explicitly, common sense makes it difficult to reject. Few would disagree that we should treat like things alike and that we have no obvious reason to accord anyone's welfare any greater significance than that of others.

So, like the postulation of the intrinsically valuable rational end of "desirable consciousness" this is another underived presupposition built into the utilitarian conception of practical reason. However, although utilitarians assume that this principle is a rational one, they do not think of it as itself an end or goal. Rather, they take it as a rational *constraint* on how utilitarian critical moralists should make the judgments of overall welfare required by the utility principle. The presence of this independent egalitarian constraint is important because it offers grounds for resisting the common criticism of utilitarianism that it does not properly respect persons as equals and is indifferent to considerations of fairness and justice.

4   Utilitarian Critical Morality

Implications and Problems

Bentham and Mill adopted a hedonistic conception of welfare because, as
children of the European Enlightenment, they sought principles of critical morality that are universal in scope yet still discriminating enough
to support interesting, nontrivial conclusions. Perfectionist accounts
of happiness and well-being tend to exacerbate, rather than reduce, the
tension between these two desiderata. Often, it will be difficult to determine whether perfectionist ideals of human flourishing are entitled to
universal standing in critical moral reflection, or whether they are merely
culturally local prejudices that should rather be the *objects* of such reflection. In the latter case, incorporating them into our critical stance will
impart cultural bias to our reflection. For example, medieval Christians
took chastity to be a universal virtue in that they thought any life will be
better for being "chaste" (whether or not most people actually succeed).
This judgment may be correct, but it would be hard to show that, in the
context of critical reflection, anyone should attach weight to it regardless
of their religious or cultural outlook.

The classical utilitarians, however, took pleasure and pain to be universal aspects of human experience, hardwired into our psychologies. They
therefore proposed that the mental states of pleasure and pain jointly comprise a quite general, uncontroversial common denominator by which to
determine the utilitarian value of anything and to compare it with that of
anything else. This assumption, as we shall see, is not actually as straightforward it seems, but the idea that hedonic states are uniquely fit to inform
universal judgments about welfare that also wield a sharp critical edge is
intuitive enough.

Sympathy and Commensurability

If I come across a human being (or an animal for that matter) that is plainly in agony, the fact that I am a militant atheist and she an ultramontane Catholic (or that I am human and it a cat) seems irrelevant to the question of whether I have a reason to help her (or the cat). Hume, who heavily influenced Bentham, thought that human agents are naturally moved by *sympathy* for the suffering of others. According to Hume, sympathy is a capacity "to receive by communication [the] inclinations and sentiments [of others] however different from or contrary to our own."[1] For the classical utilitarians, this ability to sympathize with others' suffering and joy holds out the promise of a conception of well-being that is interpersonally transparent and independent of other differences between people. If so, it provides a way for critical moral judgment to cut through cultural difference and psychological variation.

Eating chocolate may be intensely pleasurable to me, and painful for someone allergic to it, but when I see a person in discomfort because of their allergy to chocolate I know roughly what they are going through even though chocolate has the opposite effect on me. Conversely, by recalling their own pleasurable experiences, they have some sense of why I really like chocolate. More challengingly, utilitarians might on this basis be able to demonstrate that the medieval Christian is simply incorrect to value chastity so highly. The utilitarian can acknowledge that it may enhance the well-being of someone for whom sex is very painful or viscerally embarrassing; but on the assumption that most people find sex enjoyable, and experience unpleasant feelings of frustration when denied it, chastity will look like a threat to, rather than a way of enhancing, their well-being.[2]

---

[1] Hume 1978, p. 365.

[2] One proponent of this hedonistic approach, the nineteenth-century utilitarian Francis Edgeworth, even entertained the idea that eventually we might invent a device he called a "hedonimeter" (Edgeworth 2003). Just as thermometers today determine how high our fevers are, or how cold it is outside, Edgeworth's hedonimeter would be able to measure the amount of pleasure and pain that different experiences (drinking coffee, listening to an opera, orgasm) might arouse in different subjects. Few have taken Edgeworth's proposal seriously. Recently, however, the prevalence of portable electronic devices (cellphones, etc.) that allow people to regularly record their hedonic states as they lead their daily lives has led to the idea being revived (though one might reflect that it is bad enough that people are constantly checking their phones over dinner, but intolerable to encourage them to do so during sexual intercourse).

Another reason why the classical utilitarians endorsed hedonism reflects their commitment to *maximizing* welfare. It makes sense to maximize something only if it can be treated as a single, measurable magnitude. For example, we can "maximize" the distance between two objects inside a cube by placing them at diagonally opposed corners. If we were to place them at adjacent corners, they would be closer together by a measurable degree: the length of the sides of a cube can be compared with the lengths of diagonal lines between its corners. Distances are "commensurable" in this way because distance is a simple, measurable quantity. If the utilitarian injunction to maximize utility is to make sense, it seems that welfare must be measurable in this way. We must be able to measure and compare the different amounts of utility that are produced in different individuals under different circumstances.

Many have doubted, however, that this is really possible even for hedonic states like pleasure and pain. For example, some philosophers, including Plato, have doubted that pleasure and pain are mutually commensurable. It is tempting to think that the relation between degrees of pleasure and degrees of pain is analogous to that between degrees of heat and degrees of cold. But while it makes sense to say that heat and cold are on a measurable continuum, it seems odd to suggest that when I am experiencing the intensely pleasurable aroma of freshly ground coffee I am experiencing much more of the same thing that I (in some measure) lack when I am passing a kidney stone. It seems equally, if not more, plausible to say that the presence or absence of pleasure is *one* thing, and the presence or absence of pain *another*. The same seems true of many pleasures: is the pleasure I derive from a satisfying mathematical proof on a continuum with a sniff of ground coffee?

Moreover, even if the amounts of pleasure or pain that *I* experience in some instance can be compared with those *I* experience in some other instance, it does not necessarily follow that these judgments are comparable *between* persons. This difficulty particularly impressed some of the early neo-classical economists (who integrated utilitarian ideas into economic theory). W. S. Jevons, for example, saw no way to

> compare the amount of feeling in one mind with that in another ... the susceptibility of one mind may be, for what we know, be a thousand times greater than that of another. But, provided that the susceptibility

was different in a like ratio in all directions, we should never be able to discover the difference. Every mind is thus inscrutable to every other mind, and no common denominator of feeling seems possible.[3]

This is the problem of interpersonal comparisons of utility. It is a formidable problem for any version of utilitarianism.

Preference-Satisfaction

Some utilitarians have sought to avoid this problem by abandoning hedonism and instead treating welfare as a function of preference- or desire-satisfaction. On this view, my level of well-being depends on the degree to which my preferences are satisfied or unmet: I am happy to the extent that my desires are fulfilled, unhappy insofar as they are not. This move looks initially promising. Most modern economists have agreed with Jevons in accepting this view of welfare, and until recently, leading contemporary utilitarian thinker Peter Singer also endorsed it.

On reflection, however, this line makes a mess of the utilitarian view rather than rescuing it from the problem of incommensurability. We cannot plausibly measure individual well-being just in terms of the satisfaction of people's *actual* desires and preferences. For what if, as a matter of fact, I am moved by a plainly irrational preference? To illustrate such an irrational preference, consider Derek Parfit's example of "Future Tuesday Indifference."[4] You are Future Tuesday Indifferent if you desire pleasure and wish to avoid pain except when you experience them on Tuesdays. On future Tuesdays, you do not care whether you are in agony or ecstasy. But if your welfare is a function of your *actual* desires being satisfied, then we have to say that when you were in a state of unbearable pain throughout last Tuesday, your welfare was unaffected. As Parfit suggested, that is crazy.

Perhaps, however, the preference-satisfaction approach can be retrieved by focusing, not on what agents *actually* desire, but on what they *ought to* desire. This puts us back into the orbit of a perfectionist view. Mill famously argued that it is "better to be a human being dissatisfied than a pig satisfied; better to be Socrates dissatisfied than a fool satisfied."[5] Implicit

---

[3] Jevons 1931, p. 14.
[4] Parfit 1992, p. 124; Parfit 2013, p. 56.
[5] Troyer 2003, p. 102.

in this formulation is the perfectionist assumption that satisfying Socratic desires (for knowledge, wisdom, aesthetic enrichment, the realization of one's talents, the fulfillment of worthwhile projects like raising a family or excelling in a profession) is intrinsically better than satisfying more basic appetites for food, drink, and sex. On Mill's account, the former promise "higher pleasures" that are qualitatively superior to the "lower pleasures" occasioned by physical gratification. Perhaps, then, we can judge agents happier to the extent that they experience higher pleasures, since they have stronger reasons to desire them. Here, our judgment does not depend on a claim about how those pleasures *feel* as a psychological matter, but rather on the suggestion that their welfare depends on satisfying those desires they ought to have.

Mill's own discussion of these matters is strikingly close to Plato's perfectionist theory of well-being, as his references to Socrates are doubtless intended to acknowledge. Mill even borrowed one of Plato's arguments in the *Republic*, claiming that only those who have *both* experienced physical pleasures *and* been acquainted with the "higher" satisfactions of intellectual and aesthetic pursuit are in a position to appreciate the latter's greater significance for individual happiness. Similar efforts to integrate perfectionist accounts of human flourishing into utilitarianism were made by G. E. Moore and Hastings Rashdall. The resulting views are sometimes referred to as forms of "ideal utilitarianism."

We shall later see that Mill may have been right that these perfectionist views can be reconciled with a utilitarian position. However, they do not afford the utilitarian a viable response to the problem of incommensurability. For, as we noted earlier, perfectionist accounts recognize a plurality of intrinsically valuable rational ends. These tell us what we ought to desire (knowledge, acquaintance with beauty, love and respect, etc.) and what we ought not to desire (ignorance, stupidity, ugliness, the enmity of others, etc.). However, since these are desires for qualitatively different things, it is difficult to believe that they yield a simple dimension of welfare admitting of calculable degrees. The price of admitting, with Mill, Plato, and other perfectionists, that the constituents of well-being are complex and diverse is the reintroduction of the problem of incommensurability in a virulent form.

My achieving mastery of some field of study, my becoming a scratch golfer, my commanding the respect of my peers, my dearly loving (and being loved by) my children, my enjoying good food and wine, my having adequate opportunities for sexual fulfillment, my finding a good therapist all seem to be aspects of my good. But does it make sense to assume that they all enhance my life in some *one* measurable way to different degrees? Few perfectionists have thought so. They have usually followed Plato and Aristotle in insisting, rather, that these constituents of human well-being represent incommensurable goods.[6] These perfectionist accounts undermine, rather than redeem, the claim that happiness or well-being can consist in a measurable quantity that can be optimized. This is not a point about the *technical difficulty* of such measurements. The point is rather that it is *conceptually incoherent* to think that perfectionist "fulfillment" can be measured and compared along a single dimension in the way required by utilitarianism.

Desirable Consciousness

It seems, then, that the classical utilitarians were right to look to hedonism to underwrite their claims about maximizing "aggregate welfare." Preference-satisfaction accounts of welfare cannot rescue utilitarianism. But, as we have seen, the incommensurability problem threatens even hedonistic accounts of welfare. How might hedonistic utilitarianism respond to this difficulty?

In an important recent book sympathetically reconstructing the utilitarian view of Henry Sidgwick, Katarzyna de Lazari-Radek and Peter Singer make some promising suggestions.[7] Sidgwick, as I have said, prefers to speak, not of pleasure and pain, but of "desirable and undesirable consciousness." He defines "desirable consciousness" as:

> Feeling which the sentient individual at the time of feeling it implicitly or explicitly apprehends to be desirable ... when considered merely as a feeling, and not in respect of its ... conditions or consequences, or of any facts that come directly within the cognizance and judgment of others.[8]

[6] Finnis 2011, pp. 111–18; Raz 2009, pp. 321ff.
[7] Lazari-Radek and Singer 2014.
[8] Sidgwick 1981, p. 131.

This definition introduces a minimal element of *judgment*; that is, pleasure in the relevant sense is not just a "raw feel" or mere state of physical arousal. It always also involves what psychologists call "hedonic gloss," an implicit mental judgment of an experience as "liked."[9] As de Lazari-Radek and Singer note, this allows the utilitarian to respond to worries about the heterogeneity of pleasure. Enjoying a nice glass of wine and recognizing an old friend on the train feel very different, but, on Sidgwick's account, I can notice that it is a feature of both that I am glad to be having them and would desire to repeat them. This judgment of "gladness" in principle admits of comparison; I can ask myself which of the two made me gladder, and how much similar gladness I would be prepared to forgo in order to experience them again. These comparisons will clearly be very imprecise, and the problem of comparisons *between* minds remains to be addressed. But do we not make these comparisons all the time?

De Lazari-Radek and Singer make another move that is worth mentioning. They suggest that utilitarians need not, and should not, identify "desirable consciousness" with happiness. That is, they argue that "desirable consciousness" should retain its status as the ultimate end of utilitarian practical reasoning, but that happiness should be added to the list of things that utilitarians regard as having great instrumental value in relation to that end. Their point here is that we often identify happiness, less with experience as such, and more with a certain emotional disposition. If I ask you, "Are you happy in your current job?" I am not really asking you to tell me how much pleasurable experience you get at work. I am instead asking whether you are fulfilled by your work, feel that your talents are well used, are favorably disposed toward your colleagues, and so forth. Now, on a hedonistic account, these emotional states are not themselves welfare, but they may very reliably produce "desirable consciousness." Not only does this mean that these happy emotional states are instrumentally valuable, on a utilitarian view; it also suggests, as de Lazari-Radek and Singer (following Haybron) maintain, that happiness is a particularly useful deliberative heuristic, helping us simplify choices and making rational choice easier. As they put it, "The breadth and diversity of the pleasures and pains likely to result from a choice between careers make them extremely difficult to tally up." It will likely be easier "to

---

[9] Lazari-Radek and Singer 2014, p. 244.

ask: will I be stressed, anxious, or will I have peace of mind? Will I often be in high spirits, or ... irritable?"[10]

This may be the right way to construe Mill's effort to make a rapprochement between utilitarianism and perfectionism. Consider again his "higher pleasures" argument. It is "better" to be Socrates dissatisfied, one might say, because although his desires for knowledge may often be unsatisfied, he may nonetheless find happiness in the pursuit of knowledge – he will often be intrigued, absorbed, find intellectual comradeship, etc. The satisfied pig, in contrast, may not be particularly happy: he may have eaten to allay restlessness or irritation, or to distract himself from something that is bothering him ("comfort food"). These judgments about the greater happiness brought by the pursuit of the "higher pleasures" are perfectionist in structure and content, but Mill can endorse them without abandoning the utilitarian assumption that ultimately the value of anything consists in the hedonic states they produce. He can argue, as he actually seems to, that agents should adopt the "theory of life" (Mill's own term) that Socratic happiness is better than pig happiness because acting on that theory will tend to produce more utility for oneself and others.

Utilitarian Common Goods

In the last chapter, we saw that from a Platonic standpoint, liberal democratic institutions and the common good are at odds. Classical utilitarianism, however, provides a framework for reuniting them. A central element of the liberal democratic ("two atlas") view, it will be recalled, is the idea that each person should have the right to live as they choose, to invest their personal assets and property according to their own lights, as long as they respect the similar rights of everyone else to do the same. In this view, the state's primary function – the defining concern within the "public atlas" – is the protection of individuals' rights against force, fraud, and theft. The classical utilitarians thought that there was an overwhelmingly strong case for thinking of the state's functions in these terms. The reason they gave was the overriding utilitarian value

---

[10] Lazari-Radek and Singer 2014, p. 252; Haybron 2010.

of personal security, which Mill referred to as "the most vital of all interests":

> All other earthly benefits are needed by one person, not needed by another; and many of them can, if necessary, be cheerfully forgone or replaced by something else; but security no human being can possibly do without; on it we depend for all our immunity from evil and for the whole value of all and every good, beyond the passing moment, since we could be deprived of everything the next instant by whoever was momentarily stronger than ourselves … This most indispensable of all necessaries … cannot be had, unless the machinery for providing it is kept in unintermittedly active play.[11]

Mill concluded that we all therefore have overriding reasons to "join" with others "in making safe the very groundwork of our existence" by cooperating with and supporting the relevant "machinery." So, something like the modern liberal democratic state, guaranteeing individual safety, emerges in the utilitarian analysis as an indispensable requirement of the common good.

What, though, does the utilitarian have to say to the further worry, pressed by the Platonist in the last chapter, that this will not be *sufficient* to guarantee the welfare of all members of society. Should we not regulate the lives of citizens in additional ways to ensure that they not only respect each other's rights but also succeed and *live well*? After all, the Platonist need not disagree with Mill about the value of personal security. The problem with the "two atlas" view, from the Platonic standpoint, lies not here, but rather in its refusal to expand the public atlas any further into what the liberal democrat regards as the sacred "private sphere." It is this feature that (on the Platonist objection) leaves individual agents cruelly at the mercy of their own unguided judgments about what is good for them.

Like any account of the common good built around a commitment to agents' well-being, utilitarianism generates some pressure in this paternalistic direction. In their sympathetic reconstruction of Sidgwick's utilitarianism, de Lazari-Radek and Singer at one point contend that "what people want is not a reliable indicator of what will maximize their well-being over time,"[12] and note that the "experiencing self" (the true locus

---

[11] Troyer 2003, pp. 137–8.
[12] Lazari-Radek and Singer 2014, p. 279.

of utilitarian well-being) is not necessarily well represented in the voting booth. In other words, a democratic society that follows the preferences of its members need not act in ways that maximize their utility, and so (as de Lazari-Radek and Singer admit) utilitarians should at least be open to paternalism.

However, any utilitarian paternalist must contend with the immensely powerful case against paternalism mounted, on rigidly utilitarian grounds, by Mill in *On Liberty*. The argument of that book is important because, as I noted earlier, Mill himself was a perfectionist. Despite his effort to integrate a conception of human flourishing into utilitarianism, Mill nevertheless adamantly rejected the suggestion that the law be used to directly promote human flourishing. Two of Mill's arguments are particularly relevant here. First, whatever might be said for the more intimate and culturally homogenous setting of the ancient Greek *polis*, the modes of legal and bureaucratic regulation characteristic of modern states are ill-adapted to the direct promotion of perfectionist ideals. Trusting public officials, or (as in Iran) a "moral police," to impart the right character traits and personal qualities is likely futile and self-defeating. These responsibilities are better left to families, churches, and other institutions in civil society. Mill's divergent conclusions here result from applying common-good considerations to political institutions whose nature and limitations Plato and Aristotle could not have foreseen.

Second, Mill argued that from a utilitarian point of view, it is not necessarily bad that individuals lead unhappy, unfulfilled lives or are left free to advocate for, and experiment with, forms of life that put their own welfare at risk (or even sabotage it). To be sure, their mistakes, and the resulting suffering they will undergo, will diminish overall welfare. However, these errors and mistakes may also be enormously useful for individual and collective progress: we often learn a lot from them. So leaving people free to make mistakes can often help them, and the rest of us, become clearer about which choices and activities are really worthwhile. Maximizing utility therefore requires toleration and resisting the temptation to use the power of the law to interfere in agents' efforts to live by their own lights.

Mill made a parallel argument about the expression of erroneous doctrines and bad arguments. We should never, he insisted, suppress speech on the basis of its content, because having spurious arguments before us helps us become better, more critical, reasoners. As Mill correctly noted, justified confidence in one's own judgments, including especially practical judgments about what we should value and oppose, how we should conduct ourselves, etc., can be acquired only under conditions in which one has an adequate opportunity to consider the objections our own convictions invite. This in turn requires the open expression of dissent, and a disposition to take it seriously and reckon with it. The suppression of dissent only erodes the foundations on which any legitimate confidence in one's own convictions can alone be based. Those who deny this confuse rational belief with the parroting of a dogma.

This is a powerful argument against the Platonic position we described in the last chapter. It suggests that a free and open society in which agents are left to pursue their own good in their own way *is* a common good after all, because the resulting cultural ferment and debate turns out to be a precondition for, not a threat to, the intelligent discussion and pursuit of human flourishing.

Still, two worries about Mill's case deserve mention. First, one might find something manipulative in Mill's suggestion that we can learn from the mistakes, stupidity, and misery of others. Does this not exploit others' misfortune for the sake of overall welfare? We will return to this concern that utilitarianism instrumentalizes agents' lives in a moment.

Second, one wonders whether the experience of modern liberal democratic societies supports Mill's prediction that open discussion, freedom of speech, and experiments in living tend to promote overall welfare by making us better practical reasoners and more discriminating judges of what makes a life go well or badly. Having followed Mill's advice for most of the last century, the Western liberal democracies provide something of a natural experiment for his hypothesis about the salutary effects of free thought and debate. How is the experiment panning out?

There is a lot of bullshit around these days.[13] It is far from clear that its presence is self-limiting rather than self-multiplying.

---

[13] See Frankfurt 2005.

The Experience Machine

I end this chapter by considering two standard objections to utilitarianism. The first, due to Robert Nozick, targets the utilitarians' hedonistic account of well-being:

> Suppose there were an experience machine that would give you any experience you desired. Superduper neuropsychologists could stimulate your brain so that you would think and feel you were writing a great novel, or making a friend, or reading an interesting book. All the time you would be floating in a tank, with electrodes attached to your brain. Should you plug into this machine for life, preprogramming your life's experiences?[14]

Nozick thinks that no rational person would choose to plug in on these terms.

The example is intended to expose our tacit conviction that there is more to life than experience. We do not only care about *feeling* things, but also about *doing* things, and about who we are or what we become in doing them. It also matters to us whether doing those things is genuinely *worthwhile* independently of their pleasure-promoting capacities. People plugged into the Experience Machine would have no real access to these goods. They might feel good, but they could not know that what they are doing matters, or take pride in a life of successful accomplishment; indeed there is no sense in which they *do* anything. Nozick suggests that plugging into the machine is therefore tantamount to suicide.

Clearly, the Experience Machine example will not trouble perfectionists; they will be happy to agree with Nozick that well-being ("fulfillment") requires active engagement in worthwhile, non-illusory projects. But it poses a real threat to the utilitarian. If the ultimate rational end is "desirable consciousness," why should it matter how the "desirable consciousness" is produced? As long as the pleasure itself is real pleasure, the fact that its stimulus is not what it appears would seem to lack any utilitarian significance. So it seems that, counter to our intuitions, utilitarianism recommends plugging in.

Some utilitarians respond to this challenge by biting the bullet; our intuitions are simply wrong here or at least have no probative force. If such

---

[14] Nozick 2013, p. 42.

a machine really existed and was reliable, the mere presence of intuitions that lead us to have scruples about plugging in is neither here nor there. If it is *that* good, of course we should plug in! But since there is no such machine, utilitarians do not need to worry too much about the example; it casts no doubt on utilitarian recommendations in more realistic contexts of choice.

This line of response is helpful in one way: it reminds us that it matters what the alternative to plugging in is. De Lazari-Radek and Singer report some psychological research suggesting that intuitions about plugging in may be corrupted by "status quo bias" (i.e. the irrational tendency to be more reluctant to give X up if we already have it than to want to obtain X if we do not yet have it).[15] And it seems hard to deny that, if someone's only alternative to plugging in is truly *awful* (e.g. years of agony so bad that one could not engage in any activity at all), it would be cruel to criticize them for doing so. On the other hand, even if no such machine exists, one might still worry that biting the bullet will have unacceptable consequences for more realistic cases. It is often true that we can increase people's "desirable consciousness" by deceiving them, so arguing this way likely commits the utilitarian to explaining away a lot of counterintuitive judgments about more common scenarios.

I suspect that the utilitarian can do better by questioning the example itself. Derek Parfit distinguished between philosophers' thought experiments that are merely "technically" impossible and those that are "deeply" impossible.[16] The Experience Machine challenge trades on the assumption that the example is merely technically impossible (we just do not have the technology now, but there is no reason to think that we could not build the machine). However, I think it is *deeply* impossible, in an interesting way.

Nozick says that the machine can be programmed so that I can have any experience I like. He gives the example of writing a great novel. But can I have that experience without someone writing the great novel whose composition I experience in the machine? What if I want to have the "experience" of "making the next great breakthrough in theoretical physics" (I stipulate that it has to be a *real* breakthrough, not just Einstein all over again)? Don't we, the programmers, then have to *make* the next great breakthrough to give me the experience? It looks as if, in order to

---

[15] Lazari-Radek and Singer 2014, pp. 256–61.
[16] Parfit 1992, p. 388.

have such a machine, we would have to have a lot of people working on producing the real versions of the experiences the machine will replicate. Those people would be doing pretty much what human beings do anyway (writing novels, raising children, trying to make the next breakthrough in physics). Isn't "We are doing these things in case someone wants to experience them in the Experience Machine program" just an elliptical way of saying "We are doing these things for the sake of producing as much 'desirable consciousness' as possible?"

One might respond that we can set up the program so that I merely *believe* that the meaningless equations I "see" on the "pages" of my pathbreaking treatise on light go one better than Einstein. But then it is not so clear that the machine is actually giving me the experience I wanted as opposed to merely producing a generic kind of pleasurable arousal and attaching a label to it. If the choice is between "living life" and plugging into a machine that simply gives me a lot of generic pleasurable arousal, even if very intense, few would plug in, not because they ultimately value activity over pleasure, but rather because they have very good reasons to doubt that the machine can produce pleasures as rich and rewarding as those deriving from life itself.

The Separateness of Persons

Many worry that the utility principle is too willing to allow the sacrifice of the few for the sake of the welfare of the many. If we can cure cancer forever by submitting 50 people to excruciating involuntary vivisection, doesn't utilitarianism require us to do this? According to one of utilitarianism's most influential critics, John Rawls, these counterintuitive implications arise for a deeper theoretical reason: utilitarians do not take sufficiently seriously the "separateness of persons."[17] As Rawls has it, the utilitarian drive to maximize overall welfare makes sense only if we think of the collectivity of all human beings as a kind of aggregate person that seeks to maximize its own welfare. On this analogy, just as individuals sometimes sacrifice certain of their own desires in order to satisfy more of their other desires, so collectivities may sacrifice the welfare of some of their members in order to secure the happiness of a greater number of others. But, the objection

---

[17] Rawls 1999, pp. 19–24; Taurek 1977.

runs, this analogy is mistaken. Collectivities are not super-persons whose welfare conflicts with and takes priority over the welfare of the individuals comprising them. Rather, they are made up of separate, individual persons, each with their own life to lead. We should not instrumentalize or exploit their lives, as if they were mere fodder for the hive.

Must utilitarians indulge the seemingly totalitarian idea that society *as such* is a conscious collective self whose well-being is distinct from, and is of overridingly greater importance than, the well-being of its members? What gives the allegation some plausibility is the utilitarian focus on *aggregate* welfare. But to say that endorsing the utility principle implies that society *as such* is a kind of collective person with interests in its own right is a caricature.

Suppose everyone is currently (A) at the same level of welfare, and we can either

stay at (A);
move to (B): three people will be better off by 10 utiles;
move to (C): 10 people will be better off by 10 utiles.

Assuming that no one in (B) or (C) is any worse off than in (A), both are better than (A). But of these options (C) is clearly the best. When we make these judgments, are we assuming that the society is a kind of person with interests of its own? Plainly not. We are assuming merely that it is better if more prosper.

Of course things get more complicated when we relax the assumption that none of our options will make anyone worse off. Suppose we add the option to

move to (D): 100 people will be made better off by 1,000 utiles but three people will be subjected to terrible agony for two hours (−1,000 utiles).

(D) now looks like the best option from a utilitarian perspective. But should we really choose (D) knowing that three people will suffer terrible agony?

This question (and the infinite possible variants on it) raises a genuine problem for utilitarianism, and many have, under the influence of Rawls and other critics, abandoned the doctrine for this reason. The matter is too deep and complex to resolve here, but utilitarians should not give up without a fight.

Here, we should remember the earlier point that the most plausible versions of utilitarianism are "indirect." Most of the simple thought-experiment examples that philosophers use to pump their readers' intuitions about utilitarianism (like the (A)–(D) case used here) involve applying the utility principle directly to a one-shot decision. But as I emphasized earlier, the classical utilitarians were less concerned about single-case choices of this sort. They were critical moralists who were most interested in subjecting whole social practices to utilitarian scrutiny. In these contexts, we have to consider not only the specific effects of a particular choice at a given time. Rather, the critical moralist is interested in the utilitarian profile of some ongoing, society-shaping institutional configuration.

From this point of view, the question we should be asking about the (A)–(D) case is not so much whether on *this* occasion we should choose (D), but rather whether it would be valuable, from a utilitarian point of view, for institutions and society generally to adopt and enforce a positive morality prohibiting people from taking action that would inflict agony on people. In a society that adopted and internalized such a positive morality, choosing (D) would be considered completely out of the question from the first, and anyone choosing (D) would be subject to sanction – as in our society, where (D) would be considered a crime. Given Mill's argument about security, it seems that classical utilitarianism can deal with this case very easily. Imagine a society in which the prevailing positive morality *permitted* agents (anyone, private or official) to injure, kill, maim, defraud, etc. others any time they believed that doing so would "maximize utility." Under this positive morality, all of us would be insecure, and constantly anxious that our lives or children would be taken or hurt by some self-appointed utilitarian crusader. This would clearly be suboptimal, and so it seems rather easy to defend fairly traditional, intuitive prohibitions on instrumentalizing people in this way.

Of course, there are social practices of different kinds, and we might consider many possible ways to reform, change, or replace them, and these questions may not be as straightforward as determining the worthlessness of a social practice that permits people to kill one another whenever they believe that doing so will improve overall welfare. But the utilitarian might say that the complicated cases will also be ones in which the trade-offs will not involve anyone having to sacrifice anything as fundamental as their basic security and safety. All large-scale social practices impose sacrifices of one sort or another on somebody even when they do not threaten basic security. So when critical moralists judge the relative value of alternative political arrangements none of which threaten basic security, why shouldn't they do so by applying the utility principle?

5   The Social Contract

The last three chapters have considered conceptions of the common good that are organized around various notions of well-being. Along the way, we considered several objections to these views; some of these are quite serious, but it seems fair to say that none delivered a knockout blow. However, one might argue that the very diversity of the views we have considered constitutes an objection in itself, and a rather powerful one at that. Recall our discussion in Chapter 1. There, I suggested that critical moralists succeed in informing us about something to the extent that they reduce reasonable disagreement along some nontrivial dimension. Theorists of the common good hoped they could do this by adopting a welfarist approach. Their gambit was that concepts of welfare, happiness, rational interest, etc. would prove more straightforward, less unruly, than more contested political ideals like justice, the common good, rights, security, etc.

Unfortunately, however, we have discovered that, interesting and ingenious though they often are, their arguments about well-being seem to be subject to just as much reasonable disagreement as the original categories that they were trying to clarify. We have not shown that it is *unreasonable* to accept a perfectionist, fulfillment theory of well-being, to accept the utilitarians' hedonistic alternative, or to judge social institutions in terms of aggregate welfare. Equally, we have not shown that any of these views is clearly superior to the alternatives. This may lead us to lose confidence in the idea that critical moral reflection can be advanced by philosophical inquiry into the nature and conditions of well-being.

Those impressed by this objection have often suggested that rather than looking to ambitious and endlessly contestable claims about happiness and our real interests, we might instead look to more modest and tractable judgments about what agents would voluntarily agree to under defined conditions. This attempt to reformulate critical morality in terms of agreement, consent, and choice resulted in the development of the social-contract theories we consider now.

Peace in Our Time

In Chapter 1, I discussed two imaginary countries, Atlantis and Pacifica, committed respectively to egalitarian and inegalitarian conceptions of justice. Suppose that, for a time, Atlantis and Pacifica go to war. After several years of bitter fighting, the war ends in stalemate. There is a peace conference at which both sides, keen to end hostilities, make various concessions and eventually agree on the terms of a treaty to regulate their future interaction.

Some years later, after the horrors of the war have faded from popular memory, a new Altantan government starts making bellicose denunciations of Pacifican "tyranny," "injustice," and "oppression." Influential voices in the Atlantan government start calling for "regime change" in Pacifica: this is justified, they claim, because it is important to eradicate "evil" from the world. The Pacificans respond by calling the Atlantans "arrogant imperialists" whose political society is "degenerate" and morally "corrupt." The Pacifican regime threatens to roll back the concessions it made earlier. War again looms; but it is eventually averted thanks to the efforts of groups in both societies to remind their governments that they are already bound by the terms of an agreement to which they were themselves parties.

The most important thing to notice about this story is the way in which the existence of an agreement allows proponents of peace to change the topic of conversation. We can imagine the peace parties in both societies arguing along similar lines: "Look, we can argue until the cows come home about whether Atlantis or Pacifica more closely approximates true justice, furthers human well-being, or realizes the common good. Not only will we never reach final agreement, these arguments are only likely to inflame animosities. But the question of how our respective governments ought to be acting is in any case controlled by considerations that are not in dispute: we know that Atlantis agreed to respect the territorial integrity of Pacifica and we know that the Pacificans agreed to make certain permanent concessions. So instead of fighting vainly over the correct interpretation of justice, we can resolve our differences and live in peace simply by living up to our own commitments." This argument appeals to the voluntary commitments of the parties involved as a way to preempt further discussion of the merits of the two countries' moral causes.

The apparently preemptive potential of claims about agreement and voluntary commitment led the pioneers of the social-contract approach to hope that certain of our political arrangements could be justified on a similar basis. As a matter of history, the classical theorists of the social contract focused in particular on the justification of the state itself. Thus, writing in the seventeenth century, Thomas Hobbes and John Locke argued that state authority can be thought of as the product of a certain kind of voluntary agreement among the individuals who submit to it.[1] They thought that by appreciating the likely terms of this social contract, we can explain why the state is justified, why its citizens have reasons to support and submit to political authority. But as we shall see, more recently philosophers have employed social-contract arguments to defend a wider array of ethical judgments about social and distributive justice.[2]

Politics as Conflict Resolution

The kinds of agreements in which Hobbes and Locke were interested differ in an important respect from the Pacifica–Atlantis peace treaty. The latter is an agreement between already existing states. But Hobbes and Locke understood the social contract as an agreement between *individuals* to institute the state in the first place. Clearly, in order to make sense of such an agreement, we have to postulate a situation in which individuals interact prior to the institution of a state. In the jargon of classical social-contract theory, this initial situation is usually called a "state of nature." The burden of the theory is then to explain how and why, if we were in such a state of nature, we would find it rational to make mutual agreements that bring the state into being on certain terms. Voltaire famously said that "If God did not exist, it would be necessary to invent Him." In asserting a similar claim with regard to the state, the social-contract theorists presumed that political institutions are best analyzed as artificial creations of human will and choice.

[1] Hobbes 1994; Locke 1980.
[2] Rawls 1999; Scanlon 2000.

While they thought of the social contract as an agreement between independent individuals rather than between states, Hobbes and Locke nonetheless understood its function, like the Pacifica–Atlantis peace treaty, in terms of the resolution of conflict. Both philosophers describe the state of nature as a situation of instability and violence. Of the two, Hobbes's depiction of the state of nature is notably bleaker in this respect. Hobbes asserted that the state of nature would be equivalent to a war of all against all. Even when individuals in the state of nature are not openly fighting, he thought, they would operate with the (self-fulfilling) presumption that they harbor aggressive intentions toward each other.

Contrary to a popular misconception, Hobbes did not take this view because he believed that humans are inherently wicked or "evil." Rather, he thought these conflicts would be endemic because of the particular circumstances in which individuals in a state of nature find themselves. While not naturally motivated to harm others for its own sake, individuals are, he thought, naturally partial to their own interests, and are rarely altruistic. They are also prone to resent and respond angrily to slights, insults, and other perceived assaults on their pride. Hobbes contended that when these natural predilections (not in themselves symptoms of wickedness) are placed in the context of the competition for scarce resources that would characterize a state of nature, a spiral of violence and mutual suspicion is inevitable. According to Hobbes, the resulting conflicts give individuals strong reasons to band together to set up some institution capable of settling these conflicts peacefully. That institution is of course the state, which Hobbes thought of as essentially a mechanism of authoritative dispute resolution, using coercive power to enforce peaceful cooperation among citizens. Although Locke's depiction of the state of nature is more pacific, he agreed with Hobbes that it would be marked by conflict, and that the main purpose of the state is to adjudicate these conflicts authoritatively.

This underlying focus on dispute resolution, which is characteristic of the entire social-contract tradition, reflects features of the historical context within which these theories were first extensively developed. At the time that Hobbes and Locke were writing, modern centralized states, sovereign within their own territory, were not yet fully entrenched in any region of Europe. Partly for this reason, European politics was marked by endemic and violent conflicts between and within states. These conflicts were exacerbated by the bitter religious division that followed the Reformation, and by the complete failure of the Christian tradition to provide a settled account of secular authority and its relation to the divine authority claimed by the Church. Hobbes especially saw that, as long as political authority is understood as coming from above, ordained by God, its recognition will be hostage to intractable religious disagreements about how we should understand God's will. In social-contract theory, however, the authority of the state is presumed to come from below, conferred on rulers by the ruled. By understanding the terms on which rational agents would and should confer that authority, social-contract theory holds out the hope of bypassing intractable religious and ethical disagreements about how best to live and worship God and explaining why we should obey the state on a completely secular basis.

In pursuing this line of argument, Hobbes and Locke were *not* trying to convince us that we ought to acknowledge the authority of the state because people have already consented to it. They had little interest in explaining how, as a matter of fact, states either did, or must have, come into being; they understood that these facts are irrelevant. Even if it is true that *others* have consented to a government in the past, why should that give *me* any reason to believe its claims to authority are justified? Nor could this fact, if it is one, by itself explain why I ought to consent myself. The bare fact that others have done something is no reason for me to follow suit. Furthermore, it is very hard to believe that such claims are true in any case. At least in the case of the Pacifica–Atlantis peace treaty, one can point to an actual agreement signed by the representatives of the two governments. But no one remembers ever having signed any sort of social contract before being expected to submit to the authority of the state, and recorded history reveals no trace of any such agreements.

So, if the apparatus of social-contract theory is being advanced just to acquaint us with certain facts about the genesis of political societies or to establish that I am or must have been a signatory to an actual social con-tract, it is completely uninformative from the standpoint of critical mor-ality. The important question is to understand what attitude we should take to state authority: why is it rational for us to accept it on certain terms, and how far does that authority extend?

Hobbes and Locke thought that their account of how agents in a state of nature would agree to accept state authority could help answer that question because it affords us a hypothetical "thought experiment" demonstrating the *rationality* of accepting state authority given the alternatives. The point of the experiment is not to inform us about the behavior of others, but rather to force us to consider what we would find it rational to do if we attempted to live together without the aid of authoritative state institutions. They therefore ask us to imagine our way into the "state of nature" and contend that, once we do so, we will all come to appreciate the same overriding reasons to band together in a social contract establishing state authority.

To make it possible for us to imagine ourselves doing this, Hobbes and Locke ask us to assume that in the state of nature, we would all think of ourselves as bearers of certain "natural rights." It is these rights that are exchanged in the agreement that constitutes the social contract. In surrendering or transferring these rights in particular ways, Hobbesian and Lockean contractors understand themselves to be bringing the state into being on certain terms. For Hobbes and Locke, then, the rights and powers that the state acquires through the social contract are to be analyzed in terms of certain primitive rights and powers that we would presume ourselves to wield even before an institutionalized system of authority has been set up. They refer to them as "natural" rights precisely for this reason. These rights, they maintain, are not parts of a positive morality in the sense described in the previous chapters. Unlike conventional legal rights, such as my right to vote, these rights are not conferred upon individuals by the positive law in force in their particular jurisdictions. They are conceived in something like the way that people today understand "human rights": as pre-legal entitlements that rational individuals should recognize as valid independently of any institutionalized system of rules.

The Hobbesian Contract

The early theorists of the social contract differed on the precise scope of these natural rights, although all agreed that the right of self-defense or "self-preservation" was central. To explain the role they play in the theory, however, I will for the moment focus on Hobbes's account. Hobbes claimed that individuals in a state of nature would recognize not only a right of self-defense, but also a right to act on their own judgments about how best to defend themselves. But he argued that the shared recognition of this natural right guarantees that life in the state of nature will be appallingly insecure. As long as individuals retain it, everyone must feel vulnerable to predation at the hands of everyone else. For, in a Hobbesian state of nature, just as you have a right to judge me to be a potential threat and therefore to take preemptive action against me, so I am liable to form exactly the same judgment of, and have the right to take similar action against, you. The possession of these rights thus creates the self-fulfilling mutual suspicion and "war of all against all" mentioned earlier. In such a situation, individuals face "continual fear, and danger of violent death."

According to Hobbes, the nightmarish quality of the state of nature stems directly from the fact that individuals reserve the right to defend themselves as they choose. The naturally rational thing for individuals in this position to do is therefore to seek terms of peace, by signing some sort of collective treaty under which each lays down their rights to defend themselves as they choose, on condition that everyone else does the same. Hobbes argued, however, that in a state of nature individuals will be unable to assure themselves that others will follow through on such agreements even if they *say* that they are prepared to do so.

On his account, even if two individuals with guns pointed at each other are willing to agree *in words* to put their weapons down on condition that the other puts theirs down as well, in a state of nature neither party is likely to feel confident enough to put this verbal agreement to the test by actually putting *their* gun down first. In the absence of such trust, such agreements will never actually be put into effect. What is needed in situations like this is some independent enforcement mechanism capable of providing agents with a general assurance that others can be trusted to keep their word.

But Hobbes's own argument implies that such a mechanism cannot itself be put in place through direct agreement, since any simple bilateral commitment would suffer from exactly the debility we have just described. In order to be able to trust other parties enough to actually enact any such agreement, there would already need to be some enforcement mechanism capable of forcing others to keep their promises. Hobbes concluded, therefore, that to set up such an enforcement mechanism some special, nonbilateral agreement is required. This special agreement is the social contract, and the state it brings into being becomes the guarantor of all subsequent mutual commitments among members of a society.

Hobbes argued that if it is to succeed in bringing the war of all against all to an end, the social contract would have to be an agreement in which all members of a society jointly agree to lay down their natural rights and instead to follow the judgment of a third party about how best to preserve themselves collectively. This third party agency is designated the "sovereign." In the simplest case, the sovereign will be a single individual – giving rise to a monarchical regime. According to Hobbes, however, sovereignty may be also be aristocratic in form (if exercised by several individuals) or democratic (if exercised through procedures involving the participation of all citizens).

It is important to understand the precise structure of the resulting agreement. Hobbes's contract is an understanding among members of a society that each accepts the judgment of a third party – the sovereign – as authoritative for all of them. Each abandons their right to decide for themselves how best to preserve themselves on condition that all submit to the sovereign's decisions about the best means of their *collective* self-preservation. This is a nonbilateral undertaking because there is no reciprocity between the people and the sovereign. The sovereign does not surrender any natural rights in return for citizens' abandoning theirs, or even on condition that they do so. The sovereign, rather, retains its natural rights, but as a result of the agreement now *exercises* them, not simply in his/her own name, but in that of the whole community.

According to Hobbes, this is the correct way to understand the institution of the state and our relation to it. Whereas in a state of nature individuals have the right to use force to preserve themselves as they see fit, a Hobbesian sovereign retains the (unlimited) right to use force – in the form of coercive sanctions, punishments, and other mechanisms of enforcement – but now deploys it to coordinate the activities of its citizens in ways that it judges to be required for their security. On Hobbes's view, the state's right to determine rules of property, rights, and entitlements, to establish court systems to enforce these legal rights and entitlements, to identify and punish offenders, and indeed to perform all its traditional functions (national self-defense, health and safety regulations, the provision of important public goods, etc.), is simply an echo of the basic natural right to self-preservation individuals would otherwise retain in the state of nature.

It is important to stress that under the terms of the Hobbesian contract, this right is virtually absolute. Contractors give up the right to second-guess the judgments of the state about how force is to be used for the sake of collective self-defense in all cases except those in which one is in direct physical peril. For Hobbes, you can escape the state of nature and the war of all against all only if you surrender that very broad right to the sovereign. A state claiming nearly unlimited authority is, for him, the sole condition under which peace is possible.

The Rational Will

One can think of Hobbes's thought experiment as inviting us to consider a series of hypothetical questions. In the absence of a state, would we presume that each has the right to seek their self-preservation as they (individually) choose? If so, would we want to remain in a situation in which everyone retained this right? Assuming that we would not, given the resulting insecurity, on what terms would we be willing to abandon this right for the sake of peace? When we reflect on this, Hobbes thinks that we must eventually grant that the only formula likely to do the trick will be a social contract with the structure he recommends. The particular shape of this formula is important for Hobbes, not because he thought it accurately represented the way in which states were historically founded, but rather because it properly describes the relationship between state authority and our rational will. It purports to explain, without presupposing any particular positive morality, conception of human flourishing, or religious worldview, why, from the standpoint of critical morality, a sovereign state with virtually unlimited authority is a rational institution.

Understood in this way, Hobbes's thought experiment attempts to reveal something about our own rational dispositions that is not at first obvious. As we normally experience it, submission to the authority of the state seems to involve recognizing constraints on our ability to act as we would want, i.e., constraints on our own will. For example, in recognizing speed limits as authoritative legal requirements, I recognize that I am not free to drive at whatever speed I like in (say) built-up areas. But if it succeeds, Hobbes's argument enables me to see these apparent limitations on my choices as something that I should rationally will for myself, given the alternative.

Thus, in the absence of a state with the authority to enforce rules about safe driving, each of us would retain the right to drive in whatever ways we judge necessary to our self-preservation. This would likely be very dangerous for all of us: a Hobbesian state of nature equipped with cars would give new meaning to the term "aggressive driving." When we imagine the likely results of each of us retaining the right to drive our cars in whatever ways we judge necessary for our self-preservation, the irrationality of each trusting to our own wills in this way becomes vividly apparent. So it seems rational for us to defer to the judgment of a will other than our own in deciding where, how, and at what speeds to drive, as long as everyone else is disposed to do so as well. For Hobbes, surrendering judgment in this way represents the rational attitude to take to state authority, and the purpose of his thought experiment is to induce this realization in his readers. If it works, the argument makes it possible for us to think of acceptance of state authority, not as a limitation on our rational will, but actually as conforming to it at a deeper level.

Before assessing it, it may be helpful to notice the contrasts and continuities between this revised version of the social-contract argument and the structure of the common-good arguments we met in previous chapters. The two sets of arguments resemble each other in that they hinge on claims about practical reason – about what it is rational for us to choose and value. But whereas the common-good approach is organized around conceptions of our *rational interests* in achieving various forms of well-being, the social-contract argument is organized around a conception of our *rational will*. Clearly, these two notions are not sharply distinct. After all, if we are rational we presumably will our well-being. But there is a crucial difference in the way in which these two theories access these assumptions about our interests and our wills. On the common-good approach, we understand our real interests by reference to some substantive ideal of human well-being and happiness. But on the social-contract theory, there is no need to construct an elaborate account of human well-being, or for a perfectionist account of the good life. The question of what we ought rationally to will for ourselves is settled simply by reflecting on an imagined choice between pertinent alternatives.

Since, as we saw in the last chapter, disagreements about the correct conception of well-being are extremely difficult to settle, the ability of social-contract arguments to bracket this whole issue seems to count strongly in their favor. By isolating the narrower and more immediate choices at stake in the decision to accept or reject state authority, the social-contract theorists hoped, like the peace parties in Pacifica and Atlantis, to change the subject and to proceed with political justification on a less contentious basis.

Empirical Issues

As we have reconstructed it, Hobbes's argument turns crucially on a claim about the *alternative* to voluntary submission to the state. Only if we agree that Hobbes has correctly described the alternatives can we conclude that his thought experiment establishes the rationality of accepting the state and the authority it claims. Should we? This is partly an empirical question. If we are not convinced that life in the state of nature would be as insecure and as devoid of trust as Hobbes claimed, or we doubt that the alternatives he described are exhaustive, the rationality of embracing the state will seem correspondingly less clear.

But it is only partly an empirical question. This is because Hobbes's argument does not only hinge on empirical predictions about individuals' likely behavior and motivations in a state of nature. It also hinges crucially on the assumption that individuals in the state of nature would recognize certain "natural" rights. As we have seen, the shape of these rights conditions both the problem faced by individuals in a Hobbesian state of nature and the solutions available to them. So one might question Hobbes's account either by challenging his empirical description of life in the state of nature, or by questioning his normative assumptions about the natural rights individuals should recognize in the absence of a state.

The question of whether the empirical assumptions of Hobbes's thought experiment are plausible could be debated indefinitely and cannot be decided here. Still, it is important to see that there is much counting in favor of Hobbes's hypothesis. Hobbes himself defended it by inviting his readers to consider the behavior of states in the international arena. The international case is pertinent because like individuals in his state of nature, states interact with each other in the absence of any overarching global authority. Thus Hobbes noted that

> at all times kings and persons of sovereign authority, because of their independency, are in continual jealousies, and in the state and posture

of gladiators, having their weapons pointing, and their eyes fixed on one another; that is, their forts, garrisons, and guns upon the frontiers of their kingdoms, and continual spies upon their neighbors, which is a posture of war.[3]

What would be the point of this if they had nothing to fear from their neighbors?[4]

It is worth noting that a still widely influential school of international relations theory, known as "realism" (note that this is *not* the sense of "realism" we discussed in Chapter 1), is predicated on a version of this Hobbesian hypothesis. International relations realism accepts Hobbes's view that states interact under conditions of anarchy. It argues that states are therefore inevitably locked into a perennial struggle for power and scarce resources and recognize no constraints on their conduct other than strategic ones. This, it contends, is why the history of international relations is a story of *raison d'état*, preemptive attack, broken promises, mistrust, violence, and war (both cold and hot).[5] The resilience of this realist view about international relations, which we will meet again in Chapter 10, hardly shows that Hobbes's empirical assumptions about the likely terms of individuals' interaction in a state of nature are correct. But it does lend them circumstantial plausibility.

The Lockean Critique

At first glance, it seems much easier to find fault with Hobbes's normative assumptions about rights in the state of nature. The obvious suspicion is that the scope of Hobbesian natural rights is implausibly wide. Hobbes himself admitted that the effect of individuals retaining their natural rights as he understood them "is almost the same as if there were no right at all. For although one could say of anything, *this is mine*, still he could not enjoy it because of his neighbor, who claimed the same thing to be his by equal *right* and with equal force."[6] But it is tempting to object that this misses the point of having rights at all: we ordinarily think of rights as protecting us

---

[3] Hobbes 1994, p. 78.
[4] Hobbes 1998, p. 10.
[5] For a good statement of the realist view, see Mearsheimer 2014.
[6] Hobbes 1998, p. 29.

against the predations and assaults of others, not as permitting others to commit them. In other words, Hobbes's account of natural rights seems perverse because it lacks an account of natural *wrongs.* Very little, if anything, is decisively forbidden by Hobbesian natural rights. Even the killing of innocents is permitted in principle, as Hobbes explicitly admits.

Locke attempted to correct this seeming defect in Hobbes's account of the social contract. He agreed with Hobbes that self-preservation would be the overriding concern of individuals in a state of nature, but he denied that this would lead individuals to recognize a general permission to take *whatever* steps they deem necessary to further their self-preservation. Locke insisted, rather, that in a state of nature, individuals would recognize important limits on their rights to defend themselves. They would not assume that they are permitted to destroy each other on mere suspicion alone. Thus, for Locke, the state of nature is already regulated by a law of nature, appreciable by everyone, that prohibits individuals from wantonly depriving innocent others of life or property. These natural prohibitions serve as independent limits on the means individuals may select to preserve themselves. They also license the use of force against individuals who violate the law of nature; for, on Locke's view, individuals possess a natural right to punish those guilty of offenses against the natural law.[7]

One objection that one might make to this Lockean revision is that if the state of nature is *already* governed by a recognized body of enforceable rules that protect individuals against preemptive attack at the hands of others, it is no longer obvious that one needs a state at all. Anticipating this objection, Locke argued that private enforcement of the law of nature would be patchy, frequently unjust, and fraught with conflict. Violators need to be apprehended and punished; but in a state of nature victims and other interested parties would have trouble identifying the culprits, and be overzealous or unduly timid in meting out punishment. Locke predicted that this will only create further resentments and conflicts. These will be hard to settle definitively, because in a state of nature there is no impartial judge that all recognize as authorized to arbitrate these disputes. It is therefore rational for individuals to establish a neutral "umpire" with the right to adjudicate them, and this institution is of course the state. Individuals can

---

[7] Locke 1980.

do this, according to Locke, by surrendering to a third party – the state – their natural right to punish those who violate the law of nature. This is the substance of the Lockean social contract.

For Locke, then, the state is a means to settle conflicts about how to enforce an already recognized and independently authoritative body of rules. It is *not* – as in Hobbes's theory – the ultimate and unique source of *all* authoritative rules and obligations. This implies, again in contrast to Hobbes's position, that on Locke's account the state's authority is limited. For, as Locke cogently argued, if the authority of the state derives from a transfer of individuals' natural rights, the state could not acquire rights more extensive than those originally possessed by individuals in the state of nature. Since, on Locke's view, individuals' natural rights are already limited by the natural law, the state's authority must be similarly limited. Thus the Lockean state cannot have the authority to kill innocents preemptively, take their property without their consent, inflict unjust punishments, and so forth. And when the state exceeds this authority, citizens retain *in extremis* a right to overthrow the current regime and replace it. It is easy to understand why these Lockean arguments were so congenial to the American colonists in their struggle against the British crown in the eighteenth century.

Problems with Locke's Account

This Lockean view is much more attractive than Hobbes's, but it is problematic nonetheless. Is it clear that individuals in a state of nature *would* recognize the authority of a law of nature that constrains their actions in the way Locke describes? On what basis would they recognize this more extensive schema of rights and duties as authoritative? Locke's answer to this question is unclear. Although the tradition of natural law theory on which Locke drew is predominantly a Christian one, Locke often claimed that the natural law is known to us independently of revelation. Thus he sometimes suggested that it is sufficient for individuals simply to consult their natural reason; this will reveal to them immediately that killing innocents and stealing from others is wrong, forbidden by a natural law that is written on their hearts.

On the other hand, much of what Locke actually wrote about the law of nature and its basis contradicts this claim. For example, he argued that individuals would recognize the authority of the law of nature because they are "all the workmanship of one omnipotent, and infinitely wise maker; all the servants of one sovereign master, sent into the world by His order, and about His business; they are His property, whose workmanship they are, made to last during His, not one another's pleasure."[8] Locke also argued that the state ought not to tolerate atheists, claiming that "the taking away of God, though but even in thought, dissolves all" motivation to act morally: "promises, covenants, and oaths, which are the bonds of human society, can have no hold upon an atheist."[9] These claims suggest that Locke's understanding of the law of nature is inextricably linked to the assumptions of a Christian worldview.[10]

Taken literally, then, these claims would imply that as long as there are atheists and other non-Christians in a state of nature, not everyone would recognize the authority of the natural law. But is it reasonable to suppose that in a state of nature everyone would already embrace Christianity? This would appear to infect critical moral reflection with a problematic religious bias and appeal to an assumption that surely many quite reasonably reject.

What of Locke's alternative suggestion that his law of nature is self-evident to the light of natural reason independently of revelation? At this point it is open to the Hobbesian to retort, drawing on a long tradition of skeptical argument, that if there is any conception of rationality that would be self-evident to individuals in a state of nature it would be the logic of self-interest and self-preservation. However, it is doubtful whether compliance with a Lockean rule proscribing preemptive attacks against others should always strike individuals as rational in this sense. For, in a Hobbesian state of nature, strict compliance with such a rule will often expose one to a very high risk of attack. In what sense is it "naturally rational" for individuals to accept such risks for the sake of an abstract moral principle? Doesn't honest introspection compel us to admit that, were we faced with such a choice, we would regard compliance with the rule as self-evidently foolish rather than "naturally" rational?

[8] Locke 1980, section 6.
[9] Locke 2013, p. 81.
[10] See on this Waldron 2002.

By contrast, Hobbes's assumption that individuals would recognize a right to use whatever means necessary to defend themselves accords much better with this self-interested sense of rationality. Perhaps there is some richer form of "natural reason" that individuals in a state of nature would apply to their decisions; but the burden seems to lie with the Lockean to convince a skeptic that this would be the case. Locke's gestures in the direction of Christian theology are hardly encouraging in this regard. In contrast, Hobbes's position does not require any controversial theological backup. Whatever else they disagree about, atheists and Christians might (upon reflection) agree that if they found themselves in a state of nature and faced a choice between compliance with some moral rule and taking action they deemed necessary to their self-preservation, they would recognize a right to do the latter. Notice that this does not require agreement that violating the relevant rule is morally ideal; it requires only an acknowledgement that agents at least reserve the right to take otherwise morally questionable action when they judge that their own survival is at stake.

Doubts about Natural Rights

So despite the greater attractiveness of Locke's theory, we may still conclude that Hobbes's more austere and rigorously secular account of natural rights is more realistic. But in the last analysis it remains unclear that Hobbes's pared-down version of the argument is better able to answer the question with which we saw Locke's theory struggling. For in the end he, too, has to convince us that individuals in a state of nature would recognize certain "natural" rights. But is it clear that there are any "natural" rights at all?

For suppose one countered that all rights are merely creatures of positive moral conventions. It makes sense for me to claim that I have a property right in my car only because there exists in my society an accepted framework of rules and conventions that confers this right on me. If anyone doubts that I have property rights in my car, they can consult the relevant deeds and apply the pertinent legal provisions. But in the absence of such background conventions or institutional arrangements, it may seem senseless to imagine individuals being in a position to recognize that they have certain rights. On this sort of view, the notion of "natural" rights is – as Bentham put it – "nonsensical."[11] The shared recognition of rights is possible only within an established positive moral scheme and set of institutional conventions. We cannot assume that individuals would be in a position to recognize any rights beforehand.

This line of argument led eighteenth-century critics like David Hume and Jean-Jacques Rousseau to ridicule the arguments of the seventeenth-century social-contract theorists.[12] They thought the notion of a "natural" right confused for the reasons just given and concluded that classical social-contract theories are therefore caught in a dilemma. On the one hand, if individuals in an alleged "state of nature" are indeed able to recognize and discuss certain rights, moral powers, and entitlements, then it must already be the case that they interact within the framework of some set of political institutions or legal conventions whose authority is accepted. This renders the notion of a social contract superfluous: by hypothesis, individuals already find themselves immersed within exactly the institutions for which the theory of the social contract was supposed to account. So it is difficult to understand, on this alternative, how talking about a social contract could help to justify such institutions. Whether particular systems of entrenched conventional rights should command our approval or disapproval will have to be decided on some other basis (according to Hume, at least, in terms of general utility).

On the other hand, we might try to imagine a genuine "state of nature," representing the likely condition of human life purged of any social conventions or political arrangements whatsoever. Rousseau undertook such an experiment in his famous *Discourse on the Origin of Inequality*.[13] But as he made clear in that text, individuals in such a situation could have no access to the concept of a "right" at all, for in the absence of any such conventional arrangements individuals would lack any basis for recognizing that they enjoy certain rights. This undermines the notion that individuals in a state of nature would be in a position to understand themselves to be jointly participating in a social contract of the sort envisaged by Hobbes

---

[11] See Bentham 2002.
[12] Hume 1985, p. 542; Rousseau 2011, pp. 141–7.
[13] Rousseau 1992, pp. 25–109.

and Locke. If individuals do not recognize any natural rights, then they will not be able to make sense of a social contract involving an exchange of such rights.

Does Hobbes have any response to this line of criticism? How might he convince us that individuals in his state of nature would recognize the natural rights that form the substance of his social contract? One answer sometimes suggested by Hobbes's own discussion is that in this area what agents *do* is more revealing and important that what they are able to *say*.[14] While agents in a state of nature cannot refer to any settled rules or conventions to establish through discussion what rights they have, their likely behavior will nonetheless tacitly betray a commitment to natural rights of the sort he described. Thus, like nations in the international arena, they will often find themselves driven to renege on their agreements, to seize others' possessions, and preemptively attack perceived threats, and in that way implicitly claim a right to do so.

But as Rousseau later argued, this suggestion is confused. At best, we can say that agents in a Hobbesian state of nature tacitly *assert* a right to do whatever they find necessary to defend themselves. Thus we can say that, in preemptively attacking Teddy, Nicholas asserts a right to take action against a perceived threat. But it is one thing for Nicholas to *assert* such a right, and another thing for him to certify that he is *justified* in claiming it. Presumably, Teddy is not going to be convinced by Nicholas's merely arguing that he has the right to attack Teddy just because he has the power to do so. This does not seem to qualify as an adequate justification; as Rousseau pointed out, it is tantamount to asserting the principle that might makes right, which surely no one ought to accept. It would also imply, counterintuitively, that when we lack the power to do something it follows that we cannot really have a right to do it. But as Rousseau cogently asked: "What kind of right is it that perishes when the force on which it is based ceases?"[15]

These considerations suggest that force alone cannot be sufficient to justify rights claims – there needs to be some independent standard such

---

[14] For example, Hobbes 1998, p. 11.

[15] Rousseau 2011, p. 143; here Rousseau anticipates Hart's classic criticism of Austin's Hobbesian theory of law. See Chapter 2, n. 1.

as a set of conventionally accepted and authoritative rules that confer these rights upon us. But again this implies – against the current of social-contract arguments – that rights must be the *products* of political and legal institutions, not, as both Locke and Hobbes supposed, the primitive raw material from which they are made.

6 Contractualism 2.0

One might think that the objections we considered at the end of the last chapter are fatal to the contract approach. That was certainly Hume's verdict and, under his influence, that of the subsequent British utilitarian tradition. Rousseau, however, took a different view. He believed that the core idea behind social-contract arguments could be salvaged. As our discussion of Hobbes suggested, that core idea was the effort to ground political authority in the rational will of its subjects. Rousseau realized that this effort relies on an extremely compelling principle of political justification: to justify themselves, political institutions must vindicate themselves before the tribunal of each and every subject's rational will. By the lights of this principle, political institutions imposed on individuals against their rational will must be illegitimate.

Rousseau saw that Hobbes's and Locke's efforts to explain the rationality of accepting political authority in terms of a hypothetical decision to retain or (on certain terms) to transfer certain natural rights implicitly appealed to this principle. But Rousseau denied that the problematic doctrine of natural rights was needed in order to explain how political institutions might meet this contractualist standard of legitimacy. Indeed, he thought that once we understand that rights are purely conventional artifacts, the social-contract idea can be turned around to test the legitimacy of the positive moral scheme that define and allocate them.

To appreciate how Rousseau proposed to rescue the social-contract argument, consider again the Nicholas/Teddy example. Suppose Nicholas attacks Teddy in order to steal something from him – a weapon, say. As we saw before, it is possible to view Nicholas as asserting a right to attack Teddy and to take his weapon. However, as we also saw, merely asserting such a right on the basis of force is not sufficient to justify it, and in this case we have a strong intuition that Nicholas's claim cannot be justified. But once we abandon the idea that rights are "natural," our misgivings about Nicholas's claim cannot specifically be misgivings about whether he has a "natural right" to attack Teddy. They must, rather, be misgivings about the legitimacy of any conventional schemes of rules conferring such a right upon him. In questioning the justifiability of his claim, then, we are simultaneously questioning the legitimacy of some conventional scheme – call it the Nicholas Convention – that confers upon Nicholas the right to attack Teddy at will.

What accounts for our strong intuition that the Nicholas Convention is illegitimate? Rousseau's answer was that it would permit Nicholas to force Teddy to do things against his will. The point here is not merely that Teddy does not *want* to part with his weapon and therefore that Nicholas prevents him from getting what he wants. It is rather that, quite apart from his desires and wants, Teddy is being forced to submit to a will other than his own. The Nicholas Convention simply requires Teddy to submit to Nicholas's superior force. But, as Rousseau put it, "to give in to force is an act of necessity, not of will."[1] Rousseau suggested that no set of conventional rules requiring agents to submit to force in this way could satisfy the contractualist test of legitimacy. For that test requires that political institutions and conventions be in accord with the rational wills of all those subject to them. But the Nicholas Convention effectively bypasses Teddy's will entirely; it permits Nicholas to treat Teddy as if he has no will of his own that needs to be taken into account. It is difficult to see how any scheme of rules that would deny Teddy any say *at all* in this transaction could be regarded as conforming to Teddy's own rational will. We can be confident, then, that on Rousseau's analysis the Nicholas Convention cannot be reconciled with the rational wills of all those subject to it: Teddy, at least, must have a reasonable objection.

At a minimum, then, Rousseau's contractualist test requires that legitimate political institutions and conventions respect every individual's independence and autonomy, their capacity to act in accordance with their own will. Submission to legitimate conventions must be such that in submitting, citizens "obey no one but their own will alone."[2] As Rousseau also

---

[1] Rousseau 2011, p. 148.
[2] Rousseau 2011, p. 158. In this Rousseau anticipates Kant's imperative that we always treat ourselves and others as "ends in themselves" and never merely as means to

saw, this automatically presumes certain notions of equality and imparti-ality. For, on this view, the autonomous will of one individual deserves no greater or lesser consideration than the next: if even *one* person is unable to reconcile some conventional scheme of rules with their rational will, the whole scheme is thereby rendered illegitimate.

The General Will

What would an ideal set of conventions, impartially respecting each individual's autonomy in this sense, look like? Rousseau left his own answer to this question tantalizingly vague, but its outlines are clear enough to have exerted a continuing influence on political philosophy down to the present. According to Rousseau, conventional allocations of rights and obligations can be legitimate only if two conditions are met: first, the rules and principles governing their allocation must actually be approved by the full assembly of citizens to whom they apply; second, the decision procedure by which this assembly endorses those rules must itself be of a very particular kind. In Rousseau's language, the "social contract" (or sometimes: "social compact") refers, not to an exchange of natural rights by which agents leave a state of nature, but to the design of this ideal legitimacy-conferring decision procedure in which all citizens participate. The purpose of this decision procedure is to reveal the authentic will of the political community as a whole, what Rousseau called the "General Will." Rousseau distinguished the General Will from the particular wills of par-tial associations and specific individuals. These private groups and individ-uals are oriented toward their narrowly sectional interests and so cannot claim to embody the will of society as a whole.

The terms of the "social compact" that defines Rousseau's favored deci-sion procedure are roughly as follows. All citizens agree to submit to the General Will and in return receive equal privileges as co-legislators of the laws and constitutional principles in their society. In this capacity, citizens are expected to vote on the basis of a sincere consideration of what the General Will ought to be, rather than on the basis of their own personal preferences. They are also to make up their mind on their own, and not

our own ends. To be an "end in oneself" in Kant's sense is to be a self-determining, autonomous agent.

to vote in organized blocs, parties, or coalitions. Citizens must also understand that, if this General Will is to emerge at all, it must be articulated in the form of general laws (as opposed to particular executive decisions, edicts, declarations, and actions) that apply impartially and equally to all members of the relevant political community. The General Will is revealed only in rules that apply to all those who enact them.

This last provision was particularly important for Rousseau, for it implies that, in participating in the process by which the General Will is articulated, individuals enact rules that will apply equally to themselves as well as others. Rousseau supposed that as long as this is true, citizens would impose on each other only those requirements they would be prepared to endorse for themselves, since "in this institution each person necessarily submits himself to the conditions he imposes on others."[3] Under these conditions, Rousseau hoped that political institutions might genuinely embody a "form of association which defends and protects with all common forces the person and goods of each associate, and by means of which each one, while uniting himself with all, nevertheless obeys only himself and remains as free as before."[4]

This, at any rate, was Rousseau's general thought. Unfortunately, Rousseau's discussion is mired in obscurity and it is extremely difficult to extract from his texts a detailed account of what, once properly articulated, the General Will would actually require in practice. Still, it is important to notice that, under this Rousseauan revision, the aims of the social-contract approach have broadened. As we saw, Hobbes and Locke deployed social-contract arguments primarily in order to justify the authority of the state. Rousseau shared this goal, but he also described the General Will as an independent "rule of what is just and what is unjust."[5] As well as telling us when political institutions can command citizens' obedience, then, Rousseau's General Will also defines the terms on which individuals justly enjoy legal rights, civil liberties, private property, and other economic entitlements and opportunities.

There is a sense, then, in which our discussion has come full circle and we find ourselves addressing once again questions that resemble those

---

[3] Rousseau 2011, p. 158.
[4] Rousseau 2011, p. 148.
[5] Rousseau 2011, p. 114.

that Plato faced in the *Republic* – questions about what rules, roles, rights, and other social arrangements we ought to recognize as ideally just. But whereas Plato and the philosophical tradition we considered in Chapter 2 tried to answer these questions in terms of elaborate theories of well-being, Rousseau proposed to do so by asking what social principles free and equal individuals concerned to maintain their autonomy could rationally impose upon themselves. It is important, therefore, not to exaggerate the contrast between the social-contract approach and the common-good arguments we looked at in the last chapter. Rousseau helps us to see that contractualism is not so much an abandonment of the ideal of the common good as an alternative way of identifying and conceiving it. Rather than justifying claims about the common good by reference to fully fleshed out (and often controversial) conceptions of human flourishing or welfare, contractualists seek to do so on an independent, and less controversial, basis, by considering what free and equal agents would be prepared to impose upon themselves in some appropriately defined choice situation.

The Theory of Rawls

As I have said, Rousseau failed to develop this project with much clarity or rigor. But in his seminal work *A Theory of Justice*, first published in 1971, some 200 years after Rousseau's death, the American political philosopher John Rawls took it up with as much rigor as anyone could wish. Like Rousseau, Rawls's book invites us to think of the principles regulating an ideally just society as validated by a decision procedure involving the participation of all those to whom the principles are to apply. Unlike Rousseau, however, Rawls did not conceive of this decision procedure as a regularly convened public assembly through which citizens of an actual political community exert direct and ongoing control over the laws under which they live. Rather, he proposed to reformulate it as a purely imaginary meeting at which free and equal agents choose in advance, and once and for all, principles of justice to govern their interaction in some future scheme of association. Rawls's argument therefore harks back to the (I have suggested) more Hobbesian conception of the social-contract argument as a kind of thought experiment.

Rawls called this hypothetical meeting in which agents preselect the "foundation charter of their society" the "original position." In words

Rousseau might have penned, Rawls suggested that a society governed by principles chosen in his original position would come "as close as a society can to being a voluntary scheme, for it meets the principles which free and equal persons would assent to under circumstances that are fair. In this sense its members are autonomous and the obligations they recognize self-imposed."[6]

Rawls introduced another important twist on this Rousseauan idea. If, as Rawls suggested, the original position is part of an imaginary and hypothetical thought experiment, its design is entirely within our control. Philosophers can therefore tinker with the various features of the original position (the motivations of the individuals in it, their understanding of the task before them, the amount of information available to them, and so forth) until they reach a specification of it that seems most appropriate given its aim of definitively recommending a set of principles of justice. Rawls's design of the original position is therefore guided by a search for a truly fair and impartial benchmark from which to assess the justice of social institutions and practices. Simplifying considerably, Rawls's original position has the following three features.

First, the individuals in it understand themselves to be deciding how the "basic structure of society" (its laws, conventions, constitutional documents, institutional ground rules, etc.) makes available to citizens what Rawls called "social primary goods." Rawls's list of social primary goods comprises: rights, liberties and opportunities, income and wealth, and the "social bases of self-respect."[7] These goods are "primary" in that every rational person can be presumed to want them whatever else they want – without them, our ability to pursue virtually *any* activity in which we might have an interest will be impaired. They are "social" in that, unlike certain "natural" primary goods like health or intelligence, their availability is mainly a function of the basic institutional principles around which political communities are organized. Such principles directly allocate such social primary goods as rights, freedoms, and economic advantages, but have only indirect effects on people's share of natural primary goods. For example, institutional rules of this kind clearly will not

[6] Rawls 1999, p. 12.
[7] Rawls 1999, pp. 54–5.

determine how intelligent I am, or any genetic susceptibility to chronic or life-threatening diseases.

Second, individuals in the original position are motivated by the desire to obtain as many social primary goods as possible. They will therefore favor principles of justice likely to secure for themselves the best possible share of these goods. So although not positively motivated by a desire to outdo or harm others, Rawls's contractors are nonetheless essentially self-interested rather than altruistic. Like the individuals in Hobbes's state of nature, they are neither saints nor monsters.

Finally, and most importantly, Rawls's hypothetical contractors are deprived of any particular information about the society they are about to enter, about the precise social positions they occupy within that society, and about their own identifying attributes. The individuals in the original position deliberate behind a "veil of ignorance."[8] Behind this veil, individuals have access only to generic information about human life, societies, and their historical modalities. That is, they will know *that* societies are often stratified into groups enjoying different economic advantages, but they will not know to what extent this will be the case in their society, nor their own economic position or prospects; they will know *that* societies often treat individuals with different religious and ethical beliefs (what Rawls calls "conceptions of the good life") differently, but they will not know what their own "conception of the good life" is; they will know that individuals are endowed with different needs, preferences, talents, and abilities, but they will not know their own specific endowments, and so on.

The purpose of the veil of ignorance is to prevent individuals in the original position from adopting the standpoint of particular individuals with specific interests and biases. In a way that recalls Rousseau's distinction between the General Will and particular wills, Rawls's individuals act from a point of view purporting to represent society as a whole, not particular groups or individuals.

Rawls argued that individuals in the original position would select several basic principles of justice to allocate social primary goods. According to Rawls, these principles are likely to be correct because we have independent reasons to believe the original position in which they would be

---

[8] Rawls 1999, pp. 11, 118–23.

chosen represents a fair and impartial standpoint from which to evaluate social institutions in terms of justice.

Reflective Equilibrium

In later chapters we consider in detail the particular distributive principles that Rawls believed would be chosen in the original position. I conclude this chapter by considering a more general question raised by Rawls's overall strategy of justification. Suppose we were convinced that the particular principles Rawls recommended would indeed be chosen by individuals in his original position. So what? Why should the decisions of hypothetical people in an imaginary situation determine our own judgments about what sorts of social arrangements we ought to support and value as just?

Rawls offered a subtle answer to this question. It turns on the assumption that we should test theories of justice against widely shared "intuitions" or "considered convictions" about fairness and justice. According to Rawls such beliefs include (among others): the thought that the requirements of justice have a certain priority over considerations of mere expediency or advantage; the notion that it would be unfair for social arrangements to impose punitively high costs on some merely to further the welfare of (even many more) others; the idea that justice involves notions of impartiality and equality; and that to treat people justly means respecting their freedom and independence in some sense. So Rawls took himself to be addressing readers already predisposed to take such intuitions seriously, people moved by what he called a "sense of justice." He argued, however, that as it stands this pre-reflective sense of justice is too vague to settle detailed questions about exactly how social institutions ought to be arranged so as to be fully just. People moved by these same convictions about justice may still disagree about which specific political principles and patterns of wealth distribution they require. To settle these disagreements we need some way to bring our blurry general intuitions about justice into sharp focus on matters of detail.

Rawls thought the original position device provides a way of doing just this. Because the original position is a completely imaginary situation, there are many possible designs for it, in each of which different principles of justice will be chosen. According to Rawls, this feature allows us to test different theories of justice against our settled intuitions at two independent points. We can ask, first, whether the particular principles of justice a theory recommends mesh with our intuitions about what just societies ought to look like. Second, we can consider whether the choice situation in which those principles of justice would be chosen fits our intuitions about how an appropriately fair and impartial original position ought to be designed. It is possible that particular designs for the original position that strike us as intuitively fair nonetheless produce principles that seem intuitively unfair. And vice versa: intuitively fair principles might be chosen only in original positions whose design may seem intuitively unfair in important respects. By mutually adjusting the principles and the design of the original position, Rawls believed he had arrived at a theory in which both sides of his account mesh seamlessly with our intuitive beliefs about justice.

Rawls referred to this happy outcome as a state of "reflective equilibrium."[9] The virtue of a theory of justice displaying reflective equilibrium is that it taxes our intuitive sense of justice as little as possible. At the same time it systematizes our intuitions about justice and pins down their precise implications for the proper ordering of social institutions. So, on Rawls's view, we ought to pay attention to the choices of the individuals in his original position because they help us to understand the mutual relations and specific repercussions of assumptions about justice that already move us. Rawlsian contractualism is, in this sense, a sophisticated exercise in self-understanding and self-clarification.

Intuitions and Their Status

Rawls's reflective equilibrium strategy thus treats our intuitive assumptions about justice as fixed points around which we then construct a coherent theory. But do they deserve this status? One reason to doubt it is that such intuitions have been historically and culturally highly variable. As the example of Pacifica and Atlantis illustrates, our intuitive beliefs about justice often reflect our socialization into particular kinds of societies, organized around diverse social practices. Rawls himself recognized this. In his later writings, Rawls explicitly renounced any suggestion that his theory is based around intuitions about justice accepted at all times and in

[9] Rawls 1999, pp. 18–19.

all places. Instead, he argued that it should be understood as constructed from assumptions about justice that are peculiar to the liberal democratic culture of the United States and the European nations in the late modern period.

But this acknowledgement of the historical contingency of our intuitions about justice, which dramatically narrows the scope and ambition of Rawls's theory, raises at least two troubling questions for the reflective equilibrium strategy. First, why assume that intuitions and convictions about justice we inherit from our political environment can be reconciled systematically without distortion? It seems equally, if not more, plausible to expect that these intuitive beliefs are fragments of inconsistent social ideals reflecting the influence of quite incongruous historical sources and political practices. In that case, we might legitimately worry that the effort to impose seamless coherence on our intuitions about justice will succeed only in misrepresenting them, and the political cultures from which they are drawn. The concern here is that Rawls's theory is ideological in the Marxian sense that we introduced in Chapter 1 and encounter again in the final two chapters.

Second, even if they do naturally fall into a consistent theory of justice displaying reflective equilibrium, why should that establish that we have reasons to value social arrangements meeting its requirements? Here, it is helpful to recall some of Plato's qualms about democratic conceptions of justice. As we saw in Chapter 2, Plato feared that individuals socialized into democratic conceptions of justice will predictably make unnecessary and harmful mistakes about their own interests; their lives may be gravely damaged as a result. That is why Plato saw few redeeming virtues in democracy and democratic conceptions of justice.

For present purposes, it does not matter whether we think Plato's allegations about democracy ultimately have merit. The important point, rather, is that Rawls's reflective equilibrium approach seems powerless to address concerns of this general form. If we are worried that prevailing beliefs about justice (democratic or otherwise) inevitably inflict damage on the lives of those socialized to accept and act upon them, it simply seems beside the point to claim, in response, that the relevant beliefs can be worked up into an elaborate theory exemplifying reflective equilibrium in Rawls's sense. Beliefs and ideas whose acceptance is toxic to human well-being will not cease to be toxic just because they can be formulated as a philosophically systematic, self-consistent, conviction-accommodating package. This is not to say that the beliefs and intuitions from which Rawls argued *are* toxic in this way. But whether or not they are does not seem to be an issue that a reflective equilibrium approach is by itself competent to settle.

This suggests that, without some independent analysis of their relation to human well-being, we cannot safely assume that our intuitive convictions about justice form a solid bedrock on which to construct satisfactory theories of justice, and to explain their capacity to justify various political arrangements. But since, as I have emphasized here, contractualist arguments proceed precisely by *abstracting* from particular theories of well-being, and by bracketing the controversies to which they give rise, it is doubtful that they have sufficient resources to provide such an analysis. This weakness in the general approach partly explains why Rawls and his contractualist followers today face strong criticism from a perfectionist direction. Echoing the concern just articulated, many of Rawls's acutest critics insist that the contractualist attempt to justify political institutions and arrangements without a systematic account of the conditions of human flourishing is doomed to fail.[10]

In this chapter we have considered the nature and evolution of a distinctively modern idea in political philosophy, that of the social contract. We saw how the approach originated in the effort to sidestep interminable disagreement about the correct view of human well-being. But we have also seen that, despite their ingenuity, the advocates of contractualism have not succeeded in showing that political philosophers can avoid having to face these difficult questions about the conditions of human well-being.[11]

---

[10] Finnis 2011; Haksar 1979; MacIntyre 2007; Raz 2009; Sher 2009; Wall 1998.

[11] The so-called "Capabilities Approach" developed by Martha Nussbaum and Amartya Sen represents another approach to these questions. See Nussbaum 2007, esp. pp. 69–97.

Part II

Topics in Political Philosophy

7   Property and Wealth

If you should see a flock of pigeons in a field of corn; and if (instead of each picking where and what it liked, taking just as much as it wanted, and no more) you should see ninety-nine of them gathering all they got, into a heap; reserving nothing for themselves, but the chaff and the refuse; keeping this heap for one, and that the weakest, perhaps worst, pigeon of the flock; sitting round, and looking on, all the winter, whilst this one was devouring, throwing about, and wasting it; and if a pigeon more hardy or hungry than the rest, touched a grain of the hoard, all the others instantly flying upon it, and tearing it to pieces; if you should see this, you would see nothing more than what is every day practised and established among men. Among men, you see the ninety-and-nine toiling and scraping together a heap of superfluities for one (and this one too, oftentimes the feeblest and worst of the whole set ...); getting nothing for themselves all the while, but a little of the coarsest of the provision, which their own industry produces; looking quietly on, while they see the fruits of all their labour spent or spoiled; and if one of the number take or touch a particle of the hoard, the others joining against him, and hanging him for the theft.[1]

These words were written in 1785. Over 200 years later, Paley's challenging analogy has lost little of its force. Although the worst-off members of the Western liberal democracies do much better, absolutely speaking, than the worst-off inhabitants of Paley's England, economic disparities in these societies remain quite stark and seem to be widening.

And if we consider the global distribution of wealth today, the picture is little better than that painted by Paley: while affluent Americans and Europeans preoccupy themselves with seemingly trivial luxuries, many

---

[1] Paley 1828, pp. 80–1.

manufactured under appalling sweatshop conditions elsewhere, in the "developing world" a child dies of a preventable waterborne disease every 15 seconds. That is around 6,000 deaths, the equivalent of 20 unsurvivable jumbo-jet crashes, per day. In 2016, Oxfam calculated that the richest 62 individuals on the planet are as wealthy as half of the world's population. In the early years of the twenty-first century, half of the world's population survives on less than two dollars a day, and its richest 1 percent receives as much income as the poorest 57 percent.[2]

These inequalities, which some believe are endemic to capitalism,[3] strike many as perverse and even obscene. They seem very difficult to justify. Can they be? If not, which distributions might we consider justifiable? These questions form the focus of the next two chapters.

Property, Equality, Merit

The economic hierarchies Paley vividly described were not new in 1785; they can be just as easily discerned in earlier historical epochs as they can today. What *was* new in the late eighteenth century, however, was the nascent system of commercial capitalism, and its attendant emphasis on the rights of private property. In England, the agricultural revolution was already largely complete. The earlier feudal world of small peasant proprietors owing service to the nobility in return for protection and small plots of land had all but disappeared and commercial farming on consolidated, privately owned land now dominated the countryside. Although the industrial revolution was still in its earliest stages, Paley knew that the economic structures of his society were shifting under his feet, with technological innovation serving as both symptom and cause. And, like many of his contemporaries, he recognized that a renewed commitment to the overriding importance of private property was implicated in these transformations.

Still, as we have seen, he was unusually frank in acknowledging the social costs of the institution of private property in market societies: the fact that it is propped up by the often brutal use of force against those it

---

[2] For more depressing statistics, see Pogge 2002, pp. 97–8.

[3] Piketty 2014.

seems to dispossess; its tendency to distribute rewards without regard to merit or desert; its wastefulness; the fact that it condemns many to lives of drudgery and alienation; and the often extreme inequalities of wealth it brings with it. Despite all of this, Paley concluded, on utilitarian grounds, that "the balance ... upon the whole, must preponderate in favour of property with a manifest and great excess." In his eyes, the system of private property is redeemed by the incentives it affords agents to assume responsibility for conserving and efficiently exploiting the Earth's resources, to develop a highly productive division of labor, and to avoid violent and predatory conflicts over scarce resources. Yet his own discussion ends with an enigmatic concession: "if there be any great inequality unconnected ... [with its tendency to secure the efficient pursuit of wealth], it ought to be corrected."[4]

Yet how much of the inequality and deprivation that persists in our world is strictly *necessary* in order for us to obtain the advantages of private property that Paley cites? If little of it is, then Paley's closing remark implies that the rules governing ownership should be adjusted so that, as far as possible, they prevent or mitigate the "unnecessary" inequalities. A similar question arises, though Paley does not mention it, about another major concern expressed in the pigeon analogy – the question of desert. For one might suggest, as Paley does in connection with equality, that when departures from a principle of remuneration in accordance with desert are not required in order to secure the overall advantages of a system of private property, they too should be corrected.

Paley's discussion is therefore less conclusive than he suggests. At the very least, it indicates that more is at stake in our assessment of private property regimes in particular, and distributive arrangements more generally, than simple considerations of efficiency. We must also consider whether people are receiving "their due," either relative to some standard of equality, or to some (probably conflicting) notion of what they deserve or merit. It seems, then, that in order to decide whether systems of property relations are justified, we need to judge them by a complex set of standards involving considerations of both justice and efficiency.

---

[4] Paley 1828, p. 83.

Distributive Justice?

Libertarians and other defenders of largely unrestricted rights to accumulate personal wealth often try to preempt this whole discussion at the outset. In their view, emphasizing what economic rewards are due to people makes sense only if we accept an entirely unrealistic picture of the way in which wealth is produced and distributed. When we complain about some individual(s) not receiving "what they deserve," or the equal share that is (allegedly) their due, we seem to assume that our complaints are directed at some agency responsible for doling out the relevant goods in accordance with some principle of desert or equality.

But this, libertarians argue, is not normally a reasonable assumption. Economic wealth is not initially held by some benevolent, wise, impartial, and central agent and then doled out as parents might divide up a cake equally among guests at their child's birthday party, or as teachers allocate grades for their pupils' performances in accordance with merit. Rather than being centrally controlled and consciously distributed, wealth is extracted from the raw materials to be found in nature in a radically decentralized way, through the efforts of uncountable millions of individuals investing time and energy in productive projects of one sort or another, and then competing with other producers to exchange their products in ways they hope will benefit them. This complex system of production, competition, exchange, and mutual advantage is essentially blind: its distributive consequences for particular people are largely unintended, not under the control of any overarching central agency. There is therefore no one to whom one can reasonably complain when one believes that one has not received one's due.

One might resist this argument by condemning the very blindness and seeming arationality of capitalist economic exchange and urging that the state step in to plan the economy in a more rational way. Much nineteenth- and twentieth-century socialism was partly inspired by this thought. While granting that capitalism massively enhances our productive capacity, socialist critics deplored the way in which it then unleashes this capacity as an uncontrolled force of nature, indiscriminately exposing people, especially the poor and defenseless, to the often adverse effects of market competition. In response, socialists argued that the state should assume responsibility for protecting those most vulnerable to these adverse consequences, and for securing more equitable distributions of the fruits of economic growth. They suggested that, through effective planning informed by the latest economic theories, states might satisfy these distributive standards without sacrificing economic efficiency. And once states' responsibilities are understood in these terms, the question of whether (and how far) they should be sensitive to principles of equality or merit in controlling distributive outcomes becomes salient once again.

Hayek and Spontaneous Order

But this socialist argument faces two formidable and complementary libertarian objections. The first derives from economic considerations, although its most able and influential exponent, Friedrich von Hayek, transformed this specifically economic claim into a provocative thesis about the limitations of social planning more generally. Following other economists (especially his mentor Ludwig von Mises), Hayek argued that individuals can make rational economic decisions only if they have reliable information about supply and demand in the particular sector of the economy within which they are operating. According to Hayek, however, their ability to access this information depends crucially on the undistorted operation of what economists call the "price mechanism." In a free market, as they fluctuate in relation to changes in the supply of and demand for different goods and services, competitively determined prices communicate information about what people are willing to pay to have certain needs satisfied and whether investment of private resources in enterprises designed to meet those needs is likely to be profitable. This information, he argued, is indispensable for rational economic decision-making. It identifies relatively efficient ways in which existing resources (capital, talents, skills, labor, raw materials) held by private individuals and firms can be matched to meet people's needs.

Hayek claimed, however, that when states intervene in the free market in order to influence distributive outcomes, they distort the price mechanism. No matter how well intentioned, such interventions will always corrupt the information that individuals and firms need to deploy available productive resources to satisfy people's actual wants efficiently. Socialist economic planning, he concluded, is thus a self-defeating project: central planners aiming at certain distributive ideals must inadvertently sabotage the efficiency and wealth-creating properties of the free market. Sadly, the record of the Soviet-style planned economies of the mid twentieth century provided often comical confirmations of Hayek's hypothesis, as trainloads of inferior or defective goods were hauled, at great expense, to cities none of whose inhabitants had any need for them in the first place, simply to meet a "Gosplan" bureaucrat's economic target.

This argument struck Hayek as merely one illustration of several deeper truths about rational social organization, all of which (in his view) the socialists misunderstood. For one thing, he argued that if they are honest, would-be central (economic) planners must confront their overwhelming ignorance of the needs, wants, and purposes of the multifarious individuals and organizations engaged in economic and social cooperation of various sorts. Such knowledge of these purposes as can be obtained is widely dispersed and available only to particular agents with close knowledge of the various locales within which they interact with specific others. It cannot be assembled, apprehended, and then rationally acted upon by a single, central agency, as the proponents of state planning had hoped.

For another, Hayek suggested that the forms of rational social coordination that use this local knowledge best typically exemplify what he called "spontaneous order." The price mechanism itself provides a paradigm example of what Hayek meant by this. In producing and exchanging goods no one *intends* to generate prices, and yet the unintended result of economic competition turns out to be an extremely elaborate and sensitive mechanism for signaling information about supply and demand. Hayek believed that the superiority of spontaneously arising forms of coordination in economics carries over to all attempts to centralize social organization. Such (as Hayek called them) "rationalist" or "constructivist" ideals of political order are typified in the ambitious vision of Platonist perfectionism, in which a group of wise and benevolent rulers organize society in accordance with an intelligently planned conception of its common good. But for Hayek, this notion of intelligent planning from some position of central insight is a delusion: social organization is centerless, the information and knowledge needed for rational cooperation widely dispersed and recoverable only by agents who are left free to adapt to the particular locales within which they operate.[5]

[5] Hayek 1937, 1945, 1984.

Such observations led Hayek to conclude that the state can play only a modest role in regulating social and economic cooperation. At most, states should assume responsibility for formulating and enforcing a framework of open-ended ground rules or principles likely to encourage those forms of spontaneous order that promote rational social coordination. These ground rules turn out to be, in his account, those necessary and sufficient for protecting private property. Hayek regarded ground rules of this sort as "device[s] for coping with our constitutional ignorance." They "can never be reduced to a purposive construction for known purposes" but instead constitute an "abstract order" that does not "aim at the achievement of known particular results, but is preserved as a means for assisting in the pursuit of a great variety of individual purposes."[6] Clearly, adopting this conception of the state's role threatens the view that it should be responsible for securing distributions in accordance with principles of equality or merit.

Liberty and Patterns

The second, and complementary, libertarian objection to the ideal of centralized distributive control concerns the connection between private property and personal liberty, and was elegantly formulated by Robert Nozick. Nozick referred to conceptions of justice that require wealth to be distributed according to some standard of equality or merit as "patterned" theories, because they demand that particular distributive patterns ("to each in accordance with their … due, desert, need, equality, talent, effort") be maintained. According to Nozick, however, no patterned conception can be implemented without "continuous interference in people's lives." In order to preserve the required distributive pattern governments must frequently and objectionably intervene "to stop people from transferring resources as they wish."[7]

The force of this objection derives from an observation to which philosophers since Aristotle have drawn attention: private ownership gives us control over our assets and resources and is therefore intimately bound up with our sense of ourselves as free agents. When others claim the right

---

[6] Hayek 1989, pp. 5, 8, 136.
[7] Nozick 2013, p. 163.

to determine for us how we should dispose of these assets, we will feel, and arguably are, less free than we would otherwise be. Such rights have implications for my ability to view myself as in charge of my own destiny, my ability to invest in projects of personal significance, and to plan for the future on my own terms. Conversely, respecting individuals' freedom to make and pursue their own plans seems to preclude the preservation of particular distributive patterns. As Nozick succinctly put it, liberty upsets patterns.

The Entitlement Theory

This argument has clear affinities with Hayek's claims about spontaneous order. But it adds an important dimension. Like Paley's defense of private property, Hayek's argument for the free market is, in the first instance at least, a utilitarian claim about the preconditions of economic efficiency, about propitiously matching needs and resources. But Nozick's argument about liberty suggests a more principled basis for rejecting patterned ideals of distributive justice in favor of a free market. Accordingly, Nozick elaborated a challenging theory of distributive justice to bring out the freedom-based rationale for a largely unfettered free market. The resulting conception of justice – the "entitlement theory" – combines Hayek's notion of a social order constrained only by open-ended ground rules with an emphasis on respect for the freedom of individuals to form and pursue their own personal projects.[8] To capture this kind of freedom, Nozick developed a suggestion made by John Locke in a famous discussion of private property. Following Locke, he postulates that individuals come into the world with a primordial property right in their own person, a right of "self-ownership."[9] The idea here is simply that each of us enjoys a basic, pre-conventional, right to make use of our own bodies, our labor, our talents, and other personal assets as we choose. According to the entitlement theory, justice requires only respect for these rights of self-ownership.

The resulting theory is "unpatterned," in that it does not require that distributive shares approximate any standard of merit, desert, or equality.

---

[8] Nozick 2013, pp.150–82.
[9] Nozick 2013, pp. 171–2.

That is why the language of "entitlement" is central to Nozick's view: his theory incorporates the intuition that one can be entitled to property whether or not one deserves it (as when a spoilt brat inherits his father's fortune, or an arrogant bastard lands the contract even if your proposal was superior on the merits). But the entitlement theory is also (what Nozick called) a "historical" as opposed to an "end-state" theory of justice. An end-state theory assesses the justice of particular distributions at particular moments by reference to some set of criteria that specify what a just distribution ought to look like.

For example, a utilitarian might insist that, in order to be just, distributions of wealth must be shown to maximize utility. It is not clear (for reasons explored in Chapter 4) what such a principle of utility maximization could possibly mean, or what it requires by way of distributive shares. (Though it is worth noting that some utilitarians, citing the diminishing marginal utility of income, have argued that only quite egalitarian distributions are likely to satisfy the utilitarian standard.) But however utilitarians settle these details, this view clearly involves an "end-state" conception of justice in Nozick's sense. To determine whether a distribution is just, we here ask whether the current distribution meets a particular standard: does it maximize utility? If so, it is just; if not, changes are required. On an "end-state" view, the question of how the particular distributions we observe at specific times *came about* is immaterial.

In contrast, "historical" conceptions of justice like Nozick's entitlement theory assess the justice of present distributions by looking only at the sequence of past transactions that led to it and asking whether they satisfied appropriate desiderata along the way. The "historical" character of the entitlement theory can be highlighted by distinguishing between three ways self-owners might come possess external goods:

(1) they might take them from an unowned state, as when they go fishing and bring home cod for dinner ("acquisition");
(2) they might acquire them through voluntary trade or exchange, as when they buy and sell goods for an agreed price ("transfer");
(3) they might take them involuntarily from others who already own them ("theft").

The entitlement theory asserts that self-ownership rights constrain these three modes of acquisition as follows:

(1) *Initial acquisition* is "just" as long as one "leaves enough and as good" for others (Nozick calls this the "Lockean proviso," about which more later). This proviso roughly implies: agents may take (from some as yet unowned stock) whatever they want as long as others are left with enough to secure their most basic needs.
(2) *Transfer* is "just" as long as it is completely voluntary, based on mutual consent, and uncoerced.
(3) *Rectification* is due whenever someone violates (1) or (2), i.e. makes an unjust appropriation from the commons, or takes owned goods from others without their consent.

According to the entitlement theory, as long as these principles are satisfied, any resulting distributions are just regardless of any patterns they (fail to) approximate, and regardless of the shape of a distribution at any particular moment in time (i.e. whether that distribution satisfies some "end-state" standard).

Although Nozick did not develop the entitlement theory in great detail, its contours are clear enough to provide a challenging counterpoint to the socialist view. Most importantly, it seems to reconcile the system of private property with our intuition that justice requires that individuals receive their due. For while it refuses to postulate some central agency of distribution responsible for giving people "their due," the entitlement theory does not dispense with the notion of people's receiving their due entirely. Rather, in keeping with Hayek's view, it reinterprets that notion in a decentralized way, requiring that, as they interact, individuals respect each other's rights to own, invest, and transfer their property as they choose. Responsibility for giving people "their due" is displaced from the center and left to individuals to fulfill in their direct mutual encounters within a framework of laws enforcing basic property rights.

So the entitlement theory replaces the question "What does the state owe me, as a matter of justice?" with the question "What do we owe each other, as free, property-owning individuals, in the course of economic exchange?" It answers that we owe each other respect for our rights as owners of property and for the freedom these rights bring. As long as private property-holders engage in transactions that do not violate these rights (i.e. through force, fraud, or theft), the patterns of wealth distribution that result are, on Nozick's view, entirely just, no matter how unequal or undeserved they may be. Even so, Nozick's view incorporates an egalitarian feature. While it obviously rejects any requirement that individuals receive equal *shares* (this would presuppose both a patterned and an end-state conception of justice), the entitlement theory does require that agents recognize and treat each other *as equals*, in that each person is to be regarded as independent and free "self-owner," with their own life to lead, and entitled to invest their personal assets and property in pursuit of their personal projects as they choose.

Assessing the Libertarian Challenge

In the closing decades of the twentieth century, as the planned socialist economies of Eastern Europe collapsed, these Hayekian and Nozickean arguments became extremely influential and led to a resurgence of libertarian ideas, especially in Britain and the United States. They inspired hostility, not only to economic planning, but also to the welfare state and redistributive taxation more generally. These ideas are partly responsible for the widespread belief that the distribution of pre-tax income in a free market society is presumptively just, such that when governments cut taxes, they are merely returning to individuals what they are already own.[10] Indeed, some libertarians have argued that taxation for redistributive purposes is, morally speaking, a form of theft and – in Nozick's notorious exaggeration – "on a par with forced labour."[11]

There is no doubting the ingenuity and force of the libertarian arguments that underwrite these still fashionable views. But we should not allow ourselves to be carried away. It is particularly important to distinguish the case *against* a full-scale socialist state, with central planning and public ownership in the means of production, from the case *for* an unfettered free market as an agent of distributive justice. These are not exclusive alternatives: even if we reject public ownership of the means of production, it hardly follows that the only remaining alternative is a largely unrestricted scheme of economic exchange of the sort required by Nozick's entitlement theory.

---

[10] For a criticism of this view, see Murphy and Nagel 2005.
[11] Nozick 2013, p. 169.

For example, it is entirely possible that participants in a scheme of exchange could respect each other's ownership rights with religious devotion and yet produce distributive outcomes in which significant groups of people find themselves stricken with crippling poverty through no fault of their own. Some have speculated, on the basis of UN figures, that a 4 percent tax on the richest 225 individuals in the world could raise enough money to provide healthcare, food, clean water, and safe sewers for every person on the planet.[12] Suppose we accept these numbers for the sake of argument. Although imposing such a tax hardly amounts to central planning, it would be forbidden by Nozick's entitlement theory, since it would violate the property rights of the 225 by coercively exacting a portion of their (let us assume) justly earned income. But can it make sense for an adequate a theory of justice to *prohibit* redistribution that might mitigate the severe poverty and deprivation that we see around the world today, at such a modest cost to the affluent? Many find that judgment counterintuitive. Why should we believe that the right of the richest 225 to control every last penny of their already vast incomes outweighs the seemingly more urgent claims of the global poor to assistance? There is surely ample room for a moderate middle position, neither central planning nor wholly unrestricted free markets, that answers more effectively to these intuitions about distributive justice than the raw entitlement theory.

Misfortune and Injustice

To this, libertarian free marketeers might offer two responses. First, they often insist that it is important to maintain and not blur the distinction between injustice and misfortune. We do not believe that the victims of earthquakes and other natural disasters are the victims of injustices or wrongs for which we can hold someone morally responsible. On this view, we can reasonably complain that the global poor are the victims of injustice only if we can identify some agent whom we can legitimately hold responsible for an injustice or wrong.

---

[12] Yates 2003, p. 57. Whether this speculation is precisely accurate I am not competent to say; but surely it is generally plausible that relatively modest taxation of the affluent could provide adequate funds for these purposes. For further discussion see Singer 2004, ch. 5.

To be sure, if we find that particular individuals among the global poor have had property deliberately stolen from them, or have been the victims of fraud or aggression at the hands of identifiable others, we can then claim that they have been treated unjustly. (Recall that Nozick's theory entitles them to restitution under the rubric of principles of "justice in rectification"). But it is not clear that unforeseen aggregate effects of property-respecting economic exchange, even if very unfortunate, can by themselves legitimately count as instances of unjust treatment at the hands of responsible others. Such effects more closely resemble the unfortunate consequences of natural disasters, or so libertarians often claim.[13] This need not imply that agents have no duties of charity to both victims of natural disasters and those suffering from severe economic deprivation. But, libertarians claim, it is one thing to say that people ought to support worthy causes as a matter of charity and another to say that they can be justly *forced* to contribute to them. Such forcing, they insist, is simply theft, and therefore unjust. Behind this first response lies the assumption (which we will later query) that justice is, and can only be, a property of individual actions, not of circumstances, institutional arrangements, or states of affairs.

Second, one might argue that Nozick's position already has within it a mechanism for dealing with the problem of severe deprivation around the world. To understand this response, we need to look more closely at a technical feature of the entitlement theory, its account of how individuals may justly acquire private property in the first place. Leaving aside the issue of inheritance, which for Nozick would fall under the rubric of "justice in transfer." the acquisition of property in external assets occurs when individuals invest their self-owned energy in appropriating or improving those external assets ("mixing their labour" with them, to use Locke's phrase).[14] Nozick follows Locke in holding that, in "mixing their labour" with natural assets (e.g. investing energy in climbing up a tree and picking apples), agents come to own them and acquire a right to profit from any improvements they make to them.

But according to both Locke and Nozick just acquisition is subject to an important constraint: appropriation must leave "as much and as good in

---

[13] Hayek 1989, pp. 70ff., 177.
[14] Locke 1980, section 27.

common" for others to use.[15] For Locke, at least, this proviso flows from the assumption that the external resources of the world originally belong to no one in particular, but to humankind as a whole: everyone therefore always retains a residual entitlement to share in those resources and the wealth they contain.

This "Lockean proviso" is open to various interpretations. If it is interpreted strictly, it becomes impossible to satisfy: if I take one apple from the tree, others are no longer free to appropriate *that* apple for themselves and are in that sense worse off than before and so there is no longer "as much and as good" in the tree for others to appropriate for themselves. But Nozick canvasses a more realistic, weaker interpretation, according to which appropriation is legitimate as long as no one is any worse off than they would be in a "state of nature" in which the fruits of the earth are as yet unowned, and each has free access to sufficient means of survival.[16]

Clearly, this revised interpretation of the Lockean proviso is fairly relaxed. It points toward a welfare baseline (something like "adequate resources for survival") whose satisfaction is nonetheless compatible with great inequalities of wealth. Still, Nozick admits that even this weaker version of the proviso must cast a "historical shadow" into the future, forbidding subsequent transfers of legitimately acquired property that would deny some individuals the required welfare minimum. Suppose, for example, that as a result of otherwise legitimate (by Nozick's lights) transfers, a single corporation acquires a monopoly in the world's entire water supply and asserts the right to exclude others from its use and to charge for it as they please. As Nozick himself conceded, this almost certainly worsens the position of others in the sense prohibited by his proviso.[17]

The second response, then, is to point to this feature of the entitlement theory and maintain that it is sufficient to motivate a principled objection to the current pattern of global deprivation. Even if none of the parties involved in the sequence of transactions resulting in the current distribution of wealth is responsible for unjustly violating the property rights of anyone else, it might still be the case that some transfers fail to satisfy the Lockean proviso and its historical shadow. One philosopher has

[15] Locke 1980, section 27.
[16] Nozick 2013, pp. 176–8.
[17] Nozick 2013, pp. 179–80.

recently noted that "with average annual *per capita* income of about $85, corresponding to the purchasing power of $338 in the US, the poorest fifth of humankind are today just about as badly off, economically, as human beings could be while still alive."[18] Not surprisingly, mortality within this group is catastrophically high. Clearly these individuals fall significantly below the welfare baseline suggested by Nozick's interpretation of the Lockean proviso. Perhaps, then, Nozick's position would allow these severely deprived people around the world to claim a just entitlement to assistance in accordance with the Lockean proviso. If so, we would not need to abandon the libertarian view in order to accommodate that intuition.

Blame-Responsibility and Remedy-Responsibility

However, these two responses actually work against each other and serve only to expose some deep problems in the libertarian position. It will be helpful to begin by asking: how are we supposed to apply the test of legitimate acquisition and transfer implied by Nozick's revised Lockean proviso? To establish that a particular appropriation or (in the case of the "historical shadow" claim) transfer of a piece of property violates the Lockean proviso one presumably must show that it is by itself sufficient to worsen the position of others in the relevant way. This seems to be implied by the first response, which assumes that only individual actions can count as just or unjust. So an appropriation or transfer can count as unjust under the Lockean proviso only if we can hold some individual appropriator or transferrer responsible for wrongfully worsening the situation of others.

However, in many if not all cases it will be unclear that any *one* person's actions in appropriating or transferring property are in themselves sufficient to worsen the condition of others in the prohibited way. It may be that a very large number of transactions are jointly sufficient but neither individually sufficient nor necessary to cause serious economic deprivation. In such cases, we will be unable to identify specific culprits to hold responsible for causing anyone's deprivation, whether by violating their property rights or by infringing the Lockean proviso. Much of the severe economic disadvantage we observe in the world today is plausibly of this kind. Insofar as this is true, the entitlement theory will deny that such

[18] Pogge 2002, p. 203.

deprivation generates any just claim to organized assistance from those who are better off. It will tend to classify these outcomes as merely "unfortunate," like the regrettable results of a natural disaster, but not unjust.

Furthermore, taxing affluent individuals to provide assistance must itself be unjust under the entitlement theory. According to libertarians, this violates the rights of the affluent to dispose of their own justly acquired property as they choose. Since in such cases we cannot plausibly regard better-off individuals as responsible for *wronging* the severely disadvantaged, there is no basis for requiring the affluent to assume responsibility for assisting them, or so the entitlement theory asserts. While it gestures in the right direction, then, many will still suspect that this appeal to a Lockean proviso represents an insufficient response the problem of global poverty and deprivation.

As we shall see, this suspicion points to serious shortcomings in the libertarian account of justice, but we must be careful to pinpoint exactly where that account goes wrong. The problem is *not* with its claim that that we cannot fairly hold the very affluent responsible for wronging the global poor just because they are vastly richer. The entitlement theory is on strong ground in maintaining that the bare existence of huge disparities in wealth does not show that the relatively prosperous have culpably wronged those who have next to nothing.[19]

The truly problematic feature of the libertarian view lies elsewhere, in its insistence that just claims to assistance from others can *only* be grounded on claims about those others' wrongdoing. But why assume this? Aren't there other ways in which responsibilities to assist others can arise to which our conceptions of justice ought to be sensitive?

Consider here the following comments of economist Amartya Sen:

> As people who live – in a broad sense – together, we cannot escape
> the thought that the terrible occurrences that we see around us are
> quintessentially our problems. They are our responsibility ... As competent
> human beings, we cannot shirk the task of judging how things are and
> what needs to be done. As reflective creatures, we have the ability to
> contemplate the lives of others. Our sense of responsibility need not relate
> only to the afflictions that our own behaviour may have caused ... but can
> also relate more generally to the miseries that we see around us and that

---

[19] See Nozick 2013, pp. 191–2.

lie within our power to help remedy. That responsibility is not, of course, the only consideration that can claim our attention, but to deny the relevance of that general claim would be to miss something central about our social existence.[20]

The sort of responsibility Sen highlights here clearly is not the sort of backward-looking culpability for wrongdoing on which the entitlement theory focuses – what we can call *blame-responsibility*. His thought is rather that we have forward-looking responsibilities for mitigating those "miseries" that lie within our collective power to remedy. Accordingly, we can call these *remedy-responsibilities*.

To sharpen this distinction between blame-responsibility and remedy-responsibility, suppose you share an apartment with a group of friends. When you move in, you, like the others, bring your own furniture, equipment, and other assets and each recognizes a responsibility to respect your rights to these goods. If one of your flatmates deliberately smashes your plates, or steals jewelry from your bedroom and pawns it to help pay a student loan, they have culpably wronged you and owe you restitution. None of this is controversial, nor does it depend on any agreement between you and your friends: your rights to your plates and jewelry pre-exist your current living arrangements, and unless your friends are psychopaths, you can presume they all understand their responsibility not to violate them. When violations occur, the perpetrators are *blame-responsible*.

However, in sharing a living space, you and your friends assume responsibilities of the different kind introduced by Sen. To be livable, the apartment needs to be kept clean, tidy, quiet, and secure; the trash sorted, collected, and put out; the facilities (stove, fridge, bathrooms, etc.) maintained and made available to everyone on reasonable terms; and there is a general expectation that tolerable conditions be maintained so that each resident can enjoy the apartment free of nuisance or offense. These general remedy-responsibilities do not await wrongdoing to be triggered, nor, in advance of any agreement about how they should be divided up, will it be clear who exactly is responsible, and when, for doing their part. That they ought to have *some* part is, however, clear, because these responsibilities will not

---

[20] Sen 2000, pp. 282–3.

take care of themselves and so impose a general burden on the residents as a whole.

To be sure, once you and your friends have accepted some common rules – you do the trash on Tuesdays, she cleans the bathroom on Sundays, we all agree to time limits on using the shower to guarantee enough hot water for everyone, etc. – misconduct can attract blame. In this sense, remedy-responsibilities can become the locus of blame-responsibility. But in such cases blame-responsibility is a derivative rather than a fundamental element, arising from an explicit agreement to follow self-imposed rules. In itself, failing to take out the trash on Tuesday wrongs no one, and if we choose not to do it, we are hardly guilty of injustice. Still, it would be *irresponsible* for you and your friends not to do to what you can to maintain satisfactory living arrangements.

Justice enters the picture here, not at the ground level, in accounting for the importance of these remedy-responsibilities in the first place, but in considering how to divide them up fairly. Once an agreement is in place, moreover, obligations to follow it, unlike your obligation not to steal a friend's stuff, are not owed to anyone in particular, but rather to all your flatmates together. So a shorthand test for distinguishing remedy-responsibilities and blame-responsibilities, then, is to ask whether the failure to fulfill a given expectation would *culpably wrong* a specific party or merely constitutes *irresponsibility* in relation to tasks of legitimate common concern.

The entitlement theory is largely insensitive to this distinction between blame-responsibility and remedy-responsibility and this, as we shall shortly see, is its major weakness. Its leading assumption that the primary responsibilities to others that justice permits political institutions to enforce are blame-responsibilities (triggered by theft, force, and fraud) is far more tenuous than it first appears.

Justice and Responsibility

To begin to appreciate why, it is important to notice that the entitlement theory cannot deny the significance of *all* remedy-responsibilities in the context of economic justice. Even libertarians like Nozick take the provision of an adequate scheme of property rights to be an important remedy-responsibility, and most assume that that responsibility is legitimately discharged by a state. For, suppose that some population fails to establish a state empowered to establish legal institutions and police powers to protect and enforce property rights. Without such a state, their entitlements will be insecure and likely frequently violated. However, although those who violate those rights are blame-responsible for wronging their victims, the libertarian cannot claim that the bare absence of a state is *itself* a culpable injustice for which we could easily assign blame. The most she could say is that, in failing to establish a state to enforce the rule of law, this population is *irresponsible* in trusting their property rights entirely to the good will of private individuals. Like flatmates who are content to let stinking trash pile up in their kitchen, or to expose themselves to illness by failing to keep food fresh, maintain hygiene in kitchen and bathrooms, etc., the members of this population fail to assume proper collective responsibility for their common interest in protecting their basic rights. In conceding that a state (albeit a minimal one) is necessary to secure private property, Nozickean libertarians tacitly acknowledge that this task is a remedy-responsibility that can be legitimately socialized and publicly enforced.

So, it is not that the entitlement theory fails to recognize *any* publicly enforceable remedy-responsibilities. The problem is rather that, having acknowledged that one remedy-responsibility (common protection of property rights) may be justly enforced, the entitlement theory asserts that it would be illegitimate for the state to assume, and enforce, any other important remedy-responsibilities.

That assertion, however, requires defense; it is not obviously sound. Why think that the protection of private property is the *only* remedy-responsibility that can be justly socialized and enforced? Since this is a controversial claim advanced by the entitlement theory, we cannot without begging the question appeal to that theory to defend it. Libertarians must present an independent argument for their contention that individuals' claims to the assistance of others (e.g. in the form of coerced redistribution of wealth) may be justly enforced only when individuals are guilty of having wronged someone or of violating the Lockean proviso.

To appreciate the crushing burden of proof such an argument shoulders, notice that it would not suffice merely to refute the claim that justice *requires* publicly organized redistribution to assist economically disadvantaged individuals at home or globally. It would also need to refute all possible accounts with the following structure. These accounts defend organized transfers of wealth from the affluent to the (global) poor *neither* on the grounds that anyone has culpably wronged the poor *nor* by claiming that such transfers are directly required by justice. They do so merely by asserting that:

(1) eliminating severe poverty and deprivation around the world is an important remedy-responsibility, for roughly the reasons Sen canvasses; and that

(2) any adequate conception of justice should at least *permit* the state to enforce some set of arrangements for fulfilling that remedy-responsibility.

Positions along these lines incorporate what I will call the "Permission View."

The entitlement theory denies (2), the distinctive feature of a Permission View. That theory maintains that, as long as agents have acquired their property through a fully voluntary sequence of historical exchanges, they are entitled to their wealth, and it would be unjust to force them to part with any portion of it against their will (unless they have culpably wronged someone or violated the Lockean proviso). But why should the rights of affluent property owners enjoy this overwhelming priority over the need to fulfill our remedy-responsibilities to help relieve severe disadvantage?

It cannot be that the outcomes of voluntary market exchange are so sacrosanct that they must *never* be adjusted for the sake of any remedy-responsibility. As we have seen, libertarians still charge the state with the fulfillment of at least one important remedy-responsibility: the need to enforce property rights (and the Lockean proviso). As Nozick himself grants, this requires the coercive redistribution of wealth. Someone must pay the wages of the police, public defenders, judges, prison officers, and anti-trust inspectors. The costs of providing and maintaining municipal buildings and equipment (courts, prisons, weapons, police cars and uniforms, etc.) must somehow be covered. Presumably, even a libertarian minimal state must rely on taxation for these funds. So if redistributive coercion is permitted to fulfill these remedy-responsibilities, why not others? Libertarians still owe us an argument for their contention that justice *prohibits* all efforts to relieve severe deprivation and poverty by coercive means except in cases of culpable wrongdoing. Unless such an argument is provided, the Permission View remains available.

The Famine-Relief Argument

In a famous article first published in 1972, Peter Singer argued that the relation between affluent individuals in the West and victims of famine and economic deprivation around the world is exactly analogous to that between a person walking by a pond in which a baby is drowning. In both cases, Singer argued, agents can prevent catastrophe at modest personal cost. By wading into the pond, I may ruin my new suit, but in so doing I may save a baby's life. Similarly, affluent individuals who contribute 10 percent of their income to overseas aid may have less money to spend on luxury items, but in forgoing them, they may nonetheless save someone overseas from starvation. Singer concluded that, just as we would regard someone who chose to save their new suit rather than the drowning baby as acting wrongly, we should regard affluent individuals' failure to contribute more than they currently do to overseas aid as similarly irresponsible.[21]

However, Singer overlooked an important difference between the two cases. In his initial vignette, it is quite obvious who bears a responsibility to save the baby, since in the example there is only one person passing the pond, and only one baby drowning. The passer-by could not plausibly defend her inaction by saying, "How was I to know that the baby would drown if I didn't jump in to save him?" The case of global deprivation differs in this respect. Consider a more closely analogous situation.

Suppose there are X thousands of people passing, not a pond, but the much larger Lake Singer, in which 50 babies are drowning. Since $X > Y$, it is not necessary for all of the individuals passing the lake to jump in to save the babies, we only need 50 people to save one baby each. None of the passers-by can be sure that their jumping into the lake is strictly necessary. In the absence of information about what others are going to do, each may decide to leave it to someone else to save a baby, but clearly if they all reason along these lines, the babies will all drown. Since none knows whether their assistance is necessary, it is not quite so easy to accuse anyone of wrongdoing as in Singer's original, simpler example. The problem of global deprivation presents related difficulties: each person's charitable contributions will make a real difference only if many others also contribute. Lacking any assurance that others will follow suit,

---

[21] Singer 1972.

however, individuals may consider that they have a reasonable excuse for not contributing.

The lesson to draw, however, is not that a libertarian conclusion follows, and that since no one has clearly wronged anyone it must be unjust to impose enforceable responsibilities on anyone to save the babies drowning in Lake Singer, or (by extension) to assist the global poor. The Permission View again offers a more plausible alternative.

To see why, notice that the Lake Singer example exemplifies what is sometimes called a "coordination problem." Such problems arise when agents are unable to coordinate their choices effectively without the guidance of some externally imposed rule or convention. The positive morality of queuing, and the expectations of others it imposes, seems to have evolved as a solution to certain analogous coordination problems. Without the expectation that people will form a queue and abide by the rule that each awaits their turn, everyone will rush to the ticket window at once, drowning out each other's requests, and making the efficient management of their inquiries impossible. Similarly, in the case of Lake Singer, the absence of any settled rule by which passers-by can determine who is responsible for providing assistance means that individuals lack reasonable expectations about what others are going to do. This allows individuals to offer an excuse for inaction.

Notice that the problem here does not primarily arise because the passers-by are selfish or immoral psychopaths entirely unmoved by the suffering of the children and their parents. I have said only that they can cite an *excuse* for inaction, but one can offer an excuse only for actions that one presumes to be unjustified. The recognition of a general responsibility to assist, then, will not by itself solve the problem, though it may help to motivate some.

Notice also that nothing turns here on the assumption that the excuse is a valid one. It may not be. The point is that, combined with other factors ("They were closer to the lake"; "She looked like a stronger swimmer"; "But I was changing a nappy at the time," etc.) it is plausible enough to be psychologically effective in inhibiting action, resulting in a general shirking of an acknowledged responsibility.

What is needed therefore is some rule or convention determining who bears responsibility for providing assistance in such cases. An obvious candidate would be one designating certain individuals as lifeguards. Such an understanding would impose on them a recognized duty to assist anyone drowning in the lake and confer on them the authority to command the assistance of others in saving swimmers. It might also mandate sanctions against lifeguards derelict in their duties and against others who ignore instructions to assist them. The costs of compensating lifeguards and of administering sanctions for noncompliance could then be shared out equitably among those visiting the lake, perhaps in the form of an entrance fee.

Such a scheme is, in effect, a way of socializing a remedy-responsibility when, despite a firm sense that *someone* should provide assistance, agents cannot spontaneously settle the question of exactly who is answerable for doing so and on what terms. No doubt there is room for debate about the detailed merits and demerits of alternative versions of such schemes. In the case of global deprivation, for example, we would still need to consider the further issue of how much relief is appropriate. And there remain also complex empirical questions about the most effective way to design and direct relief efforts. The important *philosophical* point, however, is that it seems perverse to settle for ground rules that would render these questions irrelevant by prohibiting in advance most forms of forced redistribution as unjust anyway. Surely the rules of justice should *facilitate* rather than *impede* the fulfillment of important remedy-responsibilities. The entitlement theory seems to license just such impediments. But we should demand very strong arguments before concluding that justice actively prohibits the enforcement of schemes organizing important remedy-responsibilities, like that for relieving global deprivation. The libertarian arguments we have canvassed here do not meet this burden of proof.

Possible Replies Rejected

Libertarians might still insinuate that indulging the Permission View must eventually require something like central socialist planning, and is therefore vulnerable to all the Hayekian criticisms we noted earlier. But this worry seems misplaced. There is nothing in the Permission View that commits one to the idea that the whole pattern of wealth-holding must be determined directly by central distribution. It is entirely compatible with Hayek's claim that rational social coordination rather consists in compliance with certain ground rules that guide and constrain individuals' conduct. To be sure, a Permission View will tolerate more expansive ground rules, limiting the right to accumulate property by imposing legally enforceable obligations on individuals to contribute to efforts to relieve severe economic disadvantage and deprivation. But this still leaves us far short of central economic planning and does not require that we abandon the Hayekian notion of justice as compliance with general rules constraining individual choices. It merely amends such rules so that they permit adjustments to pure market outcomes when this would enable us to better meet our remedy-responsibilities.

Another reply that libertarians might offer is to argue that the right to private property is a *natural* right. As such, it enjoys a special sort of priority over other, purely conventional rights and preempts the sort of considerations (dire need, responsibility to relieve suffering) that the Permission View assumes can justify redistribution. But we noted the difficulties of appealing to natural rights in Chapter 5: where do such "natural" rights come from? Are they dictates of God? What sense can be made of the claim that something is someone's right "by nature"? It seems far more straightforward to assume that legally enforceable property rights are conventional, the result of artificial and therefore in principle malleable human constructions. With that assumption granted, a Permission View can again insist that in a just society, private property rights ought to be qualified so as to allow important remedy-responsibilities to be discharged.

A related line of defense sometimes canvassed by libertarians appeals to the so-called "non-aggression principle." The idea here is that aggression directed against others is inherently illegitimate. By the lights of that principle, any threat or initiation of force against a property-holder, including coercive taxation for redistributive purposes, is prohibited even if it is very well intentioned or will produce more welfare overall. But this suggestion seems no less question-begging than an appeal to "natural rights." What gives the non-aggression principle its overriding priority? It is no answer to say that it reflects the special importance of private property rights, for that simply repeats the claim in dispute. Perhaps the suggestion is that the language of "aggression" captures the special offensiveness of physically interfering in the affairs of another. But this response will help only if we assume, implausibly, that the badness of any aggression involved in coercively taxing the wealthy is far worse than the badness of the deprivation, suffering, and likelihood of death confronted by many of the world's poorest people.

It is also important to distinguish the Permission View from positions that appeal to problematic notions of *collective* culpability, which some represent as the only alternative to a libertarian understanding of justice.[22] On such views, the affluent *as a group*, or institutions like Western liberal democratic states that act in the name of affluent groups of people, are somehow collectively culpable for wrongfully harming the (global) poor. Marxists have sometimes advanced this argument with respect to the conditions of the working class. For example, Engels wrote:

> When society places hundreds of proletarians in such a position that they inevitably meet a too early and an unnatural death ... when it deprives thousands of the necessaries of life, places them under conditions in which they cannot live – forces them, through the strong arm of the law, to remain in such conditions – knows that these thousands of victims must perish ... its deed is murder just as surely as the deed of a single individual.[23]

Engels's description of these purported wrongs as "murder" is clearly rhetorical. Still, we cannot simply dismiss the idea that these deaths might be collective wrongs of some kind. However, as libertarians often insist, suggestions along these lines are open to two kinds of objection. First, they require that we treat failing to prevent certain harms as equivalent to directly causing them. But many are uneasy about collapsing this distinction between actions and "omissions." It undermines our ordinary intuitions about culpability, according to which there is an important moral difference between directly injuring someone and failing to intervene to prevent harms that will take place but for one's intervention. Second, these arguments assume that we can make sense of group culpability, of the idea that collectivities *as such*, as opposed to the individuals who make them up, can be blamed for wrongful actions. But such notions of group agency and collective blame for wrongdoing are mysterious. We might worry that when indulged, they indiscriminately and unfairly burden entirely innocent individuals with liability for "collective" wrongdoing.

It is not clear that these objections are decisive. Perhaps some suitably fair and discriminating theory of collective culpability can be worked

---

[22] For example, Hayek 1989, p. 69.
[23] Engels 1987, p. 108.

out; and perhaps – as utilitarians have often urged – we should on reflection abandon the intuitively attractive distinction between actions and omissions. But even if the original objections were decisive, this would still not suffice to defend the libertarian position, for a Permission View does not hinge on claims about anyone's (individuals' or collectivities') liability to blame-responsibility, but rather on the importance of certain remedy-responsibilities.

Dividing Responsibilities

This chapter has been largely critical of the libertarian account of economic justice. It is therefore particularly important to end by acknowledging an important virtue in the entitlement theory. As we have seen, the libertarian argument is motivated by a desire to correct the naïve assumption that there is some central agency responsible for directly allocating economic shares. Instead of viewing conceptions of distributive justice as directly recommending principles for the central distribution of economic goods, libertarians understand them as comprising various general rules and principles to guide agents' choices. Such rules specify and demarcate the responsibilities of individuals and institutions by, for example, directing agents to recognize and respect certain rights, authorizing others to fulfill various important social functions and to apply certain sanctions and penalties or require forms of compensation when the rules are broken. This is of course exactly how the rules comprising the entitlement theory should be understood. They require agents to abide by certain rules circumscribing spheres of personal control over possessions and defining individuals' and institutions' responsibility to respect and enforce these boundaries; as long as those rules are followed, the theory regards the particular distributive results as just.

This assumption that conceptions of distributive justice primarily require conformity with *general* rules allocating social responsibilities and entitlements and only derivatively with the *particular* distributions of wealth that result is a strength of the libertarian view. Hayek was correct that it is utopian to begin the discussion of economic justice by postulating an agency with an already recognized responsibility to allocate economic shares centrally. Economic exchange is too dynamic and complex, the preconditions of its well-functioning too delicate, for comprehensive central control to make much sense. We are likely to do better by formulating a general framework of rules defining an adequate "social division of responsibility," to use a helpful phrase from Rawls. On this more subtle approach, acting justly is a matter of making legitimate rather than illegitimate moves within such a settled scheme of rules, not a matter of doling out goods in accordance with some simple distributive principle.

This sound Hayekian insight also connects the present discussion with views about justice held by classical Greek philosophers such as Plato. Plato's understanding of justice is clearly very different from modern liberal and libertarian conceptions. Still, as we saw in Chapter 2, it resembles them insofar as it primarily associates injustice with improper meddling and interference. But any notion of improper interference presupposes rules and principles determining appropriate spheres of control, freedom, jurisdiction, competence, and authority. In this respect at least, the entitlement theory is at one with the classical assumption that the primary function of conceptions of justice is to settle questions about who should be responsible for what, to fix the terms on which we are entitled to dispose of our property as we choose, and to determine where our obligations to respect the entitlements and honor the claims of others begin and end.

So the difficulties we have identified in the libertarian view therefore do not lie here, but rather in its premature optimism about the sufficiency of rules that protect the privileges of private ownership. This assigns undue, or at least unargued, priority to the responsibility to protect the rights of property owners over other social responsibilities that also command our attention, such as the responsibility to mitigate extreme suffering and deprivation. As we have seen, libertarians have not adequately defended this ordering of priorities. Like Paley's arguments, their case is incomplete and question-begging.

If we have found the libertarian view wanting in this respect, however, this does not mean that we have vindicated any alternative. The larger questions of which division of roles and responsibilities with respect to the control and regulation of economic wealth is most adequate, and of how we might establish that this is the case, remain open. But we have at least clarified that this is a propitious way to frame the question of economic justice. In the next chapter, we consider these questions more closely and focus on the answers to them provided by John Rawls. His writings remain the most comprehensive and influential recent effort to grapple with the problem on these terms.

8   Economic Justice

The previous chapter concluded that the quest for economic justice is best understood as a search for some general framework of rules and principles regulating the terms on which individuals may claim and institutions adjust holdings of wealth. We saw that such rules, and their recognition and acceptance among members of a society, define a "division of responsibility" with respect to economic activity. Such rules will typically determine, for example, responsibilities to respect others' property, to acknowledge the right of specific agencies to tax individuals' wealth under certain conditions, to ensure that private and public organizations providing important social services have access to adequate resources, and the like. The question is how such rules should be configured if they are fully to realize the ideal of social justice among people who accept and live by them.

It is important to emphasize that, in formulating the question this way, we are not directly evaluating existing social institutions by in light of some already settled criterion of justice. Rather, we are asking which set of rules and principles is *worthy* of serving as such a criterion among members of a political community. In Chapter 1, we noticed that different societies and cultures have often differed over what counts as just and unjust conduct, which allocations of social responsibility ought to be recognized as just rather than unjust. To take a very vivid economic example, many human societies have practiced slavery. Such societies have therefore formulated and lived by sometimes very elaborate positive moral rules specifying the just responsibilities of slaves and those of their owners. In contrast, the positive moralities of our own societies prohibit *any* form of ownership of people as unjust, a violation of their human dignity. On this now happily dominant view, nobody has any business claiming other human beings as their property, and both individuals and institutions ought to recognize and uphold this general principle of just treatment.

Given these deep disagreements about how justice and injustice are to be conventionally recognized, we do not have the luxury of being able to point to some settled, natural conception of justice to answer our questions about how economic responsibility ought to be divided. We must rather decide between different possible conceptions of economic justice, i.e. between different possible schemes of positive moral rules that classify as just or unjust various ways of regulating, controlling, interfering in, and assuming responsibility for wealth and economic resources. Once we have somehow vindicated a preferred conception of economic justice of this form, we might *then* compare existing institutions against that social ideal. But at this stage the question is to determine which ensemble of principles regulating the holding of wealth makes the most sense as an ideal criterion of justice to apply.

Some Initial Leads

But what sort of question is this and how might we go about answering it? Our discussion of the libertarian entitlement theory in the last chapter was largely negative, but it is possible to draw from it several positive clues about what we need to take into consideration in addressing it. Five points stand out.

First, we need to take account of the likely effects of different schemes of rules on the performance of the economy. The stock of productive assets in the world is not fixed, but may itself be augmented or diminished by the terms on which economic production is socially regulated. In particular, we need to organize the rules so as to give agents adequate incentives for productive economic activity. For example, if – as opponents of equality often contend – guaranteeing everyone roughly equal shares threatens productivity by undermining incentives to work hard this surely counts against strongly egalitarian principles of distributive justice.

Second, the stock of productive assets is not simply "external" to human beings; it includes our own talents and capacity for labor. The fact that these personal resources constitute important economic assets creates worries about unacceptable exploitation and alienation. Our freedom and self-respect seem bound up with our ability to control these personal assets

Economic Justice   153

on our own terms; when others can override our own wishes in this particularly intimate sphere of concern, we are likely to feel dispossessed and
alienated from ourselves. Such worries motivate the libertarian insistence
that humans are "self-owners."[1] The idea is that agents should be thought
of as coming into the world already owning their labor and assets and
enjoying the right to exclude others from decisions about how they should
be controlled and invested. The appeal of this notion of self-ownership
derives from its ability to forbid involuntary enslavement and other forms
of exploitation.

Third, we cannot assume that individuals are equally situated with
regard to access to the means of economic prosperity. Individuals' talents
and assets are highly unequal. Moreover, different schemes of social regulation may affect differently placed individuals in very different ways. These
overall regulatory schemes are hard to change and difficult to escape,
with effects on individuals' prospects that are "profound and present
from the start."[2] Individuals are therefore potentially very vulnerable to
these effects: they can make the difference between a successful and an
unsuccessful life.

Fourth, schemes of social regulation are not themselves costless.[3] As we
saw in the last chapter's lifeguard example, they must be paid for, and this
raises questions about how these burdens ought to be fairly divided. This
question arises even in the case of the pared-down scheme of rules constituting the entitlement theory. For even that theory requires the provision
of legal services to adjudicate disputes about property rights and restitution for injury. These services do not come for free: someone must pay to
maintain the courts and to remunerate the judges and other legal officials,
and so we need to know how responsibility for providing these public services should be fairly allocated.

Fifth, as a general principle, rules of justice ought to facilitate, not impede,
the fulfillment of socially necessary tasks – the remedy-responsibilities we
defined in the last chapter.

The philosopher who has made the most sustained and influential recent
attempt to synthesize these considerations into a single, ideal conception

---

[1] See the discussion in Chapter 7, pp. 143–5.
[2] Rawls 1999, p. 7.
[3] Holmes and Sunstein 1999.

of justice is John Rawls. The rest of this chapter considers and assesses Rawls's remarkable contribution to this discussion.

Rawls on Social Justice

Each of the five considerations listed above raises questions about costs and benefits. According to Rawls, the point of a theory of justice is to tell us how we should ideally allocate these benefits and burdens. Translating into his distinctive terminology, the subject of justice is "the basic structure of society," by which Rawls meant the institutionalized framework of publicly accepted principles that regulate the "terms of social cooperation." Such cooperation, Rawls thought, is marked both by identities and conflicts of interest: "There is an identity of interests since social cooperation makes possible a better life for all than any would have if each were to live solely by his own efforts. There is a conflict of interests since persons are not indifferent as to how the greater benefits produced by their collaboration are distributed, for in order to pursue their ends they each prefer a larger to a lesser share."[4] Rawls's theory of justice is intended to identify the best set of rules for dividing these benefits and burdens, the most rational basis for settling the terms of social cooperation.

It is natural to see this problem as inviting a utilitarian analysis. After all, if the question boils down to judgments about the costs and benefits of social cooperation, surely the obvious way to proceed is to ask which set of rules would maximize the benefits and minimize the costs. However, Rawls rejected this view in favor of the version of contractualism we described in Chapter 6. Thus he invited us to think of his recommended principles of justice as the outcome of an agreement reached at an imaginary meeting – the original position. The purpose of this imaginary meeting is to decide in advance, and once and for all, on a set of principles organizing the basic structure of a political association that the persons in the original position will later share with each other.

Readers will recall that individuals in Rawls's original position deliberate behind a "veil of ignorance." The veil ensures that they have access only to general facts about human society and the modalities of social and economic reproduction. They lack specific information about

[4] Rawls 1999, p. 4.

themselves and their position in the society they are to enter after their deliberations are complete. They do not know, for example, how talented they are, or what talents are highly valued in their society. As we saw in Chapter 6, Rawls defended the veil of ignorance because he thought that it guaranteed procedural fairness and impartiality. It is worth noting, however, how well it fits in with Hayek's notion that rules of justice ought not to "aim at the achievement of known particular results" but rather to define an "abstract order" to be "preserved as a means for assisting in the pursuit of a great variety of individual purposes" of whose details we must remain ignorant. As Rawls wrote of his own proposal: "no attempt is made to define the just distribution of goods and services on the basis of information about the preferences and claims of particular individuals."[5]

Rawls preferred this contractualist approach over utilitarian derivations because in his view it better captures our considered conviction that "each person possesses an inviolability founded on justice that even the welfare of society as a whole cannot override." The intuitive problem with utilitarian conceptions, Rawls feared, is that they might recognize as perfectly just the imposition of sacrificial burdens on the few in order to promote the welfare of the many. Thus although various utilitarian principles are considered in Rawls's original position, all are rejected. Rawls reasoned that individuals would not risk endorsing principles under which such catastrophic personal sacrifices could count as just. In this way, the design of the original position captures and guarantees individuals' "inviolability" by giving them a veto over principles that would expose them to the risk of such sacrifice or unreasonable exploitation, or so Rawls maintained.

Although Rawls's individuals choose among various possible rules and principles, they understand that in doing so they are determining the terms on which they are entitled to certain fundamental goods – the "social primary goods." As we saw in Chapter 6, Rawls's list of primary goods comprises: rights, liberties, opportunities, income and wealth, and "the social bases of self-respect." The two principles of justice that Rawls recommended, therefore, represent an agreement to make these

---

[5] Hayek 1989, p. 5; Rawls 1999, p. 42.

basic goods available to members of society on certain terms. Those two principles read as follows:

(1) Each person is to have an equal right to the most extensive total scheme of equal basic liberties compatible with a similar system of liberty for all.

(2) Social and economic inequalities are to be arranged so that they are both:

    (a) to the greatest benefit of the least advantaged (the "Difference Principle");

    (b) attached to offices and positions open to all under conditions of fair equality of opportunity.

The "Difference Principle" (2(a), above) is the part of this proposal with the most distinctive and controversial implications for the regulation of economic holdings. But before we consider that principle and some of the criticisms it invites, it is important to note two aspects of Rawls's first principle that bear indirectly on the question of economic justice.

First, Rawls argued that the first principle should be "lexically prior" to the second. This simply means that on his theory, citizens' first responsibility is to secure to each other certain basic liberties. This they must accomplish *before* they contemplate redistributing wealth under the terms of the Difference Principle. To put it another way, citizens who associate under Rawlsian principles recognize *no* possible combination of economic advantages as compensating for the loss of the basic liberties protected under the first principle. Giving liberty this overriding priority over material prosperity is characteristic of the liberal tradition of political thought with which Rawls is often associated. Whether it deserves this strong priority over other social goods and values is an issue to which we will return.

Second, while the right to hold personal property (in some form) is included in the list of liberties protected by Rawls's first principle, other economic liberties are conspicuously absent. Rawls's first principle protects the "political liberties" (the right to vote and run for office), freedom of speech, assembly, conscience, religion, and freedom from physical assault and theft. But it does not protect freedom of contract, rights to inherit wealth, or the right to ownership in the means of production. This does not mean that such freedoms could receive *no* protection in a Rawlsian society. It means, rather, that Rawls did not regard them as fundamental liberties. Rawls's decision to exclude these privileges of private ownership from the list of liberties deserving the most urgent protection reflects a determination not to allow the rights of property owners to block the fulfillment of other important social responsibilities. In the last chapter, we criticized the libertarian entitlement theory for doing just this. Rawls's proposal builds on that criticism.

It is important to emphasize, however, that Rawls agreed with the libertarians that personal liberty trumps other social values. Both accept, moreover, that individuals' self-respect is crucially at stake in these judgments about the relative importance of liberty. But they disagree over whether the *kinds* of freedom crucial to individuals' sense of self-respect are essentially economic and proprietary in character. While Rawls denied this, libertarians insist on it.

The Difference Principle

Rawls's Difference Principle requires that inequalities in income and wealth must be shown to secure the highest possible benefit to the least advantaged members of society – i.e. those whose access to the social primary goods is most limited. Under this principle, when citizens find that their least advantaged fellows could enjoy better economic prospects by *either* improving *or* diminishing those of better-advantaged groups, they must recognize that justice requires those adjustments. Three points will help to clarify this requirement.

First, it has a complex relation to notions of equality. On the one hand, the Difference Principle is itself justified as a requirement of political equality. Rawls's thinking was that any society that fails to do the best it can for its least advantaged members cannot claim to be treating them fully as equals. Moreover, the principle assumes a presumption in favor of equal shares in that it permits departures from an equal distribution of income and wealth only under certain conditions – i.e. when we are sure that inequalities will work to the greatest benefit of those with the meagrest holdings in primary goods. On the other hand, the Difference Principle might in practice very often prohibit as unjust efforts to enforce a strictly egalitarian distribution. For whenever a policy of strict equality would *worsen* the situation of the least advantaged members of society, the Difference Principle would reject it. For example, if the least advantaged will do as well as possible only if already affluent groups receive even more than they currently do (perhaps in order to provide them with incentives to greater productivity), the Difference Principle will require that we accept the resulting inequalities.[6]

Second, the Difference Principle is anti-utilitarian. It disallows any economic distribution that leaves the least advantaged worse off than they could be under some sustainable alternative, whether or not it maximizes utility. Thus a Rawlsian society recognizes no responsibility to maximize wealth as such. As we have seen, Rawls argued that maximizing principles leave people, especially those least advantaged, unacceptably vulnerable to exploitation for the sake of marginal utilitarian gains. Behind the veil of ignorance, individuals in the original position are uncertain of their relative position in the society they are about to enter. Given the possibility that they may turn out to be in socially disadvantaged positions, they will regard utilitarianism and any other maximizing principle as too risky, or so Rawls reasoned. In contrast, the Difference Principle minimizes these risks. Even if they turn out to be the least advantaged members of their society, individuals will nevertheless do as well as possible as long as that principle is enforced.

Third, the Difference Principle represents a clear and explicit repudiation of desert-based conceptions of distributive justice. Rawls recognized that if left unregulated, economic exchange will be powerfully affected by the natural distribution of talents and abilities. Those who are more talented, or whose talents happen to be highly valued in their generation, will tend to do much better than others. Those naturally disposed toward hard work, too, will tend to be more successful. Common sense says that such inequalities are just because they are deserved. But Rawls rejected that view. He insisted that personal endowments of such character traits are as much a matter of luck as the social status into which one is born. Permitting distributive shares to be determined by factors so "arbitrary from the moral point of view" is therefore "improper," or so Rawls concluded. Accordingly, the Difference Principle is justified independently of, and its application insensitive to, considerations of personal desert or merit.

Rawls's decoupling of social justice from desert has proven very controversial. Many critics have challenged Rawls's suggestion that because individuals do not deserve the good fortune of being naturally rich in abilities

---

[6] For a critical discussion of incentives and the Difference Principle, see Cohen 2002, chs. 6–9.

and talents, they cannot be said to deserve any economic rewards these traits command. We consider these and other criticisms of the Difference Principle below. But before we do so, it is important to forestall a common misunderstanding of Rawls's views about desert and luck.

Some have been tempted to identify Rawls's stance with a position today dubbed "luck-egalitarianism."[7] Luck-egalitarians object to inequalities of wealth that reflect "brute luck." Jones's being a "giftless bastard" (as Tchaikowsky once described Brahms) is a function of her ill fortune in the "natural lottery" for talents. Luck-egalitarians argue that insofar as her comparatively low income can be attributed to this undeserved raw deal, it is unjust. As a matter of justice, therefore, such inequalities must be eliminated or compensated for as far as possible. Once this is accomplished, however, luck-egalitarians have no further objection to economic inequalities that reflect individuals' subsequent choices. So according to luck-egalitarians, it is reasonable to regard individuals as responsible for disadvantages resulting from their *chosen* behavior, but not for those that reflect unchosen and undeserved ill fortune.

Luck-egalitarianism deserves consideration in its own right, but the relevant point here is that Rawls's own view differs importantly. Luck-egalitarians assume that brute ill luck is already an injustice that calls for compensation or mitigation. But Rawls expressly denied this, insisting that the distribution of natural talents "is neither just nor unjust; nor is it unjust that persons are born into society at some particular position. What is just and unjust is the way that institutions deal with these facts." Unlike the luck-egalitarian, then, Rawls did not regard the Difference Principle as a device for compensating for some injustice in the genetic or social lotteries. Instead, he thought of it as a reasonable and fair basis on which citizens "agree to avail themselves of the accidents of nature and social circumstance only when doing so is for the common benefit."[8]

The Desert Objection

I now consider several objections to Rawls's Difference Principle. As already noted, many have been unhappy with Rawls's decision to exclude

---

[7] Anderson 1999; Cohen 2009.
[8] Rawls 1999, pp. 87–8.

considerations of merit or desert from his theory of justice. One such critic, John Kekes, complains that as a result of this decision, Rawls's Difference Principle has "numerous counterintuitive consequences":

> Suppose that a man and a woman are both among the least advantaged members of society. The man is a hitherto unapprehended mugger; he has never held a job; he is vicious when he can get away with it; he had moderate native endowments, but he has made no effort to develop them. The woman is the mother of several children; she and the children have been abandoned by her husband and their father; she earns meager wages by working part time at a menial job; she is doing her best to raise the children well; she has the same native endowments as the mugger but, unlike him, has used them to make great, although unsuccessful, efforts to improve her situation. According to the difference principle, the mugger and the mother are entitled to the same treatment. Their positions of inequality are due to contingencies that are arbitrary from a moral point of view ... They are entitled [for Rawls] to the same distributive shares.

> Changing the scenario a little illustrates another [counterintuitive] consequence of Rawls's position. The mugger continues as before, but the mother is no longer unsuccessful. Through her efforts ... she now has a moderately comfortable and secure ... middle class position. She has a good job, she bought a house, the children are doing well in school, and they can even afford the occasional family vacation. According to the difference principle, the contingencies of life, among which are counted the mugger's lack of effort and the mother's successful effort, are to be redressed in the direction of equality. Thus on Rawls's view, some of the mother's resources should be taken from her and used to support the mugger.[9]

But Kekes overestimates this objection. One initial point to notice is that he pursues his point by comparing a conscientious mother with someone – the mugger – whose conduct is not merely vicious but also criminal. We are likely to agree with Kekes that muggers do not deserve to have their criminal activities subsidized by taxpayers, but our immediate reaction to such people is surely that they should be apprehended and punished, something that Rawls's theory very clearly supports. Moreover, the further issue of whether those convicted of crimes should or could permissibly be

---

[9] Kekes 1997, pp. 132–3.

disqualified from receiving welfare benefits is not one that Rawls explicitly addresses, since he brackets the "nonideal" question of how social institutions ought to deal with "partial compliance" with fair and reasonable social expectations (like rules prohibiting violent theft). Because it overlooks these complications, Kekes's example is misleading and his conclusions about the counterintuitive implications of Rawls's position rather hasty.

Moreover, even if we accept that Kekes's example has counterintuitive features, it is not clear why *single* counterintuitive cases should be allowed to count against a principle that is offered as a *general* rule to follow. To take a parallel case, we all know that under the rule of law, guilty persons often go free. We also know that we could reduce the number of such injustices by relaxing the burden of proof that the state must satisfy in order to secure a conviction. But one obvious reason to resist this solution is that it runs the graver risk of the state unjustly convicting (and punishing) the innocent. Surely in most cases the guilty going free seems the lesser evil. Citing specific cases in which guilty parties have been freed and pointing out that this offends against widely held intuitions about justice would not (and should not) shake our confidence in this judgment.

Kekes's citation of a single counterintuitive case against the Difference Principle seems similarly beside the point. Individuals in the original position might know perfectly well that the Difference Principle could permit seeming injustices of the sort Kekes describes. But they might still think this a reasonable price to pay for insuring themselves against the greater evil of severe economic disadvantage and its attendant indignities. Kekes's counterexample would be decisive only if we can assume that the likely beneficiaries of a Difference Principle are all or mostly as reprehensible as the mugger he describes. But this assumption would be at best empirically questionable, and at worst gratuitously insulting.

Two final points about desert also count in Rawls's favor. First, judgments about what people deserve are notoriously controversial and hard to justify. This is partly because taking all relevant factors into consideration requires extremely complicated comparative assessments (how shall we weigh one person's superior but effortless attainments against another's heroically effortful mediocrity?). But these judgments are also difficult to justify because people often disagree about what substantive standard of merit we should apply. One person's merit is another's demerit; one person's virtue is another's vice.

A clear advantage of Rawls's rejection of desert as a general criterion for just economic shares is that it avoids the need to resolve these extremely difficult questions publicly. Kekes obscures these difficulties by focusing on a case in which our attitudes to someone (the mugger) are partly predetermined by the fact that he is a criminal. This *just means* that there already exists a well-recognized (and in this case uncontroversial) public standard by which we are licensed to think ill of him. But such cases are not really representative. The tougher cases for Kekes and other proponents of desert-based conceptions of justice are ones in which we cannot appeal to generally recognized and uncontroversial rules of conduct like those constituting the criminal law to dictate of whom we should disapprove and to specify how we should do so (by applying certain punishments, for example). Perhaps I consider the otherwise law-abiding Snodgrass to be a worthless empty-head, unacceptably unorthodox in his religious beliefs, lacking in important social graces, vulgar, pathetic, or sinful. But how would I convince others (who may quite like him) both that these judgments are correct and further that Snodgrass is *therefore* less deserving of economic rewards than others whom I deem more worthy?

Second, it is important to remember that Rawls's principles distribute social primary goods. But these are not the only goods there are. Consider ("secondary"?) social goods like gold medals, Nobel prizes, Oscar statuettes, professional recognition, promotions, academic grades, beatification, and fame. There are also goods (and bads) that consist in the personal attitudes we adopt and express toward each other. Approval and disapproval, love and hatred, attention and neglect, or respect and disrespect are obvious examples. The distribution of these goods is controlled by private organizations and individuals, often in accordance with distinctive personal or cultural standards. Rawls's two principles do not impinge on these private forms of distribution. Indeed, not only do they leave people free to apply merit-based assessments in their decisions about whom to reward, promote, respect, ignore, dismiss, and hate, they actually *protect* the rights of individuals and organizations to do so in accordance with their own conceptions of what people deserve. For example, freedom of association and of religion, protected under Rawls's first principle, guarantee the rights of religious communities to govern themselves by their own lights, and to apply distinctively religious conceptions of personal merit in recognizing and celebrating the character and achievements of some of their members. Rawls's rejection of desert therefore needs to be kept in proper perspective. It would be quite misleading to suggest that he left absolutely *no* room for conceptions of personal desert ever to influence any decisions about the distribution of goods in a just society.

The Common Assets Objection

Rawls claimed that the Difference Principle "represents … an agreement to regard the distribution of natural talents as a common asset," to be exploited to the benefit the least fortunate members of society.[10] Many critics have taken Rawls to task for seeming in this passage to introduce some sort of collective ownership in individuals' personal assets and talents. Leading this charge have been the libertarians, for whom Rawls's infamous remark about talents as "common assets" represents a repudiation of their cherished principle of self-ownership and hence an unacceptable concession to socialism. For, libertarians complain, if "society" has the right to redistribute the fruits of some people's labor and talents to others without their consent, the latter can no longer be said to be unqualified owners of these personal assets. Such assets would instead form a common pool of resources that society may allocate as *it* chooses. Those entitled to benefits under the Difference Principle in effect acquire a right to some portion of others' earnings and the labor and talents that produced them. This institutes "ownership by others of people and their actions."[11] Once we see this, we must conclude that the redistribution required under the *eg thru taxation* Difference Principle is "on a par with forced labour," or so libertarians like Nozick contend.[12]

   This criticism seems powerful because it raises the same concerns that led Rawls himself to reject utilitarian conceptions of social justice. As we have seen, Rawls's worry about utilitarianism was precisely that it would objectionably permit individuals to be treated merely as means for maximizing aggregate welfare. According to Rawls, individuals who accept such

[10] Rawls 1999, p. 87.
[11] Nozick 2013, p. 172.
[12] Nozick 2013, p. 169.

a permission must think of themselves as in principle reducible to little more than fodder for the mill of utility maximization. Believing oneself exploitable in this way, Rawls reasoned, precludes a proper sense of self-worth and self-respect. But if that's true, isn't treating individuals' talents as a common asset to be exploited to maximize the benefits of the least advantaged members of society a comparable threat to individuals' self-respect? As Nozick charged, individuals' sense of self-worth seems safe under this arrangement "only if one presses *very* hard on the distinction between men and their talents, assets, abilities and special traits. Whether any coherent conception of the person remains when the distinction is so pressed is an open question. Why we, thick with particular traits, should be cheered that (only) the thus purified men within us are not regarded as means is also unclear."[13]

Is this worry as strong as it looks? The objection alleges that the way in which successful individuals' assets are used to benefit others under Rawls's proposal is comparable to the kinds of personal sacrifice that utilitarianism could permit or even require. But when one actually thinks about the kinds of cases that led Rawls to reject utilitarianism, this comparison loses much of its plausibility. Rawls was worried that utilitarianism might permit very extreme personal sacrifices for the sake of overall utility. Perhaps the abject impoverishment of the few is a condition of the freedom and prosperity of the many; perhaps overall utility requires that some surrender any claim to basic liberties, such as the right to freedom of speech and association, or to practice one's religion in accordance with one's conscience; perhaps it requires that some be enslaved so that many more others enjoy greater well-being. Given these possibilities, Rawls thought that individuals who embrace utilitarian principles would be stalked by anxiety that at any moment the "calculus of social interests" might require them to forfeit their freedoms, basic well-being, and even their lives merely to secure marginal increases in overall welfare.

But the predicament of those liable to taxation under the Difference Principle is surely less dire in several important respects. First, they need not worry, as denizens of a utilitarian society might, about their basic liberties being sacrificed. For these basic liberties are already guaranteed under Rawls's lexically prior first principle and they are explicitly *not* subject to

---

[13] Nozick 2013, p. 228.

the "calculus of social interests." Notable among these liberties is what Rawls called "freedom of the person," in which he included "freedom from psychological oppression, and physical assault and dismemberment (integrity of the person)."[14] These entitlements, which would categorically rule out any sort of enslavement or privation of basic liberties, the Difference Principle leaves wholly untouched.

Second, those liable to taxation under Rawls's proposal are in socially advantaged positions, abundant in social primary goods. They are thus assumed to be already rich in "the social bases of self-respect," which for Rawls comprise the most important primary good of all. The question is whether these reserves of self-respect are likely to be in any significant way depleted by redistribution of some of their earned income to less advantaged citizens. In this context, comparisons with "forced labor," which evoke images of chain gangs, labor camps, manacles, and dangerously arduous physical effort, seem ludicrously indiscriminate. *Real* forced labor – of the Burma railway variety – *is* a form of servitude. Its victims are forced to work under the most degrading of conditions, without regard to their physical safety, with little or no compensation, and without recourse to complaint or protest. *Maybe* utilitarianism may sometimes require that some individuals submit to such miserable conditions. But even so, why suppose that the Difference Principle could require anything so drastic? To suggest that when compelled to forgo a portion of their presumptively ample income to support those less fortunate than themselves, successful professionals (say) undergo treatment that is comparably degrading or corrosive of their self-respect seems on its face quite ridiculous.

So obvious are these differences that it is only natural to speculate about why those impressed by this objection to the Difference Principle seem so willing to overlook them. Why are people in our culture tempted to think that their self-worth is closely bound up with their ability to retain every last penny that their talents and personal assets can command in a market economy? Why do they resent redistributive taxation to the point where they are prepared to take implausible comparisons with forced labor seriously?

One possible answer, deserving closer scrutiny than we can give it here, draws attention to the way in which post-industrial societies create new

---

[14] Rawls 1999, p. 53.

demand for goods and services, and thus fuel economic growth, by encouraging certain false needs. I mainly have in mind here demand for luxuries, and especially those goods that serve as tokens of the social status, peer-recognition, and self-definition to which many people, driven by the fads of modern commercial culture, today aspire. These phenomena may explain – though would not justify – the tendency to associate redistributive taxation with a loss of self-worth. If taxation threatens agents' ability to afford the badges of honor and recognition they seek, it becomes easier to understand why they might resent it as potentially degrading. On this view, widespread resentment of redistributive taxation by wealthy individuals is a symptom of a narcissistic anxiety about status and inclusion characteristic of the more affluent sectors of contemporary society.[15]

This suggestion is obviously speculative. Whatever its plausibility, however, we have yet to be given any convincing reason to reject the Difference Principle on the grounds that it necessarily injures the self-respect of advantaged individuals. And if the principle at the same time combats those forms of economic disadvantage that *do* tend to erode self-respect, one could conclude – vindicating Rawls's original contention – that considerations of self-respect support rather than impugn the Difference Principle.

The Relevance of Coercion

Those sympathetic to libertarian views will insist that I have missed the point of the forced-labor analogy. They will say that it is a mistake to make too much of an exact correspondence between forced labor and redistributive taxation. The crucial overlap between them, rather, is that both extract resources from people by *coercive* means. "Coercion," writes one philosopher, "… reduces the will of one person to the will of another; [it violates] autonomy not simply in virtue of that fact, but because of the symbolic gesture this fact represents. In subjecting the will of one otherwise autonomous agent to the will of another, coercion demonstrates an attitude of disrespect, of infantilization of a sort inconsistent with respect for human agents as autonomous, self-creating creatures."[16] Importantly, coercion

---

[15] Frank 1986; Milner 2016.
[16] Blake 2001, p. 268.

remains objectionable in this way even when used to promote valuable ends. We would still resent a mugging even if perpetrated by a Robin Hood who intends to "redistribute" his ill-gotten gains to the deserving poor. This suggests that redistributive taxation is after all at least on a continuum with other degrading forms of coercion. Forced labor is simply another, albeit more extreme, example.

It is true that taxation involves coercion. But that does not mean that there are no relevant differences between submitting to taxation under the terms of Rawls's proposal and being the victim of a well-intentioned Robin Hood. Here, it is vital to remember that Rawls assumed that his two principles are willingly endorsed by members of his ideal well-ordered society as settled public criteria determining just entitlements and fair treatment. Indeed, Rawls argued that individuals in the original position would reject principles that, when publicly recognized in this way, they could not willingly endorse, given general knowledge of the limits of psychological tolerance and the typical circumstances of political association. His contractualist thought experiment thus purports to test whether it is fair and reasonable to expect individuals to submit to different possible schemes of social rules and principles. On the strength of his contention that his two principles of justice survive this test, Rawls felt entitled to conclude that individuals in a well-ordered society indeed *would* willingly accept and fulfill the responsibilities those principles impose upon them and can reasonably expect that others do so as well.

Clearly we are not entitled to dismiss these claims until we have fully assessed the cogency of Rawls's overall contractualist approach. In Chapter 4 we expressed some reservations on this score, but suppose we give Rawls the benefit of the doubt in the meantime. Doing so exposes two important differences between submitting to redistribution under his proposal and being mugged by a Robin Hood. First, a Robin Hood has *no idea* and *does not care* whether his victims are themselves disposed to contribute to whatever worthwhile social causes he intends to subsidize by stealing. His direct resort to coercive threats testifies to his willingness to proceed *without regard* to his victim's own wishes. It is this assumption that the victim's own will is simply irrelevant that makes the coercion of a Robin Hood offensive and contemptuous of his victim's autonomy.

But, at least in theory, Rawls envisaged a very different situation. For, as Rawls conceived it, a well-ordered society *just is* one in which there exists willing acceptance of the responsibilities imposed by the two principles and in which it is publicly known that citizens are disposed to fulfill them. Rawls's contractualist argument is intended to determine what principles individuals concerned to reconcile their own autonomy with their sense of justice would be prepared to accept as a fair account of their own responsibilities to each other. So unlike Robin Hood, a Rawlsian state has at least some reason to think that its expectations of those it coerces are ones that citizens themselves acknowledge as fair and reasonable.

Second, and relatedly, it is Robin Hood's coercion that gives his victims their primary reason for complying with his demand for their money. If Robin Hood were not threatening them, they might see no reason at all to give him any of their money. But as we have just seen, individuals in Rawls's well-ordered society already acknowledge that they have a responsibility to assist their least advantaged fellows. The purpose of legal coercion in Rawls's view is therefore *not* to supply a reason to do something where previously none existed. Its purpose, rather, is to provide agents who already recognize good reasons to fulfill their responsibilities with an assurance that once they have done so, others will also do their part in accordance with a fair and reasonable principle for sharing out the costs.

The Sufficiency Objection

Rawls's Difference Principle seems more vulnerable to another criticism, this time one aimed at egalitarian conceptions of justice more generally. According to this line of argument, pioneered by Harry Frankfurt, egalitarianism is a confused version of a better principle of economic distribution – the principle of *sufficiency*.[17] What matters, for "sufficientarians" (with apologies), is not that everyone's shares approximate to equality, but rather that everyone receive *enough*. Imagine a society in which everyone has access to sufficient economic resources for personal fulfillment and contentment. No one is impoverished in, or deprived of, the material goods they require to meet their needs. Still, there remain large disparities in income between individuals working in different sectors of the economy.

[17] Frankfurt 1987; Raz 2009.

Sports stars and computer whizzes make a lot more than teachers and nurses. But again, even the latter have enough. Sufficientarians claim that as long as this is true, there is nothing objectionable about these inequalities. Egalitarians of course must claim that there is; to them there is something inherently offensive about departures from equal shares. But why? If everyone really has enough, why complain about those who have more than enough? Aren't such complaints simply motivated by envy, a seedy emotion with no place in dispassionate assessments of economic justice?

Rawls's Difference Principle is vulnerable to this criticism because – like stricter egalitarian views – it could require redistribution well beyond the point of sufficiency (whatever that is). For it requires not merely that the least advantaged members of society have enough in an absolute sense, but that they do as well as economically feasible relative to other members of society. Citizens who embrace the Difference Principle therefore recognize an important social responsibility, based upon justice, to ensure that people have more than enough under certain conditions. But does Rawls give us any reason to agree that, beyond guaranteeing that everyone has enough, this is an important social responsibility that conceptions of justice must recognize? This is not clear.

Sufficientarian views are not without their own difficulties, of course. We need in particular to explain what counts as enough, and this is a potentially very complicated matter. Here, it is important to stress that Frankfurt himself did not interpret sufficiency as any sort of *minimal* requirement, like the Lockean proviso we discussed in the last chapter. He thought, for example, that it requires not merely that individuals have enough to survive, but enough for a decent life.[18] So a principle of sufficiency might still require quite radical forms of redistribution. But however these details are settled, the sufficiency argument represents an important challenge to conceptions of distributive justice that pay attention – like Rawls's Difference Principle – to agents' *relative* as well as *absolute* economic shares.

Rawls's decision to make his theory sensitive to considerations of relative deprivation remains a puzzling and undermotivated feature of his theory. More so, since in his later work Rawls himself defended a sufficiency criterion in the international arena. As we shall see shortly, Rawls denied that the Difference Principle applies globally. Instead, he argued that

---

[18] Frankfurt 1987, pp. 152ff.

our responsibilities to the economically deprived overseas are exhausted by a "duty of assistance." This duty requires that affluent states transfer sufficient funds to allow societies "burdened" by unfavorable economic conditions to solve their problems by themselves. However, once affluent states have discharged this duty, they have no further responsibility to ensure that the recipient states succeed in relieving poverty and deprivation within their own borders: if the latter fail they have only themselves to blame and no legitimate complaint against the affluent states.

But as many have pointed out, applying this same logic to the domestic case undermines the Difference Principle.[19] One might well ask: if we have supplied all our fellow citizens with resources for an adequate life, why impose a *further* responsibility to improve the condition of the least advantaged *as far as possible*? What more do we really owe them? Doesn't justice require that at that point *they* assume responsibility for themselves?

Global Distributive Justice?

I now return to an issue we introduced in the previous chapter and consider the implications of Rawls's theory for the global distribution of wealth. The discussion in that chapter suggested that global inequalities of wealth are if anything of more urgent concern than disparities between rich and poor within existing states. But Rawls rejected this view. As he conceived them, his two principles apply only within states, but not beyond their borders. This view reflects Rawls's assumption, latent in his theory from the start, but more pronounced and explicit in his later writings, that only nation-states possess the sort of "basic structure" to which his theory was supposed to apply. But many now think that, in an increasingly interdependent world, this assumption that distributive justice is almost exclusively an *intranational* concern is mistaken.

Many of Rawls's early readers took his decision to focus on the just configuration of national institutions to be a residual prejudice that Rawls inherited from the philosophical tradition. They assumed that, once fully acquainted with the growth of international legal regulation since the Second World War, and with the magnitude and density of economic interdependence between nations today, Rawls would not hesitate to extend

[19] For example, Singer 2004, p. 178.

his principles of justice beyond the borders of states. Some of his "cosmopolitan" followers, indeed, blazed this trail themselves, though without Rawls's own blessing.[20]

They argued that there already exists a global basic structure whose effects on individuals' life prospects are no less "profound and present from the start" than those imposed by domestic institutions. They also claimed that Rawls's avowed hostility toward allowing "factors arbitrary from a moral point of view" to affect distributive shares requires international redistribution. For without it, individuals' economic prospects will often be determined by their place of birth. But what could be more arbitrary than permitting people's economic prospects to be determined by (for example) whether they are born in the USA or Bangladesh? These authors therefore suggested that Rawls's "original position" be mobilized to determine principles of planetary justice. One might expect that a strong case for a global Difference Principle could be mounted on this basis, and this is indeed what some Rawlsians have advocated.

But in his own later writings, Rawls opposed this cosmopolitan extension of his theory. While he accepted that global principles ought to be ratified through an international version of his original-position argument, he denied that the parties to such a hypothetical planetary agreement should be conceived as individuals, as in his main theory. Rather, he argued, the parties should be representatives of nation-states, or (as Rawls preferred to call them) of "peoples." Thus the outcome of Rawls's own international contractualist theory is not a rich conception of distributive justice for a global order of planetary equals but rather a "Law of Peoples" to govern the terms on which independent, self-sufficient, and putatively self-governing states might live together in peace.[21] As Rawls conceived it, the Law of Peoples comprises a familiar set of rules recognizing (among others) the equality and political independence of "peoples," their right to go to war in self-defense, and a minimal list of basic human rights. The only economic proviso that Rawls added was the aforementioned "duty of assistance" under which economically successful "peoples" are required to supply enough aid to "burdened" societies to allow them to achieve a "decent" social institutions by themselves.

---

[20] Beitz 1999; Pogge 2002.
[21] Rawls 2003.

Not only does it reject a global Difference Principle, Rawls's Law of Peoples does not even expect that all "peoples" themselves endorse the Difference Principle as a requirement of justice within their own borders. This particularly puzzling feature of the Law of Peoples reflects Rawls's later concession (noted at the end of Chapter 6) that his theory cannot be defended as true for all societies at all times, but should be conceived more narrowly as specifying the dominant understanding of social justice characteristic of modern liberal democracy. Given this revised understanding, the cosmopolitan temptation to write into the Law of Peoples expectations deriving from a specifically *liberal democratic* conception of justice became, for Rawls, a potentially imperialist impulse to be resisted. So while Rawls continued to insist that the Difference Principle is an appropriate principle of justice for societies (like ours) already locked into the project of liberal democracy, he denied that we can dogmatically impose it upon societies elsewhere. Their public cultures, he argued, may be quite reasonably inhospitable to liberal democratic ideals. Accordingly, the Law of Peoples embodies a principle of international toleration that resembles the "diff'rent strokes for diff'rent folks" principle we discussed (and rejected) in Chapter 1.

Particularism and Cosmopolitanism

Few find this account of global distributive justice satisfactory. There are real difficulties squaring it with Rawls's original articulation of his theory. It is therefore extremely unfortunate that Rawls died before having an adequate opportunity fully to clarify his own view of these matters. However, while most remain perplexed by his own defense of it, many insist nonetheless that Rawls's conclusion that the requirements of distributive justice are weaker at the global level than within domestic political society is essentially sound.

Some defend it on strongly "particularist" or "communitarian" grounds that Rawls himself could not have accepted.[22] "Communitarianism" or "particularism" here refers to the view that ethical standards, principles,

---

[22] For communitarian views MacIntyre 2007; Sandel 1998; Taylor 1994; Walzer 2010, 1994. For critical discussion, see the excellent Kymlicka 1992. For discussion of distinctively *national* community, see D. Miller 1995; Nussbaum and Cohen 2002; Tamir 1995.

obligations, responsibilities, duties, and our conceptions of them make sense only in the context of some shared cultural framework, anchored in actually realized forms of community or association. In other words, effective ethical norms require some strong and rich set of bonds, loyalties, and affiliations (e.g. kinship, culture, friendship, nationality, ethnicity). This "social thesis" promotes skepticism about cosmopolitan justice and the ethical universalism on which it seems to rest. The crucial particularist allegation is that the global community is too large and attenuated to provide a fertile soil for any framework of ethical principle.[23]

In its purest version, this view implies that the very notion of universal or impartial ethical values is incoherent, like the idea that someone could speak a language without *any* accent at all, as if there were some "impartially" correct way of pronouncing words that is not itself just another accent. On such a view, all ethical standards and understandings of justice must be inherently local and partial, and so-called "global justice" an oxymoron. On the strength of such assumptions, some claim that only when people share the appropriate cultural and civic affiliations can they owe each other significant economic assistance as a matter of justice. While this assumption holds among citizens of the same nation, they claim, it does not hold at the global level.

There is no doubt that strong bonds of affective or cultural affiliation can make a difference to our obligations to others. Few would deny that we owe more to our friends, family, and cultural intimates than we do to those outside these circles of concern. It is not clear, however, that cosmopolitans or universalists must deny any of this, nor that it makes ethical particularism a plausible view. But however we decide these larger questions, a more immediate doubt hangs over this argument. Does *citizenship* credibly belong in the category of those affiliations that intensify our sense of obligation to others, particularly with regard to economic justice?

This is far from obvious. In complex modern societies, the bond of citizenship is not necessarily a particularly close one, and not only in the sense that one does not know one's fellow citizens very well. The more telling point is that even when one *does* know them, one all too often finds their ways of life, beliefs, experiences, and emotional responses largely incomprehensible, alien, reprehensible, and even repellent. In some cases, citizens

---

[23] D. Miller 1995; Walzer 2010, 1994.

of the same state may not even speak the same language (think of Canada, Belgium, or Switzerland). One reason to be suspicious of this argument, then, is its unwelcome implication that whenever shared understanding and cultural intimacy are lacking among citizens (as they very often are), domestic redistributive justice may be as hard to justify as it claims it is in the global case. To adapt the aphorism about Russians and Tartars, scratch a fellow citizen and you will find a stranger. It is doubtful, then, that these particularist arguments can justify Rawls's view that justice imposes more extensive obligations to provide material assistance to economically deprived fellow citizens than to similarly disadvantaged foreigners.

Coercion and Autonomy

Others have, however, defended this conclusion in a different way, more congenial, perhaps, to Rawls's own approach. They deny that the salient difference between the domestic and the global case is that there exist cultural ties in one that are absent or too weak in the other. Rather, they suggest that the crucial difference lies in the presence – in the domestic case – of the coercive apparatus of the state itself. These powerful reserves of coercion, they argue, potentially warp the relations between citizens, leaving them especially vulnerable to abuse at each other's hands. For, unlike foreigners, one's fellow citizens enjoy ready access to these coercive resources and so represent an immediate danger to one's own autonomy. Association within the framework of a state thus creates distinctive problems that do not arise between humans operating in the wider global environment. Most important, wealthier groups may be able to use their domestic political institutions and their coercive capacity to dominate and take advantage of less well-situated groups of citizens. We need therefore to ensure that disadvantaged groups have adequate resources to counteract this risk that better-situated groups will convert economic advantage into political oppression. This requires that we attend to the relative economic position of the two groups and creates pressure toward a more egalitarian distribution of resources within states. These dangers thus lend relative economic shares, and perhaps the Difference Principle, a special significance in the domestic case that they do not enjoy in the global one, or so these authors contend.[24]

[24] Variants on this argument can be found in Blake 2001; R. Miller 1998; Nagel 2005.

One attraction of this argument is that it seems compatible with the cosmopolitan or universalist assumption that all humans *as such* are to be respected as *planetary equals*, regardless of their nationality, ethnicity, or other particularist affiliations. Some of its proponents therefore allow that at the global level, universal respect for the moral equality of all humans requires that we guarantee everyone in the world sufficient economic resources to live as autonomous, independent individuals.[25] Still, while conceding this much to the cosmopolitan, they nevertheless argue that this same principle of moral equality gives rise to additional redistributive obligations among those whose relations are structured around established systems of coercive legal regulation. Call this the coercion argument. If sound, it partly vindicates Rawls's instinct that global standards of economic justice ought to be ones of sufficiency, concerned only with individuals' absolute shares, while domestic ones ought to be concerned as well with relative shares.

Problems with the Coercion Argument

Ingenious as it is, however, the coercion argument faces several serious objections. First, insofar as it purports to establish that a concern for relative shares *cannot* be motivated beyond state borders, the argument is fallacious. For it does not follow from the claim that the terms of domestic association might trigger such a concern that there are no features of the international order that might do so with comparable or even greater urgency. At best, the argument merely reminds us that, given the relative weakness and underdevelopment of international legal governance, any oppression or objectionable coercion that does occur across states will not be imposed on victims directly through legal institutions they share. But surely such unjust relationships can often exist between agents who do not share citizenship in the same legal order. Indeed, surely it is quite plausible to think, as cosmopolitans vigorously argue, that wealthy Western states and corporations often use their position of global economic and political advantage to oppress and exploit the globally disadvantaged. In Chapter 13, we suggest that the widespread use of sweatshops by multinational corporations exemplifies unjustifiable oppression and domination. Why

[25] Blake 2001.

lower the burden of justification for such privations of freedom simply because they occur across, rather than within, state borders?[26]

Second, like Rawls's Difference Principle itself, the coercion argument remains vulnerable to a version of the sufficiency objection. Its proponents are prepared to assert that at the global level everyone has an entitlement to sufficient economic resources to permit autonomous functioning. But if the distinctively *economic* conditions for personal autonomy are already guaranteed by this global sufficiency principle, it becomes unclear why additional monetary forms of redress like the Difference Principle are needed to forestall any efforts by better-situated groups to take political advantage of their less privileged compatriots. Under the global sufficiency principle proposed by the coercion argument, everyone is guaranteed sufficient economic resources to live autonomously. If less advantaged groups are still menaced with oppression and privations of freedom at the hands of their wealthier compatriots, the obvious solution is to fortify the political procedures guaranteeing them their basic liberties and rights. But increasing their relative share of the national wealth is hardly an appropriate response to this problem. For good Rawlsian reasons, buying citizens off with economic benefits seems poor compensation for any losses of personal freedom and political liberty to which they remain vulnerable.

Of course, guaranteeing citizens their basic liberties itself costs money, and presumably the financial burden of providing them will, and probably should, fall more heavily on better-advantaged groups at home and abroad. But that's not the same as saying that a concern for relative shares of wealth enjoys a special significance within national borders that it does not enjoy without them. Rather, it amounts simply to a global expectation that, regardless of where they live, citizens are entitled to a fully adequate bundle of basic liberties. This implies a global entitlement to an adequate threshold of a primary good, not the application of a principle sensitive to relative shares.

Finally, the argument assumes that the forms of legally sanctioned coercion that exist within states create a stronger burden of justification than those that hold the international order together. But why? That the international order *is* held together by legal coercion cannot be seriously

---

[26] I am very grateful to Ryan Pevnick for many illuminating conversations about these matters.

disputed, as anyone who has been turned away at gunpoint by border guards well knows. Perhaps, as some proponents of the coercion argument maintain, the coercion involved in (say) immigration restrictions is different from that involved in the ongoing regulation and adjustment of property-holding by domestic legal institutions, and thus raises different issues.[27]

Remember, though, that all of these authors, including Rawls, require some organized redistribution across state borders. Rawls's "duty of assistance" is admittedly a rather modest redistributive requirement. But guaranteeing all persons in the world sufficient economic resources for personal autonomy, as entertained by some proponents of the coercion argument, could require very extensive redistribution. Presumably the funds for these transfers are to be gathered by coercive taxation across states, enforceable through international legal instruments. But if this amounts to the routine coercive regulation of property rights, the coercion argument turns out to have paradoxical consequences. For in calling for such coercive adjustments, it seems to require at the international level *exactly* those measures that it claims trigger a concern for relative economic position in the domestic context. But if that is so the argument plausibly undermines its own intended conclusion.

---

[27] Blake 2001, p. 280, n. 30.

9   The Significance of Borders

The position reached in the last chapter mirrors the current state of the debate about global justice. On the one hand, few would deny that the current distribution of wealth across the globe is seriously unjust. And, as we have just seen, it is difficult to find *principled* reasons for believing that criteria of international distributive justice differ from, or are less urgent than, those that apply to the assessment of domestic economic arrangements. A cosmopolitan perspective seems to be an inescapable implication of an impartial commitment to respect all individuals as equals.

On the other hand, the lack of principled grounds against cosmopolitanism does not mean that there are no valid *political* reasons to be cautious about global redistributive justice. We currently lack adequate institutional means to effect such redistribution and to guard against the possible abuses that such transnational economic authority might invite. While it may not be defensible on grounds of high principle, then, Rawls's position may still win on points.[1]

Here it is helpful to remember the predicament of individuals in the Hobbesian state of nature. As we noted in Chapter 5, Hobbes was quite clear that rational individuals in a state of nature could see that the solution to their problems lies in agreeing mutually to lay down their rights to preserve themselves as they choose. Indeed, he derived an extensive further list of quite specific rules that ideally it would be rational for peace-seeking individuals to recognize and follow, including rules prohibiting the ridicule of others, requiring that every person acknowledge every other

---

[1] Rawls's cosmopolitan critics concede that, in our nonideal world, the application of even an ideal cosmopolitan vision of redistributive justice may result in conclusions that tally with Rawls's. But this still leaves the outstanding question of why Rawls defended those modest conclusions as the correct account at the *ideal* level.

person as an "equal" and prescribing a willingness to be accommodating to others.[2]

So the problem confronting individuals in Hobbes's state of nature lies not in their inability to perceive, even in some detail, the provisions of a workable and effective mutual peace treaty to put an end to their endemic conflicts. Rather, for Hobbes the difficulty is that in order for such a treaty to come into effect, individuals would have to trust each other's word to abide by its terms. But Hobbes thought such trust must be absent in the state of nature. In his view, it can be cultivated only through the artifice of a sovereign state, deploying legal coercion to assure citizens that their fellows will make good on their undertakings. To put Hobbes's point in more contemporary terms, individuals in a state of nature have access to the *software* of peace – they have access to an algorithmic list of rules the following of which will reliably result in peaceful cooperation. But they lack the *hardware* capable of actually running the program. This, for Hobbes, can be provided only by the distinctive institutional powers of a sovereign state.

Something similar seems true of our current situation with regard to criteria of global distributive justice. Suppose we concede for the moment that Rawls has given us a reasonably compelling set of ideal criteria for economic justice. Even if we grant this, and moreover that these criteria are not *inherently* national or statist, it remains unclear that we possess the political hardware to actually run this program at the planetary level. In contrast, we have such hardware ready to hand in our domestic political institutions, and it is not too difficult to see how these institutional resources might be adapted so as to run the Rawlsian software or some alternative conception of distributive justice. For the time being, then, criteria of distributive justice will continue to seem most salient within the domestic political arena.

Still, this judgment reflects contingent facts about available political resources. It does not amount to a principled objection to cosmopolitan distributive justice as such. There is therefore every reason to follow Hobbes's example and to seek, with as much ingenuity as we can muster, a compelling rational account of the global agencies that might enable us better to live up to our responsibilities to each other.

[2] Hobbes 1994, pp. 94–9; Hobbes 1998, pp. 47–57.

International Migration

For the foreseeable future, then, the planetary political order is likely to remain fundamentally *international* rather than genuinely *cosmopolitan*. Yet, while I have suggested that this circumstance lends discussions of global distributive justice a rather utopian quality, three other sets of issues with an international dimension will, and should, continue to command the attention of political philosophers in the meantime.

The first reflects mounting concern that modern economic development is causing an unsustainable warming of the Earth's climate. The risks of climate change are obviously global in scope, and any effective strategy of mitigation will accordingly require international cooperation. The second set of issues is prompted by the problem of war. In a world of independent sovereign states, many armed to the teeth, violent conflict remains a standing possibility, and so questions about how to secure global peace and security, and about when (if ever), and how, states are justified in initiating force against each other cannot be ignored. The next two chapters are devoted respectively to philosophical questions raised by these topics.

This chapter addresses a third set of international issues, especially controversial today, to do with cross-border migration. Are states entitled to condition access to their territories, and if so on what basis? Can would-be immigrants be legitimately excluded or should states adopt a regime of "open borders"? This discussion belongs here because the question of immigration connects directly to questions about the global distribution of wealth. Regional economic deprivation has always been a major spur to migration (think of the Irish potato famine, for example). Today, some claim that when affluent Western states restrict immigration they reinforce unjust global inequalities, effectively excluding large portions of the world's population from the fruits of economic development. Thus, Jo Carens, today the leading philosophical proponent of "open borders." has compared such restrictions to "feudal barriers to mobility" that "protect unjust privileges."[3]

However, questions about immigration are about more than economic distribution. They also require attention to rights of territorial control

---

[3] Carens 1987, p. 270.

and of membership in a political community. Most of us, after all, accept an "open borders" view with regard to jurisdictional boundaries *within* states and take for granted internal free movement between cities, municipalities, townships, counties, federal states, and regions. We would be horrified if Paris, New York, California, Quebec, Wallonia, or Yorkshire set up barbed-wire fences around their borders, posted armed soldiers at points of access, and required would-be entrants to apply for special visas to enter their land. Yet nation-states do all these things routinely, thereby implicitly asserting their right to exclude immigrants as they choose.

Although immigration is today a topic of intense public debate in the Western liberal democracies, the status and scope of this purported right to exclude is rarely broached directly. Familiar disagreements over *which* restrictions should be imposed tend to presuppose that the right to exclude is itself legitimate, and open-ended enough to support protagonists' own preferred views about who should be let in and who not. But is that right legitimate in the first place? In what form?

To answer these questions, one must explain what, if anything, changes as we move from local jurisdictions like counties or cities to the level of the nation-state. Cogent answers to the question of when, and for what reasons, states may exclude migrants must therefore depend on plausible assumptions about the nature and scope of national authority. Before addressing the claims of immigrants directly, then, I begin with some remarks about these more basic features of the institutional background.

Authority: General Features

We noted in the Introduction that, unlike other political concepts (e.g. justice, the common good, human flourishing and the good life, equality, and many notions of freedom), authority is not an *ideal*, but rather an actually existing political practice. We confront it on a daily basis, when courts order us to pay a fine, police officers pull us over, tax authorities command us to cough up, or we receive a jury summons. Although they can, in principle, be configured in any number of ways, practices of political authority display several characteristic features. Some of these are generic, built into the very concept of authority itself, while others are merely ubiquitous, yet contingent, aspects of the form that political authority assumes in our present *international* global order.[4] Four of the former are particularly important.

(1) Although itself a creature of "positive morality" (as defined in Chapters 1 and 2), the distinctiveness of authority consists in the power to apply, interpret, and modify *other* positive moral expectations implicated in the same scheme of social practices. In other words, the self-regulation of positive moral norms is a central feature of practices of authority.

Developed legal systems illustrate this self-qualifying feature particularly well. For, on the one hand, we recognize domestic legal authorities by reference to various positive rules – for example, constitutional and statutory provisions, procedures like elections that confer power on specific officials (presidents, legislators, sheriffs, etc.), and those conventions by which we can determine in the moment who may exercise public authority (badges, types of documentation, uniforms, markings and lights on police vehicles, etc.).

On the other hand, legal authorities recognized in these ways are distinguished by their capacity to act upon, and alter, related positive expectations in ways denied to ordinary citizens. Police officers can apply and enforce the law by using defined powers of arrest, search, seizure, and detention; courts may designate individuals as criminals and prison officers are authorized to incarcerate them; ministers and clerks can change agents' marital status; courts, judges, and executive officials can definitively interpret and specify the content of the law in unclear or disputed cases; and legislative assemblies can enact new laws and repeal or modify existing

---

[4] They are contingent not only in that, as I have suggested, we can imagine some post-national system of global governance in which the modern state "withers away," but also in that the nation-state as we know it is a relatively recent historical phenomenon. Familiar contemporary understandings of the "nation" as a fundamental political unit would have been quite alien to people living in earlier periods. Similarly, the exhaustive division of the global political power into separate sovereign states each claiming an exclusive monopoly on the right to use force within its own jurisdiction has been accomplished only within the past two or three centuries. During much of the medieval period, for example, the right to use force was not monopolized by any secular institution, but shared out among dynastic monarchies, aristocratic families, land owners, leagues of civic corporations, and the church (which developed, and coercively enforced, its own system of canon law and, during the crusades, mustered its own armies).

ones. Normally, you and I, as private citizens, can do none of these things; indeed, we are prohibited from doing so.

The same pattern can be discerned in the context of games, professions, and other organizations, all of which characteristically operate according positive rules authorizing certain individuals to apply and change other rules within the same institutional network: referees who can call fouls or disallow goals; official bodies that can modify the rules of the game (like FIFA in soccer or the R&A in golf); deans who can promote professors and change academic curricula; tribunals convened to adjudicate disputes within an organization; or priests who can consecrate a building or determine whether, in the eyes of the Church, a "miracle" occurred, etc.

(2) The concept of authority presupposes that it can be legitimately or illegitimately exercised. No consensus exists on how to define *sufficient* conditions for the legitimacy of different forms of authority. The issue has historically been, and will continue to be, highly controversial. However, we can safely stipulate several basic *necessary* conditions. At a minimum, legitimate authority:

- must be exercised for reasons, rather than arbitrarily, randomly, or in a completely thoughtless manner;
- must represent "someone's view about how its subjects ought to behave,"[5] as opposed to reposing solely in events, indeterminate traditions, hopes, guesses, suggestions, advice, stories, completely vague or ambiguous utterances;
- while it may sometimes *override* independently important duties, obligations, claims, and norms, it cannot ignore, deny, or purport to *annul* their importance completely;[6] and
- must be exercised with at least some consideration for the interests of its subjects and not solely for the benefit of those wielding it.

(3) Although itself a way of influencing others' conduct, and even though in political contexts it almost always implies a right to use coercive force,

---

[5] I take this formula from Raz 1985, p. 303.

[6] This is an important proviso in the context of immigration because it establishes that one cannot defend a right to exclude on the grounds that states have duties only to their own citizens. As Dummett points out, it is mere "tribalism" to suggest such a thing, because states, like everyone else, have plain duties to others (Dummett 2004, pp. 116–18).

political authority is neither equivalent, nor fully reducible, to power. For example, a police officer overwhelmed by a mob may lose the power to arrest a rioter, but his *de jure* authority to do so remains intact. Conversely, a mugger uses coercive power to extort money from her victim, but neither claims nor exercises any authority over them. The relation between authority and power is thus not straightforward; its perplexing character can be highlighted by considering a final general feature of authoritative practices.

(4) Authority is to be obeyed: its exercise normally corresponds to an obligation to comply. That obligation is moreover "content independent" in a notoriously puzzling way. When someone obeys an authoritative order, she does not do so only because she judges the authority's decision to be correct on the merits. If her compliance were conditional on that judgment, it would not constitute genuine obedience, for in that case the presence of an authoritative order would be entirely incidental; she might as well have judged the matter for herself in the first place. To actually *obey* the order, then, she must comply *for the reason that* she has been instructed to do so, and not because she agrees or disagrees with its content. In other words, authority *preempts* its subjects' judgment.

For example, when a police officer orders you to "pull over!" his instruction purports to *override* your own judgments about how to proceed, presenting itself as an independent, decisive reason to bring the car to a halt on the hard shoulder. To be sure, the police officer also issues an implicit threat: "Do as I say or else I will arrest/charge/fine/imprison/flog, etc. you." But this coercive element cannot be the whole story. If that is all that is going on, the important and familiar distinction drawn above between being merely *compelled* to do something (as in a mugging) and being ordered to do so by someone (like a police officer) *authorized* to compel compliance when subjects fail to respond to the order itself, disappears.

Yet, holding on to that distinction creates a deep problem, with formal and substantive aspects. If authorities give us reasons to do things, but those reasons are independent of any threats of force, and also distinct from the soundness of beliefs or arguments about what ought to happen, they seem to have the form "Do *X just because* we say so." But what sort of reasons could these possibly be? When is someone's mere say-so ever *any* sort of a reason to do something?

The more substantive aspect of the problem concerns freedom and autonomy. If compliance with authority involves allowing someone else to preempt my own sincerely held views about what ought to happen, it seems to require agents to surrender their own judgment. But this conflicts with our sense of ourselves as autonomous rational agents, entitled to act on our own judgments about what ought to happen. The effort to explain how political authority can legitimately impose content-independent expectations on its subjects has given rise to a philosophical debate over the so-called "problem of political obligation." The first edition of this book assessed and outlined the standard positions in that debate, and so readers wishing to explore it are directed to that earlier discussion.[7] Our focus here, however, is on the more specific question of the right of states to exclude immigrants. So I turn now to those more immediately relevant aspects of political authority that, though pervasive, are not conceptually integral but rather due to the contingently *international* structure of the current global order.

re expect. based on authority alone

Territory

In our world, political authority is parceled out to independent, sovereign nation-states along two distinct but overlapping dimensions, one concerning *territorial boundaries* and the other concerning *membership*. I will discuss each in turn.

It is a commonplace that nation-states legitimately exercise their authority only within a defined territory. Land is the most obvious and pertinent manifestation of this territorial particularity: that is after all how nation-states are identified, usually with different colors, on world maps. However, the demarcation of terrain is merely a paramount, but not unique, constituent of a state's territorial reach.

This is so because a state's jurisdiction can and often does extend beyond land – e.g. to lakes, rivers, and coastal waters; to oilrigs, offshore windfarms, ships, submarines, or planes in the sky; to satellites orbiting the planet; to the frequencies on the electromagnetic spectrum constituting radio and internet bandwidth; and to citizens while abroad, as with the US Foreign Corrupt Practices Act, which prohibits American citizens and companies

---

[7] See also Klosko 2005; Simmons 1981, 2001; Wolff 1970.

from paying bribes to foreign governments or officials even when abroad. The identification of this extended territorial domain presupposes the presence of spatial boundaries that are not land-based borders (e.g. latitudes and longitudes defining the edge of a country's territorial waters, the jurisdictional bubble within which states have authority over their naval submarines as they sail, or the metaphorical locations at which US jurisdiction over its citizens under the Foreign Corrupt Practices Act yields to that of the host country). We should therefore follow Allen Buchanan's more precise characterization of territoriality as a jurisdictional category tied to specific areas including, but not limited to, land.[8]

Buchanan's conception of territory carries an important implication. If a state's territory is the totality of physical spaces within which it exercises authority, the legitimacy of its authority must partly depend on the legitimacy of the boundaries defining that state's territory. So, to fully account for the scope of legitimate national authority, we need to explain how territorial boundaries are properly fixed and modified. Unfortunately, as Buchanan correctly notes, we currently lack any settled theory of boundaries (although the effort to develop one is now a major area of research in the field[9]). Nevertheless, several rudimentary considerations are beyond reasonable dispute and would have to be incorporated into any satisfactory theory.

For one thing, although the *de facto* determinants of existing territorial limits cannot be sufficient to justify them *de jure*, any sane theory of boundaries must adopt at least a presumption in favor of leaving them as they are. The actual shape of territorial boundaries is determined by multiple historical factors, some tragic or entirely disreputable (natural disasters, inundations, conquests, crusades, imperialism, annexations, violent *coups d'état*, forced resettlements, genocides, exterminations, programs of "ethnic cleansing," etc.), others of more ambiguous value (rebellions, peace treaties, secessions, demographic shifts, campaigns of pacification, and processes of institutional consolidation, of cultural transformation, or of economic development, etc.), and still others innocent or even beneficial (the evolution and maintenance of basically just and

[8] Buchanan 2003.
[9] Banai et al. 2014; Buchanan and Moore 2003; Kolers 2009; Margalit and Raz 1990; Meisels 2009; Moore 2015; Nine 2012; Pavel 2015.

decent institutions over many generations, successful campaigns to liberate oppressed or excluded groups within a territory, the cultivation of public spirit and civic virtue, etc.). However, the complicated twists and turns of history jumble these good, bad, and ambivalent factors inextricably together. Rarely can we sift them apart and say with any confidence that the particular shape of any given territorial jurisdiction is exclusively or largely the result of desirable rather than undesirable ones. A certain degree of arbitrariness in where the lines are drawn is anyway inevitable: in many if not most cases, there simply is no reason *at all* why (e.g.) a particular lawn, hill, or forest should be Welsh rather than Roman, Belgian rather than Spanish, Soviet rather than Ukrainian. Given all of this, any suggestion that a theory of boundaries could somehow begin *tabula rasa* and then infer a complete territorial ordering of the world, just on philosophical grounds, is a nonstarter.

Still, the presumption in favor of existing territorial jurisdictions is rebuttable, and among the most important tasks a theory of boundaries can perform is to tell us when adjustments (foundings, secessions, restorations of annexed land, resettlements, decolonization, partitions, confederation, etc.) are appropriate, and on what terms. Clearly, it cannot be up to any one state, or even group of states, to determine these matters for the whole world. The belief on the part of particular states that *they* alone have the right to unilaterally determine boundaries has been a major source of international aggression and conflict – one thinks, for example, of the infamous Nazi doctrine of *Lebensraum*, and of imperialism more generally. The legitimate authority to settle boundaries, or at least specific disputes about them, cannot therefore be ascribed to any particular state within the international system; in this sense, it constitutes a minimal international "common good" in the sense defined in Chapter 2.

As we saw there, being guided by the norms and conventions of settled positive moralities is not the same thing as being bullied, intimidated, or coerced by particular others in a position to make us do what they want. It is, rather, a matter of following rules that possess an impersonal character in that they are generally accepted as valid by the participants in a particular community or practice, and commonly known to be so. Hence our earlier analogy between the positive moralities in a society and the rules of games. In both cases, the relevant rules establish a common point of reference for intelligent, engaged deliberation among participants about how to discharge their responsibility for securing the proper functioning of the relevant practices by applying or modifying those expectations.

Similarly, any international conventions about where territorial boundaries are drawn, and about how they are to be properly respected or adjusted, must be regarded as the site of a common global responsibility, not simply as *de facto* outcomes of international coercion. A theory of boundaries will therefore be constituted by general constraints and principles to guide the discharge of that common responsibility, so that all relevant interests are taken properly into account. Whether or not we agree with its content and provisions, and although it says virtually nothing about the making and unmaking of territorial boundaries, Rawls's notion of a "Law of Peoples" (see the previous chapter) at least occupies this conceptual space. It presents itself as a reasonable basis for agreement among nation-states (or "peoples") to arrange the international commons on terms that take due account of each national community's legitimate interests.

A connected, but even more important, point about territorial jurisdiction is that one cannot plausibly regard it as a generalization of primordial rights of private property in land or other assets. Rather, as Buchanan and others have stressed,[10] the right to hold private property on certain terms must be derivative of the positive legal rules that legitimate territorial authorities develop to define the terms on which agents can own things within their jurisdictions.

The point here is not just the one made in Chapters 5 and 7 that the status of private property as any sort of "natural" right is doubtful. It is also that there is nothing in the bare idea of a private property right to forbid proprietors from moving their land from one jurisdiction to another at their discretion. Just as private individuals move their money from one bank/ investment to another to secure the most favorable interest rates/returns, one can easily imagine that landowners might similarly wish to switch jurisdictions to take advantage of lower tax-rates or other legal benefits available elsewhere. This, however, is a recipe for chaos, threatening the territorial integrity of nation-states.

---

[10] Buchanan 2003; Carens 1987.

Behind these pragmatic problems lies a deeper conceptual problem, well described by David Miller (glossing Buchanan):

> [T]he idea that state S has rightful jurisdiction over a piece of territory T because T's owner O has consented to its authority depends upon first establishing that O has a (property) right to T. But if the only way in which we can demonstrate that O has a right to T is by referring to the law of S, then clearly our account becomes circular.[11]

Locke tried to address this problem by stipulating that those inheriting or acquiring at least landed property can do so only if they accept the territorial affiliation selected by its previous owners. He sought thereby to reconcile the voluntarism of his theory of property with the need for states to maintain their territorial integrity.

But, far from removing it, Locke's stipulation merely reinstates the original difficulty. Who gets to decide that agents can inherit or acquire land only on condition that they agree to accept the jurisdiction chosen by its original owner? It is hard to see how the right to make that decision derives from powers implicit in property ownership itself. If the first generation of owners can choose the national jurisdiction with which they wish to affiliate their land, why shouldn't later generations of owners enjoy the same freedom? If I build a shrine to Zeus, are those who later buy or inherit the building now obligated to preserve its sacred Jovian status in perpetuity because this was the wish of the original owner? Locke's own conception of private property and his related insistence on agents' natural freedom from subjection to others point in just the opposite direction, implying that current generations cannot legitimately tie the hands of future people in that way. So this does not seem a very promising line.

If, instead, Locke's argument appeals to the need for states to maintain their territorial integrity, it presupposes that a state's own interests may legitimately qualify the terms on which property can be voluntarily transferred. Yet that presupposition is tantamount to conceding that at least some rights of territorial control cannot be derived from, or subordinated to, privileges enjoyed by property owners.

[11] D. Miller 2003.

This also makes it implausible to think that the relation of a "people" to its territory is analogous to that of an owner to his or her private property. As Buchanan says:

> If the state territory as a whole belongs to the whole people, but if some of the land within the state is owned by some people but not others, then the relationship of the people to the state territory cannot be that of the owner of land to the land owned.[12]

The lesson to draw is that settling territorial boundaries is a special case of the more general problem of political justice as we have described it in this book. As previous chapters have emphasized, that problem is centrally about how best to divide, and prioritize, responsibility for realizing common goods among potentially competing agencies. A good way to characterize our own *international* global order is to see it as instituting an implicit hierarchy of such responsibilities, within which the territorial jurisdictions of nation-states occupy an intermediate position.

Looking *downward* from their position within that hierarchy, national authorities determine how responsibility for assets falling within their jurisdictions is to be divided. This involves not only deciding which ownable resources are public (e.g. nationalized industries, public lands) and which private property (e.g. personal goods, corporate assets, etc.) but also how responsibility for other indivisible, unownable goods should be allocated (national defense, health and safety, police protection, just public institutions, schemes of fair political representation, rights of legal representation and adjudication, respect for personal freedom, a tolerant social culture, etc.). Looking *upward*, however, the boundaries of territorial jurisdiction are themselves nested within a set of higher-order international conventions. These determine (whether defensibly or not, and often rather indefinitely compared to the highly granular content of existing domestic law) the scope and geographical limits of the responsibilities reserved to nation-states.

Membership

This brings us to the second dimension along which political authority is particularized within the current international order. If territory implies a geographically discrete jurisdiction, it also presupposes a local agency

---

[12] Buchanan 2003, p. 234.

that can exercise legitimate authority within it. Insofar as nation-states are presumed to be independent and self-determining, the relevant agents must somehow be drawn from within the resident citizenry. In this broad sense, national authority automatically involves the idea that it is exercised by a "people" physically located within the relevant territory.

Now, "peoplehood" is a slippery category. At a minimum, it excludes colonial domination, occupation, conquest, and other forms of external subjection. Beyond this uncontroversial minimum, however, identifying "the people" such that we can verify that public action is genuinely *theirs*, rather than that of some imposter, is fraught with difficulty in all but the smallest communities. In the context of today's large and populous nation-states, it is simply not feasible for "the *actual* people" to exert direct political control in any literal sense. This allows even dictatorial regimes to at least *claim* the blessing of their own "people" and govern in their name (North Korea describes itself, after all, as a "People's Republic"). Such claims are certainly spurious, but the pretense is possible at all because in any large-scale regime "the people" can find its voice only in intermediary representatives, and through institutional routines sanctioned by accepted positive moral rules and conventions. In practice, the "people's" presence is virtual, mediated through proxies and representative agents claiming to speak in its name.[13]

How a "people" can recognize itself in the actions of its government therefore raises some very thorny questions. Fortunately, we can skirt these questions here, for the only immediately relevant point is that "peoplehood" presupposes *membership*. The idea of national rule "*by* the people, *for* the people," in other words, assumes a distinction between those who belong to that body and those who do not. This implies, at least, that foreigners are non-members, and that not everyone physically present within a state's territory automatically enjoys citizenship.

To be a citizen in the relevant sense is to have rights of full civic participation – i.e. to have a formal say in shaping the decisions representing the "people's" *de facto* control over "its" territory. Typical incidents of membership in this sense include: recognized rights to hold political office; a voice in legislation both statutory and constitutional; the entitlement to form political parties, stand for election, and participate fully in political campaigns; eligibility for social welfare benefits (health care,

---

[13] See Tuck 2016.

unemployment insurance, etc.) or public honors; and guaranteed membership for one's children. Citizenship also characteristically incurs such civic obligations as liability to national or military service, jury duty, and some forms of taxation from which non-members are immune. In addition, it carries a more inchoate expectation of allegiance or loyalty, such that only members (but not foreign citizens, even those who are long-term residents) can be accused of treason.

The Claims of Migrants

The contrast between the particularity of territory and of civic membership allows us to distinguish two polar cases involving claims about the rights of states to exclude migrants. At one pole, we can ask whether, and on what grounds, states may deny persons bare access to their territory – i.e. deny their right to be physically present within a state's jurisdiction (on the understanding that they obey the local laws during their stay). The claims to enter foreign jurisdictions asserted by holidaymakers, tourists, explorers, archeologists, students, and those visiting friends or family abroad fall under this category. At the other extreme, we can ask whether, and on what terms, states may condition the right to naturalize as a full, participating member of a nation's citizenry. These twin cases are not sharply distinct. They rather define a spectrum of more complicated, mixed cases in which migrants assert various combinations of claims that receiving states may or may not permissibly deny.

For example, migrants' intentions and circumstances sometimes change, and since finding and removing people who are already (somewhere) within a territory is far harder and more expensive than turning them away at a border, authorized temporary visits can easily become much longer, unauthorized stays. Virtually all societies, then, confront the complex question of whether immigrants who have entered illegally or overstayed their legal admission but who have nonetheless established long-term, productive residency within a territory may legitimately be removed. According to recent estimates, the number of undocumented aliens in the USA today is roughly equivalent to the populations of such countries as Belgium, Greece, and Portugal. Given the scale of nonlegal migration, it is doubtful that nation-states can expel all undocumented aliens from their territory without instituting objectionable levels of surveillance (of legal citizens as well as immigrants) and deploying unacceptably brutal policies of forced deportation.

The presence of children complicates such cases even further. Despite having no legal right to be there, any children who have accompanied illegal immigrants may put down deep roots in their new location. Yet they can hardly be held responsible for their parents' decision to move (still less for the failure of the state to enforce its own immigration restrictions in their case). And, of course, some children are born to undocumented immigrants after they arrive. Kicking out innocent children is hardly reasonable; many would say they should be treated exactly like children born to legal citizens (who, after all, may themselves have committed criminal offenses far more serious than crossing a border without permission).

Here, the strict enforcement of immigration restrictions conflicts with the value of keeping families together. In 2018 the Trump administration briefly pursued an appalling policy of separating illegal migrants from their children upon arrival in the USA, turning their parents away and placing the latter in "camps." Facing widespread criticism, President Trump was forced to abandon this policy. Although he did so for party political reasons, the ethical case against orphaning children just for the sake of a border is surely overwhelming. It should move even fascists who (spuriously) attach special significance to the ties of "blood." For if "blood" is what matters, then presumably the claims of families override those of other affiliations.

Another intermediate possibility is that agents may move to another country with no intention of, or interest in, becoming full members, but simply to take up professional or personal opportunities that nonetheless require their extended presence. A company or institution may have offered them a job because they have unique skills or qualifications for the position, or perhaps their partner cannot move and wishes them to join her and start a family in her home country. Such migrants may well want to participate fully in the life of their localities (churches, social clubs, sports teams, school boards, etc.) yet not seek full naturalization. They ask for more than temporary territorial access for the purposes of leisure, study, or vacation, yet less than full citizenship. This raises the question of whether, and on what terms, states may condition "permanent resident" status.

The most challenging and philosophically interesting questions about immigration arise in this complex intermediate terrain. I cannot hope to resolve these here. However, to frame our thinking about these more involved issues, we can look to the more straightforward polar cases of bare territorial access and full membership for some initial guidance. As we shall see, convincing arguments for immigration restrictions are quite hard to find. I will consider the latter case first.

Exclusion from Membership

The case for a right to exclude migrants from full *membership* is surely stronger than that for a right to deny them territorial access. As we have defined it, membership as a full citizen implies the right to share in the exercise of national authority "by the people, for the people." Viewed from this angle, the "people" is effectively the ultimate executive body within the state. The earlier-noted complications attending the identification of this executive body in the context of large, complex, modern nation-states are serious, but they need not dislodge a fairly uncontroversial intuition: that a body of persons, whoever they are, responsible for actively governing their collective affairs enjoys some prerogative to decide who may join them in this endeavor. The standard arguments canvassed to support the state's right to exclude immigrants are at their most compelling when applied in this context.

For example, Michael Walzer has proposed an analogy between states and clubs.[14] Like other private associations, clubs enjoy considerable latitude to decide whom they want to admit as members by reference to their own self-understandings. Since the Boy Scouts define themselves as a male-only organization, no one finds its exclusion of female members particularly problematic. It is hardly unreasonable for churches to exclude known atheists from the priesthood or other official ecclesiastical roles. Similarly, one might argue that citizens wielding national powers of self-determination are entitled to attach at least some conditions on sharing that power with newcomers. Many states already prevent their existing citizens from forming political parties whose platform is inconsistent with national values. If we agree that, in principle, "peoples" have the right to control such subversion it seems a short step to allowing them to

---

[14] Walzer 2010, pp. 39–41.

deny membership to would-be citizens unwilling to profess at least broad support for national goals and values.

France, for example, has refused to naturalize Muslim residents who wear the *niqab* (which, to meet an Islamic expectation of modesty, covers the entire body except for the eyes), on the grounds that such garments are "incompatible with the essential values of the French community, particularly the equality of the sexes." In several books and articles, David Miller has defended the principle on which this policy may seem to be based, arguing that citizens have an important responsibility for preserving their distinctive national culture.[15] He is at least right that those denied membership on such grounds cannot reasonably complain that any of their basic human rights are violated by such exclusions. Exactly what our "human rights" *are* is of course controversial, but no plausible account would acknowledge a human right to be French or Dutch, or to be granted whichever citizenship one wishes.

Michael Blake has pressed a related point (though as we shall see, its implications are weaker than those drawn by proponents of the club analogy).[16] He notes that naturalizing citizens enter into a new legal relationship with existing members, such that the latter assume an obligation to protect their basic rights and secure them other basic public entitlements such as rights to legal representation, to vote or run for office, and some welfare benefits. Even if you have a (human) right, or (more simply still) even if it is highly desirable, that *someone* secure you these benefits, it does not follow that you are entitled to have them provided by the agency you prefer. Since existing members are being asked to assume responsibility for (and bear the costs of) providing these benefits to any new members they admit, they presumably have some right to refuse. Blake believes that a limited right to exclude can be derived on this basis.

These considerations are strong enough to neutralize another argument sometimes pressed by proponents of a permissive immigration regime, at least when it is advanced as grounds for granting migrants full membership on demand. Both in international law and as a matter of

---

[15] D. Miller 2005, 2016; for a different view about states' rights to condition membership, based on a quasi-Lockean notion of "associative ownership," see Pevnick 2014.

[16] Blake 2014.

common-sense justice, individuals have an unconditional right to *emigrate* from their current place of residence. The importance of this right is that it affords those menaced by injustice or oppression in their home countries a legal permission to escape. No state is, or should be, permitted to prevent those it abuses from leaving. Some suggest that this uncontroversial right of emigration entails a right to naturalize somewhere else. Since there are today no habitable regions not under the territorial control of some nation-state, one might think the right to emigrate is empty without a corresponding right of *immigration*. This argument probably works for the claims of refugees and asylum-seekers seeking stable residence, having been driven from their home countries by plagues, persecution, and strife. But, for the reasons given by Miller and Blake, it cannot justify automatic rights of membership. Having a right to marry does not automatically impose an obligation on anyone to marry you.[17]

However, while the idea that "peoples" can legitimately exclude immigrants from full civic membership seems reasonable enough in principle, it is doubtful that their discretion to do so is as wide as that enjoyed by clubs or private associations. Carens is right to note that the "deep tension between the right of freedom of association and the right to equal treatment" threatens any simple analogy between states and private organizations.[18] Peoples organized as nation-states may, as Miller argues, have a legitimate *interest* in preserving a distinctive national culture, but at the very least that interest competes with an arguably stronger expectation: that any genuinely *public* association must honor a principle of impartiality in its treatment of people with different characteristics.

So, while Eton or the Boy Scouts are certainly not obligated to accept girls, the idea that the electorate of a nation-state can be (as it once was) a male-only body offends the rudimentarily egalitarian principle that public association must be fully inclusive and not discriminate arbitrarily between people. In America today, even private employers may not discriminate against job candidates on the basis of national origin, so it is certainly not obvious that the USA can consistently deny citizenship to resident immigrants while granting it automatically to anyone born in its territories. After all, especially when they are long-term residents, one could

---

[17] For opposing views on this point, see Wellman and Cole 2011, pp. 197–203.
[18] Carens 1987, p. 267.

reasonably argue that noncitizens are just as entitled to a say in the demo-cratic process as anyone else likely to be significantly affected by legisla-tion enforced within a state's territory.

These points about equal treatment and democratic inclusion raise a more subtle issue. Consider again France's refusal to naturalize Muslims who insist on wearing the *niqab*. The French courts upheld that exclusion on the grounds that wearing the *niqab* conflicts with France's national commitment to full gender equality. Notice, however, that as stated that justification is importantly ambiguous: does it turn on the assertion that the commitment is part of France's national self-conception, or rather on the independent importance of a principle of gender equality? If the latter, it is not obvious that this case can be cited in support of Miller's claim that the preservation of distinctively *national* values is an acceptable reason to deny residents citizenship.

To be sure, one might argue (plausibly in my view), that the values of civic equality and democratic inclusion do not restrict, and may require, the freedom to wear clothes reflecting one's religious identity. On that argument, the French interpretation of civic equality is itself defective. Regardless of how that issue is decided, however, it is clear that this case is not dispositive of Miller's claim that "peoples" may condition civic membership on claims about the preservation of national culture. The real issue may be how we should interpret a universal principle of equal treatment. Carens has argued very powerfully that once the issue is viewed from this angle, there is a very strong presumption in favor of naturalizing all long-term residents, even when borders are not fully open, and even if those seeking citizenship originally entered the country illegally.[19]

What of Blake's view that a right to exclude can be derived from the circumstance that in enrolling new members, a "people" takes on a new responsibility to secure the newcomers' civic interests which it is entitled to refuse? As Blake acknowledges, this line cannot justify the right to exclude residents from citizenship currently claimed by nation-states, and leaves us well short of Miller's or Walzer's view. However, while Blake's argu-ment provides the most promising basis for a right to exclude residents from citizenship, whether it identifies a stable middle position between

---

[19] Carens 2015.

Miller's more restrictive nationalism and Carens's more permissive cosmopolitanism is unclear.

Blake implicitly assumes that a "people" will exercise its "right to refuse" citizenship when it is somehow reluctant that certain newcomers join it in the project of collective self-determination. But that reluctance might reflect different sorts of concerns on the part of existing citizens. Sometimes, it may be based on their perception of some disqualifying cultural difference. However, if Blake's "right to refuse" protects reluctance of that kind, his view becomes equivalent to that of Miller and Walzer, which he claims to reject. So, to be distinctive, Blake's argument must protect only reluctance of some other kind – presumably a reasonable fear that taking on new members will impose a burden or net cost on a society.

Yet, are such fears usually reasonable? Many affluent states today are having trouble *sustaining* their population levels; as their birth rate declines, meeting (especially) the health-care needs of their aging populations has become increasingly challenging. One might think, therefore, that adding new members, especially if they are younger and economically successful, far from being a burden, will bring net benefits. New members are not necessarily charges on the public fisc or on society more generally. To the contrary, they may inject new dynamism into the economy, help increase tax revenues, and also contribute in desirable ways to the diversity and pluralism of civil society and public life. In any case, we presumably do not want to suggest that countries in which citizenship is granted automatically at birth are justified in limiting the number of babies born to those populations within its territories statistically more likely to commit costly crimes or to place a greater burden on the existing public welfare system.

Furthermore, excluding new members may itself impose costs on existing citizens resident in a territory. If a company, sports team, or university wishes to hire people with special skills or expertise from overseas, and they will come only if they can obtain full citizenship, denying them naturalization limits the freedom of such organizations and will sometimes be costly to them. Why then should the reluctance of the "people" to naturalize certain aliens trump such voluntary, mutually advantageous cooperation across borders? Locke and the social-contract tradition insisted that the state (and the "people" it represents) cannot acquire any rights stronger than those enjoyed by individuals in a "state of nature." Would I, in such a state of nature, have a right to prevent a local organization from employing someone from far away if both parties are agreeable? If not, one might wonder how any nation-state could acquire the right to do so. Indeed, one could argue, on these grounds, that in hiring people from abroad and bringing new employees into a territory, private companies impose an obligation on their societies to naturalize them.

Exclusion from Territory

Most value freedom of movement, and some think of it as a human right. We have seen that, even if it is such a right, it does not plausibly require naturalization upon demand. Still, one might think that there remains a presumption in favor of the freedom (at least) to enter foreign territory and (more strongly) to settle and pursue one's livelihood with the willing cooperation of existing legal residents (professional colleagues, friends and relations, members of other private associations) even if one is not accorded full membership rights. How far does that presumption extend?

Consider first two relatively uncontroversial ways of defeating that presumption. First, there is in principle some finite limit on how large a population a given territory can support. If patterns of immigration are pushing a society toward that limit, refusing new admissions is surely allowable. Second, when particular individuals or groups are traveling to a foreign country with clear intent to do harm or commit a crime, the state surely has a right to exclude them.

Neither of these considerations, however, tells strongly against "open borders," at least under current circumstances. The affluent Western countries are today far from demographic saturation, and (as noted earlier), their birth rates are generally declining. So it is hard to believe that worries about overpopulation have much contemporary relevance.

The right of states to deny access to those intending harm also makes few inroads into an "open borders" position. For one thing, that right cannot plausibly extend beyond cases in which the evidence of danger is clear and reliable. Vague or unverified suspicions, the profiling of migrants based on ethnic, religious, or national background, etc. cannot reasonably trigger exclusion. Acting on them would restrict the freedoms of too many innocent individuals without an adequate reason and violate the principle of impartial treatment mentioned earlier. More generally, the right to exclude migrants on these grounds seems to be a special case of an uncontroversial domestic restriction on free movement. Even within a state's territory, the police may apprehend and detain those they reasonably believe are intending to injure others. Although the means of prevention available in the two cases may look very different, the basis for the underlying right to deploy them is the same. Clearly, this will not help the conclusion that international borders have any special significance.

Turning to the opposite end of the spectrum, I take it that the presumption in favor of free movement becomes virtually insurmountable in the case of refugees displaced by war, persecution, and natural disasters. To be sure, there is room for debate about how the burden of accepting refugees should be fairly divided among those states in a position to accommodate them. One might also wonder how bad the domestic predicament of those who go in search of asylum has to be to trigger rights to settle elsewhere. Few would say that simply facing unjust, yet quite systematic discrimination in the workplace, or even routine police abuse, are enough to impose an obligation on another country to let victims move to their territory. By that standard, countries with a better record of combatting racism (Scandinavia? contemporary South Africa?) might today be obligated to accept those African Americans living in the USA who daily confront policing and a criminal justice system that notoriously treats them far more harshly than members of the white population for no good reason.

These complications aside, however, the international community is surely obligated to find safe, stable residency for anyone fleeing clearly intolerable conditions in their home countries. When people are being buried alive in their own homes as warring parties shell each other, or face beheadings at the hands of theocratic zealots, there are no philosophically interesting reasons against helping them re-establish their lives in a place of relative safety. Viewed in this light, the callous and often xenophobic response of Western states to the recent influx of refugees from Syria and other war-torn areas of the Middle East has been a disgrace. Many of these refugees are in a situation comparable to that of a new-born baby reluctantly abandoned by its mother because she cannot look after it. Often enough, after all, the refugees *are* babies, whose parents have made the fateful decision to seek asylum elsewhere precisely in order to save their children's lives. But even when they are adults, such refugees are new arrivals hardly less vulnerable and helpless. Many arrive at the border penniless, exhausted, and sick, lacking the means to support themselves.

Does anyone think that when a jogger on her morning run discovers such a baby abandoned in the bushes, the authorities may simply let it die and refuse to accept any responsibility for looking after it? Presumably not. Yet that is not very different from what Western states do today when they turn away boats overloaded with starving refugees as they near their coasts.

What about migrants with less pressing reasons to access foreign territory? David Miller grants that genuine refugees may not be legitimately excluded from territory (at least subject to some reasonable arrangement for sharing out the burden of assuming responsibility for resettling them across receiving states). However, he thinks that the responsibility for preserving the distinctiveness of national culture may justify a right to exclude. Yet, as Blake correctly notes,[20] cities and regions also have a legitimate interest in maintaining their cultural distinctiveness, but few would say that this justifies them in denying visitors access, or that doing so is necessary to maintain it. Most, after all, retain their unique character in any case. People have been free to move between Edinburgh, London, and Barcelona for a very long time, but the three cities remain very different. So why should it be any different with states? Have Germany, Italy, and Spain lost their distinctive cultural complexion since the EU instituted free movement across member states?

Miller offers two other grounds for thinking that states enjoy wide discretion to exclude migrants from their territory. First, he suggests that once we realize "how hedged about with qualifications the existing right of free movement in liberal societies actually is," we must grant that that right is far from absolute:

> I cannot, in general, move to places that other people's bodies now occupy (I cannot just push them aside). I cannot move on to private property without the consent of its owner, except perhaps in emergencies … and since most land is privately owned, this means that a large proportion of physical space does not fall within the ambit of a *right* to free movement. Even access to public space is heavily regulated: there are traffic laws that tell me where and at what speed I may drive my car, parks have opening and closing hours, the police can control my movements up and down the streets, and so forth.[21]

---

[20] Blake 2014, pp. 527–9.
[21] D. Miller 2005, p. 195.

Miller seems to think that once we take these restrictions seriously, any presumption against restricting territorial access to migrants can be easily overcome.

Second, having interpreted the presumption in favor of free movement as a claim about a "human right," he goes on to argue that it could qualify as such a right only insofar as it protects very general and basic human interests, not highly specific, idiosyncratic preferences "like my interest in having an Aston Martin." On Miller's account, the value of free movement entitles agents only to *adequate* opportunities for meeting their basic interests. If so, it can confer on agents a right to access to other territories only when their current state is failing to secure those basic interests. As he puts it:

> A person can legitimately demand access to ... an *adequate* range of options to choose between – a reasonable choice of occupation, religion, cultural activities, marriage partners, and so forth. Adequacy here is defined in terms of generic human interests rather than in terms of the interests of any one person in particular – so, for example, a would-be opera singer living in a society which provides for various forms of musical expression, but not for opera, can have an adequate range of options ... even though the option she most prefers is not available.[22]

Miller concedes that it will be "frustrating" for his opera singer to be excluded from countries with more opportunities for her to pursue her operatic talent. But he denies that this interest is sufficiently basic or general to obligate such a country to let her enter and settle in its territory as a matter of right. Accordingly, he concludes that "insofar as all contemporary states are able to provide such an adequate range internally, people do not have a basic interest of the kind that would be required to ground a human right" to free movement.[23]

Miller overestimates the power of these considerations to justify any robust right to exclude foreigners from a state's territories. The first is beside the point. It merely reminds us that the internal free movement we take for granted within state borders is subject to various uncontroversial constraints (prohibitions on trespass, a right not to be shoved off

[22] D. Miller 2005, p. 196.
[23] D. Miller 2005, p. 196.

physical space one legitimately occupies, speed limits, etc.). This consideration would be relevant only if migrants requesting entry to a nation's territory are necessarily demanding greater free movement than current law-abiding residents possess. But why should we believe that? Migrants seeking territorial access are generally not demanding the right to break speed limits, visit national parks when they are closed for winter, or trespass on anyone's property once they are in: they are asking only for the same access privileges and immunities enjoyed by current residents, no more and no less. Given the same willingness to abide by the local rules, why treat current residents and would-be migrants differently?

Miller might respond that they are *also* demanding the right to cross an international border and therefore that they *are* asking for greater freedom of movement than current residents. One problem with this response is that it depends on empirical assumptions that need not hold: though unlikely, it is at least *possible* that the citizens of the state you seek to enter are not barred from overseas territory even as they deny you and others access to theirs.

The more serious problem is that it begs the question. Miller may be correct that restricting entry to national territory is of a piece with imposing internal rules against trespass or speeding. But that is the very point disputed by proponents of open borders. Their claim is that, at least with regard to territorial access, there is no relevant difference between

- moving 2 miles from Niagara Falls, Canada, to Niagara Falls, USA

and

- moving 5,000 miles from Honolulu to New York.

To answer that claim, Miller must highlight relevant differences that would justify access restrictions in one case but not the other. Simply pointing out that Hawaii, Ontario, and New York State restrict freedom of movement by (e.g.) imposing their own speed limits does little to reveal such differences. It remains to show, then, that Canadians in Niagara Falls should enjoy greater discretion to exclude some Americans just over the river than New York State currently does to exclude Hawaiians from its territory.

Freedom of movement in Miller's sense is also often quite legitimately restricted by formal and informal kinds of *rationing*. At peak periods, national parks or museums hosting world-famous artworks may face a problem of overcrowding. To allow hordes of campers, picnickers, and noisy tour groups to overrun areas whose natural beauty consists importantly in their emptiness and tranquility will transform and diminish their character. Similarly, it will be difficult for me to properly appreciate one of Rembrandt's very moving self-portraits if I am jostling with hundreds of other eager visitors as I approach the painting. Accordingly, in such cases access is formally rationed so as to preserve geographical character or reasonable conditions for aesthetic contemplation. However, informal rationing is also common. If there is a total solar eclipse at a particular place and time when I would like to visit, and all the hotels, trains, planes, etc. are either booked up or too expensive for me to afford, I may be unable to go when I want. Heathrow, with its paltry two runways, can also only take a certain number of incoming flights per day, again limiting *de facto* access to the UK to some degree.

These *de facto* restrictions on free movement, however, seriously threaten neither a right to, nor a strong presumption against, limiting free movement across borders. The National Park Service may legitimately ration access to the Grand Canyon, fearing overcrowding; the Louvre may similarly limit the number of daily entries to the museum; and you may not make it to London this year because all the flights to Heathrow are booked up. But none of this entails that the USA, France, or the UK have a presumptive right to deny anyone access to the world's geographical or cultural resources in their full richness. And states themselves could ration access to their land on these terms only when their territories are so overcrowded as to undermine the smooth running of daily routines. Overcrowding at that level is not a serious issue in any of the affluent Western states. Indeed, it mostly occurs in such societies today at bottlenecks created by the enforcement of border controls – such as the infamous "Calais Jungle" caused by Britain's strict policing of the Channel Tunnel.

These considerations also cast doubt on Miller's second argument, that agents have a right to freedom of movement only to the extent that their basic needs are unmet by their current states. One obvious problem is that it could easily justify objectionable *domestic* restrictions on free movement. Perhaps Miller's opera singer lives in Cumbria, and wishes to move to London to pursue an operatic career. But his argument would permit Greater London to exclude her from the city on the grounds that all her basic human needs are already met in Cumbria.

More generally, Miller's second argument tendentiously assumes that territorial access must be conceived as a "human right." But the proponent of "open borders" need not be asserting so strong a claim; she may simply be arguing that there is a presumption that anyone wishing to study at an overseas university prepared to admit them, participate in an archeological dig relevant to their research, visit people they love, or experience unique landscapes or cultures is free to do so. We can again apply the "Lockean" test mentioned in the previous section: is anyone permitted to bar someone from seeing the Grand Canyon, the Norwegian fjords, the *Pietà*, or the Sistine Chapel? May any individual prohibit others from hanging out with their grandchildren, studying with gurus or professors prepared to take them on, or exploring careers or professions unavailable in their current location? If not, the presumption goes the other way: in the absence of strong reasons to limit access, these natural, cultural, personal, and educational opportunities should be freely available to any citizen of the world.

10   Responsibility for the Environment

In the Qur'an, we find the following remarkable passages:

> Have those who disbelieved not considered that the heavens and the earth were a joined entity, and We separated them and made from water every living thing? Then will they not believe? (21:30)
>
> And We have made the heaven a roof, safe and well guarded. Yet they turn away from its signs. (21:32)
>
> [Allâh] has created the skies without the pillars that you may see. (31:10)
>
> [T]he water [rain] which Allâh sends down from the sky and makes the earth alive therewith after its death, and the moving [living] creatures of all kinds that He has scattered therein, and in the veering of winds and clouds which are held between the sky and the earth, are indeed Ayât [proofs, evidences, signs, etc.] for people of understanding. (2:164)
>
> [B]lessed is He to whom belongs the dominion of the heavens and the earth and whatever is between them. (43:85)

These passages depict Allâh creating a narrow band of living space – what we today refer to as the "biosphere" – between two environments hostile to human life: the solid rock of the Earth's crust and the vacuum of space. As the Qur'an implies, the biosphere is a common resource: no one owns it, and its benefits come like free gifts from a creator. Our physical survival and all human society depends on this protective canopy: it protects us from harmful radiation, supplies us with breathable air, keeps temperatures within a habitable range, provides us with flora and fauna that we need for nourishment, and secures resources available for economic exploitation.

Modern science has begun to demystify the invisible "pillars" that hold up the sky and supply us with the means of survival. We now understand weather

I wish to thank my former doctoral student Ross Mittiga, who works on climate ethics, for much help and insight that contributed to the writing of this chapter, and also Bob Amdur for several invaluable suggestions.

systems, the determinants of ground and sea temperature, ocean currents, and the chemical symbiosis between the atmosphere and vegetation better than ever before. However, our deepening insight into these mechanisms has brought a loss of innocence, and scientists have become increasingly concerned that our exploitation of the environment is overextending the biosphere. Two claims now command wide support among climatologists:

- the climate of the earth is changing in ways that may threaten human civilization;
- these changes are to a large extent "anthropogenic," the result of the rapid industrialization of human societies over the past three centuries.

To date, modern commercial development has relied largely on fossil fuels (coal, oil, wood, etc.), whose combustion releases into the atmosphere various gases (especially carbon dioxide [CO_2]). These gases play a critical role in the so-called "greenhouse" effect, which captures the heat of the sun and warms the atmosphere. The greenhouse effect is not in itself a bad thing: to the contrary, it is an entirely natural process responsible for keeping global temperatures within a range that supports life – like one of Allâh's invisible pillars. However, the unprecedented economic growth that has occurred since the industrial revolution has greatly increased the levels of greenhouse gases entering the atmosphere. At the same time, economic development has caused large-scale deforestation, which matters because trees and other plants absorb CO_2 from the air through photosynthesis. The worry is that, as more CO_2 and other greenhouse gases are released to meet the economic demands of a rapidly increasing global population, and as natural carbon sinks like forests decline, the greenhouse effect will spiral out of control, causing a dangerous warming of the atmosphere.

The most recent (fifth) report of the Intergovernmental Panel on Climate Change (IPCC)[1] predicts that, if nothing is done to reduce greenhouse gas emissions, by 2100 global surface temperature is likely to increase by between 2.4 and 4.8 degrees Celsius. This (it projects) corresponds to a rise in mean sea levels of between 0.48 and 0.89 meters.[2] Apart from the

---

[1] www.ipcc.ch/report/ar5/syr/.

[2] Some believe that these estimates are too conservative. One recent National Oceanic and Atmospheric Administration (NOAA) report suggests that we might see as much as 2.5 meters of sea-level rise by 2100 in the USA (US Department of Commerce 2017). Another study (DeConto and Pollard 2016) suggests 2 meters (6.5 feet) of rise globally

obvious threat they pose to populations located in low-lying areas by the sea (e.g. countries like the Maldives, Bangladesh, the Netherlands, or cities like Venice, Jakarta, New Orleans, Miami, London, and New York), these changes are also likely to increase the occurrence and intensity of severe weather events (hurricanes, powerful storms, droughts, extreme precipitation and flooding, etc.), disrupt agriculture, food production and global trade, and promote diseases and pests.

Although some dismiss these projections as alarmist exaggerations (see below), few informed citizens are now unaware of, or indifferent to, these concerns about global warming. Many already see direct evidence of a warming climate. For example, inhabitants of mountainous regions have watched glaciers retreat dramatically over recent decades, and gardeners in the northern hemisphere have noticed that trees and flowers are now blooming earlier in the spring than they remember. As a result, the problem of climate change has emerged as a major political issue. What (if anything) do political philosophers have to contribute to the discussion?

The Place of Political Philosophy

Obviously, the verification of the sorts of claims about global warming made by the IPCC and other climate scientists falls beyond the competence of political philosophers – and certainly mine. It is equally clear, however, that climate change is a political problem in at least three ways. First, it raises the general question of how much authority scientific expertise should carry in political deliberation. I will touch on this question shortly, in a discussion of climate-change skepticism.

Second, like issues about global inequality, immigration, and the justifiability of war, the challenges posed by climate change are truly global in scope. Since attempts to address them will obviously require concerted international action, one might ask whether the institutional architecture of a global order separated into autonomous sovereign states affords an auspicious format for the requisite collective action. The recent history of

by 2100. Dale Jamieson notes that the last time atmospheric CO_2 concentrations were as high as they are at present, sea level was 60 to 80 feet above its current level (Jamieson 2014, p. 108). If that is true, however, one might ask why sea levels are, despite current CO_2 concentrations, so much lower now. I am grateful to Ross Mittiga for these references.

attempts to secure an international commitment to curbing the emission of greenhouse gases, like other efforts to secure global cooperation among states, is very disheartening. Many countries are reluctant to incur the significant costs of reducing their greenhouse gas emissions without assurances that others will accept their fair share of the burden. Since international agreements are typically not backed up by reliable enforce-ment mechanisms, such assurances are often elusive. At the least, strong leadership from the most powerful countries like the United States is required. Yet, for internal political reasons, the United States has vacillated over whether to join with others in committing itself to mitigation efforts. Meanwhile developing countries like India and China have been under-standably reluctant to sign on to agreements that would obstruct their efforts to follow the path of industrialization blazed by the developed countries in the nineteenth and twentieth centuries.

These considerations support pessimism about the capacity of our broadly Hobbesian world order, divided into independent sovereign states each dedicated to pursuing their own national interest as they see it, to implement effective climate change mitigation. Yet, attempting to recon-struct a more propitious scheme of cosmopolitan governance is no less daunting a task than addressing the challenges of climate change itself, and the prospects for any such comprehensive restructuring are obvi-ously remote. Commenting on the escalating Cold War in the 1960s the satirical songwriter Tom Lehrer quipped that people had begun to "feel like a Christian Scientist with appendicitis." Lehrer's remark is an equally apt characterization of contemporary anxiety about climate change, which is tinged with a strong sense of impotence and despair in the face of challenges to which current global institutions seem hopelessly ill-equipped to respond.

However, as it raises deep political questions about cosmopolitan governance that go far beyond the preservation of the environment, addressing this underlying concern about the limitations of the extant structure of global politics would take us too far afield from the focus of this chapter. I will therefore not comment further on it here except to make the following important point about one way in which some think these limitations might be rendered irrelevant. As we have seen, the main thrust of climate-change activism has been to urge governments to cooperate in mitigating suspected anthropogenic contributors to global warming, by systematically reducing their emissions of greenhouse gases, expanding carbon sinks such as rainforests, and investing in renewable forms of energy (solar, wind, tidal, etc.). There is, however, a possible alternative to this strategy of mitigation that might obviate such measures.

Some believe that techniques of "geo-engineering" might allow us to cool the climate without requiring a reduction in emissions. To illustrate, meteorologists have long suspected that large volcanic eruptions in the past have lowered global temperatures. Such volcanos release huge quantities of volcanic ash and droplets of sulfuric acid into the atmosphere, thereby causing more solar radiation to be reflected back out into space, resulting in significant cooling. For example, the so-called "year without a summer" in 1816, which resulted in crop failures and food shortages in Europe and elsewhere, was likely caused by the eruption of Mount Tambora in the Dutch East Indies the previous year. This was a massive volcanic event, the largest eruption in at least a millennium. Researchers have estimated that, perhaps in tandem with another large volcano in the Philippines in 1814, the Tambora eruption lowered average global temperatures by 0.4–0.7 degrees Celsius.[3] Accordingly, some suggest that we could mimic these cooling effects by spraying sulfur particles into the stratosphere.

A range of other geo-engineering ideas have been proposed, including the deployment of "carbon scrubbers" to trap CO_2 that can then be buried, fertilizing oceans with iron to stimulate photosynthesis in phyto-plankton, thereby increasing the absorption of CO_2, and enriching the soil with a fine-grained charcoal called "biochar," which increases fertility (and hence crop yields) while reducing emissions of nitrous oxide (a greenhouse gas).

If we pass a "tipping point" beyond which emissions reductions could no longer prevent dangerous warming, or if, as seems highly likely, the international community fails to reduce greenhouse gas emissions, the temptation to turn to one or other of these geo-engineering strategies will become irresistible. This is politically important because states or even private agencies might decide to deploy them unilaterally, independently of any international agreements. Whether such unilateral deployments could be prevented is unclear. Since these technologies are largely untried, and will certainly have unforeseen effects, the likelihood of their having adverse consequences for some local populations is high. This could easily

[3] Oppenheimer 2003; Stothers 1984.

spark political conflict. Efforts to address climate change may therefore not merely highlight the impotence of the international community, but also risk destabilizing it.[4]

One might think that, since the prospects for effective international cooperation are so dim, philosophical discussion of the issue is a waste of time. However, while it is difficult to imagine circumstances under which states as we know them suddenly acquire a magnanimous determination to cooperate in addressing global problems like climate change, that is hardly a reason for political philosophers to go on strike until states get their act together. We can still ask how we might best preserve the environment, given what we know about climate dynamics, and it is at least possible that clarifying this question might help foster international cooperation. No doubt some of the political foot-dragging is due to willful ignorance and the ruthless pursuit of narrow national agendas. Yet, as Hobbes saw (see Chapter 5, p. 93), the deepest obstacles to rational political cooperation are as much structural as motivational, and good will will not suffice to overcome them. As in his "state of nature," each interested party may have, and know that they have, unimpeachable motives but still lack sufficient assurance that others are similarly inclined because of the structural limitations of their situation. Under such circumstances, the problem is less a lack of good will than a systemic incapacity to act on it together.

trust is not a structural issue

In the case of climate change, such structural incapacity may often reflect not merely a lack of trust between states, but also the absence of any clear consensus about what, exactly, the problem of climate change *is*, and about which principles and values should guide our responses. Is it primarily a matter a of collective prudence, of staving off disaster? Or is it also, and more fundamentally, a principled issue about the just allocation of benefits and burdens? These are questions over which people may reasonably disagree even if they are determined to take the issue seriously. They bring us to the third way in which climate change is political: it is a context in which reasonable disagreements arise among citizens and public institutions who acknowledge that they are responsible for preserving the environment about how to understand and discharge that responsibility.

---

[4] For more on this, see Corner and Pidgeon 2010; Gardiner 2013; Preston 2014.

The Prudential Dilemma

To simplify our discussion of the issues arising at this third level, then, we can make the idealizing assumption that our arguments are addressed to states and citizens who are committed to taking the problem seriously and, though naturally partial to their own interests, are willing and able to appreciate the legitimate interests and standpoints of others. Under this assumption, states (and other parties) are not indifferent to the well-being of other populations, or to the claims of justice and fairness, and are willing to abide by reasonable norms of reciprocity. These idealizing assumptions are far weaker than those made by Rawls in his theory. For, as we saw in Chapter 8, and as will be discussed in greater detail in the two final chapters, Rawls's notion of "ideal theory" presumes circumstances, not only in which agents share a sense of justice, but also in which compliance is perfect and favorable historical circumstances prevail. These stronger conditions are unnecessary, and anyway misplaced, in this context. The question of how (and on what terms) to enforce international commitments to mitigate climate change is a central, not peripheral, issue in environmental policy. Yet, to ask this question is to presuppose, contrary to Rawls's full compliance condition, that states, corporations, and other actors will sometimes be noncompliant. Moreover, climate change is on the agenda at all only because of warnings of looming environmental dangers. Its deliberative context is therefore quite unlike that which stimulated Rawls's project. Rawls's theory did not aim to resolve a pressing, contingent policy problem, but to abstract from such particular challenges in order to describe and justify quite general desiderata for an ideally just political association.

In the first instance, then, the climate change issue stems from prudential, rather than principled, concerns: what steps should states take to ensure that any risks associated with global warming are minimized and a sustainable biosphere preserved? Yet considerations of justice presumably still impose constraints on the selection and pursuit of appropriate remedies. We could, after all, eliminate any threat of anthropogenic environmental disaster at one stroke by killing off the bulk of the human population, thereby shrinking the global economy. This would no doubt be effective, but plainly such an approach is beyond all possible justification. So bare effectiveness cannot be all that matters. The difficulties begin when all the policies that we deem likely to succeed will inflict greater or lesser, more or less grave, injustices. Should states then restrict themselves, on principle, to the alternatives that require as little injustice as possible? Or is the risk of dangerous climate change urgent enough to justify, under some conditions (which?), tolerating more than minimal injustice? We cannot resolve these difficult questions here,[5] but we can at least clarify how prudence and justice interact in the context of climate policy.

But why is justice relevant at all? Some might suspect that climate change is entirely a prudential issue, a matter of cost–benefit analysis alone, in which philosophizing about justice and fairness is a distraction. A proponent of this line could agree that the threat of dangerous global warming does not justify the genocidal policy described above, but maintain that this is not because of anything to do with justice, but simply because it imposes prohibitively costly harm and suffering. And, to the extent that the risk of climate change constitutes a public policy emergency, they might argue that, just as we are prepared to suspend ordinary ethical expectations under conditions of imminent crisis, we should be willing to set aside such ideals until the danger has passed.

However, this line of thinking is implausible. Even under the direst IPCC scenarios, we are not currently in a climate emergency. Rather, we are in a situation in which there is a risk that a *future* emergency will develop; but no one is suggesting that it will materialize immediately. Our predicament with respect to global warming, then, is not akin to cases of imminent emergency (ticking time bomb scenarios, impending invasion, immediate social or political collapse) in which life-or-death decisions must be made rapidly and under highly pressured conditions.

A better analogy is provided by imagining a group of hikers who, as a result of bad weather, poor visibility, and a series of compounding navigational errors, have become lost in a vast and high mountain wilderness. Since they did not expect to be entering this region, they did not bring any maps covering it. Although they now have no idea where they are, and appreciate that they are in a potentially dangerous situation,

---

[5] These are the issues that the burgeoning literature on climate ethics addresses. For example, Caney 2005, 2009, 2010, 2014; Gardiner 2010, 2011; Jamieson 2014; Shue 2014.

they are not in immediate peril. They have enough food, clothing, fuel, and equipment to survive for some days. Suppose that some of the hikers are more experienced; not only do these more experienced members of the group have a rough memory of the topography of the area, they also have a deeper appreciation of the risks they face. They recognize the importance, for example, of not ascending to altitudes in which the weather will be worse, temperatures lower, and the air thinner, for this would cause them to tire more quickly and burn up their available fuel at a faster rate. They see clearly that theirs is a race against time: to be avoided at all costs is a situation in which they get too high and too cold, causing them to run out of fuel and provisions too quickly to keep hypothermia at bay.

Suppose that the hikers have spent the day ascending a valley that they hoped would lead to a pass allowing descent to safety on the other side. As they proceed, the gradient progressively steepens, visibility becomes minimal, and they cross the snow line. The more experienced hikers become concerned that they are getting too high. They recall that some of the valleys in these mountains lead not to watersheds permitting descent on the far side, but to a featureless, glaciated, high-altitude plateau. With the clouds down and night drawing on, they have no idea how far away the summit of the pass lies. Given these uncertainties, the experienced hikers argue that the safer option is to retrace their steps. Descending to warmer altitudes, they point out, will allow them to conserve their resources, regroup, and consider alternative escape routes. Some of the hikers reject this advice. To their more experienced colleagues they say: "Look, we've already spent a whole day advancing up the valley; the top cannot be too far away; why waste the energy we've already spent on getting this far? You're just being paranoid: we should stay the course." The hikers thus find themselves divided over the wisest course of action.

This scenario highlights some salient features of our current position with respect to climate change. Like us, the hikers are not in *imminent* danger, but, as the more experienced members of the group recognize, they have good reasons to believe that some present choices are prohibitively risky and to adopt a precautionary, safety-first, approach. And, as with the squabbling hikers, some today insist that climate experts are greatly exaggerating the real dangers of global warming.

The Place of Justice

The hikers' dilemma is essentially a prudential one; puzzles about distributive justice play no role in it. For this reason, their situation misses two important ways in which the parallel case of global warming does generate distributive concerns. The first can be appreciated by noting that in the hiker case, the costs and benefits of different courses of action will fall pretty evenly on each member of the party. If they decide to retreat, then all the hikers have wasted roughly similar effort climbing the valley; if they push on, then each assumes a similar risk of dying of hypothermia should the valley be one of those that leads, not to safety, but to the icy wastes of the plateau.

In the climate-change case, however, the costs and benefits of alternative policy responses are very unlikely to be spread so evenly among members *a)* of the global population. The rising sea levels, crop failures, economic disruption, more violent weather, and increase in disease predicted by the IPCC will almost certainly affect some areas of the earth more severely than others. The poor and economically disadvantaged are likely to be hit harder, both by climate change in the future, and by policies adopted now intended to mitigate or adapt to likely global warming.

Second, the hiker case lacks any significant intergenerational compo- *b)* nent, yet this is central to the questions raised by global warming. The developed countries of the West had the luxury of industrializing at a time when the vulnerability of the biosphere to the burning of fossil fuels was not recognized. Yet the resulting anthropogenic global warming has imposed a cost on subsequent generations. Even if one cannot reasonably accuse them of having acted recklessly or negligently, given their ignorance of the problem, one could still argue that, in virtue of the benefits they have reaped, they owe it to contemporary developing countries to shoulder *c)* more of the burden in helping them to industrialize in an environmentally responsible manner. And, of course, similar considerations apply to *our* relation to *future* generations. Whereas the hikers need only consider how their decisions will affect themselves, in thinking about climate policy, we have to consider risks and costs that will be borne by people who do not yet exist.

So, even if the problem of climate change is fundamentally a version of the prudential dilemma faced by the hikers, questions about justice and fairness are nonetheless integral to it. The hikers are responsible only for their own survival and can assume that the costs and risks associated with different choices fall uniformly among them. Neither of these simplifying assumptions holds in the context of climate change and it therefore raises both intragenerational and intergenerational questions of justice.

A third aspect of climate justice deserves mention even though (as we shall see) it turns out to be less salient than one might think. Consider the fuel, provisions, and equipment the hikers carry with them. These form a common fund of resources available to the hikers to meet their needs during their expedition. Since their carrying capacity is finite, these resources are limited, and so the hikers need to adopt rules governing their fair distribution. When they flout these rules and take more than their fair share, the culprits invite the indignation of their fellows. All of this is obvious, and it has nothing to do with the prudential dilemma created by their getting lost in the mountains. Similar expectations will apply even among hikers who know exactly where they are. The passages from the Qur'an quoted at the outset imply that the biosphere is also a common resource that serves vital human needs. In principle, then, rights to draw on the biospheric commons raise the same issues of fairness, although this has become obvious only recently, with the discovery that these resources are not, as had been previously assumed, effectively unlimited.

Should we think about climate justice along these lines? Citing Locke's famous proviso discussed in Chapter 6, Peter Singer invites us to

> [t]hink of the atmosphere as a giant global sink into which we can pour our waste gases. Then once we have used up the capacity of the atmosphere to absorb our gases without harmful consequences, it becomes impossible to justify our usage of this asset by the claim that we are leaving "enough and as good" for others. The atmosphere's capacity to absorb our gases has become a finite resource on which various parties have competing claims. The problem is to allocate those claims justly.[6]

Singer presumes, surely reasonably, that each person has "the same right to part of the global sink as everyone else." So, once we have determined how much overall emission the sink will tolerate, we can then calculate an equitable *per capita* share of annual carbon emissions. Using the target

[6] Singer 2004, p. 29.

adopted in the 1992 Kyoto Protocol, Singer suggests that each person on the planet is entitled to emit roughly 1 metric ton of carbon per year. In 2014, the World Bank estimated that the USA emits 16.5 metric tons of carbon per person and the UK 6, far above Singer's allowance. Accepting Singer's calculation for the sake of argument, his account implies that these (and doubtless other) countries have been, and are, effectively stealing from the commons on a fairly grand scale.

Singer's analysis elegantly captures one element of climate justice, but whether we should follow him in prioritizing culpability for unjust appropriations of common resources is doubtful. For it turns out that workable standards of culpability are very hard to specify in this context. We have already noted that, since in the past the industrializing nations were excusably ignorant about how burning of fossil fuels can damage the biosphere, we cannot easily accuse them of negligence or intentional wrongdoing. But there are further complications that apply even now, when agents can no longer plausibly maintain that they are unaware of the risks of high carbon emissions.

One is that it would be extremely disruptive to expect countries whose economies are habituated to high emissions levels to suddenly reduce them to levels that Singer's view would regard as legitimate. Singer suggests that emissions trading (which would allow countries to buy rights to exceed their carbon quotas) might address this problem without requiring wrenching structural adjustments to local economies.[7] However, buying the appropriate emissions rights will itself be disruptive, and politically very difficult to sell to affluent populations.

A still deeper problem concerns the difficulty of identifying relevantly culpable agents in the context of climate change.[8] In a simple case like that of the hikers, no such problems arise: if someone is stealing chocolate from their store of provisions, the culprit(s) must be one (or more) of the hikers, and it is not controversial that the discovery of a discarded chocolate wrapper in someone's backpack incriminates them. Singer's account, however, involves a statistical abstraction, pegged to total emissions by nation-states. It is not clear why we should assign national emissions totals

---

[7] Singer 2004, pp. 45–7.

[8] This is the problem that Gardiner calls the "fragmentation of agency" that arises in discussions of climate justice. See Gardiner 2011, ch. 1.

such significance. Perhaps corporations, economic sectors, or even individuals are more appropriate units of analysis. After all, we cannot infer from the fact that *per capita* US citizens emit 16.5 metric tons of carbon a year that each individual American is actually emitting this much. Some, like those who bike to work or rely on solar panels to power their homes, may emit little or nothing, while others, like those who drive SUVs or use a personal jet, may emit far more than the average. Moreover, when differences between individual emissions levels are not due to their own choices, holding individuals responsible for them will seem unfair: it is hardly your fault if you must drive to work because your city has lousy public transport; some jobs (e.g. trucking, bus-driving) make it very hard for employers to avoid causing high emissions (and why should they, rather than the companies or travelers who forgo cleaner forms of transportation, be primarily responsible?).

The intractability of these judgments about the improper appropriation of common environmental resources strengthens the case for adopting the different approach to climate justice already suggested, which focuses on the fair allocation of the burdens of any climate change mitigation or adaptation policies we choose to implement. These two approaches easily blur into each other in practice, but they are in principle distinct. The contrast corresponds to the distinction I drew in Chapter 7 between "remedy-responsibility" and "blame-responsibility." Singer's approach emphasizes the allocation of blame for appropriating more than one's fair share of common environmental resources (whether now, in the past, or in the future). The alternative view recommended here (and largely adopted by recent philosophers of climate change) would instead proceed by first determining, on prudential grounds, what needs to be done to prevent global warming from becoming dangerous and then fairly allocating the likely burdens and benefits of preventive policies. It therefore regards climate justice fundamentally as a matter of equitably assuming a remedy-responsibility, rather than of justly allocating blame for wrongful appropriation from the environmental commons. Apart from the problems about judging culpability involved in a blame-centered approach, the remedy-centered one seems anyway more appropriate because many think that the gravity of the threat posed by global warming makes the relevant "remedies" particularly urgent.

Structuring our thinking in this way need not preclude giving indirect weight to culpability for unjust national appropriations along the lines Singer canvasses. For example, such attributions may justify asking developed countries and their citizens to bear a greater share of the costs of mitigation than the globally disadvantaged. When we use (something like) Singer's account in this way, however, we are not fundamentally concerned with assigning blame for, and punishing, unjust exploitation of a common resource. We are simply using the likelihood of greater culpability to help identify those populations with weaker grounds for objecting to their shouldering a significant portion of the mitigation burden. One might think that the wealthy, or those who have benefited most from global commerce, should similarly bear most of the responsibility.[9] Certainly the liability of all of these groups would seem to be far greater than that of the global poor.

However we allocate these burdens, a more general implication of the approach recommended here deserves emphasis. Under that approach, the overall scale of the burden to be distributed – how much we need to sacrifice now – is hostage to judgments about how serious or urgent the problem of global warming will turn out to be. We can appreciate the importance of this point by noticing how it bears on the scale of our climate obligations to future generations. Since they stand to suffer most of the harms resulting from global warming, how much we owe them will obviously depend on how bad we think those harms will be. But it also depends on whether, and to what extent, policy-makers now should mark down future harms (and benefits) compared to the value they have today.

Economists and cost–benefit analysts invariably assume that we should discount future harms (and benefits) in this way. Moral philosophers, by contrast, often insist on "temporal neutrality," arguing that it is arbitrary

---

[9] For some of the challenges that attend bringing these various issues together, see Caney 2014. Much of the discussion in the literature has considered the advantages and disadvantages of three burden-distributing principles: Polluter Pays (i.e. those more culpable); Ability-to-Pay (i.e. the wealthier); Beneficiary Pays (i.e. those who have benefited most from industrialization based on fossil fuels). For discussion, see Caney 2010; Page 2011.

to privilege the well-being of any particular generation. As economist
Kenneth Arrow put it:

> Cost–benefit analysis is based on the equality of all individuals. Why does
> this not extend to the future? The fact that an individual will be alive at
> some future time instead of today does not seem to be a morally-relevant
> distinction. Hence, so it is argued, proper social policies, such as abatement
> of carbon dioxide emission to reduce the burden of climate change on
> the future, should be chosen to treat future generations equally with the
> present. This position implies that the rate of discount or, more precisely,
> the rate of pure time preference should be zero.[10]

Arrow goes on to reject this view, and to affirm the standard economist's
assumption that we should discount the future at some positive rate.
However, he acknowledges that decisions about what discount rate to adopt
are not narrowly technical or actuarial, but turn on substantive ethical
judgments suited to the particulars of the policy context under discussion.

The case of climate change, however, displays some rather special
features, notably the possibility of environmental "tipping points" beyond
which more or less serious degradation of the biosphere becomes irreversible. This feature makes it almost impossible to divorce the justification of
a discount rate appropriate for the case of climate justice from judgments
about how bad things may get for future victims of global warming. This
has led some to contemplate adopting a negative discount rate (under
which we should weigh future welfare *more* heavily than present welfare).[11]
One (though not the only) way to put the argument is this: since the future
generations who primarily matter for climate change may preside over an
environmental collapse, they will live at a pivotal point in human history
and have to manage a truly catastrophic situation. We cannot therefore
think of them as a generation just like any other, and apply a principle of
temporal neutrality. Nor should we *discount* their welfare. We should instead
give their welfare extra weight in virtue of the unique, do-or-die, world-
historical predicament they may face. This is obviously a controversial
position, but it underlines how, on the approach recommended here, intelligent thinking about climate justice now must be informed by judgments
about how dangerous global warming really is. As with the hikers, however, many today suspect that these dangers are being overblown.

[10] Arrow 1999, pp. 89–90.
[11] Fleurbaey and Zuber 2013; Litterman 2013; Mittiga 2018.

Climate Change Skepticism

In a 2003 speech in the US Congress, Republican Senator James Inhofe said: "Wake up, America. With all the hysteria, all the fear, all the phony science, could it be that manmade global warming is the greatest hoax ever perpetrated on the American people? I believe it is." Inhofe's skepticism about climate change is extreme, and his insinuation that climate scientists are willfully deceiving the public does not deserve serious consideration. Still, ordinary citizens can be forgiven for feeling unsure what to make of the dire warnings issued by the IPCC and other climate scientists. After all, they can rarely assess the evidence for themselves and recent political history provides a litany of cases in which expert predictions have been confounded by events. So it is hardly surprising that some greet confident predictions of coming environmental disaster with skepticism. There are at least three reasons to take such doubts about global warming seriously.

First, the immense complexity of the "biosphere" surely warrants an attitude of intellectual humility. The history of modern attempts to understand and master such vastly complex, nonlinear, systems is not encouraging – think, for example, of the failure of central economic planning in the Soviet bloc in the last century. Among other factors, the biosphere is affected by solar cycles, the chemistry of both air and sea, seismic activity, the dynamics of plant growth, meteorological conditions, to say nothing of the impact of human activities. Although the environmental sciences have made enormous strides, they remain in their infancy and our understanding of the relevant phenomena is still far from complete.

For example, we lack a settled theory of cloud formation, without which it is difficult to be sure how much solar radiation is likely to be reflected away from the atmosphere under different conditions. Moreover, we have gathered climate data systematically only within the past couple of centuries; our knowledge of the climate in earlier periods is therefore at best indirect and partial. Since claims about climate *change* presuppose comparisons with historical patterns, the incompleteness of our data about the past matters a lot. Even today, global temperature is hard to measure, because individual weather stations can be affected by local conditions (proximity to urbanized areas, for example). Many have also noted that temperature readings given by satellites diverge from measures taken on the ground. In the face of all this, one could reasonably think that it is mere hubris for climate scientists to claim with any confidence that they have already hit on a fully adequate synoptic model of the planetary climate system.

Second, modern history is replete with spectacular examples of scientists and technologists greatly overestimating the wisdom of their forecasts and prescriptions. Many confidently predicted that the so-called Y2K bug would bring critical computerized systems crashing down and precipitate a social and political crisis. In fact, the consequences were very mild. Conversely, the engineers who designed the *Titanic* believed it unsinkable. The pesticide DDT was touted by its developers as a safe way to kill mosquitoes and other pests, until its dangers (which almost caused the extinction of eagles and peregrine falcons in the United States) became clear. In 1968 Paul Ehrlich's book *The Population Bomb* prophesied an impending Malthusian crisis that would result in mass starvation in the 1970s and 1980s. Ehrlich approvingly cited one source saying "I don't see how India could possibly feed two hundred million more people by 1980."[12] By 2010, India's population was 2.1 billion and rates of poverty and malnutrition declined significantly during the intervening period. So, we have strong reasons to be cautious about the forecasts of experts.[13] As Matt Ridley has said, "There is no such thing as an expert on the future."[14]

Third, the emergence of consensus, even among highly intelligent people, sometimes exemplifies what William Whyte and Irving Janis (adapting Orwell's notion of "doublethink") called "groupthink":

> The main principle of groupthink ... is this: The more amiability and *esprit de corps* there is among the members of a policy-making ingroup, the greater the danger that independent critical thinking will be replaced by groupthink, which is likely to result in irrational and dehumanizing actions directed against outgroups.[15]

Groupthink is especially likely to develop when agents view themselves as crusading for something of fundamental or existential importance and

---

[12] Ehrlich 2007, pp. 39–40. I owe this example to Bob Amdur.
[13] For further reasons to be skeptical, see Tetlock 2017.
[14] Ridley 2016.
[15] Janis 1971, p. 43.

when support and funding for climate research comes from wealthy groups with vested interests, whether political, economic, or otherwise, in promoting it. Neither intellectuals nor those with resources to contribute to climate research are immune from the self-flattery that often accompanies the belief that they are saving the world. Environmentalist agitation often displays a messianic quality. Climate change skeptics regularly complain that they are vilified, reviled, and ostracized by those who accept orthodox views about global warming. Whatever the merits of the skeptics' position, I doubt that these reports of abuse are exaggerated.

Answering the Skeptics

Yet, while they show that we cannot simply dismiss climate change skepticism out of hand, these three points do not vindicate it. Nor do they support the claim that the matter is too uncertain to justify taking any action now. To begin, we should be careful to distinguish between the epistemic utility of challenging orthodoxy and the likelihood of any particular challenge being well founded. Climate change skeptics like Matt Ridley frequently defend their stance by claiming, correctly, that science crucially requires a critical attitude:

> We're told ... [by environmentalists] ... that it's impertinent to question "the science" and that we must think as we are told. But arguments from authority are the refuge of priests. Thomas Henry Huxley put it this way: "The improver of natural knowledge absolutely refuses to acknowledge authority, as such. For him, scepticism is the highest of duties; blind faith the one unpardonable sin." What keeps science honest, what stops it from succumbing entirely to confirmation bias, is that it is decentralized, allowing one lab to challenge another. That's how truth is arrived at in science ... by scientists disputing each other's theories.[16]

Fair enough, but nothing in this argument entails that those who challenge orthodoxy are more likely to be correct than those who defend it. As Mill saw, we need intelligent crackpots to keep the conventional wisdom on its toes, but the fact that they are vital solvents of mindless dogmatism neither confirms nor impugns their crackpot credentials. The plausibility

[16] Ridley 2016.

of their views must be decided independently of their value as a spur to critical reflection.

Several of the points above are, moreover, circumstantial and apply equally to positions taken by the skeptics. For example, the same skeptics who point out the uncertainty of judgment about complex systems rarely acknowledge that this proviso applies equally to their often very confident assertions that existing climate policies are doing more harm than good. Moreover, there is no reason to think that one side in the debate is more prone to groupthink than the other. The willful, self-congratulatory, "smarter-than-thou" contrarianism common among climate change skeptics can incubate groupthink just as effectively.

Similarly, the charge that climate scientists prostitute their intellectual judgment to the vested interests that fund them is offset by the consideration that researchers who dissent from the consensus about global warming often receive generous support from oil companies and others who stand to lose from mitigation efforts. It is anyway implausible to attribute the gathering consensus about climate trends and their causes *entirely* to groupthink and suspect motives. We have good reasons to worry that the increasing dependence of universities on private philanthropy threatens their intellectual independence, but the idea that the integrity of academic research has rusted away completely under the pressure of venal lobbying from outside is a fantasy.

Even more importantly, although the skeptics are right to push us to consider the important political, ethical, and economic trade-offs climate policy faces, such chiding does not show that giving these issues due consideration tends to support a wait-and-see approach. Taking them seriously might strengthen, rather than weaken, the case for taking action now to preempt any dangers associated with climate change. Particularly worth emphasizing in this context is that we often advise action to protect people against certain dangers even when the probability of their occurring is quite low. Diseases like tetanus and diphtheria are today quite rare; yet we still vaccinate children against them because 5–10 percent of those who contract these diseases will die. Many smokers will not develop cancer despite the carcinogenic properties of tobacco tar but this does not make it rational for any particular smoker to stop trying to kick the habit. In these cases, what is mainly doing the work in dictating a rational stance is our confidence that certain outcomes are unambiguous evils. There is no upside to developing lockjaw or lung cancer, and this consideration seems sufficient to justify taking action to prevent them even if the odds of our contracting them are low.

Many intuitively think about the possibility of global warming in this precautionary way, and, whatever the skeptics say, it is not clear that this intuitive approach is unreasonable.[17] Albeit at a high level of generality, we have a reasonably unambiguous picture of what environmental disaster might look like, and some real-world cases for archetypes. For example, Easter Island once harbored an isolated civilization that became sufficiently sophisticated to build the enormous statues for which it is famous. When Dutch sailors discovered it in the early eighteenth century, however, they found a rump of around 3,000 islanders living in squalor and locked in endemic and often violent conflict over scarce resources. This created a puzzle: barely clinging on, the Easter Islanders were clearly no longer capable of the elaborate public works projects of their forebears (erecting 14-ton monoliths without electricity, steam power, etc. is no easy task). What happened to them? It is now believed that Easter Island suffered an environmental disaster resulting from its inhabitants' excessive reliance on wood for the technology to build the statues and maintain other practices integral to their culture. This led earlier generations of islanders to an unsustainable deforestation of the island, condemning their descendants to "nasty and brutish" Hobbesian conditions.

Closer to home, we now know that a major cause of the American "dust bowl" of the 1930s was the excessive exploitation of the prairies of the Midwest in prior decades. Unlike the grassland they replaced, the new wheatfields that were planted during the rush to develop the prairies could not anchor the topsoil in times of drought. As a result, when the winds came, they whipped up enormous dust-storms. This destroyed farming in the region, ruined many families and businesses, promoted often deadly respiratory diseases, temporarily transformed the Great Plains into arid deserts, and led to an exodus of refugees from the affected regions unparalleled in American history.

We know, then, that uncoordinated human activity can sometimes precipitate environmentally unsustainable outcomes.[18] Social scientists have

[17] For a good philosophical account of the "precautionary principle," see Gardiner 2006.
[18] For other cases of collapse, environmental and otherwise, see Tainter 2011.

even baptized this general phenomenon, calling it the "tragedy of the commons." Such "tragedies" develop whenever the action of independent agents, though rational from their own point of view, produces outcomes in which a common resource is depleted or destroyed. Overfishing or the excessive prescription of antibiotic medications, which many fear will render them ineffective by allowing bacteria to develop resistance, provide key examples. Like diseases or natural disasters, tragedies of the commons are unambiguous evils: they are indeed *tragic*. Even if the probability of such tragedies occurring is quite low, it still seems folly not to take preemptive action to prevent them where we can.

These considerations cast doubt on the practical force of climate change skepticism. Certainly, the predictive accuracy or certainty of the projections made by the IPCC can be questioned. Yet, how much certainty do we need for precautionary action to be warranted? If it is rational to vaccinate children against a disease that they have a less than 1 percent chance of contracting but that will kill 10 percent of those who get it (roughly the numbers for diphtheria), then the answer seems to be: not much. Taking the immunization example as a guide, we should be prepared to "vaccinate" society against climate change that causes 10 percent of the global population to experience an Easter Island-type environmental disaster even if there is only a 1 percent chance of its occurring. This implies that the burden of proof lies with the skeptics to explain why their doubts about the accuracy and reliability of mainstream climate science should dislodge a safety-first stance. The threshold for reasonable precautionary action is far lower than it would need to be for a "wait-and-see" approach to be defensible.

A further implication of this line of argument is worth noting. Much of the controversy engaged by the climate change skeptics has focused on the question of whether and how current global warming is anthropogenic; hence skeptics often seize on arguments canvassing alternative explanations for observed climate change (e.g. those who claim that the recent warming of the atmosphere is better accounted for by variation in solar activity than by the burning of fossil fuels over the past 200 years). But once we see that the case is similar to those involving evils of entirely natural origin (like diseases and tsunamis), the relevance of any distinctively anthropogenic component becomes less clear.

Suppose, for example, we had good reasons to believe that imminent volcanic activity will almost certainly produce very dramatic global warming, and that preventing or mitigating it would require more or less the same policies as are today advocated to address the effects of anthropogenic climate change. Does the fact that the problem here is nonanthropogenic significantly weaken the case for taking action? It is hard to see why: we do not think that Japan has less reason to invest in sea defenses and an elaborate warning system just because tsunamis are not usually caused by human action. The reasonableness of these precautions derives from two factors alone: on the one hand, the uncontroversially hazardous character of tsunamis, and on the other, the availability of measures that provide a realistic hope of protection. If this is right, the authority of climate science in this context turns not on its ability to verify that human activity is implicated in causing harmful climate change, but rather on its capacity to reliably prescribe policies likely to prevent or mitigate its dangers, regardless of its causal genesis. The independence of these considerations is disguised in the climate debate because it turns out that in this case our best understanding of effective remedies is closely connected to a diagnosis of what is in fact causing climate change. But this connection is contingent, as can be seen by numerous medical examples in which the fact that certain treatments are effective (e.g. chemotherapy) tells us nothing about the underlying causes of the diseases being treated (e.g. genetic mutation).

To be sure, the extent to which current global warming is anthropogenic matters for judgments about how far the developed countries are culpable for harming current and future generations. But as we have seen, determining culpability for global warming is at best a secondary aspect of climate justice. The overriding issue is how to justly allocate the burdens of climate change mitigation and adaptation. Since this forward-looking orientation is primary, the significance of debates about how far global warming is anthropogenic may have been exaggerated by the skeptics.

How Bad Will It Be?

I have so far assumed, in relation to the dangers of global warming, that the costs and risks of mitigation and adaptation policies are comparable to those involved in immunization. Some may find this assumption implausible. While administering vaccines carries few costs and risks, mitigation and adaptation policies for climate change may impose considerable costs and risk of harm on current and future populations.[19] How should we judge the gravity of the dangers of global warming in relation to the possible harms resulting from implementing various mitigation measures?

It is tempting to assume that good answers to this question require only careful cost–benefit analyses (CBA) informed by empirically well-grounded accounts of the nature and likelihood of dangerous climate outcomes. Certainly, the better the empirical analysis, the more credible our estimates of the likely costs and benefits will be. However, CBA works best in highly specific contexts of choice with relatively short time horizons (e.g. should we locate the power station here or there? Are the upfront costs of transitioning to this technology justified by foreseeable scale of benefits in the short to medium-term?). But climate change is a much more indefinite problem, involving immensely complex, multi-variate, and non-linear systems, with very long time horizons. Whether fine-grained CBAs can really be dispositive under these conditions is open to doubt.

It does not follow, however, that the issue is too uncertain for intelligent judgments to be made. We need not throw up our hands or say that we might as well toss a coin. For in fact we make judgments under these conditions of uncertainty all the time and yet think it would be irresponsible to resort to a coin toss. Suppose a champion long-jumper about to compete in the Olympics is invited on a hiking trip to a rocky, mountainous, region. She politely declines: "Thanks, but I cannot afford a sprained ankle right before the Olympics." Most would say her decision is sound and sensible, but this cannot be because she has performed a rigorous CBA. In truth, neither she nor anyone else has any fine-grained insight into the risks associated with her choice. Though we cannot know this, it may in fact be certain that, if she stays home, she will slip on her stairs or suffer a car accident. Even though these would put her ability to compete in the Olympics in even greater jeopardy, we remain confident that tossing a coin would be an irresponsible way to decide whether she should join the hikers.

What accounts for this confidence? The answer, I think, is that intelligent day-to-day practical decision-making relies on various simplifying archetypes and heuristics to clarify our choices. These are drawn, on the one hand, from our ordinary notions of prudence and, on the other, from schematic models of people's particular goals and commitments. These

[19] See Lomborg 2001; Sunstein 2006.

rough working schemas tell us, for example, that a shattered tibia is a more devastating injury for a long-jumper than a concert pianist. Such judgments presuppose background, non-empirical assumptions about an agent's reasonable ends and commitments, in the light of which we can intelligently classify some outcomes as disastrous, propitious, or ambivalent. So, in thinking about how bad global warming might be, informal philosophical reflection on how seriously it threatens the legitimate goals and aspirations of civilized human existence may provide some guidance when calculations of long-term costs and benefits are very uncertain.

The developing philosophical literature on physical disability (blindness, paralysis, chronic pain, etc.) provides an unexpected source of insight here. Some theorists resist the claim that even serious physical disability must be considered bad. Elizabeth Barnes has argued, for example, that one's being physically disabled need not detract from the quality of one's life. Obviously, no one thinks that being disabled is, to use her terminology, "good *simpliciter*" in the way that love, joy, or profoundly moving aesthetic experiences automatically "enrich your life," such that "you'd be missing something if you didn't have them." But Barnes points out that it does not follow that disability must therefore be "bad *simpliciter*." We should instead see it as "neutral *simpliciter*," like having red hair. Something is "neutral *simpliciter*" in her sense if it lacks any inherent tendency to enhance or detract from one's well-being. This does not mean that there are no circumstances under which being disabled (or having red hair) will have a net negative or positive effect on someone's well-being. Under some conditions (widespread prejudice and hatred against red-haired people) being born with red hair might be a net bad for redheads. But unlike (say), suffering rape or torture, disability need not always mar a person's life.[20]

Barnes's view about the status of physical disability is controversial, but her philosophical distinction between something's being good, bad, and neutral *simpliciter* provides valuable perspective on how we should view the dangers of climate change. Suppose we distinguish between five possible outcomes of global warming, in decreasing order of severity:

(1) *Apocalypse*. Global warming becomes exponential: for example, as the Siberian permafrost eventually melts away, vast quantities of latent

---

[20] Barnes 2016, pp. 84–8.

methane are released, with the result that the Earth develops an unin-
habitable atmosphere like that on Venus (where average surface temperature is around 460 degrees Celsius, hot enough to melt lead).

(2) *Civilizational disintegration.* The Earth suffers a global equivalent of the
Easter Island collapse; human beings survive, but their overexploitation
of the biosphere knocks them back to a pre-civilizational, hunter-
gatherer mode of existence.

(3) *Compromised civilization.* Civilization continues, but only in regional
pockets excluding the majority of the human population.

(4) *Severe but localized disruption.* Many areas are largely unaffected but
others face catastrophic changes. For example, low-lying regions (the
Netherlands, the Maldives, Bangladesh) are inundated; or the Gulf
Stream shuts down as melting ice from the Arctic spreads south,
undermining the temperate climate of Western Europe and cooling it
drastically.

(5) *Systematic but moderate environmental degradation.* The global climate
changes in ways that adversely affect health and life expectancy,
increase exposure to dangerous weather, inflate pollution levels, etc.
However, civilized coexistence is not seriously undermined.

This is a rough-and-ready list, and one could easily specify finer-grained
distinctions between these bands. But it gives us enough to at least provi-
sionally see how applying Barnes's categories to the case of climate change
might work out.

(1)–(3) seem good candidates for outcomes that are bad *simpliciter*. At
least from a human point of view, each involves the absence, termination,
or radical curtailment of something inherently valuable. (5) provides
a reasonably clear case of an outcome that is neutral *simpliciter*. To be
sure, under (5) many, perhaps most, people will fare less well overall
than they do currently but not necessarily in ways that preclude them
living a basically decent life. What about (4), which is perhaps the most
likely actual outcome?[21] Whether we should regard it as neutral or bad
simpliciter is not immediately obvious, but exploring this and adjacent
questions about the status of outcomes (1)–(5) may open a fruitful line of
future inquiry.

---

[21] See on this Boisvert 2018.

Among other factors, those inclined to pursue them further would have to consider the possibility that, as long as they are not manifestly insuperable, the challenges and hardships created under (4) form valuable opportunities for human beings to display ingenuity in solving problems, providing mutual aid and adapting to new circumstances. Insofar as they do so, the case for viewing (4) as "neutral" rather than "bad *simpliciter*" will strengthen.

Moreover, whether (4) should be considered neutral or worse will partly depend on how much disruption should be considered "normal" (as opposed to "severe") given the basic parameters of life on Earth. Here, historical perspective is more informative than CBA. The threat of severe disruption has always been a part of human experience, and one must remember that it is only quite recently that large sections of the human population have been spared the scourges of famine, diseases like smallpox and polio, surgery without anesthetic, high infant mortality, illiteracy, slavery, etc. In many parts of the world, these problems persist even today. Depending on how one defines "civilization," then, some might argue that (4), or even (3), describe the normal state of play prevailing throughout the bulk of human history, including today. If so, (4) (and also (5)) might not be relevantly different from the rest of human history. To be sure, the "severe" disruption caused by global warming might, under (4), take a predominantly climate-related form, but what is fundamentally at stake in these discussions is the gravity, not the character, of likely future dangers.

A more general point about outcomes (1)–(5) is that, while climate change may well bring about one or other of these outcomes, it is certainly not the only live risk factor for them, nor the only anthropogenic one. Consider, for example: the independent threat of global pandemics (recall that the 1918 Spanish flu killed between 3 and 5 percent of the world's population); our ongoing investment in thermonuclear, biological, and chemical "weapons of mass destruction"; the consequences of population growth; human propensities toward violence and aggression (the combined death toll of the two World Wars was upward of 100 million people); or the effects of political authoritarianism, religious dogmatism and intolerance, and genocidal hatred of those perceived to be different.

Do such considerations, after all, vindicate the intuition of some climate change skeptics that global warming is not an urgent enough problem to justify significant sacrifices now? This would follow only if the possibility

[margin, handwritten:] other risks to civilization

that, as the climate warms, we are transitioning between two states that are both "neutral *simpliciter*" implies that we should focus on other problems to the exclusion of any risks accompanying global warming. But this inference is invalid.

Being in a state in which your tetanus vaccine has not been updated in the last 12 years is not bad *simpliciter:* unlike (say) suffering abuse or torture, it does not inherently detract from your well-being. Nor is being fully vaccinated against tetanus good *simpliciter:* it does not inherently enhance your life. In deciding whether you should vaccinate yourself against tetanus, then, you are choosing between two states that are neutral *simpliciter.* Yet vaccination remains an advisable precaution; you are better off having the vaccine, all things considered, because contracting tetanus *is* bad *simpliciter.* This prudential judgment would become irrational only if, for contingent reasons, taking the vaccine poses a greater risk of an outcome that would be worse for you, all things considered (perhaps you have a potentially lethal allergy to the vaccine, for example).

Applying this logic to climate change implies that we should shelve mitigation policies only when adopting them itself carries risks comparable to your suffering a fatal allergic reaction to a tetanus vaccine. In other words, even if we are currently in a state exemplifying (4) or (5), and even if that state is neutral *simpliciter*, we should refrain from climate mitigation only if it carries a serious risk of moving us to (1)–(3). That strikes me, however, as quite unlikely.

Of course, if we are confident that the costs of reducing greenhouse gas emissions or investing massively in renewable energy will be very severe, particularly for the most disadvantaged, then the vaccine analogy loses its force, because vaccines are relatively inexpensive and so a good bet given the risks. As I have suggested, however, these judgments are *very* uncertain. Whether CBA can significantly reduce that uncertainty is far from clear, though here political philosophy ought to acknowledge its own limits: if anyone is competent to decide the matter, it is certainly not philosophers. Perhaps the best political philosophy can do is to remind us that, when others attempt to work out the costs and benefits, the already precarious conditions of the world's poor should weigh heavily in their calculations.

11 War

Admittedly, there is something futile, even ridiculous, about philosophers stepping forward to offer dispassionate critical judgments about the topic of war. For one thing, war is waged today by the colossus of the modern state, bristling with weapons and armaments, some of which now possess apocalyptic power. Philosophical analysis and argument can seem an absurdly mismatched David when pitted against this monstrous Goliath. For another, war is often waged under conditions of extreme stress. As such, it is both cause and symptom of some of the darkest human impulses – fear, violence, hatred, suspicion, and the desires to inflict harm, to humiliate, to terrorize, to destroy, or to avenge. These potent human motivations have little place in, and are alas rarely influenced by, intellectual reflection of any kind.

But to picture war as simply a mindless orgy of violence would also be misleading. Wars are fought for reasons, sometimes even for the sake of moral ideals, and not usually waged on impulse alone. They are often initiated as a result of cool strategic calculation on the part of statespeople who claim, quite conscientiously and dispassionately, to be duty bound to pursue the national interest. War is also an *institution* as much as a collective manifestation of personal aggression. Soldiers often recognize and abide by written and unwritten conventions and codes of conduct. War is conducted by complex organizations – the armed forces – structured by elaborate rules of authority and deference and characterized by a very distinctive professional ethos. For that reason among others, it is also a venue for the cultivation of certain virtues – those of courage, honor, selfless devotion to a cause, and loyalty, among others. War as we know it would be unthinkable without these elements of structure, ethos, and organization.

Indeed it is precisely because war presents itself as in these ways a rationally organized practice that it often seems especially horrifying. One thinks, for example, of the famous "Christmas Truce" that occurred sporadically but spontaneously in December 1914 along various stretches of the Western Front early in the First World War. For a brief period, soldiers from both sides stepped out of their roles and trenches to fraternize with their opponents. They sang carols, drank beer, and (reportedly) even played soccer in the "no man's land" between the lines. Many cite this as an inspiring story of hope and common humanity amidst the bleak reality of war. To my mind, however, the haunting image of these men saluting and bowing to each other before returning to the trenches, like players in a game, to continue the organized killing attests to a more depressing truth about the power of institutional expectations to overwhelm sane and decent human relations.

In any case, at least in principle, the institutionalized and organized nature of war makes it available for philosophical assessment. As with any other human institution, we can ask when (if ever) it might be justified, how it should be regulated and whether (and how) it might be eliminated. This chapter considers some of these questions, although we will be able only to scratch the surface of an inexhaustible topic.

Three Views

That war is an evil is not in dispute; the interesting question is what follows from this. Three broad lines of response have developed. The first claims that while war is presumptively bad, it may nevertheless be justified in certain circumstances. On this view, not all wars are unjust, and it falls to philosophers to explain the conditions under which fighting a war might be just rather than unjust. Those who take this view defend the theory of "just war."

The second response is a pacifist one. It claims that the evils of warfare are so grave as to be beyond any possible justification. The use of violence even to promote justice is, on this view, always a losing gambit. Thus many in the pacifist tradition argue, like Ghandi and Martin Luther King, that legitimate political action must be nonviolent. While they agree with the just war tradition that war is open to moral assessment, then, pacifists doubt that resorting to arms is just or justified under any conditions.

The third response claims that if war is an evil, it is an evil like disease and natural disaster, not subject to moral assessment as just or unjust. On this view, often termed "realist," the division of the world into separate, mutually suspicious powers, restrained by no authority beyond their own conceptions of their "national interest" makes war as inevitable as the tectonic friction that causes earthquakes. The international arena is thus essentially anarchic and perhaps amoral, and it is futile to criticize wars by reference to systematically irrelevant criteria of justice.

We encountered a version of this realist view in Chapter 5, in our discussion of Hobbes's state of nature. We saw there that Hobbes's individuals retain a right to decide for themselves how best to preserve themselves against attack. They therefore possess the "blameless liberty" to launch violent preemptive attacks on those they fear might be a threat. The fact that everyone knows that they are in this way vulnerable to the suspicions of others makes war endemic in the state of nature. For, as Hobbes put it, "as the nature of foul weather lieth not in a shower or two of rain, but in an inclination thereto of many days together: so the nature of war consisteth not in actual fighting, but in the known disposition thereto during all the time there is no assurance to the contrary."[1] Hobbes draws the realist conclusion in the following passage:

> To this war of every man against every man, this also is consequent;
> that nothing can be Unjust. The notions of Right and Wrong, Justice and
> Injustice, have there no place. Where there is no common Power, there is
> no Law; where no Law, no Injustice. Force and Fraud are in war the two
> Cardinal virtues.[2]

It is a short step to the depiction of the international arena, or of civil wars resulting from the collapse of organized government, in similarly amoral terms.

I will discuss each of these three views in turn.

War and Justice

As we have seen throughout our discussions in this book, rules and principles of justice are centrally concerned with the recognition of boundaries and responsibilities. Thus such rules may often mark off spheres of

---

[1] Hobbes 1994, p. 76.
[2] Hobbes 1994, p. 78.

personal responsibility and forbid meddling by outsiders as unjust. But they may also draw the boundaries so as to license specified forms of interference with others. This will be the case, for example, when they permit defined agencies to (say) tax property-holders in order to compel them to make fair contributions to the provision of some valuable public service, or to search someone's home as part of a criminal investigation. In such cases, justice makes it someone's business to interfere in ways otherwise denied to others.

But how might justice understood in this way bear upon the regulation of war? War involves the organized use of violence by some group of people against others they designate as enemies. This cultivation of *enmity* is, I think, the defining feature of war-making, and we can normally assume that violent aggression against others is by itself sufficient to create enmity in the relevant sense. For it is surely uncontroversial that such violence will normally be unwelcome, resented, and resisted by its victims. That is why belligerence is frequently self-fulfilling, breeding enmity in those with whom an aggressor chooses to pick a fight. Michael Walzer captures this nicely when he refers to the "morally coercive" character of aggression. It involves, Walzer tells us, more than the effort to manipulate behavior through threats in the manner of a mugging. It represents a moral challenge to its victims' independence and drags them into the violent effort to vindicate their rights against that challenge.[3]

The self-fulfilling quality of belligerence also accounts for the appeal, to some, of that form of Christian pacifism that demands love for one's enemy and that one "turn the other cheek." For one can see this as a psychological tactic intended to frustrate an aggressor's intentions to incite conflict. It is, in its own way, an act of defiance – a refusal to accept an aggressor's terms. Unfortunately, however, whatever its psychological satisfactions, such defiance may also fail to frustrate an aggressor's hopes of seizing one's land, possessions, and people.

The Just War Criteria

In any case, given what we earlier said about justice, to ask whether war can be just is presumably to ask two questions: (a) under what conditions

---

[3] Walzer 2015, p. 53.

is it ever someone's place to declare others as *enemies* and to organize violent attacks against them? (b) How are "enemies" to be properly identified and how is it appropriate to treat them in the course of fighting them? The theory of the "just war" has always distinguished these questions, referring to (a) as *jus ad bellum*, the matter of what justifies a resort to war in the first place, and to (b) as *jus in bello*, the issue of *how* and *against whom* violence may permissibly be directed.

The traditional "just war" answers to these questions are easily summarized:

Jus ad bellum:

(1) *Formal and legitimate declaration:* wars must be openly declared by legitimate and recognized political authorities; thus "wars" supposedly declared by private individuals or organizations are unjust. On this view, Osama Bin Laden's 1996 "fatwa" declaring "War against the Americans Occupying the Land of the Two Holy Places" is already excluded as unjust. For neither Bin Laden nor his Al Qaeda organization is a recognized public authority with the requisite standing to make a valid declaration under this provision.

(2) *Just cause:* wars must be a response to some already unjust aggression or to grave injustices inflicted upon innocents. Just wars are therefore always defensive wars: imperialist aggression, religious crusades, commercial wars, and preventive wars are all ruled out as unjust.

(3) *Right intention:* wars must not be fought with ulterior motives. Legitimate belligerents must be motivated by a sincere and unsullied intention to respond appropriately to the just cause, whatever it is.

(4) *Proportionality 1:* the value of a belligerent's intended aim must outweigh the likely costs of fighting a war to achieve it and there must be a "reasonable prospect of success."

(5) *Last resort:* other nonviolent means of attaining a war's aim must have been fairly tried and exhausted.

Jus in bello:

(1) *Proportionality 2:* soldiers must not use excessive force, given their immediate military objectives.

(2) *Noncombatant immunity:* civilians must not be deliberately targeted or harmed. Only soldiers are legitimate objects of attack.

This list of desiderata is intricate and raises many complex issues. I will focus here on two questions: first, what is the relation between the *ad bellum* and *in bello* criteria? And second, how should the crucial "just cause" criterion be interpreted?

Before I do this, however, I note a more general issue that the very complexity of these criteria raises. Presumably the purpose of enumerating criteria for a just war is to remove confusion or disagreement about whether particular wars are just or unjust. We saw in our discussion of Rawls's notion of "reflective equilibrium" in Chapter 6, for example, that an important role for "theories" of justice is to refine equivocal general convictions into sharper criteria yielding clear critical judgments about just and unjust arrangements. Such an enterprise fails to the extent that people who accept the proposed criteria nevertheless quite defensibly reach opposed conclusions when they apply them in similar cases. If the point of "theory" is to help us discriminate, the tendency of a theory to remain equivocal counts against it.

A serious worry about the just war formula is that its complexity guarantees that it fails in just this way. With so many criteria to satisfy, open to so many possible interpretations, it seems inevitable that just war theorists will reasonably reach divergent conclusions about the same cases. To take a recent example, many just war theorists, including those speaking officially for the Catholic Church, opposed the 2003 US invasion of Iraq on just war grounds. But others used the same criteria to argue that the liberation of Iraq was a just war. One such was Jean Bethke Elshtain, an avid defender of just war thinking. Noting that "other just war thinkers may well disagree with my analysis," Elshtain modestly conceded that "the just war tradition does *not* provide a handy, stipulative tick-list. It rarely yields a unanimous knock-down argument. Rather, it is a way of analyzing and arguing based on the assertion that a resort to war justified solely on an appeal to national interest will not pass ethical muster."[4]

This strikes me as a poor defense of the just war theory. The theory is only of significant value if it helps us to vindicate judgments about war that are not already largely uncontested, like the claim that naked appeals to national interest are insufficient to justify war. No doubt asking of *any* theory that it achieve "knock-down unanimity" is to ask too much,

---

[4] Elshtain 2004a, p. 2. See also Elshtain 2004b.

but surely we need something more than just a bland concession that those who accept the same theory may reasonably reach quite opposed conclusions when they apply it in specific cases. Such academic courtesies seem especially misplaced when, as here, lives are at stake. Given the magnitude of the sacrifices we are potentially asking troops and others to bear, it seems only fair to demand that just war criteria yield pretty unequivocal conclusions. Would it seem adequate to console someone who has just lost a loved one in combat by saying: "*Arguably* he died in a just cause"? Perhaps if we are being honest that is all we can ever say, but the just war theory holds out the promise of our being able to say more. If that is an empty promise the theory fails.

In bello **and** *ad bellum*

Just war theorists usually insist on the independence of the *in bello* and *ad bellum* requirements. This independence reflects an implicit division of responsibilities between civilian officials and members of the armed forces: the former, but not the latter, are responsible for satisfying the *ad bellum* provisions. But both are responsible for seeing to it that the *ad bello* standards are met. On this view, soldiers cannot be responsible for violations of *jus ad bellum*; but both soldiers and officials can be war criminals in respect of *jus in bello*.

Insisting on the independence of these sets of criteria carries two significant consequences. First, it implies that even in a war that is not justified by the *ad bellum* requirements, soldiers remain responsible for fighting with restraint and regard for innocent life. This is important because it prevents soldiers even in spectacularly unjust military campaigns, like Nazi troops and officers, from citing this as mitigating their responsibility for any atrocities they commit in the course of fighting.

Second, the independence of *jus in bello* and *jus ad bellum* renders the just war theory strongly antiutilitarian. In particular, it rules out the view that Michael Walzer helpfully refers to as the "sliding scale."[5] According to this utilitarian view, the *in bello* requirements weaken in proportion to the justice of the cause for which we fight. Proponents of the sliding-scale view might argue, for example, that in a war of overwhelming righteousness,

---

[5] Walzer 2015, pp. 228ff.

there is a stronger justification for relaxing (say) noncombatant immunity than would apply in a war whose aim was of less urgent significance. The ends, in other words, justify the means.

True to the traditional just war position, Walzer rejects the sliding-scale argument, insisting that certain means are to be ruled out regardless of the value of our military goals. On this view, exposing millions of inno-cent civilians to the risk of nuclear incineration through the Cold War policy of "nuclear deterrence" could not be justified even if the defeat of Soviet communism was an overwhelmingly just cause. Still, Walzer admits one important exception, arguing that in genuine cases of "supreme emergency," states may suspend the *in bello* criteria. On this basis, Walzer entertains the conclusion that the British bombing of German civilian targets in the Second World War was justified, at least up until 1942, when a plausible "supreme emergency" existed. But the subsequent continuation of these raids after this "emergency" had passed, culminating in the terror bombings of Hamburg, Dresden, and Berlin toward the end of the war, represented a lapse into utilitarian calculations that the just war theory forbids.[6] Still, because this judgment invokes the independent *in bello* requirements, this lapse does not cast doubt on the justice of the Allied cause from the point of view of *jus ad bellum*.[7]

Just Cause

We have already noted that, as usually interpreted, the just cause proviso requires that just wars be defensive responses to illegitimate aggression. But what counts as such aggression? One standard answer is enshrined in current international law. Thus Article 2(4) of the United Nations Charter: "All Members shall refrain in their international relations from the threat or use of force against the territorial integrity or political sovereignty of any state." On this view, what Walzer calls the "crime of aggression" consists in assaults on the territory or sovereignty of a state.

Walzer's metaphor of criminality is important, for it underlines an implicit assumption in the traditional account of just cause. Aggression is

---

[6] Walzer 2015, pp. 255–63.

[7] For a criticism of the claim that *ad bellum* and *in bello* requirements can and should be kept apart, see McMahan 2009.

understood, not merely as an assault on the particular states attacked, but as a challenge to a broader norm of international order, according to which all states deserve equal respect as independent sovereign powers. As Vattel, the great eighteenth-century theorist of international law, has it:

> A dwarf is as much a man as a giant is: a small Republic is no less a sovereign state than the most powerful Kingdom. By a necessary consequence of that equality, whatever is lawful for one Nation is equally lawful for any nation. A Nation then is mistress of her own actions ... if she makes an ill use of her liberty, she is guilty of a breach of duty; but other Nations are bound to acquiesce in her conduct, since they have no right to dictate to her. Since Nations are free, independent and equal, and since each possesses the right of judging, according to the dictates of her conscience what conduct she is to pursue in order to fulfill her duties; the effect of the whole is to produce at least externally and in the eyes of mankind a perfect equality of rights between nations.[8]

So, for Vattel, states cannot forcibly intervene in each other's affairs "without violating the liberty of some particular state and destroying the foundations of their natural society."[9]

Walzer's understanding of the "crime of aggression" moves in close orbit around this statist conception of global politics. There already exists, he and others maintain, a discernible vision of justice ordering the community of nations, assigning responsibility for the internal affairs of nations to the separate states that govern them and imposing on them a corresponding duty of mutual forbearance. On this view, aggressive transgressions of these responsibility-defining boundaries provide just cause for war.

The obvious problem with this position is that it gives too much latitude to states to abuse their own citizens. If Vattel's statism does describe a certain vision of justice, it seems a very imperfect exemplar, as Walzer himself concedes. In a puzzling passage, Walzer writes: "[T]he boundaries that exist [between states] at any moment in time are likely to be arbitrary, poorly drawn, the products of ancient wars. The mapmakers are likely to have been ignorant, drunken or corrupt. Nevertheless, these lines establish a habitable world. Within that world, men and women (let us assume)

---

[8] Vattel 1844, p. lxiii.
[9] Vattel 1844, p. lxiii.

are safe from attack; once the lines are crossed, safety is gone."[10] But *can* we assume that such lines establish a "habitable world"? Habitable for whom? What about those persecuted by their own state for their religious beliefs, ethnically cleansed by their compatriots, or shot by the tyrants that rule them?

Such considerations encourage modifications so as to permit, over statist objections, "humanitarian intervention" to rescue individuals from gross abuses ("crimes against humanity" – torture, enslavement, "disappearance," genocide, etc.) at the hands of their own rulers. Darrel Moellendorf, for example, proposes a "cosmopolitan" account of just cause, according to which "just cause for the use of military force exists if and only if the intervention is directed toward advancing justice in the basic structure of the state or the international effects of its domestic policy." This cosmopolitan interpretation of the just cause provision requires us to consider "whether the justified claims of persons are met before one accepts that sovereignty provides a shield against the use of military force."[11] According to Moellendorf, this corrects the fundamental weakness in the statist account.

Elshtain's arguments for the justice of the 2003 American invasion of Iraq turn on a similar appeal. Since the theory of just war predates the entrenchment of modern state sovereignty from the mid seventeenth century up to the present, Elshtain argues that just cause need not be interpreted in exclusively statist terms. Citing the authority of St. Thomas Aquinas, she claims that a well-established track record of abusing its own citizens renders a state liable to military attack in defense of the victims or as "punishment" for its misdeeds; since the Iraqi regime had such a record just cause for war existed whether or not it posed any immediate or direct threat to the sovereignty of the United States.[12]

Such views invite the rejoinder that they are too permissive of military intervention. They establish, it seems, a presumption in favor of violent intervention whenever there is serious injustice in the relations between citizens and their states. But since the violation of human rights by governments, even on a large scale, is unfortunately quite common, this

---

[10] Walzer 2015, p. 57.
[11] Moellendorf 2002, pp. 159–60.
[12] Elshtain 2004a, p. 3.

position would seem to commit us to large-scale belligerence in defense of human rights around the world. More so if we follow Elshtain's suggestion that not only efforts to avert ongoing abuse but also the need to punish *past* abuses constitute just cause for war.

In response Moellendorf rightly reminds us that there are other *ad bellum* conditions that must be satisfied in order for a war to be permissible, according to the just war theory. If it is merely a necessary but not a sufficient condition for the justice of a war, the presence of a just cause does not automatically commit us to launching a military strike. For example, there must also be a reasonable prospect of success, and we must have exhausted all nonviolent alternatives.

But this response underestimates the special importance of the just cause condition. I earlier suggested that the defining feature of war-making is the cultivation of *enmity*. Here it is relevant to recall Hobbes's claim that war refers not merely to belligerent acts, or to the actual initiation of hostilities, but more basically to a possible state or disposition of two or more parties vis-à-vis each other. Thus Hobbes denied that a state of war requires actual fighting: it requires merely a "tract of time, wherein the will to contend by battle is sufficiently known."[13] The great seventeenth-century jurist Hugo Grotius opened his seminal *De Jure Belli ac Pacis* with a closely related observation. Having quoted (approvingly) Cicero's definition of war as "a contention by force," Grotius noted the etymological origins of our concept of war in words signifying multitude, diversity, disunity, and discord.[14] Enmity is an extreme manifestation of such disunity and division: it involves the open recognition of implacable causes of contention between separate individuals and groups, and precludes their peaceable unification under agreed terms.

These considerations reveal a difficulty with Moellendorf's reply that just cause is a necessary but not sufficient condition for a resort to arms, for it seems to overlook the symbolic significance of an open acknowledgement of just cause. Even in the absence of actual fighting such an acknowledgement nonetheless nurses enmity and the disposition to "contend by force." It implies that but for contingent considerations having to do with the likelihood of success, last resort, and judgments about proportionality,

[13] Hobbes 1994, p. 76.
[14] Grotius 1901, p. 18.

when states are judged to have unjustly abused their own citizens a violent military response is in principle justified.

But encouraging states to draw this conclusion seems an uncertain recipe for peace. It is difficult not to have some sympathy for Vattel's worry that allowing nations a presumptive right to intervene by force in other states' internal affairs "opens the door to all the ravages of enthusiasm and fanaticism, and furnishes ambition with numberless pretexts."[15] Under this dispensation, when states are accused of maltreating their own citizens, they have good reason to fear that these criticisms express hostile intentions, whether or not military action is actually unleashed. Insofar as this heightens a sense of enmity and therefore insecurity, this approach seems only likely to encourage belligerence and sabotage peace. The statist alternative has significant costs, too, but its proponents can argue that its redeeming virtue is an accepted norm of mutual forbearance around which states can unite in pursuit of peace, notwithstanding their other differences.

One might respond that justice is more important than peace. But that is exactly what is in dispute. For example, pacifists, to whose views we turn next, think that the evident evil of war requires that peace be preserved at all costs, even if this means tolerating some injustice. To them, war remains the greater evil. They may be wrong, but flat assertions that justice trumps peace simply beg that question.

The Claims of Peace

Many assume that just war theory and pacifism are mutually exclusive. But here some care is needed. In particular we need to notice that pacifists could be opposed to just war theory in at least two ways. They might hold, on independent grounds, that war is always unacceptable and then argue that since it regards war as sometimes acceptable, the just war framework must be incorrect. If, for example, Ghandi and King were right to insist that violence is never an acceptable means of pursuing political ends then clearly just war theory goes wrong at the outset in assuming that it can be. Clearly this radical version of pacifism represents a direct challenge to just war theorists.

---

[15] Vattel 1844, p. 137.

On the other hand, pacifists might accept the just war criteria but deny that any actual wars could possibly satisfy them. Taking their cue from those proponents of the just war theory who have admitted that the number of truly just wars must be vanishingly small, "just war pacifists" could regard the *in bello* and *ad bellum* criteria as useful reminders that the notion of a "just war" is a utopian fiction.

It is not hard to see how they might make this argument. They might agree, for example, that justice in war requires that a belligerent declare war for the sake of a just cause and without any ulterior motives at all, but argue (surely plausibly) that motives of the requisite purity are hardly ever displayed by states in the world that we know. Alternatively, they might suggest that the judgments about proportionality required by both the *in bello* and *ad bellum* criteria presuppose a degree of foresight and precision that is unattainable in the context of international conflict, and especially in the heat of battle. Rather than rejecting the theory of just war, then, pacifists who argue along these lines actually lean on it to make their case against the resort to military force.

Pacifism is often correctly associated with a commitment to nonviolence, but here too we must be careful to avoid two possible misunderstandings. First, a commitment to nonviolence is not necessarily the same as a renunciation of all forms of force as means to achieve political ends, or even of all expressions of enmity. In a memorable passage from his "Letter from Birmingham Jail," for example, the pacifist Martin Luther King made this point clear:

> Non-violent direct action seeks to create such a crisis and foster such a tension that a community which has constantly refused to negotiate is forced to confront the issue. It seeks so to dramatize the issue that it can no longer be ignored … just as Socrates felt that it was necessary to create a tension in the mind so that individuals could rise from the bondage of myths and half-truths to the unfettered realm of creative analysis and objective appraisal, so must we see the need for non-violent gadflies to create the kind of tension in society that will help men rise from the dark depths of prejudice and racism to the majestic heights of understanding and brotherhood. The purpose of our direct action program is to create a situation so crisis-packed that it will inevitably open the door to negotiation … We know through painful experience that freedom

is never voluntarily given by the oppressor: it must be demanded by the oppressed.[16]

Quite clearly these are fighting words, but they are also an admonition to fight an enemy through nonviolent means. This is not a paradoxical idea: talk of the "pen" being "a mighty sword" or of "battles" of ideas, and for "hearts and minds" need not be empty rhetoric.

Second, at least some pacifists have distinguished between the lawless violence of war, which they regard as absolutely wrong, and the "force of the magistrate," the acceptable legal use of violence to punish wrongdoers and maintain social order. This is the position taken, for example, by Quaker pacifists. It allowed William Penn, who attempted to govern Pennsylvania on Quaker principles in the seventeenth century, to reconcile his pacifism with the view that government nonetheless has a right to "terrify evildoers" through the use of violent punishment.[17] On this view, it is the cultivation of violent enmity that marks the special evil of war. But from the fact that violence is often an expression of enmity it does not follow that all forms of violence express enmity. For Penn and other Christian pacifists, penal violence channeled and restrained through legal means need not be motivated by enmity. It may rather reflect an impartial desire to see justice done, and even reflect love and benevolence toward those sanctioned, as in the case of parents disciplining recalcitrant children.

Killing in Self-Defense

In any case, pacifist views draw their strength from conventional beliefs about the wrongness of violence and especially that of killing innocents. It is precisely because war inevitably involves both of these that pacifists deny that war is ever justifiable. Against the thrust of the *in bello* provisions many pacifists are even inclined to resist the conventional assumption that *soldiers* engaged in combat forfeit the right not to be killed. After all, they argue, soldiers are rarely themselves directly responsible for any wrongful aggression in which they are engaged – they are often innocent pawns in campaigns planned and authorized by their superiors, both officers and

[16] King 1989, pp. 59–60.
[17] Penn 1682.

politicians. This presumption of innocence will seem particularly strong when soldiers are conscripts but often remains plausible even when they have volunteered for military service. Soldiers may volunteer only because they cannot find other forms of employment and few ever do so on the understanding that they may ignore orders whenever they personally disapprove of the wars they are later asked to fight.

Pacifist doubts about killing innocents in war come under the greatest pressure in the context of self-defense. Most believe that they have a right to use violence to repel physical assault, and *in extremis* a right to kill in self-defense or in the defense of others. The most natural way to defend war against pacifist objections is to extrapolate from these relatively uncontentious individual rights to the right of states to kill in defense of their citizens. Both Hobbes and Walzer, despite their many other differences, use this form of argument to defend the resort to war.

Whether pacifist views falter in the face of such arguments depends on how wide the right to kill in self-defense really is. For Hobbes, it is of course as wide as one can imagine since on his view it entails not only the right to use violence to repel an attack but also the right to decide who might be a threat in the first place. On his account, individuals in a state of nature and by extension states in the international arena reserve the right to destroy, even preemptively, whomever they judge to be a threat to their safety. We will consider Hobbes's views in our later discussion of realism. However, we can set it aside here because both pacifists and just war theorists like Walzer will agree in rejecting Hobbes's hair-trigger interpretation of the right of self-defense. The challenge posed by pacifism to just war theorists is thus to provide a principled basis for rejecting Hobbes's extremely permissive view while still leaving enough room for justified killing of even innocent soldiers in a just war.

A standard way of meeting this challenge is to appeal to cases in which pacifists would on reflection have to admit that individuals reserve the right to use violence against innocents in self-defense. Moellendorf offers two such examples on behalf of the just war theory:

> Case 1: In the middle of the night a hatchet-bearing sleepwalker attacks my housemate. I do not know that the attacker is sleepwalking, but I can repel the attack only by killing her. Case 2: A group of armed thugs has already attacked my neighbor once. I see them coming for a second attack.

I do not know that one member of the group has been urging restraint. I can prevent the imminent attack only by firing on the group, which will probably kill all of them. Does the innocence of the person in each case prohibit that person being killed?[18]

Moellendorf claims not, and concludes on the strength of these examples that "the activity of unjustly attacking defeats the presumption of the wrongness of killing innocents."

Against this, some pacifists concede that the use of violent force against attackers in situations like those Moellendorf describes is permissible but deny that this carries over into the relevant case of *states* killing innocents in wars. This was the position taken by C. E. M. Joad in a pacifist tract (still worth reading) written between the two World Wars. Denying that "the use of force is always and necessarily wrong," Joad continued:

I should find no difficulty ... answering the historic question put by military personages on tribunals to those who appeared before them pleading conscientious objection to military service in the last war: "What would you do if you saw a German coming at your wife, mother, daughter, sister, cousin, aunt, or what-not, with intent to rape her?" My answer is that I should quite certainly try to stop him with whatever means were at my disposal, and with whatever means were at my disposal I should, in similar circumstances, try to defend myself. What I should not do, is to regard the aggression of the hypothetical German as a ground for proceeding to drop bombs on *his* wife, mother, daughter, sister, cousin, aunt, or what-not.[19]

Moellendorf would respond that Joad misses the point because there is no disagreement about the targeting of civilians in bombing campaigns. This, he might remind us, is ruled out anyway by the *in bello* criteria. The purpose of Moellendorf's two cases is then not to justify killings of this sort, but rather to make room for the defensive killing of (even innocent) combatants engaged in aggressive military campaigns.

This is a fair point, but pacifists might in turn respond that until weaponry has become far more discriminating than it actually is, or until wars are fought with androids without relatives and dependents who will be

---

[18] Moellendorf 2002, pp. 152–3.
[19] Joad 1939, p. 59.

crushed or ruined by their loss, as a practical matter war still involves unacceptable collateral damage to innocents. Just war theorists will be unimpressed by this reply, since on their view as long as it is *unintended*, and every effort made to avoid it, such damage is not necessarily unjust or impermissible.

Against this, however, pacifists can argue that while such philosophical niceties about intention seem plausible when reflecting on war from a distance, they are disloyal to the lived experience of warfare. When our missiles miss their intended military targets and instead destroy (say) a school and its pupils, the relatives of the victims will surely be quite reasonably disgusted with official statements to the effect that "we didn't mean it." For the parents, the more immediate point will be that had "we" not chosen war, their children would still be alive. Nor is the unintended nature of the damage likely to assuage significantly any (quite understandable) feelings of guilt afflicting the soldier who wrongly calibrated the missile's targeting mechanism that day.

Killing Combatants

Even if we are not convinced by these counterarguments about noncombatants, several other features of Moellendorf's examples raise doubts about whether they can even justify the killing of *combatants* on the terms just war theorists usually defend it. In particular, those examples *stipulate* that killing specific attackers is the only available means to save specific victims. They also assume that we already know exactly who is attacking whom. Moreover, in both cases the attack is imminent and demands immediate preventive action. But examples with these features expose as many questions about the just war position as they remove.

For one thing, even if we concede – with Joad – that when there *really is* no alternative to killing specific attackers to save their victims, individuals and perhaps states retain the right to kill, this arguably leaves us well short of the rights to go to war against an enemy that just war theorists usually defend. The right of a state to shoot down a military aircraft that is about to bomb a civilian neighborhood is one thing. But a formal declaration of war, and initiation of hostilities, against a state whose forces (say) merely violate the territorial integrity of a state but do not immediately, or to anyone's knowledge, threaten innocent life is another. (Perhaps they are marching through uninhabited lands, are actually welcomed by the indigenous population though not by their government, or crossing into foreign airspace on a surveillance mission.)

And what of cases in which "just" war is contemplated after, and as a response to, some already consummated outrage such as an assassination, an invasion, a terrorist attack, or a massacre? In such instances we cannot plausibly maintain that attacks on combatants are necessary to prevent the relevant outrages because, by hypothesis, it is already too late to prevent them. Perhaps we are worried about similar outrages in the future. But generic anxiety of this sort is quite different from the immediate and unambiguous encounters with specific attackers and specific victims presumed in Moellendorf's discussion. It is not obvious, then, that his examples license the resort to war in such cases, though not all just war theorists will be content with that conclusion.

Another problem is that in Moellendorf's examples it is not so much the *injustice* of the attack as its overwhelming *imminence* that triggers the resort to preventive force. After all, if we knew that someone was planning a similarly unjust attack to take place next week we would not normally think that killing them is the appropriate, or even a permissible, response. In such a case, calling the police and having the would-be attacker arrested while finding the intended victims a place of safety seems nearer the mark.

This suggests that our reactions to Moellendorf's discussion may be controlled, not by considerations of justice, but by our natural tendency to identify strongly with the psychological stress experienced by individuals intimately confronting violent attack. We realize that they may not have time to consider their options carefully and their responses may therefore be largely reflexive and instinctive. But pacifists might admit that under such conditions of extreme necessity agents have an excuse for killing but nevertheless insist that this is not sufficient to establish that such killings are positively justified or no longer "presumptively wrong," as Moellendorf claims. There is an important difference between having an excuse for doing something that we recognize as unjust or otherwise wrong and claiming – as just war theorists do about killing innocent combatants in a just war – that it is actually the *right thing to do*. Pacifists might also point out here that while soldiers in combat will often face imminent threats of the sort Moellendorf describes, the civilian leaders who authorize and declare the wars that put them in such dangerous situations rarely do so under conditions of similar necessity. While soldiers may have an excuse for wrongdoing, then, the official authors of war may not. (We will return to this issue of excuse in our later discussion of realism.)

Finally, is Moellendorf's principle compatible with the *in bello* requirement that only combatants may legitimately be killed? Moellendorf says that the "activity of unjustly attacking" justifies the killing of the attackers, but often members of the civilian command (civil servants in the ministry of defense, say) are themselves implicated in this activity. *Jus in bello* confers immunity upon them, but the thrust of Moellendorf's argument points in a different direction. If we can most effectively halt imminent military aggression by killing civilian leaders rather than soldiers on the ground, his principle presumably recommends that course. Indeed, since they are more directly responsible, it seems only fair that they, rather than the (often innocent) soldiers they order around, ought to bear the costs of unjust aggression.

These considerations suggest that defending the just war position against pacifist objections is a more complex task than we may at first suppose. Whether just war conclusions are completely congruent with conventional moral assumptions about the wrongness of killing innocents is unclear. On the other hand, many will think it unrealistic to suppose that our judgments about war can ever be fully and neatly reconciled with even fairly uncontroversial moral principles. To them, insisting on keeping our moral hands squeaky clean[20] makes little sense when we think of those cowering in London Underground stations while the Luftwaffe bombs their homes, or of thousands of Muscovites fleeing in panic upon hearing that the Wehrmacht is within 50 miles of the city. We turn now to consider this sort of view, which holds that war is in some sense a special case, not fully capturable within the framework of conventional moral assessment.

Realism

Those, like just war theorists and pacifists, committed to the moral criticism of war (and of international institutions more generally), often regard

---

[20] Walzer 1973.

the refutation of Hobbesian realism as a high priority.[21] It is easy to understand this impulse. Realists often seem to assert that international politics is necessarily an amoral struggle for power unrestrained by ethical principles. But if true this makes the moral criticism of war as pointless as the moral criticism of the natural selection of species. ("Use of venom by predators is wrong!")

If realists really claim that the global order is an ethical vacuum, in which moral assessments of states' actions are systematically unavailable or beside the point, their view becomes difficult to distinguish from a broader skepticism about moral judgment in general. Accordingly, its critics often contend that realism is defensible only by sacrificing the assumption that individual conduct is itself subject to moral restraints.[22] Since few realists have been so radical as to abandon the conventional belief that individuals' choices are open to moral assessment, this line of criticism reveals a serious tension in their position. If states are engaged in an amoral struggle for power, why suppose that it is any different for individuals generally? This suggests that crude realist doctrines of this sort are either confused or merely reiterate a more generic moral skepticism with very controversial implications far beyond the international case. Given these difficulties, this rudimentary realist claim seems unworthy of serious attention.

But there is a more interesting and subtle version of the realist view. Proponents of this alternative interpretation do not claim that moral judgment is *impossible* in the international arena; nor do they draw from realist premises the conclusion that we must simply resign ourselves to the inevitability of war. Rather, they have used the realist view as a springboard for an unsentimental critical analysis of the institutions of war-making. One thinker who developed this line of argument with particular clarity was the American pragmatist John Dewey. Dewey's endorsement of a version of realism is clear from the following passage:

> Lamentations as to the gulf which divides the working ethical principles
> of nations from those animating decent individuals are copious. But
> they express the pious rather than the efficacious wish of those who
> indulge in them. They overlook the central fact that morals are relative to

---

[21] Thus Beitz 1999, part 1; Holmes 2014, chs. 2–3; Moellendorf 2002, pp. 143–8; Walzer 2015, ch. 1.

[22] This is the essence of Beitz's critique. See Beitz 1999, pp. 14, 15–17, 34.

organization. Individuals ... can be [moral]... because they are partakers in modes of associated life which confer powers and impose responsibilities upon them. States are nonmoral in their activities just because of the absence of an inclusive society which defines and establishes rights. Hence they are left to their own devices, secret and violent if need is deemed imminent, in judging and asserting their rights and obligations ... The nations exist with respect to one another in what the older writers called a state of nature, not in a social or political state.[23]

The problem to which Dewey draws attention in this passage is not the complete absence of ethical criteria by which to judge states' actions. The problem is rather that of making such norms *effective*, such that states are prepared to recognize their direction as authoritative over their own judgments about their national interests. Dewey continued:

If only there were a general recognition of the dependence of moral control upon social order, all of the sentiment and well-wishing opinion that is now dissipated would be centered. It would aim at the establishment of a definitely organized federation of nations not merely in order that certain moral obligations might be effectively enforced but in order that a variety of obligations might come into existence ... Warlikeness is not of itself the cause of war; a clash of interests due to the absence of organization is its cause. A supernational organization which oversees, obviates and adjusts these clashes ... possible only with the coincident outlawing of war itself, will focus moral energies now scattered and make operative moral ideas now futile.[24]

In a similar vein, Rousseau used a recognizably Hobbesian realism to mount a powerful critique of Hobbes's own argument that accepting the authority of sovereign states is sufficient to end the state-of-nature struggle. He argued that Hobbes's conclusions create a "manifest contradiction": "As individuals we live in a civil state and are subject to laws, but as nations each enjoys the liberty of nature." The resulting predicament "is worse than if these distinctions were unknown. For living simultaneously in the social order and in the state of nature, we are subjected to the evils of both without gaining the security of either." In this way, Rousseau

---

[23] Dewey 1939, pp. 508–9.
[24] Dewey 1939, pp. 510–11.

pessimistically concluded, "the vain name of justice serves only to safe-guard violence."[25]

The "War System"

While still essentially realist, this position is more complex than the crude doctrine that international power politics is simply an ethical vacuum. For it assumes that distinctive (and dangerous) configurations of power tend to promote and to be sustained by distinctive (and dangerous) ethical beliefs. Dewey's depiction of the international world of states as a "war system" nicely captures this point:

> It is inevitable that disputes, controversies, conflicts of interest and opinion shall arise between nations as between persons. Now to settle disputes … the experiences and wisdom of the world have found two methods and only two. One is the way of the law and courts; the other is the way of violence and lawlessness. In private controversies the former way is now established. In disputes among nations the way of violence is equally established. The word "established" is used advisedly … the world lives today under a war system; a system entrenched in politics, in diplomacy, in international law and in every court that sits under existing international law. The proposition, then, is not the moral proposition to abolish wars. It is the much more fundamental proposition to abolish the war system as an authorized and legally sanctioned institution. The first idea is either utopian at present or merely sentiment. This other proposition, to abolish the war system as an authorized, established institution, sanctioned by law, contemplated by law, is practical … Recourse to violence is not only *a* legitimate method for settling international disputes at present; under certain circumstances it is the only legitimate method, the ultimate reason of state.[26]

Here Dewey echoes Rousseau's dark thought that the most dangerous features of the current global order actually reflect ethical understandings that are "established" or "reigning" within it. The "war system" is patho-logical, on this view, not because it is an ethical vacuum, but precisely because the ethics regulating it are unduly permissive of dangerous con-duct on the part of states.

[25] Rousseau 1990, p. 186.
[26] Dewey 1939, pp. 514–15.

One might think that this view is incompatible with Hobbes's realist claim that in a state of nature "nothing can be unjust" and that "notions of right and wrong, justice and injustice have there no place." Clearly, the two views are incompatible if Hobbes is understood as suggesting that there are no ethical assumptions *at all* governing a state of nature. But there is another possible interpretation of Hobbes that corresponds to the more subtle version of realism that Dewey seems to have had in mind.

Suppose we understand Hobbes as arguing that the special conditions of the state of nature *excuse* conduct that is nonetheless without justification and perhaps indeed immoral. On this view, the extenuating circumstances of the state of nature diminish responsibility for morally questionable actions. This interpretation is supported by Hobbes's own talk of individuals' "blameless liberty" to defend themselves as they choose in a state of nature. Whether or not they are justified in choosing to defend themselves (say) by preemptively attacking a perceived threat, individuals must be excused from blame for such judgments as long as they remain in a state of nature.

But what is the basis for this supposed excuse? As we saw in Chapter 5, Hobbes's answer was that under the anarchical conditions of a state of nature, individuals will contrive a self-fulfilling mutual suspicion and mistrust. Under these conditions, individuals will be driven to assume that they (like everyone else) reserve the right to protect themselves as they choose. Overwhelmed by fear and mutual suspicion, individuals in the state of nature will find this habit difficult to kick, like an addictive drug. In this way, the duress of fear and insecurity induces a kind of collective addiction to violence as a way of dealing with perceived threats and to concomitant beliefs about agents' right to use it. While such beliefs do not amount to, and indeed preclude, a systematic consensus about what is justified or unjustified as just and unjust, they nonetheless have ethical content. The multipurpose excuse of self-preservation institutes an ethical permission, of uncertain limit, for the resort to violence. Applied to the international case, this view implies that a similar addiction to the logic of excuse is likely to develop among self-protecting states interacting under global anarchy.

The resulting possibility that states are addicted to a "war system," and habitually view violence as a legitimate means of conflict resolution, is a powerful and disturbing one. According to this Deweyan/Hobbesian hypothesis, it is in the nature of this addiction that states presume themselves and their peers to have a systematic excuse ("raison d'état") for conduct they might nonetheless acknowledge as morally questionable or as without justification. On this basis, pleas of necessity, self-defense, national interest, and the like in due course come to be accepted as legitimate excuses for wrongdoing.

Unfortunately there is considerable plausibility to this gloomy hypothesis about the addictive, even obsessive, quality of states' interest in violence as a mode of conflict resolution. One writer refers memorably to the "monstrous dissipation of resources in the search for military security."[27] Particularly striking is the famously self-defeating phenomenon of arms races, of which the nuclear proliferation during the Cold War is the most spectacular recent example. In a recent discussion lamenting the reluctance of The Cold War protagonists to renounce their ridiculously superabundant stockpiles of nuclear weapons, former US Secretary of Defense Robert S. McNamara wryly observes:

> Although any proposed reduction [in nuclear arsenals] is welcome, it
> is doubtful that survivors – if there were any – of an exchange of 3,200
> warheads (the U.S. and Russian numbers projected for 2012), with a
> destructive power approximately 65,000 times that of the Hiroshima
> bomb, could detect a difference between the effects of such an exchange
> and one that would result from the launch of the current U.S. and Russian
> forces totaling about 12,000 warheads.[28]

Writing before the outbreak of the Second World War, and before public knowledge of nuclear weapons, Joad wrote:

> Give a schoolboy an airgun and he may shoot a few sparrows or break a
> window ... give him a revolver and he becomes a public danger. One does
> not, after all, present one's children with dangerous toys, until they are
> old enough to play with them without harming themselves ... Yet these
> are precisely the gifts with which science has dowered modern man,
> with the result that he is in measurable distance of destroying himself
> through his inability to devise the political machinery which is necessary
> to canalize and direct for the public safety the powers with which science

---

[27] Stone 1984, p. 157.
[28] McNamara 2005, p. 34.

has invested him. Unless he can devise this machinery before it is too late, our civilization will follow its predecessors to destruction, and man himself may be superseded and sent to join the Mesozoic reptiles upon the evolutionary scrap-heap of life's discarded experiments.[29]

The important point Joad makes here is that the technological enhancement of the means of violence is a necessary but not sufficient condition for war to become an unacceptable menace. The sufficient conditions include institutions disposed to deploy and use lethal weapons, and the political environment likely to foster this disposition. It is just such an environment that Dewey and other realist critics intend to pick out when they speak of a "war system" that renders futile "serious efforts at disarmament."

Arguments along these lines do not so much condemn war on moral grounds as regard it as a symptom of pathological irrationality. Thus one contemporary pacifist writes:

> A man overeats, smokes heavily, drinks too much, and gets no exercise. He learns that he has high blood pressure and a weak heart. He decides to switch to filters, drink a little less, skip seconds on desserts, and walk a few blocks now and then. Is that not a step in the right direction? Certainly. But it probably will not save him. What he needs is a change in his whole way of life. We, too, can go on fueling the furnace of war and take our chances on being able to control the heat. But let us not deceive ourselves that this is likely to save us either. The whole history of civilization shows that we have never been able to resist heaping more fuel onto the fire. Or to avoid burning ourselves periodically with increasing severity. Less of that we have been doing wrong is not good enough. We must stop doing it.[30]

This argument is better understood as criticizing potentially catastrophic *imprudence* rather than censuring any sort of *immorality* or *injustice*. Indeed, as we have seen, such arguments can be viewed as condemning an irrationality itself bred by certain moral beliefs. These are the ideas that underpin what Charles Beitz calls the "morality of states," the Vattelian view that states are sovereign over their own affairs, equally entitled to respect as autonomous defenders of their national honor. It turns out, then, that a

---

[29] Joad 1939, pp. 159–60.
[30] Holmes 2014, p. 11.

consistent realism need not preclude a criticism of war, and may in fact be compatible with a broadly pacifist orientation that seeks, with Dewey, somehow to outlaw the institutions of war-making.

An Uncertain Future

This pessimistic diagnosis of the irrationality of a morality of states has not gone unchallenged. There is a rival view, according to which a world of independent nation states need not degenerate into the jealous suspicion of a Hobbesian state of nature. It turns out, proponents of this view suggest, that the best means for states to maintain order and prosperity at home tend also, at least in the long run, to deprive international conflict of the oxygen it needs to ignite. This more optimistic line of thinking can also be discerned in Hobbes. He sometimes suggested that by promoting industry and economic development within their own borders, states may eventually attain a kind of self-sufficiency, unavailable to *individuals* interacting in a state of nature, that renders war among nations pointless and unnecessary.[31]

This thought was modified and articulated more fully by Kant in *Perpetual Peace* and several other important essays.[32] Writing at the end of the eighteenth century, Kant foresaw that prosperity and commerce might also foster international economic interdependence and in turn engender collaboration and consensus among nations committed to broadly liberal democratic ideals of equal opportunity and individual freedom. Although the expansion of global commerce would itself exacerbate conflict in the short run, the long-term prognosis, Kant claimed, was hopeful. Eventually, a core of prosperous liberal democratic states could settle the terms of a "foedus pacificum" (a "league of peace") that would obviate war among them. A "perpetual peace" then becomes possible through gradual expansions of such a league until its membership encompasses the entire globe. A currently fashionable variant of this more optimistic vision is defended by proponents of the so-called "liberal democratic peace theory," which asserts that liberal democracies do not, and predictably will not, go to war with each other. In many ways, Rawls's Law of Peoples, discussed briefly in Chapter 8, represents a synthesis of these views, for it is at once

---

[31] Hobbes 1998, p. 150.
[32] Kant 1991, pp. 41–54, 93–131.

heavily indebted to Kant's vision of perpetual peace and openly reliant on assumptions drawn from the liberal democratic peace theory.[33]

In the light of recent world history, the prescience of Kant's view is striking. But while some developments – the foundation of the United Nations and the entrenchment of an increasingly rich body of international law, for example – seem to vindicate his predictions, the overall record is too mixed to allow us to embrace his optimism with wholehearted confidence. To take just one example from the other side of the ledger, we might remember that large-scale terror bombing was practiced during the Second World War not only by nasty Axis powers but also enthusiastically pioneered by the Allies in Tokyo, Hiroshima, Nagasaki, Cologne, Dresden, Hamburg, Berlin, and elsewhere. The targeting of civilians in such campaigns was not dictated by ideology. Rather, it reflected the massive mobilization of the economic infrastructure characteristic of modern warfare. Under these circumstances of "total war," traditional *in bello* distinctions between combatants and noncombatants tend to blur. Smashing the morale of the civilians who work the assembly lines making armaments or sewing military uniforms comes to seem as legitimate a tactic as cutting an army's supply lines on the field of battle.

The liberal democratic states too bear much of the responsibility for further blurring these distinctions by aggressively researching and then threatening to use "weapons of mass destruction," a term whose recent mindless repetition in the media should not be allowed to obscure its actual, quite outrageous meaning. These developments can only have encouraged the idea that terrorizing civilians is a legitimate means for promoting political ends. Such considerations naturally lead one to suspect that in their current desperation to contain nuclear proliferation and to win their self-declared "war on terror," the liberal democracies, and the community of nations more generally, are struggling to control Frankenstein monsters partly of their own creation.

Can states succeed in these endeavors? Or are they, like relapsing addicts, fated to repeat the mistakes of the past despite their best intentions, and perhaps with ever greater destructive force? Unfortunately these are open questions. It is still too early to say whether the tendency of modern statism is to eliminate or to exacerbate the problem of war.

---

[33] Rawls 2003, pp. 46–54.

12 Liberty

We have already felt the force of claims about liberty and freedom (terms I will use interchangeably) at various points in our discussion so far. In Chapter 6, we saw how Rousseauan and Rawlsian contractualists seek to justify political arrangements by asking whether agents motivated to maintain their autonomy would freely accept them under appropriate conditions. The possible impact of various forms of economic regulation on personal freedom was a persistent theme in Chapters 7 and 8, and quite obviously the existence of institutions claiming the authority to coerce agents poses a standing threat to their liberty. However, on reflection, exactly what it means for a person or society to enjoy freedom is not obvious. Moreover, although claims about freedom carry a powerful intuitive force, we have already encountered at least one argument (Plato's, discussed in Chapter 2) to the effect that political freedom is overrated.

Berlin's Wall

For good or ill, recent philosophical discussions of freedom have been profoundly shaped by Isaiah Berlin's seminal essay *Two Concepts of Liberty*, originally his inaugural lecture as Chichele Professor of Social and Political Theory at the University of Oxford.[1] When Berlin delivered it in 1958, the world was divided into two ideologically opposed blocs – the liberal democratic West and the communist East (from which Berlin himself was an *émigré*). His lecture was an effort to understand how, despite their bitter enmity, both sides of this Cold War division could nonetheless claim to be crusading for liberty.

[1] Berlin 1969.

Berlin's explanation hinged on a distinction between two rather different understandings of political liberty that emerged from the European Enlightenment. The first, a "negative" concept of liberty, to be found predominantly in English writers (e.g. Hobbes, Bentham, and Mill), takes freedom to be a function of the degree to which agents are interfered with, or obstructed. On this negative construal, freedom consists fundamentally in the *absence* of something else – forms of constraint, interference, and impediments to possible action. I am therefore free, under this analysis, to the extent that opportunities for action are available rather than foreclosed by constraints and obstacles. For example, the liberty of a man trapped in a cell is in this sense severely curtailed. In contrast, whether or not they choose to leave, someone not prevented from leaving a similar-sized room enjoys greater freedom. The point is that this option remains *available* to them insofar as certain obstacles (locked doors, chains, handcuffs, gags) are absent.

Berlin's second, "positive," concept of liberty, interprets freedom in contrasting terms, as a matter of autonomy and self-determination, and is more strongly associated with various continental European traditions of thought on which (among others) Rousseau, Kant, and Hegel were particularly influential. On a positive construal, freedom consists fundamentally in the *presence* of something – a certain sort of self-direction, independence, or autonomy. Agents who are brainwashed, enslaved, under the sway of addiction, or overwhelming emotional impulse, or subject to manipulation lack freedom in this sense. They are not masters of themselves: their actions are dictated by some alien force, i.e. something, whether inside or outside, that is not *them.*

A long-standing challenge for political philosophers has been to reconcile the existence of political authority and due respect for the freedom of its subjects. The tension between these is best seen in terms of positive liberty. To be sure, authorities may use their power to limit our options and thus reduce our negative liberty to an unacceptable degree. But institutions claiming authority are not the unique source of such interferences, so concerns about a diminution of negative freedom do not pick out something that is special to cases involving authority. The more immediate freedom-related worry about the latter rather concerns the way in which authorities preempt our own judgments about how we are to act, and thereby threaten to subject us to alien rule. This suggestion that someone other than ourselves has a right to determine our actions raises a question about positive, not negative, liberty.

This distinction, or variants on it, had been long recognized before Berlin's essay. Berlin's particular contribution was to chart the diverging historical careers of these two concepts over the course of the nineteenth and early twentieth centuries, and to explain how they eventually came to be at loggerheads, with the positive concept evolving into a rationale for very illiberal forms of totalitarianism, and the negative concept underwriting the more benign institutions of liberal democracy.

Berlin's typology has generated an extraordinarily extensive critical commentary. The resulting debate has become bewilderingly complex and is, I believe, rife with misunderstandings. To guide readers through this thicket without getting lost within it, I begin by entering two important clarifications of Berlin's distinction.

An Ideological Distinction?

First, these two concepts of liberty should not be too tightly affiliated with rival ideological traditions such as liberalism, socialism, or totalitarianism. Berlin's distinction simply picks out two differing senses in which we might say of someone that they are (relatively) free or unfree. No important political questions are obviously settled by accepting the distinction or by opting for one of the two concepts over the other. Nor are we necessarily forced to choose between them. Indeed, as the remarks about authority above suggest, we likely need to recognize both in order to do justice to the full range of ways in which freedom may matter in political contexts.

This point runs against the grain of conventional wisdom, which often assumes that these two concepts are ideological rivals or otherwise inherently opposed, so that we must at some point declare our allegiance to one rather than the other. Berlin's original discussion has caused confusion on this point because his historical story about liberalism and totalitarianism tempted his more careless readers to suppose that he thought the two concepts, and the political theories they imply, must always be at odds. On this reading, Berlin held that negative liberty is essentially a "liberal" concept of freedom and positive liberty an essentially "nonliberal" and perhaps "totalitarian" one.

Berlin did sometimes speak of his distinction as picking out "two profoundly divergent and irreconcilable attitudes to the ends of life."[2] And he certainly did argue that, as a matter of historical record, the positive concept of liberty has proven more open to political abuse by the harbingers of modern totalitarianism. Undeniably also, Berlin saw this abuse as originating in a conceptual feature of positive liberty, its association of liberty with the presence of control, self-determination, and self-discipline.[3] Berlin suggested that this allowed the protagonists of positive freedom to confuse liberty with the exercise of political control, and to indulge Rousseau's notorious dictum that citizens must sometimes be "forced to be free." As these ideas were recruited to various collective liberation movements (especially nationalist self-determination, and Soviet-style proletarian dictatorships) during the nineteenth and twentieth centuries, the cause of positive liberty paradoxically evolved into a source of oppression, or so Berlin argued. Some began to regard the exertion of certain forms of collective control and discipline as integral to the realization of the (positive) freedom of groups, nations, associations, classes, etc. And again, as a matter of history, Berlin argued that those who construed political liberty primarily in negative terms had proved themselves less prone to any of these proto-totalitarian impulses, often speaking out against them.

But despite all this, I find no suggestion in Berlin's essay that the evolution of theories of positive liberty into doctrines purporting to justify oppressive collective control and discipline was inevitable or necessary. This was, for Berlin, a contingent historical development, and he was careful to acknowledge that many political philosophers – notably Kant – deployed positive concepts of liberty in ways that need not lead to, and indeed would preclude, the confusion of liberty with oppressive collective control.[4] He also noted that concepts of negative liberty are in principle open to dangerous misinterpretation. Finally, he explicitly insisted that "it is often necessary to strike a compromise between" the two concepts because they both represent "ultimate values" with "an equal right to be classed among the deepest interests of mankind."[5]

[2] Berlin 1969, p. 166.
[3] Berlin 1969, pp. 132–4.
[4] Berlin 1969, pp. 136–9.
[5] Berlin 1969, p. 166.

This more subtle and flexible understanding strikes me as closer to Berlin's actual views. But whatever Berlin himself intended, this seems to me the correct position to adopt in any case. We should not assume at the outset that negative and positive liberty necessarily represent politically antagonistic camps or affiliate respectively with liberal and nonliberal worldviews.

Two Families of Ideas

A second important clarification is that Berlin's two concepts are open-ended categories, in each case susceptible of a very wide range of possible political interpretations. We should think of them, then, not as very definite ideas, but as two broad ways of thinking about freedom, each of which may be developed in quite different ways for a variety of political purposes despite an underlying family resemblance.

For example, when we think of political freedom in terms of negative liberty, we immediately face a number of interpretative questions. The obstacles that might limit agents' possible actions are many and varied: some obstacles make actions strictly impossible, while others make them merely more difficult; some obstacles are the result of intentional action by other agents, while others are not; some obstacles may be more readily removed by public action, while others may be more recalcitrant; some obstacles may be completely external to the agent, while others may be partly or fully internal to the agent (does agoraphobia – the fear of open spaces – reduce an agent's negative liberty? Not clear); they may or may not interfere in activities to which agents do, or should, attach importance; some obstacles result from the activities of private citizens, while some are imposed by the state; and it may or may not be possible to remove some obstacles without imposing new and perhaps greater constraints on others.

People may disagree about which of these various kinds of impediments to freedom of action are of more urgent political significance and about whether they necessarily limit political liberty at all.[6] They may also disagree about what general goals ought to guide us in seeking an appropriate division of liberty so understood. Thus some might argue that the goal ought to be the overall "maximization" of negative liberty. Others

---

[6] Carter 1999 is the best recent effort to grapple with these complexities.

might argue that the state ought to be responsible only for guaranteeing to all individuals certain basic personal liberties, regardless of whether this would maximize overall negative freedom, whatever that might mean.

So, by the time we have settled – like Rawls – on an enumerated list of basic liberties that states are responsible for securing (see Chapter 4), we will have gone far down the road of facing and resolving some of these issues. Rawls's list of basic liberties and opportunities fits very well with the notion of negative liberty, for it defines a range of protected activities – voicing opinions, participating in religious practices, forming associations of the like-minded, and participating in democratic politics – that are in specified ways not to be obstructed either by the state itself or by other citizens. But again, Rawls's account is but *one* view of which negative liberties are of most urgent political significance. Others, also concerned about an appropriate division of negative liberty, may disagree with Rawls's judgments about which freedoms are most fundamental.[7] Libertarians, for example, think that the freedom to own property is more fundamental than, and subsumes, those liberties Rawls recognized. In their view, the responsibilities of a free society begin and end with the protection of the negative freedoms associated with the right to hold, inherit, accumulate, enjoy, buy, sell, and invest personal property.

This is a legitimate view, but although libertarians often suggest otherwise, a commitment to negative liberty does not automatically establish it. One reason for this is that the enforcement of property rights has implications for the negative liberty, not only of owners, but also of non-owners. In the UK, for example, the rights of landowners are qualified by legal duties to maintain an extensive network of public rights of way (footpaths, bridleways), along which citizens are free to walk. Farmers who erect fences and other enclosures on their land are expected to maintain stiles, gates, and pathways to allow members of the public to use these rights of way unhindered. These paths total over 117,000 miles in length (almost half the distance to the Moon), and so they afford citizens a great deal of freedom to move about the countryside on foot.

In the United States, by contrast, there is no such extensive system of public rights of way, and typically landowners have few legal duties to permit members of the public to cross their land. In the absence of

---

[7] Tomasi 2012. For a critique of Tomasi, see Bird 2014.

systematic provision of public rights of way, the fences and barriers that private owners erect to deter trespassers significantly limit freedom of movement. Hiking is thus usually possible and worthwhile only on publicly owned reservations like state forests and national parks. While in the UK one can almost always devise a cross-country route between any two towns without having to walk along roads, this option is rarely available in the USA. If one tries it, one is apt to be sued, threatened at gunpoint, snared on barbed wire, or simply defeated by walls, gates, security fences, and the other barriers property owners put up to keep the rest of us out.

Clearly, then, the enforcement of private property rights can restrict as well as expand agents' negative liberty. So we cannot simply presume that a concern for negative liberty naturally favors the cause of private property, as libertarians often contend. Of course, this hardly establishes that the libertarian conclusion about the primacy of property-based freedoms is wrong. But it does mean that we cannot decide these questions about the relative importance of the different negative freedoms individuals might enjoy just by appealing to the concept of negative liberty itself. Which particular scheme of negative liberties makes the best political sense must be determined by independent considerations (e.g. whether they promote justice, equality, personal well-being, order, efficiency, security, and so on).

The Modalities of Positive Freedom

The concept of positive liberty is no more self-interpreting than that of negative liberty. The question of what, exactly, must be *present* in order for an agent to be deemed (relatively) "positively free" raises just as many complex questions.

Some of these shade into the vexed matter of the compatibility of free will and causal determination. Many, like Kant, have worried that our ordinary notions of moral responsibility, of praise and blame, are threatened by the thesis of universal causal determinism. If human actions are no less causally determined than the behavior of thunderstorms and computers, it is unclear that it makes any more sense to praise and blame them for their actions than it does to praise a tornado for missing our home, or to blame a computer for losing our data as a result of a software bug. Driven by this anxiety, Kant's entire ethical theory is built around the effort to retrieve a conception of human beings as autonomous, self-determining agents, fully responsible for their own choices. That is why a stringent prohibition on coercion and personal manipulation lies at the heart of Kant's political ethics.[8] For Kant and his many followers, when we manipulate, coerce, and exploit others merely as "means" to our own ends, we treat them as if they were little more than objects to be shoved about and bent to our will. This fails to respect their own capacity for self-direction and threatens an aspect of their (positive) freedom.

Kant's question was how *self*-determination is even possible, given our difficulties seeing anything but causes and effects in the observable world we inhabit. The more we explain behavior in terms of heteronomous causes and effects, whether they be genetic, chemical, electrical, cellular, neuronal, social, or economic, the more our conventional notions of autonomous agency seem to slip out of view. (It is worth noting here that negative liberty raises few such metaphysical difficulties. As Hobbes noted, even inanimate objects can be more or less negatively free: he gave the comparison of a body of water that is constrained to flow down a channel and water that is by contrast free to "spread" unhindered "into a larger space."[9])

However, clarifying the metaphysical status of positive freedom will not answer all questions about how it should be interpreted in political contexts. Many agree with Kant that respecting agents' autonomy is of fundamental importance, but regard the really crucial conditions for autonomy as social, political, and psychological rather than metaphysical. For example, a condition of slavery – hardly a metaphysical state – surely precludes the relevant sort of self-determination. Slaves lack the right to control their actions: their bodies, energies, and personal assets are at the disposal of their masters. They are, by definition, not masters of themselves and so not in any plausible sense positively free. It is uncontroversial, then, that the abolition of slavery is a necessary condition for securing the positive liberty of all members of society.

But the abolition of slavery cannot be a *sufficient* condition for all possible forms of self-determination or autonomy. At their most demanding, ideals of autonomy become equivalent to perfectionist doctrines of self-realization. Some theorists of positive liberty have openly embraced just this conclusion. T. H. Green, for example, argued that "real freedom

---

[8] Kant 1993, pp. 35–45.
[9] Hobbes 1994, p. 136.

consists in the whole man having found his object" or to "have realized his ideal of himself."[10] One of Berlin's major concerns about positive liberty was that when equated with perfectionist ideals in this fashion, it can become (and historically has sometimes become) an excuse for oppressive forms of paternalism. When this happens, considerations of positive and negative liberty are likely to come into conflict.

Yet these strongly perfectionist accounts of positive liberty represent only one possible species of the genus. Other theorists of positive liberty may favor more relaxed accounts of autonomy that do not invite Berlin's criticism. Perhaps to be accounted positively free it is enough simply to have a psychological constitution in which certain impulses, addictions, neuroses, or delusions are absent. Or, moving from the psychological to the social arena, perhaps it is enough that agents are not systematically subject to certain easily preventable forms of coercion and manipulation by others.

Moreover, even those who interpret positive liberty in a more demanding perfectionist fashion need not hold the state responsible for realizing the relevant ideals directly. For example, in *On Liberty*, Mill embraced a perfectionist ideal of autonomous self-development, arguing that "[he]e who lets the world, or his own portion of it, choose his plan of life for him, has no need of any other faculty than the ape-like one of imitation." Conversely:

> He who chooses his plan for himself, employs all his faculties. He must use observation to see, reasoning and judgment to foresee, activity to gather materials for decision, discrimination to decide, and when he has decided, firmness and self-control to hold to his deliberate decision ... It is possible that he might be guided in some good path, and kept out of harm's way, without any of these things. But what will be his comparative worth as a human being? It really is of importance, not only what men do, but also what manner of men they are that do it.[11]

Although Mill did not identify this ideal of self-fashioning autonomy with political liberty, it clearly falls under the concept of positive freedom. Still, Mill expressly rejected the idea that the state ought to use the law to directly promote this ideal of self-mastery. Such efforts, he thought,

[10] Quoted in Skinner 2001, pp. 240–1.
[11] Troyer 2003, p. 196.

would invariably be self-defeating. In his view, individuals are more likely to realize the ideal of autonomous self-development if they enjoy a high degree of negative freedom to pursue their own good in their own way unhindered by paternalistic legal prohibitions.

We have seen, then, that both of Berlin's two concepts admit of different interpretations, and that there may be as much disagreement about how to interpret each as about whether and when each is more relevant. In the context of many political arguments, the two concepts may moreover complement rather than exclude each other. Less depends, then, on the decision to work with one of the two concepts itself than on the various substantive concerns that lead us to assign urgent political significance to a concern for human freedom. So, although Berlin's distinction is an important philosophical heuristic, helping to clarify different ways in which freedom figures in political debate, it cannot by itself tell us why liberty matters.

Forms of Unfreedom: Coercion

The characteristic urgency that demands for freedom carry in political life is best appreciated by reflecting on the major archetypes of *unfreedom*, virtually all of which are uncontroversial bads. Consider three such archetypes: coercion, domination, and oppression. Virtually by definition, those who are coerced, dominated, and oppressed are in some sense unfree, and whether anyone should want to be subject to them is hardly worth debating: all three are presumptively objectionable. We can also assume that the circumstances of politics often foment them. The state, after all, relies heavily on coercion to regulate the lives of its citizens, constantly threatening them with penalties for failing to obey its laws. And as political organization invariably involves the few ruling the many, the resulting differentiations of power create a standing danger of domination and oppression. However, coercion, domination, and oppression are not identical phenomena, and one can learn much about why freedom is politically important by distinguishing their specific characteristics.

A mugging provides an exemplary case of coercion: the mugger accosts you as you walk along the street and makes violent threats in order to force you to hand over your money. One can understand how such a coercive transaction diminishes your liberty either (or both) in terms of negative or positive freedom, although each brings a different aspect of coercion into view. On the one hand, one can think of a coercer as interfering with the options available to you, thereby diminishing your negative freedom: he directly interrupts your journey and prevents you from proceeding until you have complied with his demands. One might also suggest that, by depriving you of your money, the mugger reduces your negative freedom in another way: if you needed the cash in your wallet to buy a train ticket to your intended destination, he reduces your immediate options.

Some theorists of negative liberty resist this further suggestion, however, because they are keen to distinguish diminutions of freedom from reductions of power. According to these theorists, it is one thing to be *unable* to do something and another thing to be *unfree* to do it. Suppose, for example, you are ill in bed, so weak that you cannot physically get up, but that the door to your bedroom is unlocked. In that case, they maintain, you are *free* to leave the room, because the door does not prevent your exit, but lack the *power* to do so. If, on the other hand, the door is locked, you would be unfree to leave whether or not you are physically able do so. Theorists of negative liberty often press this distinction between freedom and power because they want to resist the claim that redistribution of wealth to the disadvantaged increases their freedom. Public provision of welfare, on this argument, may increase recipients' *power* but not their liberty, because as long as no one is preventing them from using any resources they possess, their freedom is not at stake. Libertarians and free marketeers routinely make this argument to deny that the desiderata of a free society include a welfare state.

Whether this sharp contrast between freedom and power is sustainable, even granting a negative concept of liberty, is, however, unclear. Commentators on the left respond, with Richard Tawney, that if

> rights are to be an effective guarantee of freedom, they must not be merely formal, like the right of all who can afford it to dine at the Ritz. They must be such that, when the occasion arises to exercise them, they can in fact be exercised. The rights to vote and combine, if not wholly valueless, are obviously attenuated, when the use of the former means eviction and of the latter the sack; the right to education, if poverty arrests its use in mid-career ... the right to earn a living if enforced unemployment is recurrent;

the right to justice, if few men of small means can afford the cost of litigation.[12]

G. A. Cohen has more recently argued, in a related vein, that money can be thought of as an all-purpose "ticket" that makes certain courses of action available to agents insofar as they possess more or less of it.[13] Just as I will be prevented from catching a flight if I lack a valid boarding pass, poverty on this view can limit the options available to a person, not merely their ability to pursue them. It is certainly not obvious, therefore, that when a mugger deprives you of your train fare on the way to the station, he is merely reducing your power but not your negative freedom.

The coercion involved in your mugging, however, also implicates your positive liberty because the mugger subjects your will to his. In suffering such subjection, you are revealed to be under alien control; the mugger effectively commandeers your will to his purposes. Unlike slavery, such coercion renders us temporarily rather than permanently unfree. But as long as one is suffering such coercion, one is, like a slave, unable to view oneself as a fully self-determining being. For the moment we find ourselves in a condition of unfreedom, and it is in the light of a tacit positive account of liberty that we recognize this. Although libertarians and proponents of free markets often disavow positive concepts of liberty, it is unclear (especially given the ease with which Tawney and Cohen draw redistributive implications from a negative concept of freedom), that their categorical hostility to state coercion makes sense without it. Nozick famously characterized coerced redistributive taxation as "on a par with forced labor," but surely we resent forced labor largely because it undermines positive freedom. To be sure, prisoners of war forced by Japanese soldiers to lay the Burma railway were deprived of options. Yet the more immediately problematic feature of their situation from the standpoint of freedom is that decisions about how to direct their own energy and power that would otherwise be theirs to make were taken out of their own hands and dictated, at gunpoint, by the wishes of the Japanese army. From the standpoint of positive liberty, then, coercion exemplifies unfreedom in that it involves being forced to act against, or independently of, one's own will.

[12] Tawney 1946, pp. 224–5.
[13] Cohen 1995.

Two points about this relation between coercion and voluntary action are worth emphasizing. First, we can now see that a common definition of negative freedom – as the "absence of coercion" – is misleading. We may be troubled by coercion either (or both) because it reduces an agent's options or because it subjects them to an alien will. But only if we object to coercion on the former grounds are we appealing to an authentically negative concept of liberty. If we object to coercion as an assault on agents' autonomy and self-determination, it is a positive concept of liberty that is doing the work. When motivated by this concern, demands for the "absence of coercion" assume that what really matters is the *presence* of (some sort of) autonomy, despite appearances to the contrary. Defining negative liberty as the "absence of coercion" fudges these important differences of emphasis.

Second, although issuing violent threats is a standard way to coerce people, the connection between coercion and physical violence is contingent, not fundamental. If the secret police or the Mafia have lurid and compromising photographs of a married man having sex with a prostitute, for example, they can, by threatening to publish the pictures, blackmail him to pass along confidential information. Although such blackmail is clearly coercive, there is nothing violent about it. The threat operates here, not through a fear of physical violence, but rather through that of social embarrassment or dishonor.

It follows that self-determination, and hence positive freedom, is about more than the absence of physical threats. The relevant feature of coercion is not its physically violent character, but the ways in which it co-opts, rather than overrides, its target's will. The mugger, after all, *does* offer you a choice: "Your money or your life." The control he exerts over you is therefore more like that exercised by the blackmailer than that wielded by prison guards physically beating you back into your cell, as you struggle and resist. The mugger is betting that a resort to actual violence will be unnecessary: verbally communicating a credible and overwhelming threat, and then leaving you to comply or not, will do the job. Although in this case fear of a physical consequence forces your choices into alignment with the mugger's desires, the resulting fusion of your will with his is problematic independently of the physical nature of his threat. What is fundamentally threatened here is not your physical integrity, but your ability to recognize yourself in your own actions. In "making you an offer you cannot refuse," the mugger's coercion renders your will indistinguishable from his: your compliance is in no interesting sense *yours*. Whether physical or not, then, coercive threats undermine positive freedom by severing the connection that should obtain between an agent's actions and their own will.

Domination

Upon taking office in January 2017, President Donald Trump, citing national security and the threat of terrorism, signed an Executive Order banning citizens of seven predominantly Muslim countries from entering the United States. Almost immediately, the order faced legal challenge on the grounds that it was motivated by religious animus, and the courts suspended it pending a full review of its constitutional standing. After several reviews, the Supreme Court eventually upheld an amended version of the ban. But while many believe (including four of the justices) that the case was wrongly decided, the Court nonetheless acknowledged that, in principle, excluding foreigners *merely* on the basis of their religious affiliation is unconstitutional. In reaffirming this position, the Court continues to prevent the US government from denying people access to its territory just because they are Muslim.

Suppose now that the Chinese government enacts a similar ban, based now on an explicitly religious test: no Muslims welcome. Muslims who wish to visit China would have no comparable hope that the courts will overturn it, because the Chinese constitution denies judges any authority to override executive decisions taken by the government. As recently as 2017, the Chinese Chief Justice, Zhou Qiang, emphatically declared that China "should resolutely resist erroneous influence from the West: 'constitutional democracy,' 'separation of powers' and 'independence of the judiciary' … We must make clear our stand and dare to show the sword."[14]

According to a long-standing "civic republican" tradition of thinking about political liberty, this contrast between the American and Chinese regimes captures the essential difference between free and unfree societies. This tradition has roots that stretch back far into classical antiquity, and is especially associated with the political theory of the Roman republic.

---

[14] Quoted in the *New York Times*, January 18, 2017. www.nytimes.com/2017/01/18/world/asia/china-chief-justice-courts-zhou-qiang.html.

Thanks to the pioneering historical scholarship of Quentin Skinner and Philip Pettit,[15] however, this "neo-Roman" account of freedom has enjoyed a recent comeback. Its central feature is a determined opposition to the discretionary exercise of power by political elites, and the concomitant claim that a "people" can enjoy true political liberty only to the extent that they have at their disposal the means to prevent arbitrary "domination" at the hands of their rulers. To combat this, civic republicans recommend an active and politically engaged citizenry, the cultivation of civic virtues, a culture of civility and mutual trust, and various institutions of public accountability such as the separation of powers and an independent judiciary. They regard these measures and institutions as partly constitutive of political liberty.

Although Trump's travel ban concerns the relation between citizens of one state and others, rather than the internal relations among citizens of the same state, it nonetheless illustrates how such checks make a society free, on the civic republican account. Citizens of a regime like that of contemporary China lack any recourse to institutional means by which to force their government to reconsider or abandon policies that widen or narrow personal freedom. As long as that is true, they and their personal freedoms lie at the mercy of the government's good will. According to civic republicans, this remains true even if the government does in fact extend its citizens significant personal liberty. For example, over the past half-century, the Chinese government has liberalized its economy, moving at breakneck speed from socialist central planning to one of the most dynamic free-market economies the world has ever seen. Clearly, China now accords its citizens a far wider economic freedom that was the case 50 years ago, but civic republicans insist that as long as these liberties are enjoyed solely at the pleasure of the government's will, Chinese citizens are in a state of political subjection. Should the government decide to withdraw these freedoms, citizens lack any institutionalized recourse for restoring them. Moreover, the Chinese government in fact denies them, or sharply limits, many other liberties (freedom of speech and worship, rights to run for office, form political parties, etc.), and citizens lack any constitutional right to force the government to provide them.

Conversely, the ability of an independent judiciary in a constitutional republic like the United States to invalidate Trump's "travel ban" is, for civic

---

[15] Pettit 1999; Skinner 2012.

republicans, an indispensable desideratum of political liberty. For it ensures that the will of the governing powers is not the last word as far as citizens' (and in this case noncitizens') freedom is concerned. As long as such guarantees are absent, citizens are in a state akin to slavery, and this remains true even if, for the moment, their masters in fact accord them considerable personal freedom. Slaves owned by a benevolent master, who affords them considerable freedom to earn their own pocket money, go to town on the weekends, or to enjoy leisure time, are still slaves. Their master enjoys an unconstrained right to withdraw these freedoms at any moment.

Civic republicans therefore strongly resist the modern effort, initiated by Hobbes and continued by the classical utilitarians, to reduce all important dimensions of political liberty to claims about negative freedom. Such claims, they maintain, cannot capture the essential requirement of "non-domination" that citizens' freedoms are not subject to the arbitrary will of governing powers. In the seventeenth century, this issue was dramatized in the opposed attitudes that Hobbes and his civic republican critics took to the Ottoman Empire, at the time the standard example of arbitrary despotism. As we have noted before, Hobbes defended the modern state's claim to wield unlimited authority over its citizens. He thus defended exactly the kind of arbitrary, discretionary authority that republicans repudiate in the name of freedom. But, by interpreting political liberty as negative freedom, Hobbes was able to argue that citizens will always be free to the extent that even an arbitrary sovereign leaves their actions unobstructed. How much latitude they enjoy within the "silence of the law" will vary in different states and at different times, but Hobbes denied the republican suggestion that citizens are *necessarily* rendered categorically unfree or are enslaved by the mere existence of political rulers wielding arbitrary authority over them. Thus Hobbes famously ridiculed the claim that citizens of popular republics like Lucca and Venice are necessarily freer than subjects of the despotic sultanate of Constantinople.[16]

But republican critics of Hobbes, such as his contemporary James Harrington, insisted that the citizens of Lucca are free in a way that subjects of the sultan are not.[17] Even if the sultan is a benevolent and liberal-minded

---

[16] Hobbes 1994, p. 140.
[17] Skinner 2012, p. 86.

ruler, leaving to his subjects wide areas of negative freedom, republicans will still deny that his citizens are authentically free. They are not really free because these negative liberties are not provided at their own hands; they are rather conditional benefits enjoyed at the pleasure of an agency beyond their control. His subjects therefore remain in a state of dependence and unfreedom akin to slavery, mere "tenants" of their "heads," as Harrington put it.

Contemporary civic republicans have extended this analysis of "non-domination" in two directions. On the one hand, they have argued that the relevant forms of domination are not restricted to distinctively civic relations. Agents can suffer domination, for example, when their livelihood comes to depend on the arbitrary will of financial institutions extending them loans, or when the personal safety of women is threatened by a culture of impunity protecting sexually abusive men (what feminists sometimes refer to as "rape-culture"). On the other hand, they have argued that the civic republican conception of freedom as "non-domination" represents an important "third" concept of liberty that cannot be accounted for either in terms of negative freedom, positive freedom, or of some combination.[18]

The first extension is more compelling than the second. Surely it is at least plausible to claim that women who live in constant fear of assault at the hands of their abusive spouses because the cultural and political norms in their society permit men to act without restraint at home suffer a kind of domination that reduces their freedom. The same can be said of those hounded by rapacious debt collectors representing lenders who are free to demand repayment *at will*, even when the debtor's financial difficulties may not be in any sense their fault.

Whether these forms of domination cannot be adequately captured solely in terms of positive and negative liberty is, however, less clear. For one thing, many of the freedoms that civic republicans insist should not be enjoyed at the discretion of government (freedom of speech, assembly, worship, etc.) are clearly standard negative liberties. For another, what republicans fundamentally care about is a certain kind of (political) independence consisting in the provision of (institutionalized) means by which citizens can preserve freedoms that the powerful are constantly tempted to withdraw. Surely, citizens who are in a position to protect their freedoms

---

[18] Pettit 1999, pp. 21–31; Skinner 2001, p. 255, n. 90.

by these means enjoy a certain kind of political self-determination, i.e. a form of collective positive freedom. But for these checks, after all, they would be subject to the arbitrary rule of alien powers. Conversely, insofar as they are available, citizens are able to force their governments to respect freedoms to which they attach great importance. That they are in a position to protect themselves against despotic and alien rule arising within their own communities implies that they are guardians of their own liberties, and in this sense masters of their political destiny.

Contemporary civic republicans sometimes argue, with Philip Pettit, that this position cannot involve claims about positive freedom, because it interprets liberty negatively, as the absence of dependence, domination, or mastery. But this suggestion is misleading. Since presence and absence are opposites it is always possible to reformulate claims about a presence in terms of an absence and vice versa. The absence of obstacles, for example, implies the presence of opportunities. The presence of slavery can be redescribed as the absence of self-mastery. And, as we noticed earlier, the presence of autonomy requires the absence of coercion. To suggest that republicans are interested "merely" in the absence of domination, mastery, and dependence as if this does not automatically, and indeed more importantly, assume that political freedom requires the presence of independence and autonomy is to appeal to a distinction without a difference.

To be sure, this republican account of freedom does not involve the sort of strongly *perfectionist* interpretation of positive liberty of which Berlin was deeply suspicious, under which groups or individuals are free only when they achieve full personal or collective self-realization. But as we have noted, there's a whole family of positive conceptions, of which perfectionist self-realization views form but one subset. Republicans interpret political autonomy in very different terms, but that does not mean that their position falls outside the scope of positive freedom.

Oppression

The allegation that the structures of modern society are in various ways oppressive has been a staple of left-wing social criticism since at least Marx. Although diagnoses of the relevant forms of oppression have often been quite diverse, three connected themes consistently recur in philosophical arguments made on behalf of those oppressed.

First, oppression is usually understood as something agents suffer as members of particular groups who find themselves in a structurally disadvantaged position within some overarching system. In classical Marxism, for example, the working class is oppressed under capitalism because its systematically precarious economic condition leaves its members unable to bargain with employers in the labor market on favorable terms; they and their interests are therefore structurally subordinated within the processes by which capitalist social relations are maintained. Feminist critics have similarly argued that women are oppressed under "patriarchal" conditions insofar as their choices are limited by a variety of entrenched legal, ethical, cultural, and ideological constraints reflecting chauvinist stereotypes of femininity and protecting privileges historically enjoyed by men. Insofar as groups defined by race, ethnicity, religious affiliation, or sexual orientation face comparably systematic disadvantage, their members suffer oppression in this sense.[19]

Second, unlike most cases of coercion and (often) of domination, describing social conditions as oppressive does not require the presence of specific agents whom we can describe as denying others their freedom. As the case of a mugging illustrates, coercion usually consists in specific acts (making threats) committed knowingly by a coercer. To be dominated in the manner that worries civic republicans is, in the standard case, to be subject to the decisions and actions of some specific dominator (whether a slaveowner, a ruler, a functionary of some powerful organization, an abusive spouse, etc.) who thereby deprives someone of their freedom. Oppressive social relations, however, are not attributable to specific agents in this way, because the distinctive form of unfreedom involved is structural rather than agentic.

To appreciate this feature of oppression, consider the following contrast between oppressive and *corrupt* societies. We judge a society "corrupt" when, and to the extent that, specific acts of corruption are so endemic as to have become routine. In judging a society's corruption in this way, we appeal to independently defined archetypes of corrupt action (bribing a judge, making a nepotistic appointment, buying silence, etc.). Clearly, however, individual instances of corruption can occur in isolation, even against the background of largely clean institutional routines. One who

---

[19] For a good general account of oppression, see Cudd 2006.

bribes a judge has committed a specific act of corruption regardless of how widespread bribery is in her society. With oppression, however, matters are precisely the other way around. Oppression is not something anyone *does* or commits apart from some wider structure of subordination. To be sure, particular actions and choices can take on an oppressive character; but they do so only when set against a background framework of unfreedom. Whereas "offering" or "accepting" a bribe constitute specific acts of corruption whatever the overall character of the society in which they occur, individual conduct can exemplify or contribute to oppression only because an oppressive social structure already exists.

This helps to explain why, despite regarding capitalism as oppressive, Marx nonetheless denied that capitalist firms culpably wrong the workers they exploit. He took this line, in part, because he thought that the structures of market society largely dictate the choices and conduct of agents caught up in them; a capitalist CEO who lays off the workforce of an unprofitable factory is not in any interesting sense making a "free" choice, nor usually doing so simply because she wants to. Rather, responsible for maximizing her shareholders' returns, she is compelled by the logic of market competition to close failing enterprises. For Marx, this illustrates how the capitalist system induces (indeed is constituted by) the oppression of those who have nothing to sell but their own labor, whose lives and hopes are systematically limited by that circumstance, regardless of anyone's intentions, actions, or decisions. They are oppressed in that the horizons of their lives are objectionably narrowed by their structural position, even though we cannot attribute that outcome to specific choices, wrongs, or culpable agencies. This is an example of the "realist" style of social criticism we mentioned in Chapter 1. We will return to this line of argument in the final two chapters.

Third, precisely because they take it to be endemic to deeply entrenched social systems, theorists of oppression frequently maintain that its presence can be hard to detect, particularly from the standpoint of those socialized into them. Its manifestations are often so pervasive that agents easily mistake them for the natural order of things and find it difficult to imagine alternatives. For example, women socialized from an early age to accept certain traditional gender roles may not notice the ways in which sexist norms artificially limit their conception of what their lives should and can be. They may buy uncritically into the erroneous belief that their exclusion from the vote, their limited access to positions of social and political responsibility, and their confinement to domestic forms of life are somehow justified by their feminine nature. Thus although, on standard views, oppression is a structural phenomenon, a function of the differential power enjoyed by particular social groups, it can limit agents' freedom in an especially intimate and insidious way, distorting their self-understandings at a very deep level. Not only are victims of oppression frequently forced to navigate their way through social life behind inauthentic masks misrepresenting who they really are or what they are capable of, they may also lack any clear awareness of a tension between the expectations inscribed on those masks and their real interests and needs. Accordingly, theorists of oppression frequently attach special importance to "raising consciousness," encouraging members of marginalized groups to question their conventionally approved self-image and to open themselves to new forms of self-understanding.

Like coercion and domination, then, oppression is a complex phenomenon in which both negative and positive freedom are potentially implicated. The former, because oppression is both a symptom and a cause of structural constraints on the options available to agents under various conditions. Oppressed groups frequently face formal and informal barriers to opportunities, professional advancement, and political representation. They are often trapped at the margins of society, where they face recalcitrant social and economic disadvantages that impede their efforts to better themselves (the fact that we find it natural to speak of a "poverty trap" indicates that negative freedom is at stake, for being entrapped implies confinement). They may face discrimination and prejudice in the workplace, in educational institutions, and at the hands of the police. In some cases, the law prohibits activities in which they have a legitimate personal interest (think of the only recent decriminalization of homosexual relationships, or of religious groups unable to worship as they wish because they are persecuted by the majority). In these and other ways, reductions of negative liberty orbit the phenomena of oppression.

However, the distinctive character of oppressive circumstances probably owes more to their implications for positive freedom, which differ interestingly from those of coercion and domination. Coercion limits positive freedom by commandeering an agent's will so that it becomes indistinguishable from that of the coercer. Domination does so by leaving agents entirely subject to the arbitrary caprice of an agent or agency in a position to condition their life circumstances at will, so that they are no longer in any meaningful sense in charge of their own destinies. Oppression undermines positive freedom in a more sinister way, potentially distorting agents' ability to even recognize a conflict between their own wills and requirements imposed by a system that subordinates them to its needs. In this sense, it makes victims complicit in their own unfreedom, submitting them to something akin to voluntary slavery. On the other hand, it is exactly this positive libertarian diagnosis of oppression that encourages what Berlin saw as the germ of totalitarianism: the belief that human emancipation requires the eradication of voluntary desires that lead agents to act against their best interests.

Sweatshops

To see how these various notions of unfreedom might help us critically evaluate particular social practices, I conclude with a test case: the phenomenon of sweatshop labor. Should we regard sweatshop workers' freedom as compromised, or should we conclude (as some think) that liberty and sweatshop labor can coexist?

Sweatshops exist wherever there are concentrated and impoverished populations with few alternative options for gainful employment. This circumstance provides employers (often Western multinationals outsourcing their manufacturing) with irresistible opportunities to lower their labor costs. On any view, sweatshops are miserable places: workers face long hours performing often soul-destroying manual labor for wages hovering around subsistence. They characteristically earn a tiny fraction of the market value of their products. Working conditions are often unsafe and unhealthy. After a rash of suicides and suicide attempts by its workers in 2010, the firm Foxconn, which assembled iPhones for Apple in China, installed nets outside its main factory in Longhua to catch falling bodies. The predicament of these workers reminds one of the brutal early phases of industrial capitalism in the West that led Marx and a host of other critics to decry the dehumanizing conditions of modern factory labor.

No one envies the plight of the sweatshop worker, then, but does it follow that they are unfree? Defenders of sweatshops deny this on two grounds.[20] They argue, first, that although sweatshop workers typically have no very good options to choose from, the presence of employers with jobs available can only enlarge rather than limit their negative freedom. Even if the opportunities opened up by sweatshop employment are far from ideal, they still open avenues by which people can provide for themselves and their families. As the left-leaning economist Joan Robinson once conceded: "The misery of being exploited by capitalists is nothing compared to the misery of not being exploited at all."[21]

Second, they point out that since no one is forcing sweatshop workers to sign their labor contracts, their choice to work is free and uncoerced. Unlike blackmailers and muggers who threaten to make their victims radically worse off, sweatshop employers offer their workers a benefit. Certainly, compared to the benefits conferred by many other jobs, sweatshop employment improves workers' welfare only marginally. Still, the offer of even a very slight benefit that agents can choose to decline cannot be plausibly regarded as coercive, or so some argue. The existence of sweatshops need not, on this view, be incompatible with respect for everyone's status as equal rights-holders free to accept only those conditions to which they voluntarily consent.

These arguments are hardly decisive, however. Even if one concedes that sweatshop workers are not coerced to accept their jobs, the conditions they face once they enter the workplace are a very different matter. Sweatshop workers typically confront a management wielding virtually despotic control over their lives at work; they may be denied time to visit the bathroom when they need to, to take food breaks, or to rest when they are feeling unwell. Disobedience or open defiance are likely to be deterred by fear of being fired, and in some cases by forms of disciplinary humiliation, public shaming and even blackmail. On paper, of course, companies may be legally responsible for observing health and safety regulations in their sweatshops, but violations will usually come to the attention of the authorities only if whistle-blowers on the factory floor feel able to report them without fear of reprisals, which they may be very reluctant to do in the face of intimidation by management. Few states can monitor and inspect working conditions all the time, and companies seeking to minimize

---

[20] Zwolinski 2007.
[21] Robinson 2017, p. 45.

production costs will tend to locate their sweatshops in regions where legal regulations are anyway lightly enforced. All of this fosters a culture of impunity.

Whatever conditions hold when workers accept sweatshop employment, then, the environment they subsequently enter is frequently highly coercive. It is also plausibly one of domination, in that they can do little to call those exercising *de facto* control over their working conditions to account for abuses of power. As long as that is so, they are effectively subjects of arbitrary autocratic regimes operating within the sweatshop walls.

And, in view of the high proportion of their time given over to working under such conditions, their limited opportunities for leisure outside them, and their weak bargaining position in the labor market, sweatshop workers are also almost certainly oppressed, their lives stunted and effectively held hostage to the logic of market competition. In one important respect, however, their oppression is unlike that suffered by women who internalize sexist ideologies limiting them to narrow gender roles. Members of those socio-economic groups whose structural weakness renders them most liable to sweatshop exploitation rarely have any difficulty recognizing their subjection to corporations and employers with vastly superior market power. In this sense, their oppression is overt rather than ideologically disguised. If these considerations are sound, it is beside the point to claim, in line with the second of the two defenses enumerated above, that sweatshop owners do not coerce their workers into signing their labor contracts.

But is that claim plausible in the first place? A contingent reason to resist it arises when companies using sweatshops collude with, or lobby, local governments to lift, or overlook, health and safety regulations, and to keep prospective workers in a condition of relative deprivation, so that it is harder for them to refuse highly exploitative terms of employment. These efforts make them more or less complicit in coercive practices. But, even if no such complicity exists, the claim that workers' acceptance of sweatshop terms is usually voluntary and unforced is vulnerable to a deeper objection.

Let us grant that workers are rarely coerced into sweatshop labor in the way that muggers or blackmailers extort compliance from their victims. Is this sufficient to establish that their decision to agree to a sweatshop owner's terms must be fully voluntary? No: as Serena Olsaretti has cogently argued, while direct, culpable, coercion is *one* way in which agents can be forced to act against their will, it is not the only one.[22] We cannot simply assume that only when a culpable agent deliberately coerces someone is there any meaningful sense in which they are forced into involuntary action. Even though it is not coercing anyone, for example, an approaching tsunami may force people from their homes, and surely it would be odd to describe them as evacuating willingly.

To be sure, the evacuees do not want to drown: since here their will to survive trumps their desire to protect and fortify their homes against the flood, we cannot say that their flight finds no foothold at all in their wills. Still, I submit that we hesitate to describe their evacuation as willing or fully voluntary, because the incoming tsunami forces them to choose between options neither of which any sane person could reasonably want under normal circumstances: drown or abandon one's home to looters and the onrushing sea. Why deny that the same applies when economic conditions confront some agents only with a choice between abject, life-threatening poverty and the degrading, dehumanizing conditions of sweatshop labor? Whether an agent's decisions can plausibly be seen as unforced, voluntary, and free when their only options are so dire is doubtful. More so, when, unlike the case of the tsunami, the conditions forcing people to choose between terrible alternatives are not of natural origin, but the result of artificially created social systems subject to human modification.

One might reply, retreating to the first of the two pro-sweatshop arguments given above, that this does not show that those forced to choose between such unattractive alternatives are unfree. After all, as Olsaretti herself points out, doing something involuntarily presupposes that one was free to do it. But leaning on Olsaretti's observation for this purpose is a desperate gambit. For one thing, it would imply that blackmailers and muggers do not render their victims unfree, because complying with their demands presupposes that the latter were free to do so. More generally, this reply works only under a negative concept of freedom. The deepest doubts about the freedom of sweatshop workers, however, concern their status as autonomous authors of their own lives. This is a matter of positive liberty; claims about the degree to which they are negatively free to act in one way or another miss the relevant point completely.

---

[22] Olsaretti 2009, pp. 137ff.

13 Democratic Rule

Democracy is today a central part of the self-image of Western nation-states. This is no disinterested self-description. It is also a *cherished* self-image. Hence the celebratory, even self-congratulatory, tenor of much contemporary discourse about democracy: it is, our leaders tell us, a noble yet realistic political ideal, worth fighting and perhaps dying for. And they continually remind us how fortunate we are to live in societies committed to realizing it, and in large measure (allegedly) succeeding in doing so. The endless incantation of this view may lead us to take it too much for granted. This chapter asks whether there is anything to be said for it.

What Is Democracy?

"Democracy" is an adjective (sometimes an adverb) masquerading as a noun. Literally, it means "rule of or by the people." But this concept does not really designate some simple nameable object like a stone or a cat, still less any sort of natural kind. Rather, it refers to a possible and variable property of a particular social practice, the practice of "ruling," or (more broadly) that of "collective decision-making." The focal usages of the concept of democracy are therefore adjectival or adverbial qualifications of such practices, as in: "This decision was reached democratically"; "The legislative process in Pacifica is very undemocratic"; "Democratic procedures promote freedom."

Of course, we do often speak of certain regimes or states as "democracies" *tout court*. But we should be careful not to take such classifications too literally; they are usually best understood as shorthand for more variegated underlying claims about different regimes' decision-making mechanisms. Perhaps for certain (let's face it: often propagandist) purposes it makes sense to distinguish democracies categorically from nondemocratic regimes and associations (tyrannies, authoritarian dictatorships, corporations), but even so such distinctions tend to beg some important questions. For example, this opposition might lead us to think that tyranny and democracy are mutually exclusive. But many have worried, from Aristotle to Mill and Tocqueville, that tyranny can take democratic forms, a possibility that an exclusive dichotomy between democracy and tyranny will require us to discount. Similarly, is there any reason to assume, *a priori*, that democratic decisions could not exemplify "authoritarianism" (whatever that is), or that dictatorships could not arise democratically, or even sustain themselves through democratic means?

The Complexity of Democratic Forms

So even if excluding certain regimes as "nondemocracies" is appropriate for some legitimate purpose, the remaining ones are not helpfully understood as democracies *simpliciter*, but rather as democratic in various ways and to different degrees. These ways and degrees are far more complex than one might initially think. Jack Lively notes that "rule by the people" might mean at least:

(1) That all (should) govern, in the sense that all should be involved in legislating, in deciding on general policy, in applying laws and in governmental administration.
(2) That all (should) be personally involved in crucial decision-making, that is to say in deciding general laws and matters of general policy.
(3) That rulers (should) be accountable to the ruled; they should, in other words, be obliged to justify their actions to the ruled and be removable by the ruled.
(4) That rulers (should) be accountable to the representatives of the ruled.
(5) That rulers (should) be chosen by the ruled.
(6) That rulers (should) be chosen by representatives of the ruled.[1]

This helpful list is already complex enough, but several of Lively's provisions themselves invite further complication. For example, provisions

---

[1] Lively 2007, p. 30, parentheses added.

(1) and (2) speak of (personal) "involvement" in decision-making processes. But what sorts of "involvement" might democratic procedures require?

The obvious possibility is participation in elections, and especially voting, but it is worth noting that the association of democracy and election is relatively recent: from antiquity until roughly the eighteenth century, political theorists more often associated voting and election with elitist forms of rule – such as oligarchy or aristocracy. In contrast, democratic rule was associated with the selection of public officials by lot ("sortition"), the mechanism by which today we select jurors.[2] From this classical point of view, what we now often identify as a form of democratic rule is better described as a kind of elective aristocracy, in which political elites, organized as political parties, compete for votes in regularly held elections. There's therefore scope for debate about how democratic competitive party politics really is.

This distinction between election and sortition is also relevant to the notions of choice and representation mentioned in Lively's provisos (4), (5), and (6). For sortition is one way of choosing rulers, and it is certainly arguable that the random selection of leaders by lot would, over the long term, secure a fairer representation of social interests than majoritarian elections. Why shouldn't we pick democratic representatives in this way? This is a good question.

On the other hand, as Lively's provisions (1)–(4) imply, the selection of rulers is not the only issue that needs to be considered. There is also the question of how far policies and decisions reflect the beliefs or preferences of the ruled. If one thought that the main point of democratic participation was not to pick rulers, but to translate citizens' various opinions about public policy into an overall judgment that can be ascribed to everyone (the "will of the people"), one might think that voting, understood as a way of expressing preferences for different policies, is better suited to democratic purposes than sortition. Referenda on particular issues, for example, and direct ballot initiatives as practiced in some American states, plausibly exemplify democratic rule in this sense. Similarly, the rather elusive notion of "public opinion" plays an important role in modern democratic politics, and one standard way of accessing information about it is through "opinion

---

[2] See Manin 1997 for a discussion of the history, and Guerrero 2014 for a recent effort to revive the idea for modern use.

polls," participation in which resembles voting in elections. Against this, however, one might argue that efforts to divine "public opinion" using deliberative "focus groups" rather than through aggregate polling data, involve important concessions to sortition.

But even if we set aside sortition and stick simply with voting and election, further complications arise. Are voting procedures more or less democratic to the extent that they approximate unanimity, majority rule, or plurality rule? Which system of election is more democratic: first-past-the-post or proportional representation? There is also the question of whether the right to vote (or indeed to participate in other ways) is actually *exercised* by large numbers of people. One could hold, for example, that procedures are democratic mainly to the extent that the ruled enjoy formal rights to participate, whether or not they choose to exercise them.

Against this, though, it may seem odd to claim that a polity in which only a small minority of citizens choose to exercise their formal right to vote is fully democratic. Historically, many proponents of democratic rule have urged that formal rights to participate are necessary but not sufficient for genuine rule by the people to be realized. They argue that popular self-government in this sense requires the active and widespread participation of citizens: insofar as citizens become politically disengaged and apathetic, democratic rule becomes corrupted and eventually moribund.[3] This notion that democratic participation should be thought of as a civic duty rather than a right has however been contested by some modern theorists of democracy who claim that a degree of apathy and political disengagement may actually be functionally necessary for stable democratic rule.[4]

Finally, there are complications about the *levels* of decision-making at which one might think democratic participation is appropriate. Modern political thought, for example, has sometimes distinguished between the state and the government. This distinction tends to become elusive on close inspection, but the general idea is clear enough. The "government" here refers to the particular groups of people who actually occupy positions of official responsibility at particular times, and who therefore operate the

---

[3] Mill 1972, p. 207; Rousseau 2011, p. 198.

[4] See Pateman 1970, ch. 1; for an explicit philosophical argument against the duty to vote, see Lomasky and Brennan 2000. Brennan 2011 argues, a little differently, that citizens should vote only if they are adequately informed and motivated by concern for the common good.

organs of political control (presidents, members of parliaments or cabinets, ministers of this or that department of state, and so on) on a day-to-day basis. The "state," on the other hand, refers to the more basic and enduring legal framework within which these officials work and that circumscribes their powers, especially the constitutional rules that define sovereignty, empower legislative bodies, and authorize the various branches of government to perform various general functions.

Either or both of these loci of political power could be organized democratically. In Chapter 6, we saw that Rousseau argued that to be legitimate, forms of political rule must be subject to a General Will that can only be articulated directly by a popular sovereign. So for Rousseau the *state* must be organized democratically: sovereignty can on this view be exercised legitimately only by the full assembly of citizens. Curiously, however, Rousseau rejected the idea that the *government* ought to be democratically organized, apparently on the grounds that the majority of a population is unlikely to be sufficiently virtuous to be entrusted with the day-to-day execution of the General Will.[5]

In contrast, it can be argued that the institutions of modern representative democracy exemplify something like the reverse combination. That is, what is most obviously democratic in "liberal democracies" is the selection of governments or "administrations" to occupy positions of official responsibility for defined periods of time. The deeper constitutional framework that defines these official responsibilities, their scope and limits, and indeed the rules of democratic elections themselves, is less obviously subject to democratic control, certainly on any regular basis. The tenuously democratic nature of this constitutional background is nowhere more evident than in the practice of judicial constitutional review, which in many societies (notably the United States) gives a tiny minority of specially trained legal experts the right to override legislation supported by democratically elected governments.

Democratic Ideals

The modalities of democratic rule are thus extremely complex. Recognizing this complexity already inflicts some damage on the conventional wisdom

---

[5] Rousseau 2011, pp. 179–80; for the historical background, see Tuck 2016.

about democracy with which we began. When our leaders tout the virtues of Western democratic institutions, they frequently speak of democracy as if it were a single, simple ideal. This view implies that there is a simple scale of democracy, such that we can always compare how near or far particular regimes are to realizing "the" ideal of democratic rule. It is often combined with a unilinear theory of political development, according to which the trajectory of political societies from barbarism to maturity is a story of progressive approximation toward truly democratic institutions.

But our discussion so far tends to undermine the assumption on which all these views rest – that democracy is a unique, simple ideal. In Chapter 4, we questioned whether human well-being is reducible to some single, common measure of utility. We saw there that, insofar as well-being comes in many, incommensurable forms, the utilitarian effort to "maximize human well-being" seems incoherent. Acknowledging that there are many different and sometimes inconsistent ways for political rule to be democratic encourages a similar conclusion in the context of democracy. It is not clear that "promoting democracy" *as such* is a meaningful political project. There are only various different, and possibly conflicting, *sorts* of democratic arrangements to be promoted for various different, and similarly conflicting, *sorts* of reasons.

Given this, it comes as no surprise that the range of social ideals that are often mobilized to justify democratic arrangements is extremely wide. Below I distinguish and assess five major strands of argument for democratic rule of various sorts. This list is neither exhaustive nor comprehensive, but it is a start, and hopefully conveys the complex relations between the various different ideals at stake in democratic political forms. The first three lines of argument recommend democratic arrangements in terms of certain ideals that they allegedly promote; these I will call the *positive arguments*. The last two do so on the grounds that democratic procedures stave off certain evils or abuses; I call these *defensive arguments*.

The Positive Arguments

The Common Good Justification

The first of the positive arguments recommends democratic decision-making because it helps society to recognize and pursue its own common good. This argument has many possible forms, but the most basic version runs as follows. Promoting the common good requires rule in the interests of the ruled, but we cannot trust exclusive subgroups of citizens to supply reliable and impartial information about the true interests of the ruled. They are likely to be unduly partial to their narrow sectional interests. By comparison, a fully inclusive democratic consultation of all citizens seems more likely to identify the common good accurately and impartially. Democratic procedures are therefore our best hope for promoting a sound understanding of the public interest and for pursuing it intelligently together.

The Argument from Self-Government

This second argument defends democratic procedures on the grounds that they promote the independent value of collective self-determination or political autonomy. Behind this argument are the suggestions that a society is not free unless it follows its own will, and that "its own will" must mean the will of the people who comprise it. Since only democratic procedures can identify the popular will, they are necessary, and perhaps sufficient, conditions for realizing the value of political freedom or self-government, or so the argument maintains.

This argument assumes that political autonomy in this sense is inherently valuable. Although it therefore readily implies that self-government is a good, perhaps an aspect of citizens' common good, it is important not to confuse it with the common good justification for democracy. In contrast to the latter, the argument from self-government need not contend that democratic rule is valuable because it enables citizens to identify, appreciate, and therefore effectively pursue their shared interests. Rather, it claims that democratic decision-making is valuable simply because, in realizing collective self-government, it directly realizes something of value, whether or not citizens consciously understand that this is the case, and whether or not it helps citizens to appreciate properly their other common interests.

The Argument from Egalitarian Justice

This argument asserts that democratic procedures are required in order to achieve an equitable division of political power. Assuming that justice requires that citizens be treated as equals, it seems natural to conclude that everyone subject to political rule is entitled, as a matter of justice, to an equal say in political decision-making. Political arrangements that deny anyone subject to coercive power an equal voice in determining how that power is to be used must, this argument contends, be fundamentally unjust. Since only democratic arrangements include everyone on suitably egalitarian terms, nondemocratic arrangements must on this view be systematically unjust.

The Defensive Arguments

The Conflict Resolution Argument

Any stable society needs some mechanism for resolving conflicts among its members and between groups with opposed interests. This argument contends that democratic arrangements represent the most propitious basis for the peaceful resolution of these potentially destabilizing conflicts. Even if one were pessimistic about the capacity of democratic decision-making to identify the common good, realize ideals of collective self-government, or satisfy the requirements of justice in the distribution of political power, one could still find redeeming merit in this putative ability to manage and settle social conflict. The value of democracy, on this account, lies in its ability to avert the dangers of social instability, disorder, violence, and – at the limit – civil war.

This argument sometimes takes a purely pragmatic form. For example, some claim that the virtues of democratic arrangements consist in the following features. Under democratic decision-making procedures everyone is invited to participate in a recursive process: (a) over which no one group has exclusive control; (b) with systematically uncertain outcomes; and (c) whose results on particular occasions are always revisable and so never final. These features foster a disposition on the part of conflicting social constituencies to bargain and compromise with each other.[6] Moreover, the fact that democratic outcomes are always revisable gives those groups that lose out on particular occasions hope that their view might prevail another day. In this way, even losers come to have a stake in collaborating

---

[6] For a sophisticated version of this view, see Przeworski 1991, ch. 1.

with, rather than subverting, the rules of the democratic game. In contrast, less inclusive decision-making procedures systematically alienate the excluded groups, for by hypothesis they lack the ability to influence political outcomes and therefore any stake in the official process by which decisions are reached. This threatens order and social peace; democratic inclusion is hence an advisable preventive.

But this argument is also often formulated in terms of the desiderata of political legitimacy, and in this guise it presents a more moralized cast.[7] In Chapter 6, we saw that contractualists often argue that legitimate institutions, laws, and policies must show themselves to be acceptable to all those subject to them. Clearly, democratic procedures cannot guarantee that this standard of legitimacy is always met. However, many argue that the conditions of democratic discussion force citizens to take it seriously and therefore promote political legitimacy in this sense. In a democracy, for example, citizens hoping to advance a certain policy or proposal must often persuade at least a plurality, and if possible a majority, of their fellows to go along with it. In seeking to do so, they must address each other as equals, each entitled to their own opinions and judgments, for this notion of civic equality is part and parcel of democratic political culture. Citizens are thereby forced to couch their arguments in terms that people with diverse beliefs could all find acceptable. In this way, the discipline of democratic compromise and debate increases the chances that political outcomes will be justifiably viewed by citizens as legitimate. This in turn facilitates peace and political stability even in the face of deep moral, religious, and political disagreement, or so the argument goes.

Safeguarding Liberty against Power

This is perhaps the simplest and most familiar argument of all. It rests on the assumption that, given the frailties of human nature, unchecked power is always an invitation to abuse and oppression. As Lord Acton famously put it, "Power corrupts, absolute power corrupts absolutely." The argument is that democracy is best defended as a response to this problem. Democratic accountability is valuable, on this view, because it provides

[7] See Cohen 1989; Gutmann and Thompson 2006.

an essential means for the subordinated to check the machinations of the powerful.

Insofar as it appeals to a notion of (collective) political freedom, this line of reasoning resembles the argument from self-government. It certainly seems natural to say that when a people are deprived of ways to replace their masters, call them to account, or overrule their mandates, it is in an important sense *unfree*. As we saw in Chapter 12, classical republicans have often described this condition as a form of political enslavement. They therefore insist that political freedom requires the vigilant monitoring of rulers by the ruled. But the notion of political freedom involved in this republican argument is weaker than that to which the argument from self-government appeals. The latter argument interprets political freedom in terms of the ambitious ideal of a society identifying and following its own "collective will." But the republican argument need not rest on anything so caffeinated. It involves the less demanding notion of citizens collectively defending their (individual) liberties against the predations of political elites through mechanisms of democratic accountability.

Before raising some questions about each of these arguments, it is important to note that their very diversity reinforces our earlier conclusions about the complexity of democratic forms. It is surely misleading to suggest that the five arguments represent complementary and mutually supportive elements of a simple case "for democracy." Even a cursory inspection suggests that they do not all point toward democratic arrangements of the same sort. It is far more likely that each supports quite different, perhaps incongruous, visions of an appropriately democratic order.

The Common Good Justification

Plato's *Republic* provides the classic statement of the most important objection to this first argument. Plato's objection grants that political rule should be guided by the interests of the ruled, but questions the claim that the common good (in this sense) is likely to be effectively appreciated and pursued through democratic means. As we saw in Chapter 2, Plato believed that properly understanding the common good is an extremely complex and challenging task: for example, it requires knowledge of the conditions of human well-being. It also depends on informed insight into the complicated interplay between social forms and entrenched moral beliefs on the one hand, and the psychological dispositions of character that they tend to promote, on the other. Only those with the necessary wisdom, experience, and training are likely to be up to these challenges. Untutored democratic publics are very unlikely to be so equipped, or so Plato maintained. That is why we do not have passengers on airplanes vote on how they are to be flown, or patients to vote on the medical treatments each should receive.

This objection is often dismissed for seeming to turn on Plato's easily ridiculed claim that only philosophers are competent to rule. But this misses the point. Plato's proposal about philosopher-rulers was his suggested cure for the (alleged) ills of democratic rule, but rejecting this cure as mistaken does nothing to undermine Plato's initial diagnosis. The central doubt remains: are democratic publics competent to appreciate and intelligently pursue their shared interests?

An example may dramatize the question. Today, the manipulation of interest rates has become a major tool of economic policy. But in many states – including the USA and the UK – interest rates are determined by a largely unaccountable elite of economists working in central banks (the Federal Reserve, the Bank of England). Whatever we think about Plato's philosopher-rulers, it seems quite plausible that trained economists are more likely to control the money supply skillfully than members of the public who lack any understanding of economics. This is presumably why we do not hold democratic referenda to determine interest rates. But if we reject democratic rule here, on the grounds that the relevant issues are better left to informed experts, are there any areas of policy-making in which the presumption tilts in favor of democratic judgment? That is the question that proponents of the common good justification must answer.

One might resist Plato's argument for seeming to assume, without justification, that members of the general public are simply too dim to contribute constructively to public decision-making. This certainly looks like a rather hasty (as well as patronizing) assumption. Doubtless the public is, as a matter of fact, often *uninformed* about complex questions of public policy, like the control of the money supply. However, one might respond that rather than abandoning democracy in favor of unaccountable technocratic rule a more appropriate remedy would be to educate democratic citizens better than we currently do.

But this tempting move underestimates the issues raised by Plato's objection. For one thing, educating *everyone* to grasp the complexities of (say) monetary policy would be extremely costly, and one might wonder whether it is a rational investment of social resources, if we already have a pool of competent economists sufficient to provide the required expertise. This point only gains in force when we try to imagine educating everyone to become experts on *all* areas of social policy (foreign affairs, health and safety policy, legal reform, fiscal policy, social welfare policy, the provision of health care and benefits, the regulation of trade and industry, or military affairs).

For another, Plato's argument, at least its most striking and challenging kernel, does not really rest on the crude assumption that ordinary people are naturally stupid. The *Republic* actually defends the more subtle position that democratically ordered institutions themselves *cause* certain sorts of irrationality and stupidity. Plato's objection is that, whatever the *natural* distribution of intelligence among members of a population, democratic arrangements *artificially* corrupt citizens' capacity to identify their common interests intelligently. Seeking the common good through democratic means is, he feared, a self-defeating enterprise.

Plato's reasons for drawing this pessimistic conclusion were complex, but the essence of his worry was this. As we noted in Chapter 2, he thought that democratic political culture tends to erode those abilities and dispositions necessary to a sound and rational appreciation of the human good. It does so (he thought) because democratic notions of equality tend to imply that as long as individuals respect others' rights to pursue their own good in their own way, we ought to give their own opinions about their best interests the benefit of the doubt. But this, Plato feared, simply floods society with an indiscriminate array of opinions about the good life, some sound, many not, without supplying agents with any rational principle on which to choose intelligently between them. Under these conditions, each is left to live their own life in their own way, but (in effect) deprived of the ability to certify that their own way *really is* in their best interests.

Plato accepted that some individuals in democratic societies will reach defensible and well-grounded views about their own and others' real interests. But his point was that under democratic conditions, citizens lack any reliable way to distinguish these better views from the many other quite indefensible views also likely to emerge. Meanwhile, democratic procedures give both sets of views the same chance to influence public decisions. It is as if we were to check into a hospital in which there are as many medical opinions as there are patients, each claiming equal rights to influence decisions about how particular diseases are to be treated. Some of the opinions may in fact be correct, but under these conditions how is anyone supposed to distinguish sound medical opinion from quackery? A disposition to defer to the majority opinion in such circumstances will seem sensible only to those who have already lost their grip on such a distinction. Moreover, majority rule will predictably result in many very irrational medical decisions. Who would admit themselves to a hospital on these terms?

This Platonic characterization of democratic political culture and its irrationality is obviously controversial, but our world of "alternative facts" and of increasingly unstable and capricious democratic electorates lends some circumstantial support for his hypothesis.

Furthermore, the modern empirical research bearing on this issue makes rather grim reading for democrats, consistently finding democratic citizens to be ill-informed and worryingly prone to inconsistency in political judgment. In 1957 Anthony Downs made the striking (and rather Platonic) suggestion that we should not be surprised at this: democratic citizens, he argued, may often be *rationally* ignorant. His thought was that, given the infinitesimally small likelihood of any one citizen's vote making a significant difference to the outcome of elections, the expected benefits of voting cannot make it rational for citizens to expend much effort in acquiring reliable political knowledge, and may indeed make voting itself irrational.[8]

Finally, we might note that under our own procedures of representative democracy, public policies are rarely if ever directly formulated and discussed in detail by ordinary members of the public. Rather, they are formulated from above by members of educated, professionalized elites (economists, experts in foreign affairs, "thinktanks," etc.), and later integrated into political parties' election platforms. The general public is

---

[8] Downs 1957. For a forceful development of the implications of the Downsian view for democratic irrationality, see Caplan 2007 and also Huemer 2015. But the underlying premise of Downs's view has been called into question by Goldman 1999 and Tuck 2008.

consulted only at the very end of the process, when parties compete for votes in general elections, and given little or no power to alter the menu of alternatives on offer. The fact that few question the elitism of this practice may betray a tacit acknowledgement of the force of Plato's general critique.[9]

The Argument from Self-Government

As we saw earlier, this argument centers on the ideal of a society identifying and then following the "will of its people" This raises the obvious question of whether any sense can really be attached to the notion of a "collective will." No doubt individuals are autonomous agents with their own wills, but can this be true of collectivities? And even if it can be, is it the case that democratic procedures can tell us what the popular will is?

One powerful reason to think not derives from an observation first made by Rousseau's contemporary, the French philosopher and mathematician Condorcet. He noticed the following problem. Suppose that there are three individuals, A, B, and C, with the following three preferences (the character ">" means "are preferred over"):

Asocialists > conservatives > liberals
Bconservatives > liberals > socialists
Cliberals > socialists > conservatives.

In this case, majorities (i.e. two out of the three individuals) prefer the socialists to the conservatives, the conservatives over the liberals, and the liberals to the socialists. What, then, is the majority will? It looks like socialists > conservatives > liberals > socialists. But what could that mean? Here the socialists are preferred to both the conservatives and the liberals, but both of the latter are preferred to the socialists! This seems logically impossible, a *nonpreference*. Such "cyclical" or "intransitive" preferences are without meaning. In this case, then, no meaningful "will" can be attributed to a democratic majority.

[9] These facts also make it implausible to suggest, as some claim, that under representative democracy, the people choose the general *goals* that ought to guide public policy, and then elites of technocrats and civil servants identify appropriate means to their realization. Surely the elites determine the goals, too.

In a seminal monograph first published in 1951, the economist Kenneth Arrow proved a famous theorem generalizing Condorcet's finding. Arrow's theorem showed that there is no way to aggregate individuals' separate preferences over three or more alternatives into a transitive collective preference that does not violate various absolutely obvious democratic requirements. Specifically, it proved that the only aggregation rules capable of yielding logically coherent collective preferences involve either deferring to the judgment of a dictator or unacceptably narrowing in advance the range of preferences citizens are permitted to express.[10]

This is a disturbing result, one that puts the argument from self-government firmly on the defensive. Arrow's work inspired the development of a whole academic field, known as social choice theory, devoted to examining and deepening the sort of analysis he pioneered. Subsequent writings in this field have unfortunately only confirmed and expanded Arrow's pessimistic conclusions about the intelligibility of a popular will. Despite the ingenuity of various attempts to salvage our intuitions about the "will of the people" in the face of the Arrow/Condorcet argument, none is entirely without difficulties. The findings of social choice theorists therefore pose a serious challenge to the argument from self-government, and indeed to the very concept of democratic self-government.[11]

It is important to stress, however, that social choice theory need not rule out all conceptions of, or arguments for, democracy. For example, many social choice theorists retreat to the conception of democracy proposed by the twentieth-century Austrian economist Joseph Schumpeter.[12] Schumpeter rejected the notion of a popular will as a utopian fiction (for reasons independent of Arrow's result), but held that democracy could still be meaningfully understood as a process by which oligarchically organized elites (political parties) compete for votes in just the way that corporations compete for consumers of their products and services. On this view, elections are like ruled-governed games with winners and losers; but they do not and cannot communicate information about a popular will, except perhaps in a purely metaphorical sense. But since it dispenses with claims about a popular will, this way of understanding democratic rule

[10] Arrow 1986.
[11] For further analysis, see Bird 2000.
[12] Riker 1988; Schumpeter 2008.

clearly cannot rescue the argument from self-government. It seems to have a greater affinity with the defensive arguments, and especially the conflict resolution arguments, considered below.

But even if we were able to make sense of the notion of a popular democratic will, the argument from self-government would still face another kind of objection. The argument assumes that there is something inherently valuable about a group of people knowing their democratic will and pursuing it. But this assumption faces serious pressure from two different directions.

From one side, there are obvious doubts about the relative importance of the "will of the people" and the will of the individuals to be ruled by it. Some would suggest that compared to the value of individual autonomy, collective autonomy has little inherent ethical importance. It is all too easy to imagine cases in which the popular will (somehow determined) poses a threat to the autonomy of particular individuals. It is such cases that inspire familiar liberal worries about the "tyranny of the majority" over the individual; the standard response is to define certain constitutional rights protecting individual freedoms with which democratic majorities cannot tamper. But this significantly qualifies the scope of discretion left to the democratic will, supposing it to be identifiable; and as we noted earlier, such rights are often actually enforced through rather undemocratic judicial means.

One might still suggest that this area of discretion is wide enough to permit significant and valuable forms of democratic self-rule. But here the claim that collective autonomy in this sense is inherently valuable faces pressure from another direction. We suggested earlier that the argument from self-government regards the realization of rule in accordance with the will of the people as valuable independently of whether it actually promotes citizens' shared interests, or whether it helps citizens correctly to appreciate their common good. But is this assumption plausible? Imagine a democratically organized people that autonomously chooses unwise policies. By following the "will of the people," they ruin the economy, condemn many in their society to poverty, ill health, and insecurity, and bring about the decay of their major cultural and educational institutions. Should citizens of this society cheer themselves with the thought that "at least we did it to ourselves"? If this seems hollow consolation, it may indicate that collective self-rule is not really inherently valuable in the way the argument from self-government claims.

It seems likely, then, that our beliefs about the value of democratic self-government are conditional on its consistency with individual autonomy and with the effective pursuit of society's common interests. But we have also seen that democratic arrangements do not necessarily secure either of these seemingly more important goals, and may actually threaten them. So whether there is anything left over in the ideal of collective self-government that specifically supports democratic arrangements remains open to debate.

The Argument from Egalitarian Justice

The main difficulty facing this argument comes to light once we distinguish between what are often termed "substantive" and "formal" conceptions of equality and justice. According to this familiar distinction, which is another of those that turn out to be harder to draw when one looks closely, it is one thing (say) to enjoy *formally* equal rights to participate in decision-making, but another to actually receive the *substantive* treatment appropriate to one's standing as a civic equal. For example, members of minority groups might enjoy a formally equal right to participate in democratic elections under the principle of one person, one vote. But clearly this is not sufficient to prevent winning majorities from denying to members of the minority groups whatever civil liberties and economic opportunities are necessary for them to enjoy genuine *substantive* equality. Guaranteeing substantive equality thus seems to require principled limits on the scope of democratic procedures. So, even if we accept egalitarian conceptions of justice it is unlikely that they provide unqualified support for formally egalitarian democratic arrangements.

In reply one might still insist that, even if not *sufficient*, equal inclusion in decision-making is *necessary* to meet the requirements of egalitarian justice. The problem here, though, is that the relevant notion of equal inclusion is hopelessly ambiguous and admits of an indeterminate range of interpretations, from the unduly weak to the implausibly strong. At the weak end of the spectrum we have: one (adult) person, (at least) one vote. (Even Mill accepted this principle.) Other (increasingly strong) interpretations include: one adult, (no more than) one vote; one adult, (no more than) one vote plus a meaningful range of options over which to choose; one adult, (no more than) one vote plus an equal right to run for office; equal liability to be called up by lot to hold office; an equal right to veto (legislation? constitutional provisions?); equal consideration (or representation?) of individuals' interests (by whom?) ... Here again we must face up to the sheer diversity and complexity of possible democratic arrangements. Is it clear that any of these forms of "equal inclusion" is strictly necessary for true civic equality, and that if some are, they demand procedures that we would on reflection want to call democratic?[13]

The Conflict Resolution Argument

One might think that this penultimate argument does not really raise any philosophical issues because it hinges on simple empirical judgments about the preconditions for political stability. If true this is bad news for the argument, for given the enormous number of very undemocratic regimes that have stably persisted for long historical periods, it is surely impossible to believe on purely empirical grounds that democratic arrangements are in any sense necessary or even advisable for political stability.

But we cannot dismiss the argument so easily, for it is a mistake to assume that in the present context questions about political stability raise only empirical issues of this simple kind. This assumption wrongly overlooks the important issue of how we should *conceptualize* political stability for various purposes (including that of measuring it empirically), a matter that raises questions that are largely philosophical in nature. For example: is a society appropriately "stable" if its formal legal structure remains invincibly resilient despite widespread and violent disruption of citizens' personal lives? What if the regular, uniform functioning of a society's institutional routines is based on fear or bought at the price of brutal indoctrination and psychological repression? These questions indicate that political stability comes in different shapes and sizes, and that not all kinds of stability are equally worth wanting. A more charitable way to interpret the conflict resolution argument, then, is to see it as making a claim about the capacity of democratic procedures to obviate unacceptably repressive ways of maintaining political stability.

[13] For a fuller discussion of political equality, see Beitz 1989.

It is natural, for example, to interpret the "legitimacy" version of the argument along these lines. That version, remember, emphasizes the capacity for democratic deliberation to yield outcomes that citizens could, and should, regard as at least "legitimate" despite any conscientious doubts they might have about them. Animating these legitimacy arguments is the hope that citizens with opposing views on divisive questions can nonetheless find a reasonable basis on which to "agree to disagree," and thereby reconcile themselves to political outcomes otherwise distasteful to them. One can construe the more pragmatic version of the argument in a similar way: what makes democracy valuable, on this account, is its tendency to foster dispositions of compromise and a willingness to play by certain recognized rules, even if the resulting outcomes run counter to the preferences of some of the parties involved.

Interpreted this way, then, neither argument is claiming crudely that democratic arrangements are a unique or important precondition for any sort of political stability whatever. Both are, rather, concerned to avert those forms of political stability based on fear, repression, manipulation, violence, indoctrination, and strife. Instead, they seek political arrangements that achieve political stability through (to resurrect an archaic term) voluntary "complaisance" on the part of citizens.[14] Complaisance of the relevant kind promotes a form peaceful social cooperation based on mutual compromise, accommodation, respect, and tolerance. In this way, democratic procedures secure political stability and resolve conflicts without sacrificing civility and a sense of concern for others or imposing undue psychological burdens on citizens.

But even if we accept that complaisant stability of this kind is valuable, and perhaps somehow more "legitimate" than alternative varieties, one can still question whether democratic procedures are the best way to promote it. As before, empirical doubts remain: is it clear, for example, that democratic discussion and procedures tend to promote complaisance in practice? Or do they more often sabotage the required attitudes by exacerbating and polarizing political disagreement?

But there is a more fundamental philosophical objection to this proposal. The question of what ideally complaisant citizens ought to recognize as a decent or "legitimate" compromise is one that, in principle, can be

---

[14] See Hobbes 1994, p. 95.

answered independently of any actual democratic process. For example, we know that appropriately complaisant citizens should not simply impose their preferred policies on other citizens with conscientious objections; rather, they should be willing to make concessions and reach an accommodation that even the objectors could regard as legitimate or at least reasonable. Suppose, however, that a particular policy to which significant social groups reasonably object is nonetheless supported by an overwhelming majority. Is there reason to believe that democratic arrangements will encourage members of that majority to seek accommodations with the objecting minorities? Will democratic procedures in such a situation not simply invite majorities to press home their advantage and uncompromisingly impose their will on the minority? Here, democratic procedures seem unlikely to foster appropriately complaisant dispositions. As Thomas Christiano has noted, it might be better in such cases to refer the matter to some impartial outside arbitrator capable of dispassionately identifying an appropriately legitimate or reasonable compromise on which all citizens could agree.[15] This, after all, is how we promote complaisance in the context of legal disputes; and legal decisions are rarely reached in democratic ways. It is not clear that democratic procedures always compare favorably to such nondemocratic ways of achieving complaisance.

Safeguarding Liberty against Power

It is difficult to quarrel with the general proposition on which this final argument is based – that unchecked political power is a threat to those subject to it. Still, this proposition is as much a challenge to democratic rule as a defense of it. After all, democratic procedures necessarily empower particular majorities and coalitions. There is no immediate reason to assume that these groups are any less likely to abuse this power than the narrower, more exclusive groups empowered under less democratic procedures. We have already noted the familiar worry that the will of the democratic majority may often act in a "tyrannical" fashion, suppressing the freedoms of the minority.

This argument does not then point exclusively toward democracy, but rather toward a mixed form of rule, in which political power is dispersed

---

[15] Christiano 1996, pp. 51ff.

among various different agencies, some democratic, some not, that can check and balance each other. This notion of a "mixed" constitution, denying exclusive power to any social group, is an ancient one, going back at least to Aristotle, and as noted above, it powerfully shaped the modern republican tradition. But insofar as a successfully "mixed" republican constitution has some democratic elements, it must, by hypothesis, include much that is nondemocratic, and perhaps antidemocratic. This is one reason why the founders of the American republic were often at pains to deny that they were proposing any sort of democracy.

At best, then, this general argument generates an extremely qualified defense of democracy. On the one hand, it abandons the idea that democracy is a necessary means for the realization of strong positive ideals (justice, the common good, the popular will), arguing instead that such value as democratic procedures possess consists in their capacity to check the abuse of power. On the other, it does not give democratic procedures any presumption over the (unmixed) alternatives, assuming instead that in principle democracy is no better or worse than any other simple form of rule. This is hardly a ringing endorsement of democratic practices.

Although we have found serious limitations in all five arguments we have considered, we should remember that the arguments we have looked at do not form an exhaustive list. Moreover, perhaps advocates of democratic rule can circumvent the most serious difficulties confronting their view by combining elements from the five arguments discussed separately here. Still, enough has been said to expose the conventional wisdom about democracy in the liberal West as deeply complacent. While our discussion has not shown that the widespread contemporary support for democratic ideals is ultimately misplaced, it should dent our confidence in them. The rationale for democratic rule is a far more complicated matter than our leaders generally acknowledge; indeed, the very identification of different political forms as "democratic" or "undemocratic" is fraught with usually unrecognized complexity. If we are honest, then, our concepts of democracy are ambiguous and unsettled, and our sense of its value haunted by long-standing yet still unstayed doubts. These received views certainly do not form simple intuitions that we can conveniently take for granted as fixed points in an appropriately critical reflection about politics.

PART III

Changing the World

Ideal Futures and Past Injustices

14 Critical Enlightenment, Ideology, and Materialism

This book has throughout treated political philosophy as a practice of critical reflection, inviting agents to step back from the most familiar and taken-for-granted features of their social and political milieu and to consider them with fresh eyes. The hope is that, by introducing critical distance on the organized routines in which agents are immersed, we can help them to acquire for themselves a wiser, more perceptive, and more enlightened appreciation of the value and limitations of their forms of life. In the preceding chapters, I have tried to illustrate how, and to what effect, this critical project can be carried forward in a variety of political contexts.

For the most part, we have evaluated the arguments considered along the way by assessing their cogency, validity, and soundness in a fairly unselfconscious way. However, it is worth highlighting two more specific dimensions along which they may succeed or fail. On the one hand, it matters how far they make good on their claim to speak from a standpoint of genuine critical detachment as opposed to being biased, partisan, tendentious, or question-begging.

On the other hand, they succeed insofar as their conclusions are genuinely *informative* rather than trivial. Political philosophy achieves little if it merely adds its voice to denunciations of injustice, suffering, abuse, venality, tyranny, genocide, torture, rape, oppression, racism, arbitrary exclusion, etc. Denying that such things are bad is simply inhuman, and civilization is in deep trouble if it thinks we need philosophy to assure us that this is so. No doubt powerful rhetoric (denunciatory or hortatory) has its place as a means of political mobilization or inspiration. But rhetorical intensification is better left to leaders, orators, and artists. Political philosophy has a different role. As an intellectual enterprise, its aim is to enlighten, not arouse.

These two desiderata, especially the second, frame the final pair of chapters comprising Part III of the book, which address a roiling contemporary debate about what it means for critical reflection in politics to be *informative* in the required sense. The controversy has arisen because Rawls's influential investment in (what he called) "ideal theory" has lately come under sustained attack from critics who charge that this idealizing approach fails to provide agents with the sort of information they need to cultivate an appropriately critical attitude in politics. Indeed, some think that, intentionally or not, Rawlsian "ideal theory" actually sabotages the project of political criticism, disguising, or distracting us from, real-world problems that most urgently invite scrutiny. Rather than adopting an idealizing orientation, these critics instead urge a "non-ideal" focus that they claim is better suited to detecting and characterizing the most salient forms of oppression, injustice, and abuse prevailing in our world.

In addressing this debate, we return to an issue left hanging at the end of Chapter 1, where we introduced Marx's misgivings about traditional philosophical appeals to rational introspection in political argument. Those who today criticize "ideal theory" tend to share those misgivings and have often been heavily influenced by Marx. Like him, they recommend a more historically informed, and realist, approach. However, contemporary exponents of this approach are often more interested in the plight of "identity groups" (women, transgender people, the racially stigmatized, those of nonheterosexual orientation, etc.) than in the distinctively economic forms of oppression on which Marx focused. Some (though not all) of them would, indeed, characterize themselves as "scholar activists" who regard "raising consciousness" about the injustice and oppression faced by such groups as a legitimate and vital educational goal. For this reason, the issues in play here also touch on broader, and today increasingly bitter, disputes about "political correctness," the charge of "left-wing indoctrination" in the university classroom, and the legitimate purposes of politically engaged scholarship.

Part III takes up some of these concerns by viewing them in the context of the discussions conducted in the preceding chapters. They provide an occasion to review some of the main arguments considered in this book and to assess how far, and in what sense, they carry concrete political significance as opposed to being of academic interest only. Before turning (in Chapter 15) to the debate over "ideal theory," then, I first discuss the senses in which the arguments advanced by political philosophers might claim to enlighten their addressees.

What Is Critical Enlightenment?

The expectation that political philosophy be somehow *informative* is implicit in the very idea that it is a mode of *inquiry*. All investigation, whether empirical, historical, interpretative, legal, philosophical, or theological, shares this enlightening aim. As we saw in Chapter 1, to be informative inquiry must somehow narrow the range of reasonable disagreement about whatever is under scrutiny: police investigations are informative to the extent that they remove reasonable disagreement about whether X should be charged with a crime; inquiry into the meaning of a poem or gospel provides information when it successfully narrows the range of plausible interpretations; and scientific experiments are informative insofar as they falsify hypotheses that would otherwise command reasonable support. Yet it is clear that the character of the enlightenment sought in different fields of inquiry, and the standards by which we recognize research as illuminating rather than trivial, will vary depending on the kind of question being asked. And, right from the start of this book, we noticed a crucial difference between the "normative" questions addressed by political philosophers and the more purely descriptive ones that scientists and other empirical researchers pursue. Let us consider this contrast a little more closely.

Fundamentally, empirical or descriptive research answers to our natural curiosity about phenomena whose behavior and characteristics are opaque or in some way perplexing. To be sure, we also often hope that it uncovers processes, materials, forces, etc. that will turn out to be practically useful in (e.g.) medicine, pharmacology, engineering, manufacturing, power-generation, climate change mitigation, etc. Accordingly, those sciences that seem most likely to enhance our technological capacity to address concrete needs will tend to attract a larger share of the available support for research and exploration. Still, while it plays a legitimate role in determining how scarce resources should be divided among different fields of inquiry, the likelihood of utilitarian application cannot by itself define the underlying point even of purely empirical investigation.

Ultimately, we seek information about these phenomena just for its own sake; as inquisitive creatures, we cannot help being perplexed when things do not make sense. When our puzzlement is only partially alleviated, we become frustrated. Thus, we do not recognize breakthroughs in (say) physics, cosmology, or archeology solely by calculating the likelihood that they will cure cancer, give sight to the blind, make people less depressed, or anything of this kind. It is enough simply that experiments, observations, or new excavations settle hitherto unresolved puzzles, or inform us why we should be puzzled about something we had previously thought straightforward. For example, the 1799 discovery of the Rosetta Stone did nothing to alleviate the problems of daily life. Yet it is rightly celebrated as a major intellectual advance because it gave us a key to decipher the hieroglyphic language of ancient Egypt, yielding new insight into its civilization. Conversely, research in these areas fails insofar as it makes no progress in removing or clarifying the original puzzles that piqued curiosity in the first place, as when initially promising explanations are shown to be unconvincing or speculative, or when theories purporting to reveal new information about a subject turn out, on closer inspection, merely to repeat what we already know.

In principle, arguments in political philosophy can succeed or fail to enlighten in a formally analogous way. However, the kind of information sought in critical moral reflection is quite different. Here, we are not seeking descriptively adequate beliefs about phenomena observable from a third-personal standpoint (planets, quarks, historical artifacts, etc.). At stake in normative inquiry, rather, is a set of *practical* questions about how rational agents should conduct themselves in the world, especially (in political philosophy):

- Are institutions and social practices X, Y, Z worth any support, allegiance, time, and energy we or others give to them?
- Or do X, Y, Z instead waste, exploit, diminish, and even ruin the lives of those either subjected to them or implicated in their reproduction?

These practical questions largely disappear from view when, for the purposes of social science or historical study, we treat the relevant social practices as observable phenomena to be analyzed and understood empirically, from a third-personal standpoint. They do not register within that perspective because they are fundamentally *first-personal* questions. That is, they crop up when agents reflect on the meaning and point of their own activities and investments of time from a point of view with which they identify or, when they are considering the predicament of others, can at least sympathize (by imaginatively putting themselves into their shoes). They acquire appreciable importance only from inside the point of view of a rational agent responsible for his her or her own attitudes and conduct. In one way or another, all of the topics we have considered in this book have this first-personal, conduct-regarding dimension.

For example, the disagreement between Plato and the classical utilitarians about how to understand human well-being does not pit two empirical characterizations of "human nature" against each other. Each represents, rather, a distinctive account of what, viewed from the inside, rational agents should desire and hope for themselves. Similarly, Hobbes's defense of the state does not claim to compel our attention because of its empirical accuracy, but because it engages the perspective of rational agents concerned for their security and self-preservation. When we have evaluated competing claims about justice, whether in the context of economic distribution, immigration, climate change, or the decision to go to war, our primary concern was not to compare and contrast different schemes of positive morality as they manifest in different societies. Rather, we have asked whether they propitiously balance concerns that no reasonable person could simply ignore: especially (on the one hand) the rational desire to advance their own interests and (on the other) the importance of various responsibilities to others. Again, our discussions of freedom and democracy have implicitly explored whether agents under a variety of political conditions (being blackmailed, working in a sweatshop, living under majority rule, etc.) have reasons to defend, appreciate, resent, reform, or even revolt against them.

Albeit in different ways, and at various levels of generality, then, all of the arguments we have considered claim to inform agents caught up in possible or actual social worlds what would constitute a rational attitude to their situation. Some purport to show, for example, that we should accept our role as subjects of legitimate political authority on certain terms and under certain conditions (e.g. Hobbesian or Lockean social-contract theory). Others claim to identify grounds on which you or I might validly complain that we are victims of oppression or injustice (e.g. Nozickean charges that taxation for redistributive purposes is akin to "forced labor," or Rawls's argument that the claims of the "least advantaged" should carry special weight among people committed to social justice). In some cases, they imply that we may be complicit in indefensible political practices (e.g. the enforcement of immigration restrictions or endemically irrational forms of democratic rule) and that we should reconsider any unreflective allegiance we have to them.

These arguments may or may not be convincing. But whether or not they succeed, they are all implicitly addressed to agents willing to submit their own (acquiescent, approving, disapproving, outraged, admiring, etc.) attitudes toward their political circumstances to critical scrutiny. In asking themselves whether those attitudes are well founded (e.g. their support for welfare redistribution or their hostility to immigrants), agents tacitly acknowledge some responsibility for ensuring that the conditions of human life are adequate, benign, and propitious. If there were literally *nothing* anyone could do to alter those conditions in any respect, these questions would not even occur to us. However, as we noted in the Introduction, the enormous historical variety of human communities provides some assurance that change is possible, and that we are in some way responsible for it.

Assuming responsibility for such change is not fundamental to purely scientific or descriptive inquiry. To be sure, science and other academic fields are themselves organized, institutionalized practices for whose flourishing participants are responsible (securing adequate funding, teaching well, encouraging important research, etc.). As noted earlier, we also often hope that science will discover new technologies that can change human society. And, obviously, communities of researchers working in these areas are responsible for changing (updating, modifying, clarifying, and where necessary dropping) beliefs about the subject matter under investigation as new data come in. Yet the fundamental *point* of empirical inquiry is not to *change* its subject matter – the phenomena under investigation (space-time, history). To the contrary, their primary aim is to map their actual contours as they find them, to conform their intellectual judgment as far as possible to what they discover (e.g. about black holes or the French Revolution).

Yet, inquiry in political philosophy plainly *is* primarily directed toward enhancing the community of which the political philosopher is a member. Its critical ambitions are implicitly tied to a project of collective self-improvement; its subject matter is defined by the merits of possible changes in how we organize ourselves politically. To this extent, we should cautiously endorse Marx's famous "Eleventh Thesis on Feuerbach": "Philosophers have hitherto only interpreted the world in various ways; the point, however, is to change it."

How to Change the World

But what kinds of "change" are realistically within the purview of political philosophy? As we shall see, Marx's own views on this point must be modified or weakened in several ways. However, in a suitably qualified form, we can and should retain his Eleventh Thesis, at least its second clause.

Presumably, neither Marx nor we are seeking "change" just for the sake of it. Rather, we want change that would in some way enhance the conditions of human life. No one disputes that existing political arrangements are far from ideal; injustice, crime, violence, corruption, oppression, institutional arrogance, and complacency remain ubiquitous, and rarely escape the glare of the modern news media. A basic task for political philosophy, one might think, is to help identify rational grounds for distinguishing welcome and unwelcome change. Although the assumption that current circumstances are non-ideal is uncontroversial, people reasonably disagree about where the most urgent problems are, what kinds of problems they are, and how we might address them. So it seems reasonable to suggest that political philosophy is informative insofar as it reduces these reasonable disagreements.

All of the arguments discussed in this book can be seen in this light. For example, from the start, we have noted that "justice" purports to be a value-conferring property, and so the struggle to theorize it adequately is implicitly guided by the goal of specifying exactly how norms of just cooperation could and should make human life better. Classical utilitarianism quite explicitly advanced the "Utility Principle" as an uncontroversial yet enlightening standard for intelligent social reform, and the more specific discussions in later chapters all canvassed arguments purporting to inform us of ways in which the world might be improved. Perhaps the abolition of sweatshops would advance the cause of freedom; perhaps the world would be more just if borders were open. Implicit in all of this is the idea that by thinking these issues through, we may be able to fill in some nonobvious details about what would constitute an advance from our currently non-ideal position. By imparting definite, well-grounded content to otherwise vague hopes for a better, freer, more just, world, these arguments purport to enlighten us about the desirable direction of change, orienting us more clearly to futures worth wanting.

Marx's Doubts: Ideology and Materialism

One might expect this suggestion to be unobjectionable, even banal. As it turns out, however, Marx thought that this was exactly the wrong way to approach changing the world. The reason for this reflects his deep suspicion of what he called "ideology."[1] As noted in Chapter 1, Marx used that term in a much wider sense than we do today. For us, "ideology" denotes rival political allegiances like "conservatism," "socialism," "liberalism," etc. Marx's category of "ideology" certainly includes these clustered political commitments, but it also covers virtually the whole repertoire of conscious ideas and concepts that agents use to make sense of their world. It includes, for example, religious and moral ideas, positive norms and beliefs about their value and importance, theoretical classifications of natural and social phenomena, philosophical ideals of rationality or well-being, the specialized technical concepts developed by experts, aesthetic categories, the language of emotions, and much else. In Marx's sense, "prayer," "nation," "race," "obligation," "justice," "murder," "biology," "minuet," "ambition," "freedom," and "love" are all ideological concepts.

To say that Marx was suspicious of such concepts is not to suggest that he thought that ideological consciousness is always bad. Ideology on his very broad construal is clearly something we cannot do without. Ideological categories allow us to cope with an extremely complex world; they regiment and simplify what would otherwise be beyond any mind to assimilate. Indeed, in some sense these categories *constitute* the world as we experience, interpret, and navigate it. So it is not that Marx wants to criticize people for *having* ideological consciousness.

His worry, rather, is that, whatever their value or functions along other dimensions, ideological beliefs and forms of reflection are ill-adapted to the enterprise of social criticism. If, as Marx thought, such beliefs and patterns of conscious reflection are *features* of the historically particular social practices that produce them, they cannot be sufficiently independent of

---

[1] Marx's account of ideology, whose features I elaborate below, is laid out canonically in the early part of his work *The German Ideology*. See Marx and Engels 1978, pp. 148ff.

those practices to afford real critical purchase on them. That is why, in his view, the ideological beliefs that dominate in societies at particular times very often stand in an apologetic and protective relation to ruling classes and institutions, purporting to justify their activities and controlling position. More generally, Marx thought they mystify the relevant forms of life, disguising their real character.

As we saw in Chapter 1, Marx thought that the only way to get an appropriately critical grip on the *status quo* is to understand it historically. To expose the real character of existing modes of life, we must on his account explain how and why they developed from earlier ones. However, his views about the pervasiveness of mystifying ideological frameworks drove him to insist that the only genuinely informative modes of historical analysis must be "materialist." That is, they must resist completely the temptation to make the historical process legible as a story only of the evolution of conscious attitudes and beliefs about the social and political order.

This is not to say that a materialist approach to history should say nothing about the ways in which those conscious beliefs – i.e. "ideology" – change over time. To the contrary, Marx thought that materialist historical analysis can loosen the grip of prevailing ideological misrepresentations of existing social and political arrangements precisely by explaining how and why such ideologies develop under definite historical circumstances. For it postulates that such ideational shifts are merely the superficial, or "epiphenomenal," results of deeper seismic forces that really cause historical change. It is these deeper forces that his materialism sets out to lay bare, by looking underneath the conscious ideas, thoughts, and beliefs that dominate agents' thinking at different historical periods and exposing their material underpinnings.

To illustrate, consider the glittering starbursts of exploding fireworks. These vivid visual and aural impressions constitute the experience of a firework display, but they tell us little about, and indeed obscure, how they are produced. For this, we need to study the combustion of different materials, the chemistry of gunpowder, the mechanics of propulsion, gravity and air pressure, and so on. It is important here that firework displays succeed precisely insofar as they *distract* the viewers from all of this technical substructure. After all, they do not want to celebrate Guy Fawkes Day or the Fourth of July boring themselves to tears calculating the trajectory of rockets, determining the quantities of propellant required for shells with a given weight, reviewing circuit diagrams for the ignition mechanism, etc. They just want to enjoy the results. Similarly, on Marx's materialist account, the ideological categories populating agents' ordinary, first-personal consciousness of their social world, while central to lived experience, will normally obscure and direct attention away from the material forces that have historically shaped that world.

According to Marx's materialism, the historian will not be able to reveal the operation of these underlying forces by canvassing historical explanations of the form "slavery ended in the modern world because agents came to the conclusion that it is wrong," or "the French Revolution resulted from disillusionment with the absolutism of the *ancien régime*." Such explanations remain at the level of conscious ideas and so, on Marx's view, provide no information about the real agents of historical change. To understand these historical dynamics, the analyst must instead decipher the deeper struggles for physical control over nature and the processes of economic production they represent.

The details of Marx's account of how conflicts over economic resources explain the real character of social and political forms of life are not our concern here. We need only note the basic character of his materialist approach, which can be captured in the following analogy. For Marx conscious beliefs about the goodness or badness of forms of social and political life (which on his account must be ideological) are to the real character of those forms as pain or its absence are to disease and physical health. Pain often accompanies disease, but it is a symptom, not a cause, of the underlying problem. No informative diagnosis of the nature and etiology of a disease will waste much time trying to clarify exactly what the pain feels like from the perspective of the patient. To concretely improve the patient's condition, we need to understand what is physically going on and, if possible, intervene to stop it.

In relation to "changing the world" for the better, Marx thought that philosophizing about the goodness, justice, or the utility of actual or possible political arrangements is a bit like encouraging a cancer patient to write a poem about her pain. The poem may be eloquent and moving, but it will not supply actionable information about how to cure her illness. On Marx's account, philosophical speculation about ideally just societies, the justification for open borders, war, or democratic representation, etc. is bound to be similarly superficial and ineffectual, trading idly on mere ideological symptoms while failing to come to grips with the material and historical conditions that produce them. To actually *change* the world, those material conditions must themselves be removed or altered.

Clearly, on Marx's view, such material transformation cannot be an intellectual task: his own account entails that it can be accomplished only through concrete historical action. However, as in medicine, that does not mean that an intellectually sophisticated diagnosis is of no value. Ultimately, of course, it is up to me to exercise more to lower my blood pressure – the doctor, after all, can hardly go to the gym for me. Yet her diagnosis of high blood pressure can still enlighten me about how I should change my lifestyle. Marx's historical materialism is supposed to be informative in an analogous way. On the one hand, by helping agents appreciate the vanity of philosophical reflection that chases its own ideological tail, it disposes them against wasting their time on it; on the other hand, it purports to pierce through the mystifying illusions of prevailing ideologies to disclose the material structures that actually control their lives, showing them not what to think, but (as Lenin put it) "what is to be done."

This strong materialist view would imply that virtually all the arguments considered in this book waste the time of proactive world-changers. Igor Stravinsky famously described jazz as "a kind of masturbation that never arrives anywhere." And that is essentially Marx's verdict on philosophical discussions of justice, economic inequality, freedom, the common good, and so forth: they are merely improvisational riffs on ideological themes with few actionable implications for changing the world.

Marx's strong materialism is, however, needlessly extreme and does not justify throwing this book into the flames as we march to the barricades.

Moralizing Criticism

On one point Marx is absolutely correct: a historically realist understanding of agents' actual political situation is an excellent way to help them achieve critical perspective on it. However, it does not automatically follow that they can do so only by viewing their history through a narrowly materialist lens. No doubt ideas and beliefs are not the sole determinants of historical evolution, but why deny them any significance at all? Surely, to return to a point made in Chapter 1, the difficulty of identifying plausible arguments for excluding women from the franchise played *some* role in getting women the vote. Did not resistance to gay marriage in the West collapse so easily in part because, as a result of public debate, the supposed grounds for treating heterosexual and homosexual love as relevantly different were exposed as threadbare?

Furthermore, it is not obvious that historical analysis must be materialist in order to open up the critical perspective on familiar social practices that realists rightly seek. Consider, for example, the work of Michel Foucault, the author of several pioneering historical studies of sexuality, medicine, and practices of legal punishment.[2] Foucault's writings extravagantly violate Marx's materialist canons, focusing almost entirely on the attitudes, beliefs, and types of "knowledge" that in his view constitute different social régimes. His historical conclusions are of course open to question (as indeed are Marx's). Yet, no one who reads his work could reasonably deny that, if it is sound, it opens a critical angle on the conventionally accepted self-image of penal institutions, professional medicine, and prevailing norms of sexuality, despite its radically nonmaterialist character. Sometimes, after all, optical illusions can be exposed optically: we can put the two lines, or the two images, side by side, and *see* that they are actually the same length/color, without needing to investigate the physiology of perception.

Marx's position is also too sweeping in that his own reasons *for* adopting a stark materialism do not necessarily tell *against* the arguments presented in this book. His materialist turn was motivated by his strong aversion to two styles of political criticism, one moralistic and the other naïvely utopian. As we shall see, his reasons for rejecting these two defective forms of political criticism are entirely valid, yet they need not implicate the philosophical arguments about justice, well-being, the common good, or concepts of freedom and democracy that we have explored in this book. Those who look to those arguments as a source of information about the desirable direction of social change can and should agree with Marx in rejecting these two modes of critical reflection.

The first is the stance that Marx deprecated as "moralizing criticism" and that realists today like Raymond Geuss sometimes identify with an "applied ethics" approach in political philosophy.[3] Now, the contemporary

---

[2] Foucault 1982, 1988, 1990, 1994, 1995.
[3] Geuss 2008.

debate over the "applied ethics" model is bound up with a broader concern about the commitment to "ideal theorizing" that Geuss and others often attribute to proponents of that model. We will consider this wider critique of "ideal theory" in the following chapter, but that is not the distinctive and problematic feature of "moralizing criticism" or "applied ethics" that I want to pick out here.

Political criticism is "moralizing" in the offending sense, rather, when it evaluates social and political practices *solely* by asking whether those practices encourage or discourage the agents who live within them to fulfill their *moral* duties. In such an approach, critical moral reflection is circumscribed by a prescriptive account of morally upright conduct – a presupposed table of ethical imperatives that dictates what agents must to do avoid moral blame or attract praise. That table is then used to identify forms of political action that are morally forbidden, required, or permitted. This view reduces political criticism to moral casuistry: once we have drawn out the implications of individual morality in the special case of public life, all relevant critical questions have been answered.

Marx (and his contemporary realist successors) rightly reject this approach as naïve and limited. Clearly, it can only be as good as its underlying assumptions about the content of moral rectitude. The problem is that in the context of critical reflection, those assumptions are typically either trivial or question-begging. Certainly, the moral duty not to lie gives us a reason to criticize politicians who deceive the electorate, but that inference hardly requires *philosophical* explanation. No *argument* is needed to justify the conclusion that Donald Trump should not lie so much. Where our moral duties are already pretty clear and uncontroversial, then, we can apply them to politics without the assistance of philosophical analysis.

Consider, on the other hand, the argument that, as long as capitalist employers scrupulously fulfill their moral duties to their workers (i.e. not enslaving them, not coercing them into signing their labor contract nor deceiving them about its terms, not stealing their property, etc.), we can have no grounds to criticize the capitalist system. This argument exemplifies "moralizing criticism" but it is doubly question-begging. For it (1) depends on the suppressed, but as yet undefended, premise that a social system attracts valid criticism only to the extent that it fosters immoral conduct, and (2) presupposes, again with no argument, that prohibitions on force, fraud, and theft exhaust the moral duties that apply.

Marx's own critique of capitalism centered on (1). For, as we saw in Chapter 12, he denied that the oppressive character of capitalism can be captured in terms of culpable moral wrongdoing on the part of those holding economic power in capitalist societies. Indeed, he thought it was vital for the critic to understand how the availability of an accepted positive morality marking force, fraud, and assault as immoral assists in lending a semblance of legitimacy to their power. The general acceptance of that positive morality allows capitalism to claim for itself the shimmering aura of justice and morality, thereby implying that it commands our rational approval. For Marx, however, that implication is an archetypical case of ideological misdirection, disguising underlying defects of capitalist social relations. It disposes agents against accepting a truth about capitalism that he thought historical materialism alone can reveal: not so much that it is an immoral system, but that it is in various demonstrable ways "verrückt" – crazy and irrational.

Whether or not we accept Marx's verdict on capitalism, we can agree with him that the "moralizing critic" is fated either to be a superficial moral casuist (like a pedantic grammarian constantly calling out split infinitives) or to beg the question of the rationality of positive moralities in place in particular historical circumstances. But are the arguments explored in this book vulnerable to this objection because they have indulged "moralizing criticism" in this sense?

The language of "critical morality," which has been central to our approach, may suggest so, but in this context the word "moral" does not carry the narrow meaning adopted by the "moralizing critic." Following Hart's definition, we have understood critical moral reflection as an effort to step back from accepted positive morality (including conventionally accepted beliefs about agents' moral duties not to lie, kill, maim, etc.) and to assess their political implications on an independent basis. The independent considerations we have brought to bear have almost always involved claims about our well-being, about what we have reasons to want, about our overriding rational investment in survival and self-preservation, and about how we should think intelligently about risks and dangers. In Chapter 2, we developed an argument of Plato's that is every bit as critical of what Marx would have regarded as "bourgeois" morality (Auden's two-atlas model) as Marx's own criticism of capitalism. We saw later that classical utilitarians also wished to interrogate the dogmas and taboos of traditional morality by considering their implications for suffering and welfare. In Chapters 8 and 10 we raised critical doubts about the implications of the "morality of states," including ones that suggest that it leads to irrationality akin to that manifested in addiction. None of this is "moralizing" in the sense that Marx rejected.

It is true that our discussions of justice have invested heavily in the language of "responsibility." But in Chapter 7, we explicitly rejected the tendency, implicit in Nozick's entitlement theory, to restrict the relevant responsibilities to those involving culpability for moral wrongdoing (in the manner of "moralizing critics"). Rather, we defended an expanded notion of "remedy-responsibility" which concerns not a fixed list of moral duties, but rather the importance of: efficiently performing tasks of legitimate common concern, better addressing human needs, alleviating unnecessary suffering, and, especially, solving coordination problems arising when agents motivated by individually rational incentives inadvertently produce collectively irrational outcomes. I submit that one cannot plausibly characterize any of this as indulging in "moralizing criticism" of the kind Marx and contemporary realists repudiate.

We can state the point another way by putting pressure on the medical analogy we earlier used to illustrate Marx's materialism. For on reflection it is not clear that even medicine can be pursued in a purely materialist manner, despite its focus on bodily functioning. To make wise decisions in the hospital, doctors and surgeons must be guided by various conscious beliefs about what constitutes health and disease, and important philosophical questions arise here, too. For example, should we consider depression and mental disorders as diseases in the same sense as cancer or the common cold?

Is such a question answerable – can it even be posed? – on a strictly "materialist" basis? It seems more plausible to say that our understanding of health is bound up with patently *nonmaterialist* assumptions (which Marx would therefore have dismissed as ideological) about the nature of well-being like those we entertained in the context of perfectionism and classical utilitarianism. As Plato thought, medicine is a good model for political philosophers to follow, and it is so precisely because it reveals that there is plenty of room between ideological illusion and a narrow materialism for philosophical argument to make intellectual progress.

The Blueprint Model

The discussion in this book has also not indulged the other style of political criticism that Marx rightly rejected – what I shall call the "Blueprint Model." To put it crudely, the Blueprint Model conceives of the political philosopher as an expert engineer of the future, occupying something like the role of sage or prophet – a kind of secular Moses leading us to liberation. According to this model, critical moral reflection should be entrusted to a group of specially trained experts who deploy their unique skills and insight to discern the outlines of an ideal utopia in which all goes well, everyone flourishes, and all unnecessary obstacles to the enhancement of human powers are overcome. Our job is to accept their vanguard guidance on trust, help settle some of the empirical details, and then implement the blueprint as best we can.

Some will be surprised to hear Marx cited as a *critic* of the Blueprint Model because this portrayal conflicts with a widespread misconception, encouraged by his conservative critics, that he was himself a blueprint theorist. On this common view, Marx's political theory proposed a utopian plan for a communist society to be followed like a recipe for *soufflé*. This misconception is implicit the slogan, endlessly repeated by his critics today, that "wherever communism has been tried, it has failed."

The principle behind this slogan is entirely fair: if the *soufflé* collapses every time, the recipe is clearly defective. No argument there. The problematic assumption is that Marx was committed to providing something akin to a recipe or blueprint. In fact, not only did Marx refuse to offer any such blueprint, he also spent pages angrily denouncing those who took anything like this approach seriously. Unfortunately, however, modern revolutionary Marxist movements and regimes have done Marx's critics a huge favor by themselves indulging aspects of the Blueprint Model. In this way, his own followers have often lent popular objections to Marx's political ideas greater credence than they deserve and have contributed to the distorted and ignorant picture of his actual views that still prevails today.

In any case, it is instructive to appreciate what is wrong with the Blueprint Model. This will enable us to see, not only that it has played no role in the arguments of this book, but also why its rejection does not support Marx's hardline materialism.

I have deliberately used the metaphor of a "blueprint" to characterize this model because it helps to bring out the deep mistake on which it rests. That metaphor is from engineering, and imports from that context a certain picture of concerted rational action. On that picture, we start with a reasonably determinate goal, like building a bridge across a river; we then hire professionals who possess relevant expertise in bridge building, the effects of wind and tidal currents on large structures, the stability of alluvial soil, etc.; once the engineers have put in the necessary mental labor and drawn up a plan (the "blueprint"), we then we organize teams of workers to perform the manual labor required in an appropriate sequence. As the work proceeds, the planners and workers consult each other from time to time as unexpected challenges arise and call into question the feasibility of plan A. We then make appropriate adjustments to yield a modified plan B. We repeat the process (as needed) for plans B, C, … Z, until eventually we have a bridge that does not sink into the mud.

However, political philosophy is nothing like this. Indeed, to properly understand the structure of critical reflection in politics we must virtually *reverse* this picture:

(1) The Blueprint Model presupposes that we have already settled on a fairly clear goal. But in the political case, we have no clear goals, only rather vague ideals of justice, well-being, freedom, the common good, human flourishing, democratic self-determination, etc., that command reasonable disagreement. The project is not to implement a blueprint with a clear aim in mind, but to try to get clear on exactly what these aims amount to and require of us in the first place.

(2) Non-ideal problems in politics are not, as in the engineering model, as yet unknown impediments that will emerge only during the implementation phase, and to which our original blueprint must be made to conform in order to become "feasible." To the contrary, it is the manifest presence, persistence, and (often) high visibility of certain non-ideal problems (poverty, disadvantage, unhappiness, suppression of harmless pleasures, oppression, discrimination, inequality, coercion, domination, exclusion, racial hatred, stupid democratic decisions, etc.) that typically *initiate* critical reflection in the political case. Since these descriptions come with attitudes of disapproval already baked in, we

are drawn into reflection about whether we are right to let our attitudes be dictated by our ordinary conscious concepts in this way. To revive the distinction we drew right at the start of Chapter 1, we may then encounter arguments with a "defusing" or "mobilizing" character. In the former case, the relevant arguments will imply that we must learn to live with the underlying problems, even if they are in some measure still a matter of regret. In the latter case, they will encourage us to think about taking action to eliminate them.

(3) Arguments of either kind may be enhanced by consulting experts with special expertise in history, sociology, economics, public choice theory, etc. to help us think about these problems by informing us of relevant facts. However, whereas in the Blueprint Model, expertise confers authority to dictate a plan of action, in critical morality any deference due to experts should extend only to their areas of technical or empirical competence. On the point of political importance – whether our attitudes of approval or disapproval are justified, and if so whether they warrant acquiescence (defuse) or efforts to change things (mobilize) – no person or group of persons, in virtue of their characteristics or social position (not even their momentary unanimity on some specific issue), has final authority to decide the matter for all.

The reason for this goes back to the points made about the notion of the "common good" in Chapter 2. Ultimately, the questions that arise in critical morality are about what *we* want to do with or about *our* shared life. This does not mean that the question of what "we" should do is entirely arbitrary – whatever *we* decide at some particular time and place goes. This is the mistake embedded in the rhetorical question beloved of populists like Nigel Farage or Donald Trump: "Must we keep running the referendum until the people get the correct answer?" What the populists overlook is that the outcomes of votes conducted on a particular occasion are no more probative than the judgment of a particular individual or cabal. If we let such outcomes decide some dispute, it is rarely because we think that they are any more likely to be correct. As with the Pacifica–Atlantis truce discussed in Chapter 5, we typically do so, rather, when we see little prospect of resolving a dispute on the merits, and so we agree to abide by an arbitrary tie-breaker, like friends who agree to go to whichever restaurant wins a coin-toss.[4] But in critical morality we precisely *should* keep the conversation going as long as necessary for us to ensure that we have thought the matter through carefully – in effect indefinitely. As we do so, we should try our best to be guided by the strongest reasons we can offer, and to ignore the stupid or weak reasons. This requires something agents find very difficult: that they be prepared to admit that they have been thinking about something incorrectly, incoherently, implausibly.

If this involves trying to discriminate within the universe of beliefs and conscious attitudes that Marx would have classified, categorically, as "ideological," so much the worse for his effort to somehow step outside the ideological dimension entirely and relocate it within a deeper reality of material or economic conflict. As I said in the Introduction, the point is to distinguish between the beliefs and attitudes that are defensible rather than foolish illusions. To do this, we do not have to erect a false dichotomy between, on the one hand, the power of material forces (and the social groups or movements that wield them) and, on the other, any and all conscious political beliefs, attitudes, or commitments.

Rather than requiring materialism, resisting the Blueprint Model means being constantly vigilant against confusing the force of a reason or argument with the power or supposed authority of the person, worldview, or organization advancing it. Critical moral reflection is in this sense essentially democratic; it is for all-comers; no one is too small, too insignificant, too peculiar to consider the arguments for themselves, or to be denied standing to object to the orthodox view. The Blueprint Model, however, is managerial and highly undemocratic in its orientation.

I hope it is clear that the arguments canvassed in this book have not been offered in this rank-pulling, managerial mode, as if I and the reader are part of a nocturnal council of experts trying to craft a plan to be

---

[4] As David Cameron, the British Prime Minister who called the Brexit referendum in 2016, implicitly recognized. Believing that the likely outcome would be "remain," he hoped that resorting to a referendum would finally settle a long-festering rift within his own Conservative Party over Europe, much as a coin-toss might resolve the friends' disagreement over where to eat. Unfortunately, his gamble misfired spectacularly. Far from resolving the domestic dispute within the party, the "leave" vote caused it to metastasize into a toxic national division, one that is likely to take generations to heal.

accepted on trust and then implemented. I have done my best to identify the more and less plausible arguments along the way, but if readers find the judgments reached in this book problematic, objectionable, implausible, and can show why, that is all to the good. Send me an email.

Change and Reconciliation

There is one final respect in which Marx's views may need to be qualified. Marx was an avowed proponent of "a ruthless criticism of everything existing." Such criticism, he said, should be "ruthless in two senses: the criticism must not be afraid of its own conclusions, nor of conflict with the powers that be."[5] Given Marx's emphasis on the violent, revolutionary overthrow of existing arrangements, it is therefore natural to read his call to "change the world" as hellbent on upending the existing order at all costs. Not everything that Marx wrote is consistent with that rather crude view of the purposes of intellectual reflection on existing social and political practice. However, if he did intend that view, he wrongly conflated critical moral reflection with willful antagonism.

The difference between the two can be highlighted by considering again our distinction between defusing and mobilizing arguments. It is clear that mobilizing arguments dispose us toward changing the world in some way. But what of defusing arguments? In one sense, they protect the *status quo* by allaying our doubts and fears about it. However, that does not mean that they change nothing. A world in which agents become more acquiescent in certain practices, when otherwise they would be disposed to resist them, is still a world that has changed in an important way. That change may be good or bad, but it *is* change of a certain kind.

Rawls argued that among the central roles of political philosophy presupposed in his later theory is the effort "to calm our frustration and rage against our society and its history by showing us the way in which its institutions, when properly understood from a philosophical point of view, are rational." Thus he hoped that his theory might "reconcile us in part to our condition," where "our condition" refers to our involuntary enrollment in institutions committed to the ideals of liberal democratic

---

[5] Marx and Engels 1978, p. 13.

freedom.[6] In these passages, Rawls comes very close to endorsing Hegel's view that the point of philosophical reflection in politics is to explain the inner rationality of existing forms of life, with a view to helping us feel at home within them.

Marx strongly objected to this Hegelian view, and I am inclined to agree. But if we should follow him in rejecting it, the reason is not that Rawls and Hegel here abandon the ambition of "changing the world" and instead identify political philosophy with the goal of "keeping everything as it is." To move people, by argument, from a state in which they are alienated from and frustrated by their social world to one in which they affirm and value it, is *not* to keep everything as it is (as if a successful course of psycho-therapy that jogs a person from debilitating depression back into vitality changes nothing). However subtle the shift may be, it is in some measure to change the world, because as I suggested in the Introduction, we cannot in the end separate political actions and practices from the attitudes informing our willing (or unwilling) participation in them. If we object that Rawls and Hegel promote an irrational quietism, then, the basis for our complaint is not that their arguments are ineffectual, but rather that they induce *undesirable* change, reinforcing certain social routines that in fact should command our suspicion.

In the next chapter, we will consider a claim along these lines leveled against Rawls and the type of "ideal theory" he has developed. According to this objection, such "ideal theories" engender a premature and unin-formed acquiescence in patterns of racial oppression and exclusion.

---

[6] Rawls 2001, pp. 3–4.

15   Ideal Theory, Race, and Reparation

In this final chapter, I consider the claim that philosophers should resist the lure of *idealization* as they try to think about the meaning and significance of justice, the common good, freedom, and other political values. This injunction has stimulated a stormy contemporary debate among political philosophers, and in the wider public, about how we can best address the plight of those groups – especially those defined by categories of race, ethnicity, indigeneity, gender, or sexual orientation – who today face discrimination, exclusion, marginalization, and often a systematic threat of violence at the hands of public and private agencies.

The prevalence of these phenomena of subordination cannot be reasonably denied. Even in advanced Western liberal democracies, women are still underrepresented in legislative assemblies and within the leadership of public and private organizations, are typically paid less for the same jobs, remain unacceptably vulnerable to rape and sexual assault, and face routine forms of harassment, intimidation, and abuse at work, in the classroom, in restaurants, gyms, and other semi-public spaces, as well as at home. Gays, lesbians, "trans," and transgender people face comparable challenges, often compounded by moralizing intolerance.

Racism of more and less insidious kinds also stubbornly endures. This is especially true in the United States, but it remains a worldwide problem. In many countries, racially marginalized groups confront discrimination in the workplace and in access to educational institutions. Racial prejudice infects the operation of many criminal justice systems, so that membership of communities defined by race increases one's risk of being convicted for crimes, punished harshly for them, and (as in case of African Americans) subjected to the use of sometimes lethal violence by the police. Patterns of economic disadvantage invariably correlate to greater or lesser degrees with racial classifications. Overt expressions of racial hatred occur regularly, and more subtle forms of racial animus and implicit bias are quite routine. A racist subtext has wormed its way into recent public discussion of immigration in Europe and America. In the United States, the ghost of white supremacism, which many complacently assumed had long since been exorcised, has re-emerged with unabashed virulence since the election of Donald Trump. The author of this book teaches at an American university whose grounds were invaded, in August 2017, by torch-bearing fascists chanting the Nazi slogans "Blood and Soil" and "Jews Will Not Replace Us."

That anyone ought to be deeply troubled by all of this, I take it, goes without saying. However, whether the shameful persistence of these non-ideal realities requires political philosophers to avoid certain ways of approaching their subject, and to adopt others perhaps better suited to addressing them, is not so obvious. This question has recently become a major point of controversy in the field. Many now argue that the dominant paradigm in political philosophy over the past half-century – that pioneered by John Rawls – is hopelessly ill-equipped to respond adequately to these problems and must therefore be abandoned.

The feature of Rawls's approach that invites this objection is its avowed commitment to "ideal theory." As we noted earlier, Rawls proposed that, to propitiously organize our thinking about complex and difficult questions about justice, we should begin by abstracting from the messy reality of the present and consider what a just society would look like given ideal circumstances. Settling on an account of justice for the ideal case will then allow us to make headway with more pressing questions that arise in our non-ideal circumstances. With a target at which to aim, intelligent judgments about the gravity and urgency of current injustice, and about how best to address it, can be oriented at an attempt to approximate, and move toward, the more just world portrayed by the ideal theory, or so Rawls suggested.

Against this, Rawls's critics have maintained not only that his effort to specify an "ideal theory" of justice is unnecessary,[1] but also that it diverts

---

[1] The attack on "ideal theory" has been mounted from many directions, and proponents of "non-ideal" or "realist" alternatives often represent quite opposed views, so the discussion here will necessarily be selective. A helpful overview is provided by Rossi and Sleat 2014. A sample of the range of positions currently in play in the debate can be gleaned from Farrelly 2007; Geuss 2008; Mills 2005; Sen 2006; Wiens 2015; Williams 2005.

our attention away from the oppression and injustice that is actually faced today by groups like those just mentioned. Far from *facilitating* an intelligent, informed, critical response to their problems, an ideal-theoretic approach only obscures their character, and postpones a serious reckoning with them, or so claim the critics.

On the strongest versions of this objection, indeed, Rawls's idealizing approach is actually complicit in perpetuating these enduring forms of injustice and oppression. Insofar as that allegation can be made out, his approach would exemplify ideological delusion of exactly the sort for which (as we saw in the previous chapter) Marx believed social critics should be constantly on the lookout. Accordingly, much as Marx hoped to unmask the ideological mystifications that conceal oppressive power structures, Rawls's critics have attempted to document the ways in which he unwittingly transformed academic political philosophy into an auxiliary conduit through which existing patterns of oppression and injustice are intellectually reinforced. To put the objection in language introduced in Chapters 1 and 14, "ideal theory" promotes a "defusing" attitude toward existing injustices that in fact invite a "mobilizing" response.

This debate raises too many very complex issues to be resolved here. However, I hope at least to clarify the terms of that debate and to explain some of the very serious difficulties that the line of objection just described faces. My aim in elaborating those difficulties is certainly not to acquit Rawls of the charges leveled against his own version of "ideal theory," for I think it is very important in this context not to get drawn into a scholastic discussion of the particular details of his elaborate theory. To this extent, the critics are surely right that Rawls's apparatus can distract us from what matters. Rather, I want to draw attention to some of the problems that attend the effort to recruit Marx's model of political criticism to the context of identity-based oppression set out above.

Liberalism: A Red Herring

Let me begin by immediately conceding one point to Rawls's critics. As I have argued throughout this book, political philosophers ought not to define their activities in relation to conventionally recognized traditions of thought. If, as I have claimed, the object of the exercise is to introduce critical distance on the prejudices of the day, we ought not to simply assume that familiar patterns of political affiliation (liberalism, conservatism, libertarianism, socialism, "the left," "the right," etc.) are any sort of reliable guide to the fundamental issues at stake in political life. These groupings are simply too parochial, too confused, and too closely interlinked with fallible and self-promoting institutions to deserve the benefit of the doubt. That is why I have chosen not to organize this book around these divisions.

For much of the past half-century, however, political philosophers have often preoccupied themselves with the question of the adequacy and internal coherence of a particular, historically local political tradition: that of "liberalism." Rawls himself encouraged this fixation. In his later career, he explicitly recast his account of justice, which he originally advanced as a non-affiliated general theory, as an effort to "construct" a systematic, self-consistent model of "political liberalism." When connected to his "defusing" remarks about "reconciliation" discussed at the end of the last chapter, this aspiration creates the unfortunate impression that he took defending "liberalism" to be among the most important responsibilities for political philosophers to take on. Alas, rather than resisting this tendency, many of Rawls's critics took the bait and fell into the trap of supposing that the political faultline between "liberalism" and its rivals is a good guide to where the most important and philosophically interesting issues lie. Yet there is absolutely no reason to make that supposition.

To reject this tendency is not necessarily to oppose any of the political practices or ideals for which self-described "liberals" have historically struggled. Freedom of speech, equality before the law, and checks on the arbitrary abuse of state power are all vital historical achievements that we should not want reversed. But our appreciation of these accomplishments should depend neither on their credentials as "liberal" nor on our desire to remain loyal to a tradition that defines our supposedly "shared" values. Rather, it should reflect our considered view that in upholding these principles our societies are better, more just, more humane, more likely to promote human good, more rational, and so on. That these also happen to be "liberal" principles by some lights is, or should be, quite incidental to this judgment.

To the extent that mainstream literature in recent political philosophy has ignored this point, and treated the word "liberal" as interchangeable with "good" and "illiberal" as synonymous with "evil," it is vulnerable to the charge of ideological obfuscation. Strictly speaking, however, this is not an issue about "ideal theory." The problem here, rather, is the willingness to let our philosophical perception be controlled by the very sorts of orthodoxy that we are supposed to be submitting to critical scrutiny. So, the issue about idealization raises independent issues, to which I now turn directly.

Ideal and Non-Ideal

Laura Valentini has usefully distinguished two ways of contrasting ideal and non-ideal theory (she also mentions a third, about feasibility, but I ignore it here).[2]

An ideal theory, first, might be one that assumes, counterfactually, political circumstances in which agents are fully reasonable and disposed to comply as a matter of course with all valid or defensible expectations made of them by the positive morality of their society. As Rawls said, we assume "full compliance." This idealizing move is normally justified on the grounds that it simplifies an otherwise intractable set of questions: it allows us, its proponents say, to abstract away from noisy features of the existing political world and focus more clearly on the problems that would remain to be solved in their absence. In a similar way, the laws of motion in classical mechanics are easier to understand and state if one pretends that friction is not an issue.

If one understands ideal theory in this way, then a commitment to "non-ideal" theory will involve a refusal to make this simplifying assumption, and a skepticism about the value of doing so. The case for non-ideal theory in this sense is that to assume "full compliance" is willfully to ignore the most urgent injustices that command our attention. If we want to help change the world for the better, we need to focus on the actual problems of the world, not settle into the philosopher's armchair fantasizing about an ideal world in which those problems are imagined away. This is an evasion, or so claim the critics.

The second contrast that Valentini picks out understands ideal theory as setting a "target" at which to aim, an orienting vision of where we ought to be heading that we can then use to make intelligent judgments in the here and now about how to advance toward the target. This way of conceiving

---

[2] Valentini 2012.

ideal theory cannot be charged with ignoring concrete, non-ideal realities, for it entails its own view about how we should conduct ourselves in
non-ideal circumstances. That is, we should regard our current non-ideal
world as a transitional state and do what we can to chart a trajectory of
improvement.

This second construal invites an independent criticism from those who
today attack ideal-theoretic approaches. This criticism does not focus on
the vanity of spending time specifying principles of justice for a world
that does not exist, but rather questions the value of thinking about non-
ideal problems in this transitional way. That transitional optic is implicitly
forward-looking: it takes an interest in the non-ideal only for the purposes
of projecting a road to the future. This, the critic might complain, alienates
us from the reality faced by victims of serious oppression and injustice.
These people are being shafted *now*, and often belong to communities that
have been being shafted for a very long time. The African American community, for example, has experienced an appalling succession of injustices,
abuses and indignities, from colonization, kidnap, transportation, slavery,
Jim Crow, lynchings, police abuse, segregation, "massive resistance," to *de
facto* confinement within underprivileged and toxic urban ghettos. When,
in the face of all this, protest groups invoke the powerful slogan "Black
Lives Matter," they are *not* interested in "mattering" as *dramatis personae* in
some grand transitional narrative controlled by an academic's ideal theory.
They simply want the abuse to stop, and for adequate restitution for the
past injustices that they and their kin have suffered, and whose effects continue to deny them anything like a decent (to say nothing of equal) opportunity for a good life.

So, we have two basic objections to ideal theory:

(1) Dreaming of full compliance and the need for justice under that rad-
    ically counterfactual condition distracts attention from more urgent
    injustices we confront today.
(2) An exclusively forward-looking approach to non-ideal problems
    suppresses the more urgent backward-looking problem of compensa-
    tion for past injustice.

Since Rawls's theory incorporates both of Valentini's two idealizing elements – full compliance and transition guided by a target – it invites both of
these charges.

Mills on the "Racial Contract"

Each of these objections plays a role, along with much else, in Charles Mills's provocative and recently influential critique of "ideal theory," which the balance of this chapter explores. Mills is best known for his 1997 book, *The Racial Contract*, which he followed up with several important essays developing its main argument.[3] In these works, Mills offers a radical reinterpretation of the social-contract tradition as implicitly (and sometimes explicitly) imbued with the ideology of white supremacy. According to Mills, the limitations of Rawlsian "ideal theory" have to be seen in this light: they are not merely idiosyncrasies of Rawls's own position but rather reflect the racially inflected logic of the Western social contract tradition itself.

The tendency for "ideal theories" to divert intellectual attention away from the historical modalities of racial oppression, and their exponents' typical lack of interest in non-ideal questions about reparation for past injustice, emerge in this account, not merely as philosophical mistakes, but rather as intellectual symptoms of a much more sinister social reality, what Mills calls the "racial contract." This contract corresponds to the actual *modus operandi* of Western modernity, whose history has been importantly constituted by racial slavery, discrimination, domination, segregation, and abuse.

Mills's postulation of a "racial contract" purports to explain the disturbing coexistence of two seemingly contradictory phenomena: the liberating impetus of the modern Enlightenment and the brutal reality of racial slavery, domination, and oppression. How can it be that these oppressive structures not only emerged but also *flourished* as the most inspiring universalist commitments of the Enlightenment (to put reason at the disposal of human improvement, to dispense with blind allegiance to tradition and religious dogma, to uphold the equal dignity and worth of all human beings, to secure the freedom and autonomy of thought, mind, and speech) were gaining ground?

A natural way to parse this incongruity, and the account favored by partisans of the Enlightenment tradition, is to understand it in terms of *hypocrisy*. On this view, we should simply say that the Enlightenment

---

[3] Mills 1997, 2005, 2008.

philosophers, and the theories of the social contract they pioneered, basically got the ideals right. The problem is that the actual practice of Western
societies, even as it professed those same ideals, radically betrayed them,
especially with regard to race. Modern Western history should be read as
an as yet incomplete unfolding of the attempt to live up to its own, essentially sound, humanist ideals.

Mills rejects this hypocrisy narrative as naïve. In taking this line, Mills
offers a critique that mirrors, and is modeled on, Marx's account of modern
capitalism. For, like Mills today, Marx also rejected hypocrisy narratives
about capitalist forms of life, for reasons suggested in the previous chapter.
As we noted there, Marx maintained that capitalism promoted a particular set of moral ideals – the rights and freedoms of property-owners,
an imperative of respect for voluntary choice, and absolute prohibitions
on aggression, theft, and fraud. Marx is precisely *not* accusing capitalism
of hypocrisy in relation to these ideals. To the contrary, he wants to draw
attention to the fact that judging market society by the lights of such moral
standards actually protects it from critical scrutiny. Critics who confine
themselves to applying those standards will fail to notice that the morality
of respect for private property and voluntary choice commands acceptance
within capitalist societies because it serves the function of *legitimating* the
historically distinctive economic formation it represents.

On Marx's account, to subject capitalism – or any social system – to
serious critical assessment requires one to set these moralizing ideals to
one side and comprehend it on a more historically realist basis. When we
do this, we discover that capitalism is an irrational social form, in which
agents are made to serve the needs of the system, rather than vice versa.
We begin to appreciate how, rather than respecting the freedom of individuals (as on the official story), capitalism is oppressive and dehumanizing,
"mutilating" members of the working class into "mere fragment[s]" of a
human being.[4]

I argued in the last chapter that Marx's critique – whether or not it is
ultimately sound – is better off without the baggage of his "historical materialism." The Marxian critic should simply admit that "dehumanization,"
"oppression," and "irrationality" are not really material categories, but
important abstract concepts that capture, without relying on moralizing

[4] Marx 1992, p. 482.

assumptions, phenomena of which we have very strong reasons to disapprove. As Mills rightly notes, to reject "ideal theory" is not necessarily to renounce all forms of abstraction in critical reflection, for sometimes we need such abstractions to give an adequate diagnosis of the irrationality of problematic social practices.[5] This is exactly what Marx attempted in his mammoth, never completed, *Capital*, whose title itself refers to a theoretical abstraction that he used to illuminate the real structure of market society.

Mills's notion of a "racial contract" is supposed to perform the same function within his critical account of Rawlsian ideal theory. Rejecting the hypocrisy narrative as a naïve form of "moralizing criticism" or "applied ethics," Mills instead argues that racial injustice is integral to the categories of social-contract theory that Rawls mobilizes in his theory of justice. In this way, he wants to expose the idealized social contract that Rawls's theory proposed as complicit in racial domination. Far from giving us a set of ideal, humanistic standards by which to properly recognize racial oppression and injustice, Rawls's framework actually conceals its real character and, like the larger social contract tradition itself, diverts intellectual attention so that the problem of race is ignored, trivialized, and misdescribed.

This is clearly an ambitious and challenging line of argument. Does it succeed? To help answer that question, we can identify five distinct, though not necessarily mutually exclusive, claims that are wrapped up in Mills's critique. In different passages, Mills complains that the contractualist tradition and its Rawlsian "ideal-theoretic" descendants:

(1) directly express conscious racist attitudes held by their proponents, tainting these intellectual frameworks with racial animus;

(2) embody racist assumptions, so that regardless of contractualist thinkers' actual attitudes, their theories are skewed in a way that overlooks or reinforces concrete structures of racial domination in the world;

(3) embody "whiteness," where this is identified with the outlook of a dominant and unrepresentative racial group, enjoying massive privileges, whose members experience the social world and conceive of their interests in relation to those of others in distorted ways;

[5] Mills 2005, pp. 174–6.

(4) disguise, obscure, or obfuscate racist practices, rendering them invisible and promoting ignorance about their character, prevalence, and historical sources;

(5) acknowledge racist practices but misdiagnose them in narrowly moralistic or juridical terms merely as failures to fulfill moral duties to treat others decently, or to properly enforce formal civil rights, so that their deeper, structurally oppressive character goes unnoticed and appropriate remedies are not considered.

Similar criticisms have been voiced by other critics of ideal theory, often with respect to other identity categories. All of them deserve careful consideration, and they raise more issues that I can possibly address here. However, as we shall see, each also faces some hard questions. I will take them in turn.

Racist Expression

The first charge to consider is whether the social-contract apparatus itself (and any "ideal theory" built on it) is tainted by the racially invidious attitudes of its leading exponents. Mills is perfectly correct on the facts here; indeed, one of his most valuable contributions has been to document the depressing frequency with which racial slurs appear in at least the major historical contributors to the social contract tradition (Locke, Hobbes, Kant, etc.).[6] This is a disturbing fact about these individuals, but its larger philosophical significance is open to doubt.

The main problem here is that the point seems fundamentally *ad hominem* – addressed to the particular authors and their racial attitudes, but not necessarily implicating their thought or the character of their philosophical influence in any deep way. Now Mills deploys considerable ingenuity arguing that we cannot easily disconnect the personal from the philosophical in the context of these authors' theories.[7] Mills contends, for example, that once we realize that Kant's writings contain several hair-raisingly white-supremacist remarks, his famous (and to many inspiring) commitment to the inherent dignity of all persons and the equal respect that it commands takes on a different complexion. We are forced to view that commitment

---

[6] Mills 1997, pp. 62–72.
[7] Mills 2017, pp. 94–105.

as racially conditioned in a way that is integral to Kant's own conception of the social contract; and for Mills, this is not just a point about Kant *the man*, but also one about the conceptual structure of his theory.

Even if we agree with Mills on that point, a more important issue remains – that of how the work of historical authors is *received*. Kant is a famous and widely read philosopher because his audience has been impressed enough by his work to believe it is worth engaging with, developing, applying, criticizing, etc. If we are trying to characterize social contract theory as a wider ideological phenomenon (as Mills is), it matters a lot *why* the writings of its leading exponents have intrigued later generations of readers. Any later currency acquired by that theory must reflect its attractiveness to members of that audience.

However, I find it hard to believe that Kant's (or Locke's or Hobbes's) racial attitudes, even if we interpret them as integral to these thinkers' own philosophical activity, explain why social-contract theories have been taken up and pursued seriously by political philosophers in subsequent generations, and especially today. Most of the latter have been completely unaware of Kant's racist attitudes; only recently have those attitudes become widely known. As Mills himself mentions, their discovery typically occasions shock and disappointment among Kant's admirers and those who have found something worthwhile in social-contract theory. Certainly Rawls would have been (and if he knew of it doubtless *was*) disgusted by Kant's racism.

Yet surely the fact that those most responsible for promoting a theoretical paradigm to prominence in intellectual discussions are repelled by, rather than attracted to, such racist attitudes tells against the claim that that paradigm, and any ideological role it has played, is inherently racialized. After all, if racist sympathies were an important motivation within that intellectual community, we might expect its members to be enthusiastically commending and developing the work of "scientific" racists and eugenicists like Count Gobineau, Francis Galton, Madison Grant, and Alfred Rosenberg alongside Hobbes, Locke, Kant, and Rawls. For the most part, however, these far more conspicuously racist writers attract only their mistrust and contempt.

Racist Assumptions

Turning to the second item on the earlier list, Mills claims that the very concept of the person that is baked into social contract theory presupposes certain racially problematic assumptions. His reason for thinking this appears to be that the theory presupposes some account of who counts as a person, and this creates conceptual space for racist assumptions to creep in, such that nonwhite people are subject to categorization as "sub-personal" or as nonpersons in virtue of alleged mental or other inferiority.

Mills is obviously correct that such invidious assumptions can be added to the social contract framework, but I see no reason to hold this against the framework rather than against the assumptions and those seduced by them. We already knew that, on racist views, nonwhite people count for less. While one could perhaps argue that contractualist views ought to have some mechanism built into them to protect themselves from the thoughtless prejudices of their exponents, one could equally well respond that the assumptions about racial inferiority involved are so obviously false that all the blame should fall on the people stupid and insensitive enough to fall for them.

Moreover, when Mills uses this line of argument to implicate contemporary versions of social-contract theory in racist practices, he winds up defaulting to the hypocrisy narrative that he claims to avoid. He writes, for example, that

> [i]n contrast to the Lockean-Nozickian ideal of a polity of self-owning proprietors respecting one another's property rights and in contrast to the Kantian-Rawlsian ideal of a polity of reciprocally respecting persons … the actual polity is one in which the property rights of non-self-owning people of color are systematically violated and rights, liberties, income, and wealth are continually transferred from the nonwhite to the white population.[8]

But this objection seems to indict actual practices of racism, slavery, deprivation etc. precisely on the grounds that they depart from the ideal of equality postulated by Rawls, Nozick, Kant, and Locke. It is true that Mills here points out that, under slavery, African Americans did not enjoy the rights of self-ownership. But that would imply that they have no rights to violate, which is inconsistent with Mills's later claim that they have suffered injustice because their rights are violated. Either they have the rights or they do not; if they do, it is because we believe they are equal

[8] Mills 2008, p. 1383.

persons like everyone else. So here, it looks as if Mills is actually *appealing* to the standard assumption of equal human dignity that all plausible contemporary versions of social-contract theory themselves endorse, not giving us a reason to be suspicious of it.

"Whiteness"

In postulating a "racial contract" among whites to advance their "common interest in maintaining global white supremacy"[9] Mills identifies oppressor status with "whiteness." This third claim is conceptually distinct from the previous two because it is not centrally concerned with the prevalence of racial animus or of beliefs about racial superiority or inferiority. For the point here is really one about a privileged group – "whites" – that uses its disproportionate social power to advance interests that can be thought of as its own.

Now, on Mills's hypothesis, the relevant privileges are wielded by and on behalf of a group that is defined racially, in this case by "whiteness." But it does *not* follow that hostile or demeaning attitudes toward *other* racial groups are essential to any oppression involved, even if those privileges are exercised at the expense of those other groups. What fundamentally justifies diagnoses of oppression or privilege is some *structural* disparity in power, not the presence of any particular attitudes toward others. A social situation in which the privileges of greater power accrue to a specific racial group will almost certainly *breed* racist attitudes and beliefs and likely exacerbate any pre-existing ones. But it is difficult to see how such attitudes could themselves be sufficient to engender oppression or privilege without some independent, structural power disparity playing a more fundamental background role.[10]

Read this way, Mills's position is formally analogous to Marx's critique of capitalism, for here Mills uses the term "whiteness" very much as Marx uses the word "bourgeois." In Marx's account, the "bourgeoisie" refers to an economic *class* defined by the unchallenged *de facto* power it enjoys under capitalist conditions. The "bourgeois" are for Marx a distinct class in that

---

[9] Mills 1997, p. 114.

[10] As Mills notes at one point, "*Whiteness is not really a color at all, but a set of power relations*" (Mills 1997, p. 127; italics in original).

their ownership of the "means of production" (i.e. their having surplus capital to invest in enterprises [manufacturing, service provision, etc.]) gives them effective control over society, allowing them to take advantage of those workers (the "proletariat") who lack access to capital and who therefore have nothing to sell but their labor. This creates a structural disparity in power, a form of class domination, that Marx believes is ideologically obfuscated under capitalist conditions by the mantra that worker and capitalist meet on the market as equals, with the same basic rights to property and security, so that everything looks fair, voluntary, and aboveboard. But Marx's argument does not identify structural oppression with any attitudes of contempt toward, or assumptions about the inferiority of, workers on the part of bourgeois. These attitudes and beliefs may well develop under capitalist conditions, but the oppressive character of the conditions themselves is for Marx an independent and more basic phenomenon.

However, if he intends a structural argument of this sort, Mills's actual characterization of "whiteness" seems rather incongruous. At various points Mills speaks of "white moral psychology," of "white" experience, white "normativity," "white cognitive distortion," "whites' sense of what is just," of "white" "reflective equilibrium," of "white" ethical discourse and of the "actual moral/political consciousness of (most) white agents."[11] These remarks suggest that Mills understands "whiteness" in terms of a characteristic set of attitudes and experiences. Yet insofar as his complaint is one about structural privilege, it is not clear what role the supposed experiences and psychological attitudes of representative whites has to play. Claims about how agents experience and develop certain attitudes to their world from their own points of view are notoriously difficult to verify. A significant advantage of Marx's structural approach is that it does not require the critic to rely on such claims. Thus, on Marx's account, we recognize who is "bourgeois" and who is a "proletarian" not by looking at anyone's physical appearance, mode of dress, cultural tics, social attitudes, psychological well-being, the kinds of books they write, personal experiences, or even their prosperity (for after all many a bourgeois has been ruined by the fierce competition of the market). Rather, we identify these classes simply in terms of their respective access to economic power.

[11] For example, Mills 2005, pp. 172, 175; Mills 1997, pp. 57, 91, 93.

But one wonders whether Mills's category of "whiteness" is a comparably stable and informative guide to the structure of existing patterns of oppression. Is it obvious that simply *being* white implicates one in such structures? Mills himself recognizes some complications here, noticing that it is one thing to be a white *beneficiary* of racial oppression and another to be so deeply inculpated in it as to be, in effect, a *signatory* to his racial contract.[12] But there are other difficulties. Is it only "whites" who have benefited from racial oppression? How about Asian-Americans, Latinos, or even middle- and upper-class people of African descent employed by Western businesses that participated in or benefited from past exploitation of nonwhite groups?

These considerations suggest that, as Marx thought, class relations may capture the relevant disparities more effectively than identity categories. Mills himself sometimes identifies "ideal theory" with "*ideology*, a distortional complex of ideas, values, norms, and beliefs that reflects the nonrepresentative interests and experiences of a small minority of the national population – middle-to-upper-class white males – who are hugely *over-represented* in the professional philosophical population."[13] Here, he not only introduces class position and gender categories, but also reminds us that in virtue of their professional (academic) affiliation, philosophy professors are largely unlike the larger "white" population. So, one wonders exactly what work "whiteness" can really do in this context. No one doubts, of course, that certain racial groups have been (and still are) victims of appalling and systematic oppression, but one might reasonably conclude from these remarks that an account of racial injustice does better to focus on the magnitude of what they have *suffered* and less on the distinguishing characteristics of those (very diverse) individuals, groups, and institutions that have inflicted that suffering on them.

Complicity, Complacency, and Solidarity

Mills's emphasis on distinctively "white" experiences, attitudes and "moral psychology" raises other tricky questions. He asserts that attitudinal and experiential structures common among "whites" hinder them from a

---

[12] Mills 1997, p. 11.
[13] Mills 2005, p. 172.

4. Said (Palest.

fully sympathetic appreciation of the experiences of domination, exclusion, discrimination, hatred, and abuse to which people of color have routinely been subjected. On Mills's account, the lack of interest that "white" ideal theorists like Rawls have shown in questions of race is an intellectual manifestation of this pervasive complacency and insensitivity toward racial oppression within the white population. His claim here is not that being white makes it impossible to understand the predicament of racially oppressed groups, but rather that the emphasis on "ideal theory" among white political philosophers attests to, and perpetuates, a refusal on the part of whites to acknowledge their deep complicity in racial subordination. That is why Mills believes that opposing "ideal theory" in political philosophy is so important: by rooting it out, we erode one of the ideological forces that allow white eyes[14] to be averted. His hope is that a historically informed non-ideal theory of racial oppression can dig out the painful truth from underneath the evasions and denials of the dominant white culture, thereby helping to force a long overdue reckoning.

As a criticism of "ideal theory," this line of argument is plausible only if we assume that pursuing such theorizing must imply indifference to racial injustice, or come at the expense of efforts to understand its true historical dimensions. I will shortly question that assumption, but here I want to ask whether it is obvious that, as a sociological or psychological fact about Western societies like the USA, "whiteness" does hinder sympathy for the injustices and oppression suffered by nonwhite groups both now and in the past.

That racism and racial injustice have proven astonishingly recalcitrant is undeniable, but whether this automatically provides evidence of indifference, complacency, or an unwillingness on the part of the white population as such to assume responsibility for its role in racism is unclear. One reason to doubt that it does is that some forms of racism depend on agents' inner psychological attitudes that are very difficult for others (from the same racial communities) who disapprove of them to change. Sometimes, one simply has to wait for generations of bigots to die off, and this can take a long time.

Whether the glacial pace of change in this area supports claims about the poverty of "white" attitudes also depends in part on whether the

[14] Mills 1997, p. 70.

political system affords the means to make successful and/or rapid inroads into the problem. If it is extremely difficult to pass legislative and constitutional programs that would address these problems in a really comprehensive way, and it is unlikely that even very sweeping reforms will have immediate effects, their persistence could just as well be evidence of a warranted sense of despair and futility on the part of people who *do* care as a reason to suspect insensitivity to or complicity in racial oppression. When, in August 2017, white supremacists marched in Charlottesville, they were met by crowds of angry protesters, many of whom were white; public reactions to these events (and to Donald Trump's notoriously tepid criticism of the white supremacists) in the news media – dominated by white commentators – was overwhelmingly angry and hostile. The case is anecdotal, of course, but it is difficult to reconcile with a uniform narrative of "white" indifference to racial bigotry. It rather suggests that where it is relatively easy to coordinate collective action against racist practices (e.g. demonstrating, marching, denouncing, or protesting, as opposed to enacting systematic legislative remedies), many members of the white population do not hesitate to act, even at considerable personal risk (one protester was killed, and many others injured, in the riot that ensued).

Finally, one might ask how Mills knows that the "moral psychology" and experiences associated with "whiteness" tend to impair a deep understanding of the experiences of those nonwhite persons who, because of their racial affiliation, are subjected to abuse, discrimination, exclusion, exploitation, etc. A white American will, by definition, not know *exactly* what it is like for an African American to experience (say) regular, racially freighted harassment at the hands of white police officers. But "whiteness" *per se* does not guarantee immunity to any number of closely adjacent experiences: sexual assault; abuse by priests or teachers as a child; being bullied almost to the point of suicide by peers at educational or military institutions; domestic violence; being driven into demeaning forms of prostitution or exploitative sweatshop labor; being ostracized or ridiculed for one's appearance, chronic illnesses, sexual orientation, or other personal characteristics; the humiliation of homelessness or poverty; the social defeat of long-term unemployment, and so on. The point here is not so much that Mills's category of "whiteness" carries with it a high risk of negative racial stereotyping of its own (whites as bigots, whites as uncaring, whites as arrogant, whites as shameless, whites as closed-minded, whites as people with limited moral imaginations, whites as ignorant, etc.), but more that emphasizing the mutual unintelligibility of experiences of abuse suffered under different conditions threatens efforts to foster desirable solidarity among the oppressed, excluded, and hated.

Invisibility and Distraction

Mills writes: "By the apparently innocuous methodological decision to focus on ideal theory, white philosophers are immediately exempted from having to deal with the legacy of white supremacy in our actual society."[15] This fourth charge is one of distraction leading to evasion: the labyrinths of ideal theory lead philosophical discussion into a strange and unreal "raceless" outlook in which the harsh reality of color lines are bleached out – "whitewashed," as Mills likes to pun. As I hinted above, however, the plausibility of the allegation that ideal theorizing distracts philosophers from thinking in a historically realistic way about important non-ideal problems depends on the degree to which we think that these are mutually exclusive intellectual foci. I do not think that is obvious.

To be sure, if (as in Rawls) engaging in "ideal theory" *just means* assuming "full compliance" for the purposes of simplifying the analysis, then it must be true that, *while doing it*, one is not thinking about the myriad phenomena of non-compliance (including racism, discrimination, etc.). However, it does not follow that ideal theorizing *is the only thing one ought to do*. Even though they may not be activities that, logically speaking, one can do simultaneously, one could still divide one's time between them and believe that both are important aspects of one's role as a social critic. And the bare fact that one thinks that "ideal theory" might have an important role, and can answer some questions that one could not address satisfactorily in other ways, does not automatically establish that it must then become like an intellectual black hole, exerting an irresistible gravitational force on one's thinking, so that ever greater sectors of one's attention, research time, philosophical imagination, etc. are sucked into its orbit until eventually any consciousness of non-ideal problems is completely suppressed or overwhelmed. Indeed, there is no logical presumption in favor of dividing attention between these activities according to any particular ratio. It is

---

[15] Mills 2008, p. 1385.

perfectly possible to believe that ideal theory has *some* importance but that non-ideal theory of a Millsian sort has even greater importance.

Mills might reply that the logical possibility of doing "ideal theory" without being distracted from non-ideal realities is irrelevant because we can document how Rawls's idealizing orientation actually *has* misdirected the attention of political philosophers away from issues of race and other identity-involving injustices. On this point Mills makes a good case: it *should* surprise us that philosophers (including Rawls himself) who have claimed to take social justice seriously have written so little that explicitly addresses the history of racial injustice in the West. This gives at least circumstantial evidence that idealizing modes of reflection about justice can distract attention from politically urgent questions.

Still, two qualifications are worth entering. First, while it is true that Rawls wrote little about race and non-ideal theory, it is misleading to suggest that during the period of his greatest influence, theorists showed no interest *at all* in issues of racial injustice. From the 1970s to the 1990s there was a vigorous and often philosophically sophisticated discussion of "affirmative action" policies adopted in the United States as measures intended to compensate for the effects of past racial injustice on the present generation of African Americans (and for other groups, including women). Many of those who contributed to those debates (Thomas Nagel, Judith Jarvis Thomson, Ronald Dworkin) were strongly influenced by Rawls's work and in some cases were his pupils.[16]

Second, although it is true that *A Theory of Justice* abstracts from the particular histories of any particular society (and so says little about the specific patterns of racial oppression that mark Western modernity), Rawls made very clear that in his view the "most important social primary good" is what he described as "the social bases of self-respect." Rawls was not always precise about what he meant by this phrase, but the general idea is clear enough: he had in mind the plight of agents who are daily demeaned as inferior, and who face systematic disrespect and social humiliation. It is impossible to believe that, as he formulated *A Theory of Justice* in the 1950s and 1960s against the backdrop of the American civil rights movement, Rawls did not have the experience of the African American community in mind. So in this sense, an awareness of the problems of racial injustice

---

[16] See the essays collected in Cohen et al. 1977 and also Amdur 1979.

informs even Rawls's theory, albeit *sotto voce*. It should not surprise us that, much more recently, scholars like Tommie Shelby have found in Rawls's theory a propitious framework for theorizing patterns of racial injustice in a non-ideal world.[17]

Justice, Affirmative Action, and Reparations

The fifth and final charge that I consider recruits and extends Marx's objection to "moralizing criticism" into the domain of racial oppression. As I suggested in the previous chapter, we have good reasons to agree with Marx's claim that phenomena of oppression, exclusion, and subordination are not reducible to the mere failure to observe formal, juridical equality[18] or to fulfill narrowly moral duties. Mills must be right that this point applies in spades to the various forms of racism and racial oppression that have persisted in the West for a long time. Apart from the issues about structural privileges and power disparities already mentioned, there are several other dimensions of the racial case that moralistic or juridical categories are ill-placed to capture.

For one thing, those categories tend to focus on deficiency in relation to rules and standards. The operative metaphors here are ones of privation, failure, and falling short of some expectation. But the presence of racial domination, oppression, and subordination implies not merely a deficiency or privation of something, but rather the active presence of an evil or malformation. To characterize such phenomena, we need a framework that is not merely privative, but one that characterizes how oppression contributes to a warping of the social fabric. Humiliation, dehumanization, and stigma can all be added to the list of features of racist social practices that cannot be reduced to a mere failure to fulfill moral duties, but that actively distort the human scene.[19] So Mills is right to emphasize the contrast between immorality, formal injustice, and racial oppression.

On the other hand, there is a tension between that emphasis and the second of the two general complaints about "ideal theory" that I mentioned

---

[17] Shelby 2007.
[18] Mills 2005, p. 177.
[19] For an argument defending restrictions on "hate speech" that turns on a claim about how hateful, abusive language can actively toxify social life, see Waldron 2014.

earlier. Recall that that second objection asserts that adopting an "idealizing" focus encourages us to pass over and suppress "backward-looking" questions about compensation for past injustice in racial and other contexts. But does it make sense to say that we need a nonmoralized, structural focus on oppression to sensitize ourselves to these backward-looking, compensatory questions?

Ordinary language suggests one reason to think not: it does not sound right to demand reparation for oppression, dehumanization, structural privilege, or domination. As Marx thought, these phenomena demand not compensation or reparation, or any form of *redress*, but rather (at a minimum) *mitigation* and (at a maximum) *overthrow*. These are actually forward-, not backward-looking categories. Compensation makes sense as a backward-looking requirement, and so presupposes past injustice or wrongdoing. But this takes us away from the structural diagnosis of oppression, and back toward what Marx deprecated as "moralization," although in this case we should surely be reluctant to trivialize the wrongs that were suffered by (e.g.) slaves in the ante-bellum American South. So it seems that we still need a more traditional, justice-based set of standards to recognize the conduct that calls for proper compensation.

One might suspect, however, that these moralistic or juridical categories are a trap, because they allow the beneficiaries of past racial injustice to resist proposals for reparations by arguing that, since they were not responsible for the wrongs of the past, they should not be on the hook for compensation. But Bernard Boxill has provided an argument that undermines that worry.[20] He reminds us that debt can be inherited: if white slaveholders in the nineteenth century, and others at the time who failed to resist what they should have known to be unjust (after all, there *was* an abolitionist movement), wronged the victims of slavery and owed them compensation, then those who inherited their land and perhaps other property acquire that debt as well. And at each stage in the sequence, the US government's failure to oversee the required transfers is itself a responsibility that it has yet to adequately discharge. Ironically, Boxill supports this argument by invoking Locke – one of Mills's contractualist bêtes noires. So perhaps the social contract tradition is not so useless in this context after all.

[20] Boxill 2003.

A final point deserves mention: as Amdur suggests,[21] the question of who should pay the costs of compensating the victims of past injustice is a central, not peripheral, one, certainly on any non-ideal view. He makes a persuasive case that in respect of racial injustice in the United States, direct and substantial cash reparations, levied on the general population (in much the way Germany paid reparations to the Jews after the Second World War), is a more appropriate remedy than affirmative action programs. The latter, he argues, impose the costs on the wrong people (non-minority applicants for prestigious positions) while doing little to benefit those (members of disadvantaged minority groups who remain stuck in the ghetto) who seem most strongly entitled to redress. Whether reparation on this scale should be paid, however, depends on a further issue: how urgent is the need to make reparation for past wrongs in relation to the independent importance of assuming proper responsibility for removing injustice *now* and into the future? If these require different things, we have to choose between giving greater weight to the claims of the past and treating the interests of the future as more urgent.

However we decide that question, scholastic philosophical oppositions between "ideal/non-ideal" or between "forward"- and "backward-looking" stances likely oversimplify the options. To say that, in moving one way or the other, we are merely orienting ourselves to "the" future or "the" non-ideal, is to impose an unnecessarily rigid and alienating framework on our situation. For what we are really doing, whether we recognize it or not, is orienting ourselves in different ways to each other, remapping the public atlas (in the sense discussed in Chapter 2) as we go.

Since we *are* our social world, how we *think* about why we do, do not, or should proceed in one way rather than another will rarely leave that world untouched, for better or worse.

[21] Amdur 1979.

References

Amdur, Robert. 1979. "Compensatory Justice: The Question of Costs." *Political Theory* 7 (2): 229–44.

Anderson, Elizabeth S. 1999. "What Is the Point of Equality?" *Ethics* 109 (2): 287–337.

Aristotle. 1981. *The Politics*. Edited by Trevor J. Saunders. Translated by T. A. Sinclair. Rev. edn. Harmondsworth, UK; New York: Penguin Books.

Arrow, Kenneth J. 1986. *Social Choice and Individual Values*. 2nd edn. New Haven, CT: Yale University Press.

   1999. "Inter-Generational Equity and the Rate of Discount in Long-Term Social Investment." In *Contemporary Economic Issues*, vol. 4: *Economic Behaviour and Design*, ed. Murat Sertel, 89–102. London: Macmillan.

Auden, W. H. 1991. *Collected Poems*. Edited by Edward Mendelson. Repr. edn. New York: Vintage.

Austin, John. 1995. *The Province of Jurisprudence Determined*. Edited by Wilfrid E. Rumble. Cambridge Texts in the History of Political Thought. Cambridge; New York: Cambridge University Press.

Banai, Ayelet, Margaret Moore, David Miller, Cara Nine, and Frank Dietrich. 2014. "Symposium 'Theories of Territory beyond Westphalia.'" *International Theory* 6 (1): 98–104.

Barnes, Elizabeth. 2016. *The Minority Body: A Theory of Disability*. Oxford: Oxford University Press.

Beitz, Charles. 1989. *Political Equality: An Essay in Democratic Theory*. Princeton, NJ: Princeton University Press.

   1999. *Political Theory and International Relations*. Rev. edn. Princeton, NJ: Princeton University Press.

Bentham, Jeremy. 1838–43. *The Works of Jeremy Bentham*, published under the Superintendence of his Executor, John Bowring, 11 vols., vol. 1: *Principles of Penal Law*. Edinburgh: William Tait.

   1988. *A Fragment on Government*. Edited by J. H. Burns and H. L. A. Hart. Cambridge Texts in the History of Political Thought. Cambridge; New York: Cambridge University Press.

1996. *An Introduction to the Principles of Morals and Legislation.* Edited by J. H. Burns and H. L. A. Hart. Collected Works of Jeremy Bentham. Oxford: Oxford University Press.

2002. *Rights, Representation, and Reform: Nonsense upon Stilts and Other Writings on the French Revolution.* Edited by Philip Schofield, Catherine Pease-Watkin, and Cyprian Blamires. Collected Works of Jeremy Bentham. Oxford; New York: Oxford University Press.

2014. *Of Sexual Irregularities, and Other Writings on Sexual Morality.* Edited by Philip Schofield, Catherine Pease-Watkin, and Michael Quinn. Collected Works of Jeremy Bentham. Oxford: Clarendon Press.

Berlin, Isaiah. 1969. *Four Essays on Liberty.* Oxford: Oxford University Press.

Bird, Colin. 2000. "The Possibility of Self-Government." *American Political Science Review* 94 (2): 563–77.

2014. "Why Not Marx?" *Critical Review* 26 (3–4): 259–82.

Blake, Michael. 2001. "Distributive Justice, State Coercion, and Autonomy." *Philosophy and Public Affairs* 30 (3): 257–96.

2014. "The Right to Exclude." *Critical Review of International Social and Political Philosophy* 17 (5): 521–37.

Boisvert, Will. 2018. "The Conquest of Climate." Global Warming Policy Forum (GWPF), Opinion: Pros and Cons, March 10. www.thegwpf.com/will-boisvert-the-conquest-of-climate/.

Boxill, Bernard R. 2003. "A Lockean Argument for Black Reparations." *Journal of Ethics* 7 (1): 63–91.

Brennan, Jason. 2011. *The Ethics of Voting.* Princeton, NJ: Princeton University Press.

Buchanan, Allen. 2003. "The Making and Unmaking of Boundaries: What Liberalism Has to Say." In *States, Nations, and Borders: The Ethics of Making Boundaries,* ed. Allen Buchanan and Margaret Moore, 231–61. Cambridge: Cambridge University Press.

Buchanan, Allen, and Margaret Moore, eds. 2003. *States, Nations, and Borders: The Ethics of Making Boundaries.* Cambridge: Cambridge University Press.

Caney, Simon. 2005. "Cosmopolitan Justice, Responsibility, and Global Climate Change." *Leiden Journal of International Law* 18 (4): 747–75.

2009. "Justice and the Distribution of Greenhouse Gas Emissions." *Journal of Global Ethics* 5 (2): 125–46.

2010. "Climate Change and the Duties of the Advantaged." *Critical Review of International Social and Political Philosophy* 13 (1): 203–28.

2014. "Two Kinds of Climate Justice: Avoiding Harm and Sharing Burdens." *Journal of Political Philosophy* 22 (2): 125–49.

2016. "The Struggle for Climate Justice in a Non-Ideal World." *Midwest Studies in Philosophy* 40 (1): 9–26.

Caplan, Bryan Douglas. 2007. *The Myth of the Rational Voter: Why Democracies Choose Bad Policies*. Princeton, NJ: Princeton University Press.

Carens, Joseph H. 1987. "Aliens and Citizens: The Case for Open Borders." *Review of Politics* 49 (2): 251–73.

2015. *The Ethics of Immigration*. Oxford; New York: Oxford University Press.

Carter, Ian. 1999. *A Measure of Freedom*. New York: Oxford University Press.

Christiano, Thomas. 1996. *The Rule of the Many: Fundamental Issues in Democratic Theory*. Focus Series. Boulder, CO: Westview Press.

Cicero. 2009. *The Republic and The Laws*. Edited by Jonathan Powell. Translated by Niall Rudd. Oxford; New York: Oxford University Press.

Cohen, G. A. 1995. "Freedom and Money." *Filosoficky Casopis* 48 (1): 89–114.

2002. *If You're an Egalitarian, How Come You're so Rich?* Cambridge, MA: Harvard University Press.

2009. *Why Not Socialism?* Princeton, NJ: Princeton University Press.

Cohen, Joshua. 1989. "Deliberation and Democratic Legitimacy." In *The Good Polity: Normative Analysis of the State*, ed. Alan Hamlin and Philip Pettit, 17–33. Oxford: Blackwell.

Cohen, M., T. Nagel, and T. Scanlon, eds. 1977. *Equality and Preferential Treatment: A "Philosophy & Public Affairs" Reader*. Princeton, NJ: Princeton University Press.

Corner, Adam, and Nick Pidgeon. 2010. "Geoengineering the Climate: The Social and Ethical Implications." *Environment: Science and Policy for Sustainable Development* 52 (1): 24–37.

Cudd, Ann E. 2006. *Analyzing Oppression*. Studies in Feminist Philosophy. New York: Oxford University Press.

DeConto, Robert M., and David Pollard. 2016. "Contribution of Antarctica to Past and Future Sea-Level Rise." *Nature* 531 (7596): 591–7.

Dewey, John. 1939. *Intelligence in the Modern Word: John Dewey's Philosophy*. Edited by Joseph Ratner. New York: Modern Library.

Donaldson, Sue, and Will Kymlicka. 2013. *Zoopolis: A Political Theory of Animal Rights*. Oxford: Oxford University Press.

Downs, Anthony. 1957. *An Economic Theory of Democracy*. Boston: Addison Wesley.

Dummett, Michael. 2004. "Immigration." *Res Publica* 10 (2): 115–22.

Edgeworth, Francis Ysidro. 2003. *Mathematical Psychics and Further Papers on Political Economy*. Edited by Peter Newman. Oxford: Oxford University Press.

Ehrlich, Paul R. 2007. *The Population Bomb*. Cutchogue, NY: Buccaneer.

Einstein, Albert. 2012. *Relativity: The Special and General Theory*. Translated by Robert W. Lawson. Repr. edn. Overland Park, KS: Digireads.com Publishing.

Elshtain, Jean Bethke. 2004a. "But Was It Just? Reflections on the Iraq War." *Nexus: A Journal of Opinion* 9: 1–9.

2004b. *Just War against Terror: The Burden of American Power in a Violent World.* New York: Basic Books.

Engels, Friedrich. 1987. *The Condition of the Working Class in England.* Edited by Victor Kiernan. London: Penguin Books.

Farrelly, Colin. 2007. "Justice in Ideal Theory: A Refutation." *Political Studies* 55 (4): 844–64.

Finnis, John. 2011. *Natural Law and Natural Rights.* 2nd edn. Oxford: Oxford University Press.

Fleurbaey, Marc, and Stephane Zuber. 2013. "Climate Policies Deserve a Negative Discount Rate." *Chicago Journal of International Law* 13 (2). https://chicagounbound.uchicago.edu/cjil/vol13/iss2/14.

Foucault, Michel. 1982. *The Archaeology of Knowledge.* New York: Pantheon Books.

1984. *The Foucault Reader.* New York: Pantheon.

1988. *Madness and Civilization: A History of Insanity in the Age of Reason.* New York: Random House.

1990. *The History of Sexuality.* New York: Vintage Books.

1994. *The Order of Things: An Archaeology of the Human Sciences.* New York: Vintage Books.

1995. *Discipline and Punish: The Birth of the Prison.* New York: Vintage Books.

Frank, Robert H. 1986. *Choosing the Right Pond: Human Behavior and the Quest for Status.* New York: Oxford University Press.

Frankfurt, Harry. 1987. "Equality as a Moral Ideal." *Ethics* 98 (1): 21–43.

2005. *On Bullshit.* Princeton, NJ: Princeton University Press.

Gallie, W. B. 1956. "Essentially Contested Concepts." *Proceedings of the Aristotelian Society* 56 (1): 167–98.

Gardiner, Stephen M. 2006. "A Core Precautionary Principle." *Journal of Political Philosophy* 14 (1): 33–60.

ed. 2010. *Climate Ethics: Essential Readings.* Oxford; New York: Oxford University Press.

2011. *A Perfect Moral Storm: The Ethical Tragedy of Climate Change.* Environmental Ethics and Science Policy. New York: Oxford University Press.

2013. "The Desperation Argument for Geoengineering." *PS: Political Science and Politics* 46 (1): 28–33.

Geuss, Raymond. 1981. *The Idea of a Critical Theory: Habermas and the Frankfurt School.* Cambridge; New York: Cambridge University Press.

2005. *Outside Ethics.* Princeton, NJ: Princeton University Press.

2008. *Philosophy and Real Politics.* Princeton, NJ: Princeton University Press.

Goldman, Alvin I. 1999. "Why Citizens Should Vote: A Causal Responsibility Approach." *Social Philosophy and Policy* 16 (2): 201–17.

Grotius, Hugo. 1901. *The Rights of War and Peace*. Translated by A. C. Campbell. Westport, CT: Hyperion.

Guerrero, Alexander A. 2014. "Against Elections: The Lottocratic Alternative." *Philosophy and Public Affairs* 42 (2): 135–78.

Gutmann, Amy, and Dennis Thompson. 2006. *Democracy and Disagreement*. Cambridge, MA; London: The Belknap Press of Harvard University Press.

Haksar, Vinit. 1979. *Equality, Liberty, and Perfectionism*. Clarendon Library of Logic and Philosophy. Oxford; New York: Oxford University Press.

Hare, R. M. 1981. *Moral Thinking: Its Levels, Method, and Point*. Oxford: Oxford University Press.

Harrison, Edward. 1989. *Darkness at Night: A Riddle of the Universe*. Cambridge, MA: Harvard University Press.

Hart, H. L. A. 1963. *Law, Liberty, and Morality*. Stanford, CA: Stanford University Press.

1994. *The Concept of Law*. 2nd edn. Oxford; New York: Oxford University Press.

Haybron, Daniel M. 2010. *The Pursuit of Unhappiness: The Elusive Psychology of Well-Being*. Oxford: Oxford University Press.

Hayek, F. A. 1937. "Economics and Knowledge." *Economica* 4 (13): 33–54.

1945. "The Use of Knowledge in Society." *American Economic Review* 35 (4): 519–30.

1984. *Law, Legislation, and Liberty*, vol. 1: *Rules and Order: A New Statement of the Liberal Principles of Justice and Political Economy*. Chicago: University of Chicago Press.

1989. *Law, Legislation and Liberty*, vol. 2: *The Mirage of Social Justice*. Chicago: University of Chicago Press.

Held, David. 1980. *Introduction to Critical Theory: Horkheimer to Habermas*. Berkeley: University of California Press.

Hobbes, Thomas. 1994. *Leviathan: With Selected Variants from the Latin Edition of 1668*. Edited by Edwin Curley. Indianapolis, IN: Hackett.

1998. *On the Citizen*. Edited by Richard Tuck and Michael Silverthorne. Cambridge Texts in the History of Political Thought. New York: Cambridge University Press.

Holmes, Robert. 2014. *On War and Morality*. Princeton, NJ: Princeton University Press.

Holmes, Stephen, and Cass R. Sunstein. 1999. *The Cost of Rights: Why Liberty Depends on Taxes*. New York: Norton.

Horkheimer, Max. 1982. *Critical Theory: Selected Essays*. New York: Continuum.

Huemer, Michael. 2015. "Why People Are Irrational About Politics." http://rintintin.colorado.edu/~vancecd/phil3600/Huemer1.pdf.

Hume, David. 1978. *A Treatise of Human Nature*. Edited by P. H. Nidditch. Oxford: Oxford University Press.

    1985. *A Treatise of Human Nature*. Edited by E. C. Mossner. Repr. edn. London: Penguin Books.

Jamieson, Dale. 2014. *Reason in a Dark Time: Why the Struggle against Climate Change Failed – and What It Means for Our Future*. Oxford; New York: Oxford University Press.

Janis, I. L. 1971. "Groupthink." *Psychology Today* 5 (6): 43–6; 74–6.

Jevons, William S. 1931. *Theory of Political Economy*. 4th edn. London: Macmillan.

Joad, C. E. M. 1939. *Why War?* London: Penguin Books.

Johnston, David. 1996. *The Idea of a Liberal Theory*. Princeton, NJ: Princeton University Press.

Kant, Immanuel. 1991. *Political Writings*. Edited by Hans Siegbert Reiss. 2nd edn. Cambridge Texts in the History of Political Thought. Cambridge; New York: Cambridge University Press.

    1993. *Grounding for the Metaphysics of Morals; with, On a Supposed Right to Lie Because of Philanthropic Concerns*. Translated by James W. Ellington. 3rd edn. Indianapolis, IN: Hackett.

Kekes, John. 1997. *Against Liberalism*. Ithaca, NY: Cornell University Press.

King, Martin Luther. 1989. "Letter from Birmingham Jail." In *Civil Disobedience*, ed. Paul Harris, 57–71. Lanham, MD: University Press of America.

Klosko, George. 2005. *Political Obligations*. Oxford; New York: Oxford University Press.

Kolers, Avery. 2009. *Land, Conflict, and Justice: A Political Theory of Territory*. Cambridge: Cambridge University Press.

Kymlicka, Will. 1992. *Liberalism, Community and Culture*. Oxford: Clarendon Press.

Lazari-Radek, Katarzyna de, and Peter Singer. 2014. *The Point of View of the Universe: Sidgwick and Contemporary Ethics*. Oxford: Oxford University Press.

Lear, Jonathan. 1992. "Inside and Outside the 'Republic.'" *Phronesis* 37 (2): 184–215.

Litterman, Bob. 2013. "What Is the Right Price for Carbon Emissions?" *Regulation* 36 (2): 38–43.

Lively, Jack. 2007. *Democracy*. ECPR Classics. Colchester, UK: ECPR Press.

Locke, John. 1980. *Second Treatise of Government*. Edited by C. B. Macpherson. Indianapolis, IN: Hackett.

    2013. *A Letter Concerning Toleration*. Edited by Kerry S. Walters. Peterborough, ON: Broadview Press.

Lomasky, Loren E., and Geoffrey Brennan. 2000. "Is There a Duty to Vote?" *Social Philosophy and Policy* 17 (1): 62–86.

Lomborg, Bjørn. 2001. *The Skeptical Environmentalist: Measuring the Real State of the World*. Cambridge; New York: Cambridge University Press.

MacIntyre, Alasdair C. 2007. *After Virtue: A Study in Moral Theory*. 3rd edn. Notre Dame, IN: University of Notre Dame Press.

McMahan, Jeff. 2009. *Killing in War*. Uehiro Series in Practical Ethics. New York: Oxford University Press.

McNamara, Robert S. 2005. "Apocalypse Soon." *Foreign Affairs* (May/June): 28–36.

Manin, Bernard. 1997. *The Principles of Representative Government*. Themes in the Social Sciences. Cambridge; New York: Cambridge University Press.

Margalit, Avishai, and Joseph Raz. 1990. "National Self-Determination." *Journal of Philosophy* 87 (9): 439–61.

Marx, Karl. 1992. *Capital: A Critique of Political Economy*. Vol. 1. Translated by Ben Fowkes. London: Penguin Books.

Marx, Karl, and Friedrich Engels. 1978. *The Marx–Engels Reader*. Edited by Robert C. Tucker. 2nd rev. and enlarged edn. New York: Norton.

Mearsheimer, John J. 2014. *The Tragedy of Great Power Politics*. The Norton Series in World Politics. New York: Norton.

Meisels, Tamar. 2009. *Territorial Rights*. 2nd edn. Law and Philosophy Library 72. Dordrecht, the Netherlands: Springer.

Midgley, Mary. 1992. "Philosophical Plumbing." *Royal Institute of Philosophy Supplements* 33 (September): 139–51.

Mill, John Stuart. 1972. *Utilitarianism, On Liberty, and Considerations on Representative Government*. London: Everyman.

Miller, David. 1995. *On Nationality*. Oxford Political Theory. Oxford: Clarendon Press.

2003. "Liberalism and Boundaries: A Response to Allen Buchanan." In *States, Nations, and Borders: The Ethics of Making Boundaries*, ed. Allen Buchanan and Margaret Moore, 262–72. Cambridge: Cambridge University Press.

2005. "Immigration: The Case for Limits." In *Contemporary Debates in Applied Ethics*, ed. Andrew I. Cohen and Christopher Heath Wellman, 193–206. Oxford: Blackwell.

2016. *Strangers in Our Midst: The Political Philosophy of Immigration*. Cambridge, MA: Harvard University Press.

Miller, Richard W. 1998. "Cosmopolitan Respect and Patriotic Concern." *Philosophy and Public Affairs* 27 (3): 202–24.

Mills, Charles W. 1997. *The Racial Contract*. Ithaca, NY: Cornell University Press.

2005. " 'Ideal Theory' as Ideology." *Hypatia* 20 (3): 165–83.

2008. "Racial Liberalism." *PMLA* 123 (5): 1380–97.

2017. *Black Rights/White Wrongs: The Critique of Racial Liberalism*. Oxford: Oxford University Press

Milner, Murray. 2016. *Freaks, Geeks, and Cool Kids: Teenagers in an Era of Consumerism, Standardized Tests, and Social Media*. 2nd edn. London; New York: Routledge.

Mittiga, R. 2018. "Before Collapse: A Political Theory of Climate Catastrophe." Unpublished Ph.D. dissertation, University of Virginia.

Moellendorf, Darrell. 2002. *Cosmopolitan Justice*. Boulder, CO: Westview.

Moore, Margaret. 2015. *A Political Theory of Territory*. Oxford Political Philosophy. Oxford; New York: Oxford University Press.

Murphy, Liam B., and Thomas Nagel. 2005. *The Myth of Ownership: Taxes and Justice*. Oxford; New York: Oxford University Press.

Nagel, Thomas. 2005. "The Problem of Global Justice." *Philosophy and Public Affairs* 33 (2): 113–47.

Nine, Cara. 2012. *Global Justice and Territory*. Oxford: Oxford University Press.

Nozick, Robert. 2013. *Anarchy, State, and Utopia*. Repr. edn. New York: Basic Books.

Nussbaum, Martha Craven. 2007. *Frontiers of Justice: Disability, Nationality, Species Membership*. The Tanner Lectures on Human Values. Cambridge, MA: The Belknap Press of Harvard University Press.

Nussbaum, Martha Craven, and Joshua Cohen. 2002. *For Love of Country?* New Democracy Forum. Boston: Beacon Press.

Olsaretti, Serena. 2009. *Liberty, Desert and the Market: A Philosophical Study*. Cambridge: Cambridge University Press.

Oppenheimer, Clive. 2003. "Climatic, Environmental and Human Consequences of the Largest Known Historic Eruption: Tambora Volcano (Indonesia) 1815." *Progress in Physical Geography* 27 (2): 230–59.

Page, Edward A. 2011. "Climatic Justice and the Fair Distribution of Atmospheric Burdens: A Conjunctive Account." *The Monist* 94 (3): 412–32.

Paley, William. 1828. *The Principles of Moral and Political Philosophy*. Boston: Whitaker.

Parfit, Derek. 1992. *Reasons and Persons*. Repr. edn. Oxford: Clarendon Press.

2013. *On What Matters*. Vol. 1. Edited by Samuel Scheffler. Oxford: Oxford University Press.

Pateman, Carole. 1970. *Participation and Democratic Theory*. Cambridge: Cambridge University Press.

Pavel, Carmen E. 2015. *Divided Sovereignty: International Institutions and the Limits of State Authority*. Oxford; New York: Oxford University Press.

Penn, William. 1682. *A Frame of Government of Pennsylvania*, excerpts online at: www.constitution.org/bcp/frampenn.htm.

Pettit, Philip. 1999. *Republicanism: A Theory of Freedom and Government*. Oxford Political Theory. Oxford: Oxford University Press.

Pevnick, Ryan. 2014. *Immigration and the Constraints of Justice: Between Open Borders and Absolute Sovereignty*. New York: Cambridge University Press.

Piketty, Thomas. 2014. *Capital in the Twenty-First Century*. Translated by Arthur Goldhammer. Cambridge, MA: The Belknap Press of Harvard University Press.

Plato. 1992. *Republic*. Edited by C. D. C. Reeve. Translated by G. M. A. Grube. 2nd edn. Indianapolis, IN: Hackett.

Pogge, Thomas. 2002. *World Poverty and Human Rights: Cosmopolitan Responsibilities and Reforms*. Cambridge; Malden, MA: Polity.

Preston, Christopher James. 2014. *Engineering the Climate: The Ethics of Solar Radiation Management*. Lanham, MD: Lexington Books.

Przeworski, Adam. 1991. *Democracy and the Market: Political and Economic Reforms in Eastern Europe and Latin America*. Cambridge; New York: Cambridge University Press.

Rawls, John. 1999. *A Theory of Justice*. 2nd edn. Cambridge, MA: Harvard University Press.

  2001. *Justice as Fairness: A Restatement*. Edited by Erin Kelly. Cambridge, MA: Harvard University Press.

  2003. *The Law of Peoples. With "The Idea of Public Reason Revisited."* Cambridge, MA: Harvard University Press.

Raz, Joseph. 1985. "Authority, Law and Morality." *The Monist* 68 (3): 295–324.

  2009. *The Morality of Freedom*. Repr. edn. Oxford: Clarendon Press.

Ridley, Matt. 2016. "Global Warming versus Global Greening." The Global Warming Policy Foundation (GWPF) Annual Lecture, the Royal Society, London, October 17. www.thegwpf.org/matt-ridley-global-warming-versus-global-greening/.

Riker, William H. 1988. *Liberalism against Populism: A Confrontation between the Theory of Democracy and the Theory of Social Choice*. Prospect Heights, IL: Waveland Press.

Robinson, Joan. 2017. *Economic Philosophy*. Repr. edn. New York: Routledge.

Rossi, Enzo, and Matt Sleat. 2014. "Realism in Normative Political Theory." *Philosophy Compass* 9 (10): 689–701.

Rousseau, Jean-Jacques. 1990. "The State of War." In *Reading Rousseau in the Nuclear Age*, ed. Grace Roosevelt, 185–98. Philadelphia: Temple University Press.

  1992. *Discourse on the Origin of Inequality*. Translated by Donald A. Cress. Indianapolis, IN: Hackett.

  2011. *The Basic Political Writings*. 2nd edn. Translated and edited by Donald A. Cress. Indianapolis, IN: Hackett.

Sandel, Michael J. 1998. *Liberalism and the Limits of Justice*. 2nd edn. Cambridge; New York: Cambridge University Press.

Scanlon, T. M. 2000. *What We Owe to Each Other*. Cambridge, MA: The Belknap Press of Harvard University Press.

Schumpeter, Joseph A. 2008. *Capitalism, Socialism, and Democracy*. New York: Harper Perennial.

Sen, Amartya. 2000. *Development as Freedom*. New York: Anchor Books.

2006. "What Do We Want from a Theory of Justice?" *Journal of Philosophy* 103 (5): 215–38.

Shelby, Tommie. 2007. "Justice, Deviance, and the Dark Ghetto." *Philosophy and Public Affairs* 35 (2): 126–60.

Sher, George. 2009. *Beyond Neutrality*. Cambridge: Cambridge University Press.

Shue, Henry. 2014. *Climate Justice: Vulnerability and Protection*. Oxford: Oxford University Press.

Sidgwick, Henry. 1981. *The Methods of Ethics*. Indianapolis, IN: Hackett.

Simmons, Alan John. 1981. *Moral Principles and Political Obligations*. Princeton, NJ: Princeton University Press.

2001. *Justification and Legitimacy*. Cambridge: Cambridge University Press.

Singer, Peter. 1972. "Famine, Affluence, and Morality." *Philosophy and Public Affairs* 1 (3): 229–43.

2004. *One World: The Ethics of Globalization*. 2nd edn. The Terry Lecture Series. New Haven, CT: Yale University Press.

2009. *Animal Liberation: The Definitive Classic of the Animal Movement*. Updated edn. New York: Harper Perennial.

2011. *Practical Ethics*. 3rd edn. New York: Cambridge University Press.

Skinner, Quentin. 2001. "A Third Concept of Liberty." *Proceedings of the British Academy* 117: 237–69.

2012. *Liberty before Liberalism*. Canto Classics. Cambridge: Cambridge University Press.

Stone, Julius. 1984. *Visions of World Order: Between State Power and Human Justice*. Baltimore, MD: Johns Hopkins University Press.

Stothers, R. B. 1984. "The Great Tambora Eruption in 1815 and Its Aftermath." *Science* 224 (4654): 1191–98.

Sunstein, Cass. 2006. "Irreversible and Catastrophic." *Cornell Law Review* 91 (4): 841.

Tainter, Joseph A. 2011. *The Collapse of Complex Societies*. New Studies in Archaeology. Cambridge: Cambridge University Press.

Tamir, Yael. 1995. *Liberal Nationalism*. Princeton, NJ: Princeton University Press.

Taurek, John M. 1977. "Should the Numbers Count?" *Philosophy and Public Affairs* 6 (4): 293–316.

Tawney, R. H. 1946. "English Politics Today: We Mean Freedom." *Review of Politics* 8 (2): 223–39.

Taylor, Charles. 1994. *Multiculturalism: Examining the Politics of Recognition*. Edited by Amy Gutmann. Princeton, NJ: Princeton University Press.

Tetlock, Philip E. 2017. *Expert Political Judgment: How Good Is It? How Can We Know?* New edn. Princeton, NJ: Princeton University Press.

Tomasi, John. 2012. *Free Market Fairness*. Princeton, NJ: Princeton University Press.

Troyer, John, ed. 2003. *The Classical Utilitarians: Bentham and Mill*. Indianapolis, IN: Hackett.

Tuck, Richard. 2008. *Free Riding*. Cambridge, MA: Harvard University Press.

    2016. *The Sleeping Sovereign: The Invention of Modern Democracy*. Cambridge: Cambridge University Press.

US Department of Commerce. 2017. National Oceanic and Atmospheric Administration. National Ocean Service, Center for Operational Oceanographic Products and Services. "Global and Regional Sea Level Rise Scenarios for the United States." https://tidesandcurrents.noaa.gov/publications/techrpt83_Global_and_Regional_SLR_Scenarios_for_the_US_final.pdf.

Valentini, Laura. 2012. "Ideal vs. Non-Ideal Theory: A Conceptual Map." *Philosophy Compass* 7 (9): 654–64.

Vattel, E. 1844. *Law of Nations*. Philadelphia: T. & J. V. Johnson.

Voltaire. 2005. *Candide, or, Optimism*. Translated by Peter Constantine. New York: Modern Library.

Waldron, Jeremy. 2002. *God, Locke, and Equality: Christian Foundations in Locke's Political Thought*. Cambridge; New York: Cambridge University Press.

    2014. *The Harm in Hate Speech*. Cambridge, MA; London: Harvard University Press.

Wall, Steven. 1998. *Liberalism, Perfectionism and Restraint*. Cambridge; New York: Cambridge University Press.

Walzer, Michael. 1973. "Political Action: The Problem of Dirty Hands." *Philosophy and Public Affairs* 2 (2): 160–80.

    1993. *Interpretation and Social Criticism*. Cambridge, MA: Harvard University Press.

    1994. *Thick and Thin: Moral Argument at Home and Abroad*. Notre Dame, IN: University of Notre Dame Press.

    2010. *Spheres of Justice: A Defense of Pluralism and Equality*. New York: Basic Books.

    2015. *Just and Unjust Wars: A Moral Argument with Historical Illustrations*. 5th edn. New York: Basic Books.

Wellman, Christopher Heath, and Phillip Cole. 2011. *Debating the Ethics of Immigration: Is There a Right to Exclude?* Debating Ethics. Oxford: Oxford University Press.

Wiens, David. 2015. "Against Ideal Guidance." *Journal of Politics* 77 (2): 433–46.

Williams, Bernard. 2005. *In the Beginning Was the Deed: Realism and Moralism in Political Argument*. Edited by Geoffrey Hawthorn. Princeton, NJ: Princeton University Press.

Wolff, Robert Paul. 1970. *In Defense of Anarchy*. New York: Harper.

Yates, Michael. 2003. *Naming the System: Inequality and Work in the Global Economy*. New York: Monthly Review Press.

Zwolinski, Matt. 2007. "Sweatshops, Choice, and Exploitation." *Business Ethics Quarterly* 17 (4): 689–727.

Index